Radical Larkin

Also by John Osborne:

LARKIN, IDEOLOGY AND CRITICAL VIOLENCE (2008)

Radical Larkin

Seven Types of Technical Mastery

John Osborne
Director of American Studies, University of Hull, UK

First published 2014 by
PALGRAVE MACMILLAN

Palgrave Macmillan in the UK is an imprint of Macmillan Publishers Limited, registered in England, company number 785998, of Houndmills, Basingstoke, Hampshire RG21 6XS.

Palgrave Macmillan in the US is a division of St Martin's Press LLC, 175 Fifth Avenue, New York, NY 10010.

Palgrave Macmillan is the global academic imprint of the above companies and has companies and representatives throughout the world.

Palgrave® and Macmillan® are registered trademarks in the United States, the United Kingdom, Europe and other countries.

ISBN 978–0–230–34824–0

This book is printed on paper suitable for recycling and made from fully managed and sustained forest sources. Logging, pulping and manufacturing processes are expected to conform to the environmental regulations of the country of origin.

A catalogue record for this book is available from the British Library.

A catalog record for this book is available from the Library of Congress.

Typeset by MPS Limited, Chennai, India.

Dr Jane Thomas
Wythnos fu unnos, f'annwyl

Contents

List of Tables

Acknowledgements

The author and publishers acknowledge the following permissions to reprint copyright material: Faber and Faber Ltd and Farrar, Straus and Giroux, LLC, for quotations from *The Complete Poems of Philip Larkin*, excerpts from *Selected Letters of Philip Larkin, 1940–1985, Letters to Monica* and *Required Writing*; and Faber and Faber Ltd for excerpts from *Jill, A Girl in Winter, Further Requirements* and *Trouble at Willow Gables*. Previously unpublished material is quoted by kind permission of Jeremy Crow and the Society of Authors as the Literary Representative of the Estate of Philip Larkin. Maurice Rutherford's poems are quoted by permission of the author; Carol Rumens by permission of Picador; and Grace Nichols by permission of Bloodaxe Books. Richard Cole's cover graphic is reproduced by permission of the artist. Every effort has been made to trace copyright holders, but if any have been inadvertently overlooked, the author and publishers will be pleased to make the necessary arrangements at the first opportunity. The author would like to thank Monica Kendall for invaluable assistance in the preparation of this text.

List of Abbreviations

All references to the works of Philip Larkin are incorporated in the text using the following abbreviations:

AGW *A Girl in Winter*
AWJ *All What Jazz*
CP   *Collected Poems*
EPJ *Early Poems and Juvenilia*
FR   *Further Requirements*
J   *Jill*
LM   *Letters to Monica*
RW   *Required Writing*
SL   *Selected Letters*
TCP *The Complete Poems*
TWG *Trouble at Willow Gables*

As explained in the Introduction, I have referenced both the *Collected Poems* (1988; revised, 1990), edited by Anthony Thwaite, and *The Complete Poems* (2012), edited by Archie Burnett, in a double citation. Hence, 'This Be The Verse' (*CP*, 180; *TCP*, 88). All other citations may be found in the endnotes.

Introduction: A Textuality that Dare not Speak its Name

Phonocentrism

An orthodoxy in aesthetics is a revolution in waiting.[1] A consensus alerts us where to concentrate the attack. Until very recently the *doxa* in Larkin studies was, in Andrew Motion's words, that 'the poems *are* autobiographical'.[2] As Larkin's biographer he would say that, wouldn't he? But so did the other three authorities who dominated the field: Anthony Thwaite, Trevor Tolley, James Booth. 'All Larkin's work is fundamentally autobiographical,' says Booth. 'He is a highly "visible" poet, who seems to have no inhibition about addressing the reader in his own, natural tone.'[3] This assumption of a pure, immediate vocality prior to inscription leads Booth to the confident assertion that 'In only four of his mature poems does Larkin create speakers who are clearly distinguished by sex or social context from himself.'[4] Once Larkin has been nominated 'speaker', all those other personages inhabiting the text can be divided into the 'spoken to' or 'spoken about' and their identities imported from the life. As the poems themselves characteristically avoid nominals and pronominals, the sexing and racing of narrators or addressees, our first objective is to reverse this argument and demonstrate that underneath the naturalness and orality attributed to Larkin's verse is a textuality that dare not speak its name.

One way we can proceed is by examining with what difficulty these critics provide *an exegesis of writing entailed to a repression of writing*. For in order to present Larkin's poems as 'speaking' in his 'voice' they must deny the textuality not only of his texts but also of their own. Theirs are scripts that try (and fail) to hide their own inscriptedness. As early as 1969, Thwaite was struggling to *naturalize* the methodology:

> Larkin needs no prolegomena, no exegesis: there is no necessary bibliography, no suggested reading, except the poems themselves. In a straightforward Wordsworthian sense, he is a man speaking to men [...] What Hardy taught Larkin was that a man's own life, its suddenly surfacing

1

perceptions, its 'moments of vision', its most seemingly casual epiphanies (in the Joycean sense), could fit whole and without compromise into poems. There did not need to be any large-scale system of belief, any such circumambient framework as Yeats constructed within which to fashion his work: Larkin has dismissed all that as the 'myth-kitty'. Like Parolles in *All's Well* he seems to say: 'Simply the thing I am shall make me live'.[5]

It is a nice paradox that in adumbrating the view that Larkin's poems speak in his own voice, unmediated by literary citation, Thwaite himself has repeated resort to citation: Wordsworth, Hardy, Joyce, Yeats, Shakespeare – five intertexts in four sentences. Moreover, the analogy with Parolles is silently lifted from a 1960 review in which Larkin described Betjeman as 'destined to be one of those rare persons who can say, "Simply the thing I am shall make me live"' (*RW*, 131). Uneasily aware that mockery might be incurred in deploying Larkin's Shakespeare citation to claim he is anti-citational, Thwaite suppresses the debt. This is an intertextuality that can neither be dispensed with nor acknowledged.

Thwaite's *Poetry Today* (1985) provides further evidence that as phono-centrism is the primal condition of this hermeneutics so writing is its primal repression. Acknowledging neither his own 1969 essay on Larkin nor Larkin's 1960 review of Betjeman, Thwaite avers:

> unlike any other important British poet, Larkin has constructed no system into which his poems can snugly fit: like Parolles in Shakespeare's *All's Well*, he seems to say 'simply the thing I am shall make me live'.[6]

As Thwaite twice recycled Larkin's Betjeman review without referencing the source, so subsequent commentators endorse Thwaite's bias against the textual by recycling *his* text, again without acknowledgement. Hence Timms in the 1970s:

> 'Simply the thing I am shall make me live', says Parolles. We might adapt the words, and say that Larkin's style and tone and choice of subject-matter simply come from the thing he is.[7]

Or, more succinctly, John Whitehead in the 1990s, 'In Larkin's case *le style* soon became *l'homme meme*.'[8] In every case the claim that Larkin the speaker trumps Larkin the writer involves denial of the critic's own dependence upon previous writings.

Shakespeare is believed to have based the plot of *All's Well* upon a tale from Boccaccio's *Decameron* which William Painter Englished in his two-volume *Palace of Pleasure*, a collection of European stories ancient and modern. If these texts are aligned in an ancestral chain we have Whitehead (1995), Thwaite (1985), Timms (1973), Thwaite (1969), Larkin (1960), Shakespeare (*c.* 1603), Painter (1566) and Boccaccio (*c.* 1353) – eight levels of intertextuality mobilized to suppress text in favour of speech. It is true, of course, that the name of Shakespeare's character derives from the French *parole* whose meaning, 'word', is more usually applied in spoken than written contexts. But the crowning irony is that the immediatist truth doctrine appealed to by Parolles in the line 'Simply the thing I am shall make me live' issues from the mouth of someone who the irreproachable Helena warns us in the very first scene is 'a great way fool, solely a coward' and 'a notorious liar' (Act I, Sc. I, lines 111–12). A Shakespeare text repeatedly cited in validation of the authenticity of the natural speaking self advises the exact opposite: that the bluff, I-am-what-I-am, I-tell-it-like-I-see-it persona is the very mark of the hypocrite, not to be trusted.

A metaphysics of presence

In *Phaedrus*, Jacques Derrida reminds us, Plato equated speech with presence and writing with absence, thereby inaugurating a Western intellectual tradition of favouring the former over the latter.[9] The presence of the speaker validates the spoken utterance, simultaneously authoring and *authorizing* the statement; whereas a piece of writing exists separately from its author and so lacks legitimation, shifting meanings according to context or readerly point of view. Thwaite, Tolley, Motion and Booth are reading Larkin's poems in the absence of the writer; but by pretending that the poems are spoken rather than written, received by ear rather than eye, the product of an oral rather than a scribal practice, they conjure up his absent presence in verification of their interpretations. One touchingly literal illustration of this is the way Tolley's *My Proper Ground* (1991), *Larkin at Work* (1997) and *Early Poems and Juvenilia* (2005) all begin by thanking Larkin for his help – as though Tolley were receiving spirit-message endorsements from beyond the grave. The warning to the reader is clear: 'to quarrel with my judgements is to quarrel with Larkin who has given them his *imprimatur*'.

The phonocentric bias of this criticism, with its reliance upon a metaphysics of presence, is intimately connected to the belief that Larkin's poems mirror his life. Tolley credited Larkin with the 'notion that poetry was not merely the preservation of an experience, but that it should begin with something that actually happened and be true to what did happen'.[10] Thwaite concurs, declaring of masterpieces like 'Church Going', 'The Whitsun Weddings' and 'Dockery and Son': 'All of these start from some quite specifically recalled incident.'[11] In the chapters that follow I shall be at some pains to demonstrate that the consensual claims that this or that poem was prompted by biographical incident – the visiting of an English parish church for 'Church Going', Winifred Arnott's photographs in 'Lines on a Young Lady's Photograph Album', the Hull-to-London train journey of 'The Whitsun Weddings', the death of Eva Larkin as inspiration for the completion of 'Aubade' – are invariably reductive, often false. The immediate point I wish to register is the more general one of methodological principle. The authocentric critic purports to anchor a poem's meaning in the writer's life, replacing the instability of literature with the stability of the lived reality. In practice, this usually entails displacing the instability of a primary text onto the instability of secondary texts like biographies, autobiographies, hagiographies, kiss-and-tell memoirs or gossip columns.

It might plausibly be claimed that the real difference between a poem or a novel on the one hand and a biography or autobiography on the other is not that one is fiction and the other fact but that both are fiction and only the former admits it. In *Notes of a Son and Brother*, for instance, Henry James entirely rewrote those letters of his brother William the volume purported to preserve. The first major biography of Thomas Hardy was actually an autobiography, filleted of anything revelatory and falsely attributed to his second wife. *The Autobiography of Alice B. Toklas*, in which the eponymous subject endlessly praises her lover Gertrude Stein, was actually written by, *ahem*, Gertrude Stein. The self-serving *Autobiography of Malcolm X* was written by Alex Haley whose account of his attempts to trace his own slave ancestry, *Roots*, was part plagiarized from Harold Courlander's novel *The African*. With homosexual acts illegal in the UK until 1967, biographies and autobiographies routinely suppressed their subjects' gay experiences – as in Robert Skidelsky's life of the economist John Maynard Keynes.[12] Of course, all are diligent paragons of candour compared to those unlettered celebrities whose ghost-written memoirs avalanche from the presses in time to deepen the sorrows of Christmas.

As for Larkin, he deliberately ensured that any life would indeed have a hole in the middle by arranging from his deathbed for the destruction of the 30 volumes of his private diaries. Lacking this anchorage (if such it was) his 'life' has gone through various 'editions': the 'hermit of Hull' – decent, monastic, chaste; the beastly male chauvinist, running three mistresses in tandem and still requiring a stash of porn to slake his depraved cravings; the blushing violet of *Letters to Monica*, forever apologizing for his low sexual appetency while flaunting his woman's atomizer, mauve bed sheets, pink toilet paper, lemon braces and dyed mauve socks; or the spiritually questing courtly lover of Maeve Brennan's memoir. Celibate, satyr, androgyne, prig? Asexual, heterosexual, homosexual, bisexual? Take your pick.[13]

This instability of the biographical text continually betrays critical attempts to bring biographical equilibrium to the unstable literary text. For example, it is a commonplace in Larkin studies that the 'Arnold' of 'Self's the Man' is, in Richard Bradford's words, 'Larkin's colleague and junior in the library, Arthur Wood'. However, Ronald Drinkwater, a University colleague with whom Larkin lodged in his first year in Hull, believes himself the poem's butt, 'Arnold' being an anagram of his name.[14] The point is not that critics like Motion, Dunn and Bradford are wrong to make a link to Wood, but that the biographical terrain they think brings fixity is itself disputed ground. The same is true with the posthumously published love poems. Booth identifies Betty Mackereth as the addressee of 'Morning at last'. However, Winifred Dawson, Bradford and Brennan herself assign Maeve Brennan that honour. Motion hedges his bets between the two. Similarly, Booth and Mackereth identify Betty as the addressee of 'When first we faced'; Motion and Dawson opt for Maeve; Maeve says it could be her *or* Betty; Bradford says Maeve *and* Betty. As for the addressee of 'Love Again', Booth says Betty in *Philip Larkin: Writer* (1992) and Maeve in *The Poet's Plight* (2005) – the latter exhibiting the usual textual amnesia about its forerunner.

Larkin's anti-textualism

The biographicalist claim that (in Tolley's words) Larkin wrote 'poems based on personal experience, not on material derived from literature', and that his 'poetry leans strongly towards structures encountered in normal conversational use of speech' with 'a conscious rejection of [...] intertextuality', has a pre-modernist simplicity and force.[15] This 'representational aesthetic has been under attack at least since the time of Mallarmé', and the more radical critical schools to appear in the twentieth century, those of the Russian Formalists, the Anglo-American New Critics, the structuralists and deconstructionists, to greater or lesser degrees, 'rejected mimesis' in favour of text-centred theories. Séan Burke has suggested that 'we have entered a postrepresentational era [...] no-one any longer takes seriously the ideal of pure realism' and 'modernist and postmodernist fiction has moved [away] from representational modes'.[16]

Faced with these alarming theoretical developments the default position of biographicalists is intentionalism: *the views the author said determined the writing are the views the critic says determine the reading.* Larkin is a considerable help here, his own theoretical writings adopting a Luddite approach to theory, as when he declares 'You must realize I've never had "ideas" about poetry' or 'I make a point of not knowing what poetry is or how to read a page' (*RW*, 76, 79). On occasion this anti-intellectualist posture is used to project a man-in-the-street, I-may-not-know-much-about-art-but-I-know-what-I-like populism:

> Some time ago I agreed to help judge a poetry competition – you know, the kind where they get about 35,000 entries, and you look at the best few thousand. After a bit I said, Where are all the love poems? And nature poems? And they said, Oh, we threw all those away. I expect they were the ones I should have liked. (*RW*, 76)

He also presented as a virtue of his own style that it was so transparent as to obviate analysis: 'I may flatter myself, but I think [...] there's not much to say about my work. When you've read a poem, that's it, it's all quite clear what it means' (*RW*, 53–4).

Larkin would sometimes give a more advanced explication of this *faux naive* stance, contextualizing it in relation to the historical crisis of modernism:

> the term 'modern', when applied to art, has a more than chronological meaning: it denotes a quality of irresponsibility peculiar to this century, known sometimes as modernism [...] My own theory is that it is related to an imbalance between the two tensions from which art springs: these are the tension between the artist and his material, and between the artist and his audience, and that in the last seventy-five years or so the second of these has slackened or even perished. In consequence the artist has become over-concerned with his material (hence an age of technical experiment). (*AWJ*, 11)

The modernist readiness to pursue technical innovation at the expense of audience understanding has historically specific causes. 'One was the emergence of English literature as an academic subject, and the consequent demand for a kind of poetry that needed elucidation' (*RW*, 216). This development poses a direct threat to the integrity of the poet: 'the danger is that he will begin to assume unconsciously that the more a poem can be analyzed – and, therefore, the more it needs to be analyzed – the better poem it is'. The threat is especially acute in the case of 'the campus poet' who might 'unconsciously start to write the kind of poem that is earning him a living' as an academic (*RW*, 89). The threat to poetry itself is that it no longer has to speak for or to a lay readership since it now draws its sales as a set text on the university syllabus:

> at bottom poetry, like all art, is inextricably bound up with giving pleasure, and if a poet loses his pleasure-seeking audience he has lost the only audience worth having, for which the dutiful mob that signs on every September is no substitute. (*RW*, 81–2)

Larkin was appalled by this replacement of a voluntary with a compulsory audience: 'I should hate anybody to read my work because he's been told to and told what to think about it' (*RW*, 56). The mid-century institutionalization of modernism by the academy had severed poetry from the general reading public.

A second historical determinant identified by Larkin was the rise to global dominance of the USA. Larkin drew comparisons between modernist poets like Pound and Eliot, their works replete with classical references, and turn-of-the-century American tourists hoovering up European culture. On occasion he would extend the analogy to the workings of international capital, claiming that this 'typically American' attitude 'that you can order culture whole' has 'led to a view of poetry which is almost mechanistic, that every poem must include all previous poems, in the same way that a Ford Zephyr has somewhere in it a Ford T Model' (*FR*, 19). From the poet's point of view, this 'means that before anything worthwhile can be written everything worthwhile must be read' (*FR*, 14). From the punter's point of view, 'you have to be terribly educated' to enjoy modern literature.

The paradigm in which a native English continuity faces invasion by the Yanks is defined by an undergirding set of antitheses: national versus international, populist versus elitist, transparent versus obscure, traditional versus experimental, phonocentric versus textual. And at his most reductive, Larkin invariably appoints the same man captain of the home team:

> it was Eliot who gave the modernist poetic movement its character in the sentence, 'Poets in our civilization, as it exists at present, must be *difficult*'. And it was Betjeman who, forty years later, was to bypass the whole light industry of exegesis that had grown up round his fatal phrase, and prove, like Kipling and Housman before him, that a direct relation with the reading public could be established by anyone prepared to be moving and memorable. (*RW*, 129)

Requiring no elucidation, Betjeman's poetry side-steps the university curriculum, academic explication and the rhetoric of critical theory:

> for him, the modern poetic revolution has just not happened; there has been no symbolism, no Ezra Pound, no objective correlative, no rediscovery of myth, no *Seven Types* or *Some Versions*, no works of criticism with titles like *Communication as Discipline* or *Implicit and Explicit Image-Obliquity in Sir Lewis Morris*. (*FR*, 163)

How does he manage it? 'What Betjeman achieves is done simply by saying what he thinks and feels, without minding if he is laughed at. And the further he gets from his fellow-poets, the nearer he gets to his readers' (*FR*, 327). Moreover, Larkin defines his own project in very much the same terms:

> There is a sentence or two of Leslie Stephen, which Hardy used to be very fond of, I can't remember it exactly, but it's something like 'The poet's task is to move our feelings by showing his own, and not to display his learning, or mimic the fine notes of his predecessors [...]' I've always thought it is a magnificent motto, for me anyway, it is the kind of thing I should like to think I did. (*FR*, 30)

We are squarely back in biographicalist territory, the poet emoting directly with the audience as though speaking *in propria persona*: 'poetry should begin with emotion in the poet, and end with the same emotion in the reader. The poem is simply the instrument of transference' (*FR*, 65). Once again, however, one cannot help noticing that the admonition to the poet 'not to display his learning, or mimic the fine notes of his predecessors' is delivered via the fine notes of Larkin's predecessors Hardy and Stephen. The textuality of the text is never more apparent than when denied.

Larkin as professional intertextualist

We have no reason to doubt Larkin's distaste for the fact that under the conditions of modernity poetry 'is thought to be difficult, like higher mathematics, something that can't be understood without preliminary study and teaching'.[17] Nor is his own popularity with the general public to be denied: his poems, even ones as formidable as 'Aubade', regularly top national reader polls. The fact remains that however useful as an approach to Betjeman the phonocentric argument unfolded in the previous section accords ill with aspects of Larkin's life, his poetic practice and his aesthetic theorizing.

One way we can broach this difficulty is by reminding ourselves that as a librarian Larkin was a guardian of historical taxonomies, a professional intertextualist. For all his strictures against 'the campus poet' he was, in a sense, of that company, conducting his poetic career from university libraries in Leicester, Belfast and Hull. At Hull he excitedly devised and administered the Compton Fellowship which brought to the campus for a year apiece the poets C. Day Lewis, Richard Murphy, Peter Porter, Ian Hamilton and Douglas Dunn, each of whom was given an office in the Brynmor Jones Library from which to conduct exactly the sort of writing classes he claimed to deplore. In the event, Larkin was most disappointed at the low student pick-up – perhaps the undergraduates had taken him at his word!

It is also relevant that in such essays as 'Operation Manuscript' (1967) and 'A Neglected Responsibility' (1979) Larkin was a leading campaigner for the purchase and preservation of contemporary writers' drafts. He was in no doubt that 'the lack of interest shown in modern literary manuscripts by British libraries reflects an identical lack of interest by British universities', adding that 'in the 1950s I worked as a librarian in a university where the head of the English department would not sanction the purchase for the library of texts by living writers' (*RW*, 102). The man who wanted to keep contemporary poetry off the syllabus now berates the universities for complying! Moreover, his interest in literary manuscripts was not just archival but showed a fascination with the very scribal processes his phonocentric praise of Betjeman had seemed to belittle. This fascination encompassed poets' calligraphy ('Why should two such dissimilar poets as Roy Fuller and Vernon Watkins have the same, vivid, flourishing, romantic kind of script?'), their writing equipment ('William Plomer's different-coloured inks') and their stationery:

> Ted Hughes slits open a large brown envelope and writes on the blank inner side, Edmund Blunden uses the back of an illustration from a Sotheby's catalogue. Others reach for paper showing where they are – Keith Douglas at the Middle East RAC Base Depot, or Edwin Muir at Battle Abbey College. Now and then we find the luxury of a notebook. Andrew Young had one; Roy Fuller's [is] red and wirebound. (*FR*, 119)

And always the palimpsestic multi-layerings of the inscription are presented as vital to a scholarly understanding of how poems are produced:

> this is primary source material: this is what he wrote, how he wrote it, what he corrected, what he left. A manuscript will show how much trouble he took, how many drafts were necessary; a cancellation may clarify a meaning, for a writer will often put down the 'prose' word while groping for the 'poetic' one. (*FR*, 120)

This text-centred approach to how poems are created is complemented in Larkin's most considered account of how poems should be received:

> Hearing a poem, as opposed to reading it on the page, means you miss so much – the shape, the punctuation, the italics, even knowing how far you are from the end. Reading it on the page means you can go your own pace, taking it in properly; hearing it means you're dragged along at the speaker's own rate, missing things, not taking it in, confusing 'there' and 'their' and things like that. And the speaker may interpose his own personality between you and the poem, for better or worse [...] And of course this fashion for poetry readings has led to a kind of poetry that you *can* understand first go: easy rhythms, easy emotions, easy syntax. I don't think it stands up on the page. (*RW*, 61)

Larkin's pronouncements on Hardy and Betjeman emphasized emotion ('the poet's task is to move our feelings by showing his own') and vocal immediacy ('simply by saying what he thinks and feels') at the expense of the materiality of the text ('the poem is simply the instrument of transference'). Such an account dematerializes what it claims to admire, evaporating literature – whose defining characteristic is that it is *written* – in the interests of an unimpeded emotional encounter. To wish for the poet and audient to commune direct is to annul the very artistry that made communion desirable. But now all the key terms have been reversed: the oratorical gives way to the graphological, talk to text; words are what we see, as well as what we see through; the acid test is whether or not 'it stands up on the page'; and the person conducting that test is not a listener but a *reader*. If anyone shares my conviction that the penultimate sentence quoted above is all too applicable to Betjeman ('easy rhythms, easy emotions, easy syntax'), it is worth remarking that even as he put the finishing touches to the long praising review article 'Betjeman En Bloc' Larkin wrote privately to Monica Jones, 'I'm *sick* of Betjeman: cosy secret Tory weapon [...] nostalgic & snobbish & that' (*LM*, 247).

Burnett's new broom

In some of his most telling remarks Larkin accords the artwork a degree of autonomy usually associated with modernist aesthetics: 'I wanted to write such a lot [...] and I wanted to do it not for *my* sake but for *its* sake – responsibility is always to the *thing* & not to yourself or the filthy reader' (*LM*, 222). The man who earlier wanted to reduce the poem to a megaphone for transmitting emotion from poet to punter now says the opposite: the text is the thing, and the writer and reader can go hang! This reification of the text extended to the production values of his books. Jean Hartley of the Marvell Press, publisher of *The Less Deceived*, has noted 'Philip's interest in the technicalities of the book's production and its format'. 'Together we discussed type sizes and faces, pagination, blurb, binding, and we agreed on a lovely strong pink, his favourite colour, for the dust-jacket.' It was Larkin who chose Garamond in preference to Bodoni for the type-face.[18]

A similar care and attention characterized Larkin's approach to all matters editorial. Reviewing a revised edition of Betjeman's *Collected Poems* he observed:

> It is in print again now with some of the more obvious misprints removed, but 'Chirst' on page 123 surprisingly remains, and 'I know that I wanted to ask you' on page 143 should surely be '*what* I wanted'. I hereby offer to correct the proofs of Betjeman's next book of poems for nothing, if that is the only way to protect them from such blemishes. (*FR*, 216)

As for his own *Collected Poems*, we know he wanted such an edition but not what he wished it to include. Although he carefully preserved and dated all his poems, complete and incomplete, published and unpublished, as though for posterity, his Will was contradictory as to how the unpublished material was to be disposed. Of one thing we may be assured, he would have expected the highest editorial standards to be observed in any posthumous publications.

When Anthony Thwaite's edition of the *Collected Poems* (1988) appeared, just three years after Larkin's death, it was criticized on two counts: first, that its chronological presentation of the poems shattered the structural integrity of the individual volumes; second, that by including a mass of material not published by Larkin the editor flooded with inferior works a canon of impeccable quality. Both complaints were unfair: the first because Larkin's individual collections remained in print for those wishing to admire the skill and ingenuity with which he sequenced their contents; the second because poets as great as Larkin always generate a demand for completeness that sooner or later must be met – so better never than late. For a quarter of a century this edition dominated the field, its expansion of the Larkin *oeuvre* and its chronological format revolutionizing critical understanding of his aesthetic evolution. Reasonably comprehensive yet compact enough to be portable, it appealed to scholars and lay readers alike. As I continue to find it indispensable when considering matters chronographical, I have incorporated it into the referencing system for the present volume.

This is not to deny that there were problems. The temporal ordering of the contents that made the volume revolutionary had the unfortunate side-effect of entrenching biographicalism. When the *Collected Poems* was followed in 1993 by Motion's biography, itself remarkably authoritative for a work written so soon after the subject's death, a critical industry was spawned in which scholars, whether admirers or detractors, did little more than key the compositional to the personal. Again, the complaint that Thwaite included too much unpublished material might better be expressed as a complaint that he did not include all of it, since he thereby ensured the publication of a supplementary volume. Matters were not improved when Thwaite produced a second *Collected Poems* (2003) which responded to adverse criticism by retracting all the posthumously published material included in the first version (the words *genie* and *bottle* come to mind). For a moment there were in circulation two very different volumes with the same author, editor, title and publisher, the second much the inferior of the two. However, the nadir came with Tolley's edition of the *Early Poems and Juvenilia* (2005) which compounded its textual flaws – of which, more anon – by making no attempt at a 'fit' with existing publications. Hence, Tolley reprinted all the poems from Larkin's first collection, *The North Ship* (1945), despite the fact that they were already available in both Thwaite *Collecteds* and as a separate volume.

Chaos was finally dispelled with the publication of *The Complete Poems of Philip Larkin* (2012), edited with an introduction and commentary by Archie Burnett. This includes 'all of Larkin's poems whose texts are accessible' (*TCP*, xiii). These texts, meticulously checked against primary sources, are organized into four categories: the four volumes published in Larkin's lifetime 'preserved as collections' (117 poems); other poems published in the poet's lifetime but not gathered in a collection (36 poems); poems not published in the poet's lifetime (403); and unpublished poems of uncertain date (10 poems). Of the grand total of 556 poems, 413 had not been published by Larkin, though 84 had been included in Thwaite's first *Collected* and 202 in the Tolley.

Burnett brings to this compilation a level of editorial accuracy and detail surpassing all prior editions. In his 'Introduction' he says of the Tolley, 'its text of the poems contains 72 errors of wording, 47 of punctuation, 8 of letter-case, 5 of word-division, 4 of font and 3 of format' (*TCP*, xiii–xiv). Sean O'Brien described *Early Poems and Juvenilia* as having been 'lovingly assembled', but Burnett's tally is 139 errors (one every two and a half pages) – not *that* lovingly, then. Burnett adds that the Appendix in which Tolley lists 'the contents of the eleven typescript booklets prepared by Larkin before publication of *The North Ship*' is also 'full of errors':

> the earliest collection is not *The Happiest Day* but *The Happiest Days*; the title of the poem *Young Woman Blues* should be *Young Woman's Blues*; the opening line 'Turning from these obscene verses to the stars' should not contain 'these'; the date of *Further Poems* is June, not July, 1940, and its subtitle is not 'Nine poems of depression' but 'Nine poems of depression and dismay'. (*TCP*, 675)

And so on. Burnett is no more impressed with this critic's other contributions to the debate:

> A.T. Tolley's account, 'Philip Larkin's Unpublished Book: "In the Grip of Light"', *Agenda*, 22.2 (Summer 1984), 76–86, is deeply flawed. From the list of contents he omits *Winter*, *Getaway* and 'At the chiming of light upon sleep'; he lists two poems, 'If hands could free you, heart' and 'Kick up the fire, and let the flames break loose', that are not in the collection; he gives the title *To a Very Slow Air* as *Slow Song*; he adds the title *The Dedicated* to 'Some must employ the scythe', which is untitled in ITGOL; and he omits the titles from 'Her hands intend no harm' and 'There is an evening coming in'. (*TCP*, xxix)

Professor Burnett charitably forebears to mention that when four years later this article was reprinted in George Hartley's symposium *Philip Larkin, 1922–1985: A Tribute* (1988) Tolley let stand every one of these errors. A quarter of a century later Tolley excused the flaws by claiming that the piece was written in 'collaboration' with Larkin.[19]

Despite the egregiousness of his mistakes, the old guard has closed ranks in Tolley's defence. James Booth and Janet Brennan, editors of *About Larkin*, the journal of the Philip Larkin Society, nominate him 'the doyen of Larkin scholars'. Describing Tolley as a 'lifelong devotee of Larkin's work', O'Brien sniffs at the whistle-blower: 'While the facts may be on Burnett's side he sounds like Malvolio, and we know what happened to him.' In a recent issue of *About Larkin* Terry Kelly accuses Burnett of being 'tough on [...] Tolley', asking 'can any substantial volume be completely blemish-free' and 'should academics in glass houses tempt fate by throwing stones?' The fact that Kelly had greeted *Early Poems and Juvenilia* as 'a handsome volume, meticulously edited by A.T. Tolley' may suggest that, like O'Brien, he chides Burnett for exposing an incompetence he himself failed to identify.[20] Of course there are errors in *The Complete Poems*, just as there will be in the present volume; but there is a glaring difference between ordinary human fallibility and outright negligence. For obvious reasons, Burnett concentrates his (f)ire on Tolley's editorial and bibliographical endeavours. He has no cause to remark that in his critical monograph *My Proper Ground*, Tolley 30 times refers to *All What Jazz* without once getting the title correct; repeatedly misspells the name of jazz legend Billie Holiday, a Larkin favourite; mangles the names of the composer Claude Debussy, the novelist Arnold Bennett, of George Moore's masterpiece *Esther Waters*, of Yeats's poem 'Lapis Lazuli', of the poets Baudelaire, Oliver St John Gogarty and Allen Ginsberg (misdating his greatest collection, *Howl*, into the bargain), of the Larkin scholar Janice Rossen and of at least ten Larkin poems (sometimes, as with 'If, My Darling' and 'The Card-Players', getting the titles wrong in different ways in different places – sometimes on the same page). Although in singling out Tolley for attack Burnett risks making him seem interesting, the reality is that surer editorial footings were vital if the scholarly debate was to move from an author-centred to a text-centred hermeneutics. Whatever its demerits, Burnett's edition of *The Complete Poems* has a textual authority that provides these new foundations.[21]

A test case

Larkin died in 1985. No-one now under 40 (and few enough aged 50) can really be said to have known the man. The future of his reputation is passing irrevocably out of the hands of those who knew him and into the hands of those who did not – a reality starkly underlined by the recent deaths of his intimates Kingsley and Hilly Amis, Monica Jones, Maeve Brennan, Jean Hartley, Judy Egerton and Ruth Bowman. Recognition of the inevitability of this process, and of the concomitant need for a post-authocentric reading strategy, was delayed by the posthumous revelations that the poet could privately be racist, sexist and boorish. In what Clive James described as 'a rush of dunces', such guardians of political correctness as Lisa Jardine, Bryan Appleyard, Tom Paulin, Terry Eagleton and John Newsinger pilloried Larkin in the print and broadcast media.[22] Although their tone was much more vitriolic than anything that had gone before, their methodology was essentially the same as that of the four Larkin defenders with whom this Introduction began: indeed, it was two of the latter – Thwaite in his edition of Larkin's *Selected Letters* (1992) and Motion in his biography of the poet (1993) – whose disclosures ignited the biographical conflagration.

That Burnett's textual rigour has mercifully brought this phase of the debate to a close may be demonstrated by considering the way the meaning of 'The Winter Palace' has been contested by Booth and Paulin, respectively representatives of the 'pro' and 'anti' lobbies. As we shall see, despite the violence of their disputations they are climbing the same biographical mountain from different sides. Over the years, Booth has regularly denounced on aesthetic grounds Paulin's politicized readings of Larkin:

> Paulin's 'historicism' reduces literary analysis to political polemic, abolishing the simply 'historical' in favour of ideology. Such historicism bears a similar relation to history as spiritualism bears to spirituality, or Scientology to science.[23]

Booth's principal allegation is that of brutal insensitivity to the art of poetry: 'Deaf and heavy-footed, Paulin barges through Larkin's delicately constructed verbal devices.'[24] When it comes to explicating 'The Winter Palace', however, Booth shares with Paulin the fundamental predicate that author and narrator are one. *Philip Larkin: Writer* describes the poem as one 'in which Larkin welcomes his own growing absent-mindedness, in the hope that it will render him oblivious to approaching death'; while *Philip Larkin: The Poet's Plight* categorically identifies 'the ageing poet' as protagonist. The argument is circular: the assumption that the poem is autobiographical leads to the conclusion that 'The Winter Palace' takes place 'inside his head' and we know it is Larkin's head because his poems are autobiographical.[25] It is precisely this tautological conflation of poet and protagonist that licenses Paulin to visit upon the narrator the uglier biographical disclosures. Larkin is a 'reactionary' who 'loves the unchanging' and who 'is opposed to the historical process'. In 'The Winter Palace', 'a lacklustre complaint about ageing', the 'quasi-Fascist' poet equates his lost youth with a lost Imperial Eden, the title nostalgically invoking the Tsarist regime's palace in St Petersburg. 'Ageing is like being a monarch besieged by revolutionaries. Change is a revolutionary process, the completed revolution is death.'[26]

It is true that 'The Winter Palace' is about a change for the worse – the encroachment of old age, short-term memory loss, the possible onset of Alzheimer's disease. In this context it may be disproportionate but it is not self-evidently false to invoke the Russian Revolution as a poetic symbol of disaster. Two writers incomparably greater than Paulin who might be expected to know more about the subject than he, Alexander Solzhenitsyn and Joseph Brodsky, both Nobel Prize winners forcibly exiled from the Soviet Union, separately estimated that the communist regime was through a mixture of deliberation and incompetence responsible for the deaths of over 60 million of its own citizens – quite apart from those it murdered in other countries. For Paulin to write at the end of the twentieth century, when the cadavers had been tallied and the statistics published, as though the Russian Revolution was unquestionably *a good thing*, any hint to the contrary proof of one's 'fiercely pro-Imperial sentiment', is stupefying.[27]

Once again a conflation of author and narrator leads directly to a *folie circulaire* in which twin propositions constitute each other's proof: because Larkin is a reactionary he takes the Tsarist institution as his presiding symbol and the choice of that symbol is confirmation that he is reactionary. If we sever that connection between poet and protagonist, or put it in parentheses, reading the poem as constitutive rather than reflective of its narrator, then the very title appears richly polyvalent and every valence suggestive of a different subjectivity. For not only are there many Winter Palaces dotted around the globe – some, like that in Beijing, internationally famous – but many of them are associated with freedom struggles. The Winter Palace in Vienna, for example, is associated with Prince Eugene of Savoy's resistance to invasion from the Turkish Empire. Arguably the most spectacular Winter Palace of them all is that at Machu Picchu, the cold-weather retreat of the Incas high in the Peruvian Andes. Some commentators believe that this became the last and secret city of the Incas after their civilization was brutally conquered by Spanish colonizers in the 1500s, the site remaining unknown to the outside world until its discovery by Hiram Bingham in 1911. The title Paulin interprets as a reactionary invocation of the Tsarist imperium may just as plausibly be read as an allusion to an indigenous culture under imperial attack: the poem's sick narrator retreats deep into the self to try and escape 'whatever it is that is doing the damage', just as the Incas retreated deep (and high) into their mountain fastness in the hopes of surviving the alien invasion. The modern view is that Machu Picchu's populace succumbed to smallpox brought over by the Spanish, which accords with Larkin's illness/damage conceit.

'The Winter Palace' is a poem about age, amnesia and the disintegration of self. If Paulin wants to explore the political implications of the title, an entirely proper enquiry, and one which Booth effaces, he might have the decency to admit that Larkin's tactical refusal to specify *which* Winter Palace thwarts attempts to conscript the narrator to one side of the Right/Left binary. Each of the locations we have identified, in a list that is far from exhaustive – Russia, China, Austria, Peru – carries distinct cultural and ideological resonances and constitutes the narrator differently. This rendering the narrator populous, expanding the narratological franchise beyond the flatly biographical kenning of either Booth or Paulin, enforces rather than enfeebles the poem's address to mortality: as if to say, with *Deirdre of the Sorrows*, in the face of death all parties are on the same side. The losing one.

Had Burnett not intervened, there we might have left the battle of the biographicalists, Booth and Paulin contending over 'The Winter Palace' like two bald men fighting over a comb (as Borges has it). Thwaite unveiled the text in *Collected Poems* (1988) as one of a number of 'previously unpublished poems' that 'deserve to stand with his best already known work' (*CP*, xxiii). Over the next two decades critical comment was largely admiring, as when Terry Kelly described it as among 'his most compelling and utterly distinctive poems'.[28] Though 'not without regret', Burnett has had the poem 'removed from the canon' for the following reasons:

The basis of the text printed in *Collected Poems* (1988) [...] is a typescript with holograph corrections in pencil. Lines 3–4 are represented in

Collected Poems as: 'I spent my second quarter-century / Losing what I had learnt at university'. The problem is that Larkin cancelled 'Losing' at the start of line 4 and provided no alternative, and that he also cancelled lines 3–4 with a wavy line. Further, he drafted alternative versions of the lines below the typescript text, but, unfortunately, these drafts achieve neither a final version without uncancelled alternative versions nor a couplet that, like the rest of the poem, rhymes or half-rhymes [...] Given this state of affairs, it seems best to acknowledge that Larkin did not finish work on the poem, and leave it at that. (*TCP*, xix)

As Burnett emphasized when challenged by Kelly: 'you can't print something the poet cancelled (as though he hadn't done so), and you can't print it as though there were no further inconclusive drafts'.[29] In short, the shared biographical certitudes of the Booth and Paulin interpretations are built on a text Burnett shows to be corrupt.

Destabilizing biographical tenets

Burnett's new broom sweeps clean in other ways. The 324 pages of poetry are accompanied by 338-page commentary. This not only offers readers variant wordings and improved dating of poems, showing in many cases durations of years between start and finish, but also a series of glosses comprised of pertinent Larkin quotes and a digest of critical opinion. It might be thought that garlanding the poems with so many of Larkin's own comments would endorse biographicalism, but the effect is quite otherwise. Larkin is repeatedly caught in contradictions between theory and practice, or between one correspondent and another, deliberately obscuring his poetic sources or simply forgetting the most elementary facts about this or that poem's composition. Burnett's greatest coup in this regard is to shatter the *ne plus ultra* of biographicalism by demonstrating the falsity of Larkin's account of the genesis of 'The Whitsun Weddings'. For nearly a quarter of a century Larkin insisted:

Every now and then you will see some happening or situation that prompts you to think that if only you could get that down, in a kind of verbal photography, you would have a poem ready-made. This was what I felt some years ago when I happened to see a series of wedding parties at a succession of stations on the way to London one hot Saturday afternoon. (*FR*, 87)

Critics swallowed this authorized version whole: the life-into-art aesthetic; the photographic realism; the author as narrator; the direct transferral of the original emotion to the audience as though the poem was an open door to a swathe of experience ('There's hardly anything of me in it at all. It's just life as it happened.'[30]). However, Burnett has discovered a private letter from a few months before Larkin's death in which Larkin admits 'when I came to look up the genesis of "The Whitsun Weddings" I found that not only did it not take place at Whitsun, but that I actually got out of the train at Grantham and took a motorbus to the Midlands to see my family [...] Twenty years or so had made me believe the poem rather than what actually happened!' (*TCP*, 411). As we shall see in Chapter 4, there is textual evidence to corroborate this revision.

Less conspicuous destabilizing of authocentric tenets occurs across Burnett's commentary. For example, Motion states that 'soon after returning to Pearson Park in early January 1967 Larkin stopped keeping his diary for a while. He tells us so in the poem "Forget What Did", which he began on 30 January (and didn't finish until 6 August 1971).'[31] As Larkin's diaries were destroyed at his death this statement is completely unverifiable. In her memoir Maeve Brennan quotes Larkin telling her that 'Forget What Did' 'directly concerns you', and she surmises that his jealousy of her new admirer was too painful for him to record in his diary. This too is beyond substantiation.[32] Bradford links 'Forget What Did' with 'Vers de Société', 'The View' and 'The Life with a Hole in it' as 'bitterly autobiographical' works whose very 'syntax seems crippled by [...] pain'. The shared theme, he declares, is less Larkin's troubled affair with Maeve than his sense of encroaching mortality, and he cites a letter to Amis of 11 August 1972: 'I keep seeing obits of chaps who've passed over "suddenly, aged 55", "after a short illness", "after a long illness bravely borne, and 57" [...] No it doesn't bear thinking about.'[33]

In all three interpretations, the biographers' awareness of the teleology of Larkin's life and work tempts them to see in the poem's abandoned diary intimations of subsequent authorial silencings: the drying up of Larkin's poetic inspiration; the physical destruction of his diaries; his premature death. Burnett puts these essentially senescent, almost valedictory readings in doubt by simply noting that Larkin used the expression 'forget what did' as early as 1950 and that in 1952 he told Patsy Strang 'I am trying to write a little unrhyming poem about giving up a diary' (*TCP*, 449).[34] As both details date from Larkin's twenties, well before he met Maeve Brennan, two decades before his letter to Amis and 35 years before his death, none of the prevailing biographical interpretations survives intact. 'Forget What Did' was conceived by a young man not an old one. How stable by contrast is Marion Lomax's observation that the title 'Forget What Did' is a quotation from Susan M. Coolidge's schoolgirl novel *What Katy Did* – an intertextual reference which Burnett acknowledges, as Motion, Bradford and Brennan do not.[35]

My own view is that it would do no harm to Larkin studies if for the foreseeable future we desisted from visiting the (imaginary) certitudes of the life upon the work but rather visited the (real) polyvalency of the work upon the life. Unlike his hero Wilde, Larkin put his genius into his poetry and only his talent into his life. Using the latter as the key to the former is a hermeneutical spoonerism. Larkin knew this full well: in life, which is true, he was false; whereas in art, which is false, he was true. Henceforth the concept of the author might better be regarded as a creation than a creator of the text.[36] After all, most Larkin lovers are acquainted with the writings not the man – and within a generation *all* Larkin lovers will be thus situated. In such a hermeneutics the text originates at the end of the writing process, not the start; with the reader, not the writer. Intentionality is redefined as an *effect* of the text not a cause. Anyone wishing to utilize the concept is obliged to locate where in a text and by what textual means the Intentionality Effect is created. Otherwise, intentionalism is an instrument of obfuscation, supposedly all-pervasive but nowhere identifiable, like phlogiston before Lavoisier or ether before the Michelson–Morley experiment. Similarly, we should accept that literary narrators do not construct their stories as speech but are constructed by them as text. What sort of narrator a specific work constructs is a key question for the reader to contemplate, probably with a limited plurality of plausible answers, as we saw with 'The Winter Palace', rather than the foregone conclusions of the biographicalist. This in turn means that the true purport of the poem is to be identified with what the text says, rather than what the narrator says, Larkin being an adept at what in the realm of the novel is known as 'unreliable narration'.

Above all, this new agenda entails an enhanced attention to and respect for those technical means by which the poems achieve their effects – means too often elided as authorial expressivism. Once again this brings us into conflict with Larkin's stated views:

> I would say that I have been most influenced by the poetry that I've enjoyed – and this poetry has not been Eliot or Pound or anybody who is normally regarded as 'modern' – which is a sort of technique word, isn't it? The poetry I've enjoyed has been the kind of poetry you'd associate with me, Hardy pre-eminently [...] people to whom technique seems to matter less than content. (*FR*, 19)

His most notorious statement of this position put an even more contemptuous spin on the word *technique*:

> I dislike such things not because they are new, but because they are irresponsible exploitations of technique in contradiction of human life as we know it. This is my essential criticism of modernism. (*AWJ*, 17)

Larkin's poems need rescuing from this cod *stylophobia*. Concentrating upon the formal strategies, the textual operations of these texts, brings out a Larkin he and the biographicalists repress: master of ellipsis, ekphrasis, narratology and allusion; self-conscious disruptor of lyric traditions of considerable antiquity; familiar of modernist aesthetics; and radical stylistic innovator. Like Empson with the poets of the eighteenth century, I wish to applaud formal qualities in Larkin's poems that he would have been horrified to acknowledge. But this is to say no more than that Larkin could afford to forget his technical expertise, so deeply had it become part of his sensibility.

Prospectus

The present project was undertaken with the following aims and objectives: to offer in-depth studies of some of Larkin's 'greatest hits'; to choose them from across his career span (from 1947 to 1977) and analyse them one per chapter; to show that Larkin's poems sustain and reward the most protracted and searching analyses, one measure of his genius being an extraordinary ratio of *latent* to *manifest* content whereby poems of one or two pages elegantly convey what critical prose needs thousands of words to explicate; to demonstrate that Larkin's texts, for all their apparent ease of access, rely upon formal strategies and technical devices as sophisticated as those of the more obviously 'difficult' authors in the modernist and postmodernist tradition; to demonstrate that these strategies and devices are largely deconstructive in effect, interrogating and unsettling conventional assumptions about 'reality' and showing them to be part of an ideological rather than a natural order; to call upon a range of contemporary critical theories in unpacking the texts in such a way as to establish that Larkin is indeed 'deep' enough to require a theorized hermeneutics; in the process to demolish the stereotype (in which he sometimes colluded) of Larkin as an old-fashioned, middlebrow, narrowly English realist; to achieve this by concentrating upon one deconstructive technique per chapter per text; to select works which not only come from across Larkin's career span and exemplify different technologies of greatness, but which also address discrete 'themes' – the need to resist idealizations, the competing attractions of solipsism and sociability, the death of God, the arbitrariness of national and gender identities, the enhanced significance of orgasm in post-Victorian culture, and the unredeemability of death – so that each chapter concentrates upon one work, one technique and one principal area of meaning; and to discuss the texts in chronological sequence so as to honour the developmental within the *oeuvre*. Of the 30 critical books and 70 or so worthwhile essays on Larkin, approximately 90 per cent employ a biographical approach (even when they think they do not). The present volume attempts seven in-depth demonstrations of the advantages of a text-centred methodology. The contestation will be justified to the extent that there emerges from these pages a Larkin more compellingly rich in meanings than the one we know from the critical consensus. All of which is another way of saying that this is the first critical monograph to benefit from Archie Burnett's editorial excellence.

Although *A Girl in Winter* is the only work in the sequence for which masterpiece status is not being claimed, it merits inclusion on several grounds: as the most underestimated work in the Larkin canon; as his greatest work of the 1940s; and, above all, because it anticipates so many of the techniques of the major poems. It remains undeniable that not just the novel but every one of my chosen works might be replaced by others quite as compelling: 'Next, Please', 'Toads', 'Toads Revisited', 'I Remember, I Remember', 'Mr Bleaney', 'Here', 'Self's the Man', 'Ambulances', 'Dockery and Son', 'Afternoons', 'The Trees', 'Livings', 'The Old Fools', 'The Building', 'Sad Steps' ... But this is evidence less of the folly of my choices than of the mature Larkin's astonishingly high strike rate. It is also ungainsayable that Larkin's genius encompassed many more techniques than may be dealt with in seven essays. Gillian Steinberg's beautiful *Philip Larkin and His Audiences* (2010) offers a full-length analysis of Larkin's strategies for engaging and positioning readers 'as active participants in the poems, inviting them to take responsibility for their interpretative acts and to view the reading [...] of poems as a consciously synthetic act'.[37] Her work accords with mine but covers techniques that I do not – indeed, covers them so well that repeating her endeavours is redundant.

I remain awkwardly aware of ways in which the aforementioned aims and objectives went unfulfilled. As stated, I planned to explicate seven techniques in seven texts, less in homage to the screen musical *Seven Brides for Seven Brothers*, an allusion Larkin might have approved, than to Empson's *Seven Types of Ambiguity*, a work I revere but he affected to despise. In Chapters 2 and 3 (and, to a lesser extent, 6) an adequate account of the stated technique required more than one poem to be adduced as evidence. A glance at the Contents page will confirm that the finished work explicates seven techniques in *11* texts – which doesn't have quite the same ring to it. Again, ellipsis and citation proved so pervasive as to be impossible to confine to their respective chapters, the other techniques depending upon them. These are among the ways in which practice usurped theory – or, if you will, the operative intention usurped the programmatic intention, the implied author the real one. May my defeat be the text's triumph, so that by failing I may succeed!

Critics commonly find that protracted acquaintance with a loved author is a prelude to divorce. Putting individual artworks under the microscope for 10–15,000 word molecular examinations has increased rather than diminished my admiration for Larkin's genius. The success of this book entirely depends upon the extent to which it similarly enhances the reader's enjoyment and understanding of Larkin's artistry. That is the primary objective.

1
Radical Ellipsis: *A Girl in Winter*

The theory of the rupture

In *Larkin, Ideology and Critical Violence: A Case of Wrongful Conviction* (2008) I propose that Philip Larkin developed a set of poetic techniques that allowed him to instantiate unfixity in the very fabric of his verse.[1] These techniques include ellipsis, a four-act structure with closing reversal, asymmetrical stanza lengths and rhyme schemes, plus a battery of disaggregative linguistic devices such as split similes, negative qualifiers, oxymora and rampant paronomasia. Together these techniques constitute the implements of a home-grown deconstructionism. I then go on to demonstrate how this deconstructive approach was applied by the poet to the subjects of nationality, gender, politics and subjectivity, the effect in every case being such as to denaturalize, de-essentialize and destabilize the discourses of power. The volume concludes that Larkin responded to 50 years of unparalleled slaughter, much of it in the name of utopian certitudes, by creating at the mid-century a literature of radical scepsis. Not only do his poems sabotage conventional pieties regarding church, state, nationality, marriage, gender, race and capital, but in the process they play a central role in the cultural transition to postmodernist indeterminacy.

In this chapter I wish to establish *A Girl in Winter* (1947) as the most underestimated work in the Larkin canon by showing how it anticipates both the deconstructive strategies and the assault upon identitarian certitudes that I have attributed to the mature poems. This entails quarrelling with the well-established view, most recently aired by Richard Palmer in *Such Deliberate Disguises: The Art of Philip Larkin* (2008), that

> until the late 1940s Larkin's poetry and prose fiction are almost entirely without distinction [...] [W]hat is extremely unusual – possibly unique – about Larkin's early work is not just its mediocrity but the fact that it does not remotely telegraph the poetry that would ensue, either in quality or

in the specifics of style, tone, choices of form, governing preoccupations and subject matter. I can think of no other writer of the first rank of whom something analogous could be said.[2]

This theory of the rupture between the prose works of the 1940s (bad) and the poems of the 1950s (good) might seem self-evidently reductive and implausible granted the anticipative or rehearsive relation of sections of the novel to 'Afternoons', 'Wedding-Wind', 'Poetry of Departures', 'Dockery and Son', 'MCMXIV', 'Toads Revisited', 'The Whitsun Weddings', 'Scratch on the scratch pad', 'Show Saturday', 'High Windows', 'Aubade', 'To the Sea' (and, more distantly), 'All catches alight', 'To My Wife', 'An April Sunday', 'Reference Back', 'Self's the Man', 'The Explosion' and 'The Life with a Hole in it'. Nonetheless, it is a sufficiently widespread orthodoxy as to constitute an impediment to a proper grasp of Larkin's development.[3]

As well as mounting a challenge to this theory of the rupture, I wish to extend to the consideration of *A Girl in Winter* an assault made in *Larkin, Ideology and Critical Violence* upon another orthodoxy. This is the view, initiated by the man himself and subsequently adopted (usually to his detriment) by critics like Charles Tomlinson (1961), David Lodge (1977), Blake Morrison (1980), Wilfrid Mellers and Rupert Hildyard (1989), Neil Corcoran (1993), Ian Gregson (1996), Andrew Duncan (2003), Keith Alldritt (2003) and Randall Stevenson (2004), that Larkin is 'anti-Modernist'. When it comes to our novel, Professor Trevor Tolley epitomizes the conventional view (as he is apt to do):

> The idiom of the novels, despite the deft handling of flashback and narrative viewpoint in *A Girl in Winter*, is that of straightforward realist narrative by a third person narrator. We encounter none of the innovations of Modernism, such as the interior monologue or distortions of form.[4]

As we shall see, *A Girl in Winter* owes rather more to modernist aesthetics than Tolley allows. In addition to which its study of a displaced person instantly renders it kin to such classics of exilic modernism as Joyce's *Ulysses* (1922), Hemingway's *A Farewell to Arms* (1929) and Camus's *La Chute* (1956); while its total secularism relates it to the central crisis of modernity, the death of God, and places it at the opposite pole from the religious realism then in vogue in England, as exemplified by the Catholic converts Evelyn Waugh (whose *Brideshead Revisited* was published two years earlier) and Graham Greene (whose *The Heart of the Matter* appeared the year after).[5]

A Girl in Winter and modernist aesthetics

A Girl in Winter shares with early poems like 'Femmes Damnées' an intense engagement with the modernist inheritance. Larkin told John Haffenden: '*Jill* has always had the edge over *A Girl in Winter* as far as sales go, which rather surprises me because that's a much more sophisticated book – written, shaped, a Virginia Woolf-Henry Green kind of novel' (*FR*, 48–9). It is worth reminding ourselves that at the time when *A Girl in Winter* was being written, 1944–45, these were unusual role models for the 22-year-old Larkin to choose. Though she always had her supporters, Woolf's reputation as one of the greatest English modernists was far less secure than it is today with critical heavyweights like Muriel Bradbrook, Q.D. Leavis, Wyndham Lewis, F.R. Leavis and Graham Greene all denigrating her achievement. As for Henry Green, 'who was having a great creative period in the forties, producing an extraordinary set of novels – a combination of realism with the aesthetic approach, an avant-garde approach to things like dialogue', he was as grievously underestimated then as he is now (*FR*, 32). Woolf's novels *Mrs Dalloway* (1925) and *Between the Acts* (1941), like Joyce's *Ulysses*, provided prototypes for Larkin's endeavour to limit his plot to a single day. Henry Green's *Party Going* (1939) offered a more stringent example of the Unity of Time, the story covering a mere four hours, the 'action' of the novel being stilled by an immobilizing fog in a manner that possibly influenced a late chapter of *A Girl in Winter*. Give or take a prologue or epilogue, this 24-hour span has latterly become a paradigm for such classics of postmodern cinema as *Rebel Without A Cause* (1955), *Pulp Fiction* (1994) and Paul Haggis's *Crash* (2005).

Other modernist precursors may have helped Larkin arrive at his tripartite structure in which the present time of the story is interrupted by a huge mid-section flashback, for this is the pattern of *Kangaroo* (1923) by D.H. Lawrence and of William Faulkner's *Light in August* (1932). This in turn may have facilitated Larkin's use of a three-act structure in the poems 'March Past', 'Places, Loved Ones', 'Reference Back' and 'Send No Money' before he went on to develop his classic four-act structure with closing reversal in such masterpieces as 'Reasons for Attendance', 'Poetry of Departures', 'Toads', 'Self's the Man', 'Toads Revisited', 'Dockery and Son', 'Vers de Société' and 'High Windows'. At a later stage in the present argument I shall want to suggest that the tripartite format of *A Girl in Winter* already contains an embryonic anticipation of the four-act model.

Less structural, but still symptomatic, are the echoes of the 'Only connect' theme from *Howards End* by E.M. Forster; the motif of paralysis from Joyce's *Dubliners*, the last story of which, 'The Dead', may have suggested the snowy setting; a disquieting beetle-crushing metaphor perhaps derived from Kafka's *Metamorphosis*; a possible indebtedness for the name Anstey to *Eyeless in Gaza* by a favourite Larkin novelist, Aldous Huxley; glancing invocations of Fitzgerald's *The Great Gatsby* and Hemingway's *In Our Time*, *The Sun Also Rises* and *A Farewell to Arms*; together with Larkin's usual gentle dewfall of Eliot allusions. If this *is* realism, as Tolley avers, it is clearly realism *after* modernism.

'Mind the gap': from modernist montage to radical ellipsis

In modernist aesthetics the term montage is applied to the intercutting of parts of an artefact in the hope of achieving a presentational immediacy not possible when they are subordinated to a chronological and discursive narrative. It encompasses flashbacks, proleptic flashes, parallel montage (continual intercutting between two geographically or temporally disjunct scenes), sudden jumps between the fictive and the documentary – in fact, any direct juxtaposition of materials without explanatory *copulae*. It is what the film director Godard spoke of when, answering the question of whether his films had a beginning, a middle and an end, he replied: 'yes, but not necessarily in that order'.[6] It is what T.S. Eliot described, in a formula we shall return to, as 'the suppression of "links in the chain", of explanatory and connecting matter'.[7]

Montage is a recurrent feature of William Faulkner's work. In *The Sound and the Fury* he juxtaposes four different versions of the same story as told by four different participants in it, each section adhering to the 24-hour model described above. No one version can be said to be authoritative, the reader having to compile a definitive account from the versions provided. Other Faulkner experiments with montage include *The Wild Palms*, which presents two apparently unrelated stories in alternating chapters; *As I Lay Dying*, which is made up of 59 sections of unequal length unequally distributed between 15 characters; and *Light in August*, whose comparatively straightforward narration is startlingly interrupted by a flashback lasting seven chapters – the identical number to that of the mid-section flashback of *A Girl in Winter*.

Montage is a term usually associated with cinema, and the widespread modernist use of the technique is not to be separated from the growth of the new medium. At least three seminal modernist artefacts – D.W. Griffith's *Intolerance*, Eisenstein's *October*, Abel Gance's *Napoleon* – are products of the first great experimental phase of film. It was Eisenstein, in innumerable articles and in the books *The Film Sense* and *Film Form*, who most successfully theorized the modernist ideal of montage as a collision of unlikes with the seams exposed. It may also be relevant that Eisenstein once approached Joyce with a view to filming *Ulysses*, the modernist poet Louis Zukofsky getting as far as the writing of a scenario. (Prior to writing his major works, we remember, Joyce opened the first cinema in Dublin.)

In proposing his theory of dialectical montage as an alternative to the continuity editing of mainstream realism, Eisenstein made use of arguments akin to Bertolt Brecht's concept of 'audience alienation'. Brecht said of his preferred style of acting, the very opposite of the Stanislavsky or Method school, and of his use of unrealistic sets with texts and slide projections: 'they do not set out to help the spectator but to block him; they prevent his complete empathy, interrupt his being automatically carried away'.[8] Similarly, Eisenstein proposed that the value of juxtaposing disjunct shots lay in the fact that it forced the audience to think, viewers being actively engaged in a struggle with the filmic language rather than passively consuming an easily extractable subject matter. That is to say, the function of Eisensteinian montage, as of Brechtian alienation, was to keep the audience in a conscious state of mentation, not only about the represented reality but also about the reality of the representation.

Eliot's formula – 'the suppression of "links in the chain", of explanatory and connecting matter' – is less sophisticated, implying an original chronological narrative that is jazzed up by periodic erasures. In practice, however, as a swift glance at the opening of his first masterpiece will verify, Eliot's use of gaps still served to 'alienate' readers by inviting them to fill in the ellipses while frustrating their attempts so to do. I have elsewhere suggested that 'The Love Song of J. Alfred Prufrock' is 'the single work by any author most often alluded to in Larkin'.[9] The poem famously begins:

> Let us go then, you and I,
> When the evening is spread out against the sky
> Like a patient etherised upon a table;
> Let us go, through certain half-deserted streets,
> The muttering retreats
> Of restless nights in one-night cheap hotels
> And sawdust restaurants with oyster-shells:
> Streets that follow like a tedious argument
> Of insidious intent
> To lead you to an overwhelming question ...
> Oh, do not ask, 'What is it?'
> Let us go and make our visit.
>
> In the room the women come and go
> Talking of Michelangelo.[10]

There are many aspects of these marvellous lines that reward investigation but what concerns us here is the way they are divided into *strophe* and *distich* by an enlarged typographical space. If we assume that the women coming and going *after the typographical hiatus* are in the room towards which Prufrock was tending *before the hiatus* then we can fill the ellipse with a realist concretization of the text: the narrative, we deduce, has elided the humdrum travelogue leading Prufrock to his social gathering in much the same way that when a movie cuts from a shot of its protagonist in a car to one of him knocking at a door we unhesitatingly explain the montage jump in terms of *arrival*. In the case of 'Prufrock', however, this is not the only speculation we might try out for its hermeneutical value: it is perfectly possible to read the entire poem as an interior monologue, Prufrock's 'stream of consciousness', the montage jump signifying the distracted manner in which he flits from one subject to another and back again, the discontinuous thought process *never getting anywhere*. This psychological malaise might lead us to the further conjecture that he does not get anywhere *physically* either, the fact that he has been to such social gatherings on innumerable prior occasions – 'I have measured out my life in coffee spoons' – allowing Prufrock to anticipate exactly what will await him in that room and thereby providing a strong disincentive for attendance.[11] This explanation shifts the burden of meaning away from a realist hermeneutics of chronological travel and arrival to a modernist one of psychological paralysis, alienation and *ennui*. When we remember that this is but the first of a succession of montage jumps, each of which gives rise to further deliberations – sometimes such as to cause a revision in the hermeneutical choices made about earlier ones – then we can truly claim that this favoured Larkin role model offered exemplary tuition in the deployment of *aporia*.

What makes Larkin's use of ellipsis the more extreme is its application in realist contexts where it is the less expected, the more eviscerative. So much so, indeed, that commentators routinely ignore or explain away these black holes in the text, refusing to address the ramifications of their absent presences. In the case of *A Girl in Winter* there are two such glaring gaps in representation, the first concerning the protagonist's origins and the second the denouement of her story, a sizeable minority of critics 'filling in' the former while the latter is universally ignored. This rendering determinate of that which the text holds ambiguous twists meanings out of true and renders Larkin's putative realism endorsive of realities it actually drains of verifiability. For if the classic realist text is a jigsaw which the author has already completed leaving the reader as a passive consumer; and the modernist text is a scrambled jigsaw requiring the reader's active engagement to complete the picture; the Larkinian text is a jigsaw whose apparent realism only serves to emphasize that vital pieces are missing and the puzzle can never be resolved.

The governing ellipse: the protagonist's identity

As with so much of the Larkin debate, critical discussion of *A Girl in Winter* is characterized by presupposition and error. Tolley tells us not once but twice that the novel was completed in July 1945; only to add, again twice, that Larkin was 23 years old.[12] At least one of these statements must be wrong as Larkin in July 1945 was aged 22. The novel concerns Katherine Lind, a European refugee during the Second World War, whose country of origin is never specified – an ellipse, or gap in representation, entailed to a major *aporia*, or gap in readerly comprehension. This has not prevented critics from assigning her a national identity, though they disagree as to what it is: Lolette Kuby categorically states that she is French; both the *Larousse Dictionary of Literary Characters* and the revised version published as the *Chambers Dictionary of Literary Characters* are adamant that she is German, a view shared by Carol Rumens and Birte Wiemann; Tom Paulin suspects that she is German but puts a side bet on her being Polish; while Andrew Motion and Nicholas Marsh more vaguely surmise that she is 'originally from somewhere in middle Europe'.[13] Booth unhelpfully declares that 'The form of her Christian name suggests that she is French or Belgian, rather than Eastern European or Scandinavian, as her surname might imply.'[14] In fact, the francophone spelling of the forename is Catherine with a C, whereas Katherine and its variants (Katharine, Katherina, Katarine, etc.) are the norm in such countries as Germany, Holland, Sweden, Finland, Russia and Greece, some of which *are* 'Eastern European or Scandinavian'.

The question that these critical responses fail to address is, what is the function of the ellipse, what is its role in the text, what does the silence say? It is not enough to propose (as, in effect, Stephen Cooper does) that where Katherine comes from does not matter, what matters is that she is not English, the novel intersecting the viewing of masculinity through female eyes with the viewing of England through foreign ones.[15] This is a necessary but not an adequate explanation, the truth but not the whole truth – though, indeed, it carries Cooper's argument a deal further than was reached by the critics enumerated above. For the first thing to observe in endeavouring to answer the question *what does the silence say*, is that the novel was written not just about but during the Second World War; and that one of the effects of any war, none more than this, is a universal resort to national stereotypes – such as those aggrandizing one's own side and denigrating the enemy. (At this very time the British children's comic *The Beano* carried a cartoon strip entitled 'Musso the Wop' – 'He's A Big-A-Da-Flop' – in which the Italian dictator's military boots were laced with strings of spaghetti!) The second point to register is that Larkin's use of ellipsis encourages and confounds readers' attempts to identify not just Katherine's nationality but her language, ethnicity, religion and class. Which is also to say that the *aporia* at the heart of the text problematizes pre-established taxonometric grids and dominant labelling strategies, making unknowability a central theme in a world given over to identitarian certitudes, many of them murderous.

After all, it is not the case that Katherine has no national statehood or culture but that, not knowing what they are, we try out different options in different combinations, assessing their explanatory value. Reading her identity as now French, now German, now Belgian, now Polish, brings out different shades of meaning, all of which are part of the novel's purport; but the fact that we cannot close on a decisive answer serves to dramatize the dissonances within the unisonant discourse of cultural belonging and to embarrass the reductively patriotic constructions of subjectivity in the name of which contending armies fight and die.[16]

Valid and invalid readings of the ellipse

When six years before the present time of the novel the schoolgirl Katherine Lind visited her English pen-pal Robin Fennel (1936 to judge by her Olympic badge), he says: 'If we'd lived in prehistoric times, before England was an island, I could nearly have taken you home. The Thames used to flow into the Rhine' (*AGW*, 172). This is the closest the novel comes to specifying a geographical origin for Katherine. However, the Rhine passes through or adjoins Switzerland, Lichtenstein, Austria, France, Germany and the Netherlands; and Robin says *near* the Rhine, so other countries may be in play. Moreover, Robin's statement might encompass tributaries of the Rhine, such as the Meuse, which would add Belgium to the six countries listed above.

When Katherine and Robin meet again in 1942, and she tells him 'of the events that had led to her arrival in England' as an exile the year before, she 'chose to tell them in a way that freed them of much of their unpleasantness' (*AGW*, 230). Nonetheless, even the emotionally insensitive Robin is moved by their horror: '"Filthy business," he said when she had finished. "It's pretty grim, isn't it."' And, again: '"I'm sorry for you," he said. "You've had a rotten time."' (*AGW*, 231–2). However, such was the speed of Hitler's conquest of Europe that even by 1941 the list of countries from which Katherine might have fled is long and includes most of those contiguous with the Rhine: Austria was absorbed in the *Anschluss* of 1938; Czechoslovakia and Poland were occupied in 1939; Denmark and Norway fell in the spring of 1940 with Luxembourg, Holland, Belgium and France succumbing by June; Yugoslavia and Greece had been conquered by April 1941 and by the end of that year so had western republics of the Soviet Union including the Ukraine.

Katherine's surname does little to narrow the range of candidates for home country and may add an ethnic complication to our considerations. Lind is common across north-west Europe, having strong linguistic associations with Swedish, Danish, German, Dutch and Scottish. Perhaps the most famous Lind up to the date of the book's publication was the great nineteenth-century soprano Jenny Lind, popularly known as 'the Swedish nightingale'. On the other hand, these rather 'Aryan' associations are counterbalanced by the fact that some prominent Linds were Jewish. The novelist Jakov Lind was born in Vienna in 1927, survived inside Nazi Germany under an assumed Dutch identity, before moving to London and becoming a major European writer, first in German and then in English. He died in London in 2007, shamefully neglected in his country of adoption. Other snippets that we glean about Katherine's family – that her grandfather was a silversmith, that her parents are intellectuals – are not at odds with the possibility that she is Jewish (though hardly conclusive either).[17] The utility of this consideration is that it provides a pressing motivation for Katherine's exile: the biggest argument against it is that the novel nowhere addresses the enormity of the tragedy engulfing European Jewry. That Katherine is not shown worrying about the fate of family or friends is psychologically implausible in such a context. To argue for her Jewishness is simultaneously to argue for an ellipse in the text that drains it, not of verifiability, but of humanity.

With neither geography, political history nor nomenclature narrowing the range of contenders, the reader may wonder if incidental detail encodes Katherine's origins. Is the passing reference to the dance music on Radio Luxembourg a nudge in that direction? (*AGW*, 94–5). Are the resemblances between Katherine and the vivacious 'Polish airgirl' of the 1943–44 poem 'Like the Train's Beat' a hint that she comes from Poland – with a confirmatory pun when in 1936 the Fennel siblings go punting 'with a pole' (*CP*, 288; *TCP*, 11; *AGW*, 87)? A consideration of Katherine's native tongue suggests that the answer to both these questions is negative and also helps us narrow the range of viable options.

When Katherine visits the Fennels in the 1930s, Robin proposes that they spend a couple of hours each day conversing in her language which he has studied at school. This overwhelmingly suggests (but does not prove) that she is either a French or German speaker, few English schoolchildren in the inter-war years being taught the alternatives at issue – Dutch, Flemish, Luxembourgish, Czech, Polish. This same argument vanquishes any lingering thoughts one might entertain that Katherine is a refugee from Finland, Estonia, Latvia or Lithuania – a victim, not of Hitler's conquests, but Stalin's. If we use this premiss to sieve pertinent details from the text we find that every piece of substantiation, for the one language or the other, refuses on closer inspection to yield the expected verification. For instance, Katherine arrives on her first visit to England at the ferry port of Dover. Robin, who has come to collect her, remarks 'that it was a perfect day for seeing across to France' (*AGW*, 75). Conflating these two pieces of information might lead to the deduction that Katherine had travelled from the visible part of France, embarking at Calais. This would be wrong. Calais is 21 miles from Dover whereas Katherine's was a 'crossing of thirty miles' (*AGW*, 73). Boulogne and Dunkerque better fit the facts; but while both are in northern France, direct rail links between Dunkerque and Belgium opened in 1936, the year of Katherine's visit, and already existed between Belgium and other contender countries, so that one is again unable to establish a single point of origin.

Similarly, the fact that the schoolgirl Katherine wears a badge from the 1936 Berlin Olympics might be thought to betoken that she is German. However, not only were participating athletes and officials from all nations issued with such emblems, but various badges were commercially available to advertise and subsidize the Games. Thus, 400,000 badges of the five interlocking Olympic rings were for sale internationally in 1935. The year following, another badge was produced in an edition of 675,000 for sale to visitors. None of these involved Nazi insignias, though other badges again did incorporate a swastika. Katherine's badge is not proof of her German nationality, let alone of any Nazi affiliations (anyway negated by her exilic status). Much the same holds true with the other evidence one might adduce as proof that she is German. Some of the reasons she gives for not re-establishing contact with the Fennels when she escapes to England during the war might hint that she is from an enemy state: 'it might even be that they would dislike dealing with her because of her nationality [...] It might even be socially awkward for them to meet her again' (*AGW*, 22). However, other formulations from this same passage shift the emphasis from a possibly problematic homeland and place it squarely upon a problematic English xenophobia: 'the English, she found [...] were characterized in time of war by antagonism to *every* foreign country, *friendly or unfriendly*' (my emphases). Again, reference to 'a beer-garden' back home might seem more Germanic than French; but such establishments were as common in Holland, Belgium, Luxembourg and Austria as in Germany, and were not unknown in France – especially the more northerly departments, like Alsace-Lorraine, that are close to the River Rhine (*AGW*, 156).

The schoolboy Larkin accompanied his father on two short trips to Germany in 1936 and 1937 and always claimed to have loathed the experience: 'I think [they] sowed the seed of my hatred of abroad' (*RW*, 47). Commentators like James Fenton see Larkin's exaggerated xenophobia and indifference to childhood as a cloak for his father's Nazi sympathies. This line of biographical speculation underwrites the widespread view, here articulated by Carol Rumens, that the apparently open question of origins is actually closed:

> A close reading reveals, in fact, a great many clues as to Katherine's nationality – too many for us not to suppose that they have been deliberately deployed. Larkin has not only fully worked out Katherine's origins; he wishes his readers to know what they are, without going so far as to tell us straight. Added together, the clues seem to point clearly to that enormously difficult place in the family psyche, *père et fils* – Germany.[18]

However, Rumens renders the case for Germany determinate only by suppressing contrary evidence – as when we are told that the Fennels assumed Katherine to be Catholic, a presupposition they would scarcely make about a German, two-thirds of whom are Protestant (*AGW*, 93). In April 1939, five years before commencing *A Girl in Winter*, Larkin went on a ten-day school trip to Brussels, Antwerp and the Belgian Ardennes, enjoying the local cuisine ('the food was superlatively good') and culture (cinema, opera, art galleries and historic sites), speaking French throughout, and subsequently co-authoring a report for *The Coventrian* that described it as 'the best and jolliest holiday we have ever spent'.[19] The Ardennes comprise the western part of the uplands across the Rhine Basin and therefore fit with what limited geographical specificity the novel provides. Belgium, unlike Germany, was overwhelmingly Catholic. It is remarkable how completely this joyous Belgian holiday has been erased from the record in the interests of promoting the myth of Larkin's xenophobia. However, I am not trying to render certain that Katherine is Belgian but to render uncertain the prevalent view that her German origins can be vouchsafed by the slanting of evidence from Larkin's childhood holidays.

There is one last piece of evidence we need to assess, a potentially vital clue, which the present writer is unable to identify and no previous commentator has alluded to. During her summer visit Robin surprises Katherine by saying 'in her own language' the words 'And so you rose up to see the dawn' (*AGW*, 129). Her reaction may simply be one of pleasure at his courtesy in speaking to her in her own tongue. However, it may also be an act of recognition as the sentence sounds like a quotation, possibly a line of poetry. Robin is already showing the linguistic aptitude that will later lead him to study Languages at Cambridge University (*AGW*, 239). But he is not a bookish young man, so if the quote is genuine, rather than something Larkin has invented for the fictional occasion, it is likely to be from a highly canonical source, most probably a schoolroom classic. Of course, even if a fellow reader is able to identify the French or German original of that line, as I am not, it will decisively establish Katherine's linguistic rather than her national identity. If the source is French it will prove she is francophone, not that she is from France (she might as readily be a Walloon from French-speaking Belgium); if German, it will still leave open the possibility that she comes from Austria or Switzerland. In the absence of that identification we are left with a startling fact (though one that no critic has bothered to remark): Larkin wrote during the Second World War a novel whose central character and presiding consciousness is impossible to securely recruit to either the French or German, Christian or Jewish sides. At the very least this must stand as a devastating reproach to the divisive national and racial ideologies undergirding international conflict. To return to our earlier question, the function of the *aporia* regarding Katherine's origins is to keep so many different options in play, often involving countries on opposing sides, that essentialist assumptions regarding race and nationality are systematically undermined. Katherine Lind is escaping an evil ideology, not an evil race.

Nation, empire, gender: 1936

Alan Brownjohn and Richard Palmer concur in the view that the theme of *A Girl in Winter* is so rarefied as to be fugitive, ephemeral: 'The gentle ambivalence of Katherine's attitude to the Fennels and to her adopted English existence during the war is not quite enough of a theme to sustain interest [...] the substance remains elusive.'[20] As neither registers how Katherine's francophone and Germanic associations call each other into question, it is no surprise that they also miss how incisively Englishness is deconstructed when perceived through her doubly deracinated consciousness. Although the novel is narrated in the third (rather than the first) person, we witness no scenes at which she is not present, free indirect speech being employed to combine in a complex simultaneity objective and subjective nuances: by looking through Katherine's eyes we see what she sees but we also see her. As an alien, she defamiliarizes the familiar, allowing English readers to observe themselves from outside, most especially with regard to the overlapping sites of Englishness, British imperialism and gender.

We have already noted that six years prior to the present time of the novel Katherine spent a summer in England at the home of her pen-pal, Robin Fennel. An account of this initial visit constitutes the lengthy (107 pages, nearly half the novel) mid-section flashback which, in plot terms, centres upon Katherine's infatuation with her fellow 16-year-old correspondent. Katherine's seaborne arrival at Dover, train journey through Kent to London, and car journey from London to the Fennel home in Oxfordshire, offers her a panoptic view of the country. There is the same kaleidoscope of traditional English scenes ('Occasionally she saw white figures standing at a game of cricket') and modern despoliation ('there were innumerable hoardings, empty petrol drums and broken fences lying wastefully about') as we find later in 'The Whitsun Weddings' – a connection we shall pursue in Chapter 4 (*AGW*, 80). Again, the sequestered nature of the foreign country Katherine sees from her boat – 'the white-cliffed island drifted nearer' – is echoed in miniature by the sign on the Fennel's stretch of riverbank: 'Private. No Landing Allowed' (*AGW*, 73, 87). That the river in question is the Thames; that the house is close to Oxford; that Katherine is taken to visit Shakespeare's birthplace of Stratford; that the name Fennel denotes a common English herb sometimes used in salads; and that Robin's name is that of the most emblematic of English birds – all these details lightly but insistently identify the Fennel household with the condition of England. '[T]he Fennels were nothing if not English' (*AGW*, 22). The place of England within the British Empire is also gestured in, as when Robin explains:

> 'Take what you can see now [...] Small fields, mainly pasture. Telegraph wires and a garage. That Empire Tea placard. And you know, don't you, that Britain is a small country, once agricultural but now highly industrialized, relying a great deal for food on a large Empire. You see, it all links up.' (*AGW*, 96)

This connection is confirmed in the person of Jack Stormalong, a family friend, who holds a Colonial Office post in India and recounts exotic adventures killing tigers, sometimes from the back of an elephant. Jack's unlikely surname makes him a shallow modern avatar of that outgoing English spirit of maritime exploration encapsulated in Stormalong John, the buccaneering hero of many old sea shanties ('I'd sail this wide world 'round and 'round, To my way hay, Stormalong, John!').

Glorious summer weather and the incipience of heterosexual love give Katherine's holiday a richly languorous quality: 'Here with the Fennels, time had a different quality from when she was at home. She could almost feel it passing slowly, like thick cream pouring from a silver jug' (*AGW*, 101). She finds Robin physically attractive – 'she thought him beautiful' (*AGW*, 128) – but is taken aback by his regal manner: 'It couldn't be natural for anyone of sixteen to behave like a Prince Regent and a foreign ambassador combined' (*AGW*, 90). However, she grasps that his grace derives in part from the easy presumption of power of the English public school class and that this can swiftly pass from precociousness to stultification:

> In five years' time it was quite possible he would no longer be remark-able, but at sixteen his almost supernatural maturity suggested that he drew on some inner spiritual calm. Looking at him one evening when he happened to be fingering the piano, she was overwhelmed by a sense of barren perfection. He had reached, it seemed to her, a state when he no longer needed to do anything. (*AGW*, 109)

Robin has peaked at 16: by inhibiting further growth, the system of values that presently makes him mature for his years will shortly make him immature.

One index of this is the fact that he wants to go into the Diplomatic Service on a career path equivalent to that of the crass Stormalong. In describing his plans, his sister Jane foreshadows the ghastly predictability of English bourgeois life: 'He will marry at thirty – I can't remember for the moment what post he'll be holding then' (*AGW*, 115). The same well-drilled perfectionism is there in Robin's sporting pursuits: his attempt to explain punting to Katherine is mechanically 'by the book'; while his tennis game is 'fast, neat, open', but so 'unvarying' that she swiftly deduces that the way to beat him is to 'break up the pattern he imposed' (*AGW*, 100). This is not Robin's fault: he is the product of his training. The Fennels have impeccable manners but are emotionally unexpressive. Their household library consists of 'a set of the Stud Book' and a few 'cheap novels, picked up on summer holidays' (*AGW*, 102). It is presumably a comparable cultural impoverish-ment that has made Jack the sort of young man who enthuses about killing Indian tigers but does not have a word to say about the peoples of India or their ancient civilization. On this evidence, the modern English are too insular, too incurious, to be the custodians of a world empire, India achiev-ing independence a decade later in the very year of the novel's publication.

Katherine's parents are described as 'intellectual and given to strange actions', as though they are not just cultured but bohemian (*AGW*, 154).

Unlike the bourgeois Fennels who are entranced by Jack's anecdotes, Katherine found 'listening to the half-intelligible ramble of this English Colonial Official was irritating' (*AGW*, 169). In this homogeneous society, she advocates the virtues of lateral thinking, difference and hybridity. Explaining her tennis victory over Robin, she says: 'If I play as you play, I lose. So I play differently' – something of a credo, that, for young Larkin's relation to the ideology of the day (*AGW*, 101). When Jane ponders whom to marry, Katherine unhesitatingly replies: 'Oh, a foreigner [...] Someone opposite to you' (*AGW*, 154). This same espousal of opposites as a form of resistance to the monolithic – Katherine, we remember, has affinities with two entirely different linguistic groupings involving half-a-dozen nation states – is there when she meets Robin's intended compliment, 'you're almost one of the family', with the challenging response: 'It would be amusing if I were [...] Don't you think families with a foreign side are more interesting? They become much stronger.' In what may be a case of the insidious, half-meant anti-Semitism, so familiar in polite English society at the time, Robin cryptically replies: 'That's what the Jews think, isn't it' (*AGW*, 158). As this conversation almost certainly takes place in 1936, by which time the Nazi persecution of European Jews was underway, Robin can hardly be congratulated on proving his fitness for the Diplomatic Service.[21]

That this critique of English values is 'othered' in gender as well as national terms is suggested by Katherine's sporadic but intense moments of communion with the 25-year-old Jane. Early in the visit, Katherine is mortified when she spills tea on her bedding, but Jane responds with a fit of laughter:

'Lord, that was funny.'
'Funny?'
'Well, it seemed funny to me.' She gave a subdued snort. 'I like that kind of thing – do you know what I mean? Something really outrageous [...] It's the kind of thing that makes life worth living.'
'What do you mean?'
'Something that really upsets –' (*AGW*, 106)

This may suggest that under the governance of men, women are reduced to the role of agents of misrule; but it also hints at the spontaneous emotional freemasonry that can ignite among the disempowered. On another occasion Jane momentarily relinquishes the bonds of family for those of 'sisterhood' by warning Katherine that, appearances notwithstanding, 'Robin is ordinary, down to the last button' (*AGW*, 107). Again, where Robin's rule-book instructions fail, Jane succeeds in teaching Katherine to punt by encouraging her to follow her own body rhythm. To Katherine's surprise and romantic disappointment, it was Jane who persuaded Robin to invite her to visit England because she thought Katherine 'exactly the kind of person I should have liked to know myself' (*AGW*, 149). Jane's explanation punningly encompasses several levels of meaning: you are the kind of person I should like to know; you are the kind of person I should like to know me; you are the kind of person I should like to know the better to know myself.

Katherine toys with inviting Jane on a reciprocal visit to her country but this idea, and the incipient sorority, yields to the pressure of prescribed gender roles. Jane, we learn, left school at 16; engaged in desultory office work, some of it arranged by her father; and now pretends to 'help mother' while unenthusiastically awaiting a proposal of marriage. When Katherine earlier asked Robin what does his sister do, he seemed incredulous that the question should even arise: 'Do? Nothing much' (*AGW*, 138). On another occasion he says of Jane, despite being nearly a decade her junior: 'She can make lemonade. I think it was what she was put on the earth to do' (*AGW*, 83). Conversely, Jane defers to the idea that her young brother is her superior: 'As you've no doubt gathered, Robin has the brains of the family' (*AGW*, 151). Yet Jane's interest in other societies is arguably the more passionate and developed. According to Robin, her 'favourite literature [...] is written by people who travel about with a gun and a typewriter': Hemingway's *Death in the Afternoon* (1932) and *Green Hills of Africa* (1935), about Spanish bullfighting and big-game hunting in Tanzania respectively, had just appeared. Jane not only nudged her brother into entering a pen-pal scheme but then took the initiative in inviting his correspondent to England; and she is far more desirous than Robin to use the visit to glimpse cultural alternatives – 'The only times she paid willing attention were when Katherine said anything about her own home, how it differed from theirs' (*AGW*, 96, 117). She contrasts the existential intensity of her interest with Robin's more detached, data-gathering approach: 'I like to *know* about places [...] All you care about is the birthrate and the standard of living. I want to know what I should feel like if I lived there' (*AGW*, 96). Moreover, her interest in Katherine's birthright is born of an alienation from her own: 'I am English, more's the pity' (*AGW*, 113).

It is therefore difficult to believe that differences in personality or intelligence are determining the divergent destinies of the Fennel siblings rather than society's different gender expectations. When this long mid-section ends, rather abruptly, with Jane's announcement that she has accepted Jack's proposal of marriage, she sounds cheerful about it (perhaps more with relief than genuine enthusiasm), but the reader feels deflated. As his preposterous surname suggests, Jack's ebullient exterior life masks the absence of an interior one. Robin's interest in 'abroad' points logically towards a degree in Languages and a diplomatic career, Jane's equivalent interest leads to a fleeting friendship with Katherine and marriage to a man who is not worthy of her. The brother accesses the world direct, the sister only as mediated by relations of dependency.[22]

Nation, empire, gender: 1942

This summer interlude in which the critical is blended with the idyllic is sandwiched between two sections set in wartime England in what is almost certainly the winter of 1942. These episodes extinguish all traces of the idyllic by forcibly demonstrating that under wartime constraints English xenophobia has intensified, gender relations have become so polarized that the sexes become parodies of themselves, and the British are exposed as unworthy custodians not just of a great empire but also a great world language. These themes are explored in relation to four locales: the branch library of a provincial city where Katherine has worked for nine months in her second year as a refugee; the dentistry to which Katherine takes a colleague for treatment; the suburban home of Miss Parbury, prospective fiancée of Katherine's boss; and Katherine's tiny flat, where she receives a visit from Robin. Of these, the second may be regarded as supplementary to the first, providing corroboration rather than new information – as when the dentist gives Katherine yet another reminder of her foreign status by tartly referring to 'the law – the law of *this* country' (*AGW*, 46).

The library where Katherine works is mainly staffed by unmarried women – Miss Brooks, Miss Holloway, Miss Feather, Miss Green – ruled over by the formidable Mr Anstey (near anagram of nasty).[23] Old fashioned, pompous and authoritarian, Anstey operates in the 'unbreakable belief that all things depended on him, and that he managed, despite an overwhelming weight of work, to administer every detail efficiently' (*AGW*, 21). Despite his bad teeth, spectacles and stench of pipe-smoke, Anstey looks down on the surrounding world as though from a very great height, scorning university 'johnnies', condescending to foreigners (he reproves Katherine for her lack 'of what we English call savvy or gumption or ... *nous*') and equating his female staff with a stereotype of scatty womanhood, 'her head full of jazz-tunes or boy-friends or the latest "movie", or whatever they call them' (*AGW*, 17–18). How Larkin, a great fan of both jazz and cinema, must have relished writing that last sentence!

Katherine abominates Anstey but gradually comes to see that his bluster signals fear not confidence. 'Mr Rylands was the real head,' Miss Green explains, after Katherine has helped her to the dentist. 'He was a very different kind of person altogether. Young and very well-educated. He had a university degree. But when the war started he had to go into the army, unfortunately' (*AGW*, 37). This view is later confirmed by Miss Holloway:

> 'Anstey isn't that bad, you know. He's really quite decent. You see, he's got where he wanted to get, now, because of the war, and he's deadly afraid that afterwards he'll be stood down again. That makes him suspicious of everything and everybody. And he longs to be efficient, but he just isn't a big enough man for the job.' (*AGW*, 222)

The problem, then, is more systemic than personal. Anstey has been over-promoted in accord with a patriarchal culture that would sooner place incompetent men in jobs vacated by competent ones than call upon the services of talented women.

This point is epitomized in the physical inadequacies of the men who prosper in the absence of the 'able-bodied' called into active service. Just as Anstey is 'thin, wizened' and bespectacled, so the dentist 'was slightly deaf', 'wore spectacles' and 'half-resembled an idiot boy' (*AGW*, 16, 41). Again, the description of Katherine 'standing on a table in the Reading Room to fit a new bulb in one of the lights, while old men stared aqueously at her legs' seems rather an account of aged impotence than active lechery (*AGW*, 25). That patriarchal power is more seeming than real, more performative than intrinsic, acquired rather than given, is conveyed in the theatrical imagery applied to the men – not least to the melodramatic huffing and puffing of Anstey: he spoke in 'a voice that might be used on the stage'; 'He made a theatrical gesture'; 'he continued with an unfunny theatrical leer' (*AGW*, 18, 20, 208). Elsewhere, Jack Stormalong 'theatrically drank a quantity of beer'; 'two slightly-intoxicated soldiers [...] grabbed theatrically' at Katherine and Miss Holloway; and at the novel's close we observe Robin 'play the gay officer, and in due course [...] play the forsaken boy' (*AGW*, 164, 222–3, 241). That intelligent women can only exert a modicum of control indirectly by answering this male performance of power with an equally theatrical performance of subservience is just as deftly established: 'Miss Feather, perhaps alone of the staff, had the knack of keeping Mr Anstey fairly close to the point: she inserted submissive, insinuating remarks that gently urged him back to the path she wished him to follow' (*AGW*, 20).

As with the Fennels and Stormalong in the 1936 sequence, the personnel, the institutions and even the names of the characters take on a considerable symbolic value. For instance, as well as being a near anagram of 'nasty' and a possible nod in the direction of Aldous Huxley, Anstey is the name of a village near Leicester, not far from Larkin's home town of Coventry. The village is in the middle of the Midlands, a contender for the title of *omphalos* of England. That Anstey shares its name grants him an umbilical relation to Englishness, making his inadequacies representative. His 'outlandish Christian name' of 'Lancelot', invoking a romantic hero of the Arthurian cycle as recounted by innumerable English authors from Sir Thomas Malory to Lord Tennyson, satirically intensifies the connection (*AGW*, 187). As England heads an international empire, so Anstey heads a library that is repeatedly shown to be a depository of world culture: Katherine and Miss Brooks 'met [...] by a special display shelf on Japan'; questions are asked about a misplaced 'book on Uganda'; shortly thereafter, 'Katherine turned back and went to the Africa section' (*AGW*, 14–15). Even the parochial Anstey dimly grasps that 'human knowledge is the same in England, France, Germany or anywhere on God's earth' (*AGW*, 19). Yet Katherine observes that the English homes she visits are devoid of intelligent literature, while she alone seems to regret the fact that 'library assistants are forced to do everything to books except read them' (*AGW*, 22).

This pervasive English philistinism extends to the language in which the said books are written, the non-anglophone Katherine being shocked to discover that her command of the language exceeds that of the natives: 'It's hard to understand English at first, you all speak so carelessly'; 'she could not fathom what these English people meant'; 'the housemaid [...] passed some unintelligible remark to her in uncouth English' (*AGW*, 59, 143, 103). It is indicative that when Anstey pompously lectures Katherine on her lack of 'what we English call savvy or gumption or ... *nous*', his anglocentrism blinds him to the fact that the words he attributes to 'we English' are all of foreign provenance: *savvy* is a corruption of Spanish *sabe*, cognate with the French *savoir faire*; *gumption*, the *OED* tells us, is 'Scotch'; while *nous* is Greek for mind or intellect. By such deft detailing, the novel uses the library as a microcosm of a monoglot patriarchal culture that is inefficient, ill-read, poorly spoken, emotionally repressed, aesthetically retarded and utterly unappreciative of the enigmatic foreign woman in its midst.

It might be thought that the best a society of such rigid sexual segregation has to offer is to be located in some essentialized female realm of nurturance and self-effacement. If anything, however, the horrors of the male-dominated urban world of work are exceeded by those of the feminized suburban domestic sphere. This is revealed when Katherine returns a lost handbag to a Miss Veronica Parbury, who is on the point of becoming engaged to Mr Anstey. The journey to her home on the outskirts of the city presents a terrible indictment of middle England with its littered buses, 'dirty hedges', 'secretive curtains' and drab houses with a 'yard of earth in front of them' and 'depressing yard' at the back. Miss Parbury, though scarcely 30 years old, 'was one of the people who do not look right till they are nearly fifty, when their eccentric appearance harmonizes with the caricaturing onset of age' (*AGW*, 190–3). Her 'soulless' home smells of cooking, she wears a 'sickly lemon necklace' and the cup of tea she offers Katherine is 'virulently sugared' (*AGW*, 201, 194). Looking round the sitting-room, Katherine is reminded

> how ugly the English houses were. This room was overcrowded with gimcrack furniture, and the furniture overcrowded with trifling ornaments and photographs, fancy matchbox stands and little woolly dogs made out of pipecleaners. On the wall were a few framed, coloured photographs, extraordinarily unpleasant to look at.

As with the bourgeois Fennels, Katherine is quick to remark that 'there were no books in the room' apart from some 'dreary rubbish, such as a Holiday Haunts for 1928' and 'a small book of Common Prayer lying on the sideboard' (*AGW*, 193–4). Observant readers will catch that early use of Larkin's characteristic pun on the word 'lying'.[24]

'There was nothing masculine in the room,' Katherine notes, underlining the aesthetic impoverishment of the abjected feminine side of patriarchal culture. Instead, she quickly discovers, the oppressive weight of the maternal hovers above their heads in the literal form of Miss Parbury's bedridden mother – paralysed, dazed, speechless, and prone to the cruel delusion that her self-sacrificing daughter is trying to poison her. By answering the grotesquerie of the male workplace with this nightmare vision of the matriarchal household, the novel suggests that each sex becomes a travesty of itself when pushed to extremes by a code of gender apartheid. Certainly, the reader may be forgiven for howling with appalled laughter when Veronica Parbury, drowning in vulgarity and repression, sympathizes with Katherine's exilic condition: 'When you think of it, we've nothing to grumble at in England' (*AGW*, 195). If the Parbury household is a microcosm of Britannia, that female domain in whose defence the men have gone away to fight, the novel seriously poses the question what there is worth killing or dying for.

While the visit has confirmed Katherine's revulsion at the tawdry depthlessness of English culture, it has offered her some important lessons about relationships. She is moved to discover that an ogre like Anstey can give and inspire love; and even more touched at Miss Parbury's lack of self-pity despite the threat to her marriage plans posed by her mother's condition: 'she was not', we are told, 'a tragic personality' (*AGW*, 198). It is true that in the very next scene Katherine reacts to Anstey's latest sermon by resigning – a glorious anticipation of the '*Stuff your pension!*' moment in 'Toads' (*CP*, 89; *TCP*, 38). However, like Jane's hasty marriage, this gesture may signify that women make impromptu decisions, often ill-advised, not because they are inherently impulsive, but because a social reality in which all the power is held by men pressures them into acting opportunistically. Nonetheless, Katherine realizes 'with annoyance' that her glimpse into Anstey's emotional life means 'that she could not hate him as simply as she had done'; while the example of Miss Parbury challenges her to reconsider her outsider's commitment to self-sufficiency (*AGW*, 204). These lessons are put to the test in the final episode of the novel.

An ellipse for a climax

Her European past obliterated by the war, her alienation from English cultural life reinforced by her disaffection with patriarchy, Katherine has lived in England for nearly two years, and in this particular city for nine months, without establishing a single friendship. When she invites Miss Green to her flat for a cup of tea after the latter's tooth extraction, she candidly admits that her unworthy library colleague is her very first guest: 'I don't know anyone' (*AGW*, 55). At the centre of her psychological estrangement, as it is at the physical centre of the novel, is her remembrance of her summer with the Fennels: 'It was the only period of her life that had not been spoiled by later events, and she found that she could draw upon it hearteningly, remembering when she had been happy' (*AGW*, 185). And at the centre of that memoration is her unresolved attachment to Robin:

> He was in the forefront of a time when she had come to this same strange country, and had been welcomed by strangers and taken in among them [...] And she thought in some way he might lead her back to it. (*AGW*, 216–17)

Her admirable self-reliance and reluctance to exploit a chance acquaintance with what might look like a begging letter are in danger of cryogenizing her emotions at an immature stage; for the fact that she still harbours her teenage feelings for Robin might be regarded as a refusal to grow up. It is in this sense that, although 22 years old, she remains a *girl* in winter.[25]

Her eye caught by Jack's unusual surname while scanning the newspaper for cinema times, Katherine happens upon an obituary announcement of the death of his and Jane's daughter. Her spontaneous letter of condolence elicits a warm reply from Mrs Fennel followed a week later by a note and a visit from Robin, the one on the morning and the other the evening of the narrative's diurnal span. Confronting Robin is Katherine's opportunity to confront the legacy of her past and embrace the future; but what ought to be the climax of the novel is, in more than one sense, profoundly anticlimactic.

Robin arrives late and tipsy, 'swaggering' in his military uniform, and immediately starts mauling Katherine in a thoroughly boorish manner: 'then he was after her again [...] He was coming at her again' (*AGW*, 226–7). When she refuses to have sex with him,

> A dark, wounded look came into his face, like the look of a child that has been refused something it believes its due [...] Was she supposed to be flattered, that he had considered it worth while making a special journey on the off-chance of sleeping with her? (*AGW*, 235)

Robin is revealed as a boy in man's clothing, exactly as Katherine half-predicted six years earlier when wondering if his teenage perfection was a sign that he had peaked. This immaturity she attributes to national factors: 'Why, he was years younger than she was: it must be his English upbringing' (*AGW*, 238). Empowered by patriarchy, the juvenile Robin arrogantly assumes that Katherine will gratefully comply with his sexual demands. 'Someone must have given him the idea that he fascinated women' (*AGW*, 235). However, there is every suggestion that he lacks the expertise to consummate the relationship to their mutual satisfaction. 'She let him kiss her. He did it eagerly but without grace, like a boy learning to smoke' (*AGW*, 232). His technique seems not to have improved since he was 16 when, at the end of Katherine's summer visit, 'He ducked his head and kissed her inexpertly with tight lips [...] It was not a bit like lovemaking' (*AGW*, 173). Now that 'She felt superior to him', Katherine decides that she can accede to his request to stay the night: 'It would be no more than doing him an unimportant kindness' (*AGW*, 241, 243). The indifference with which she agrees leaves him more crestfallen than triumphant. Moreover, '[s]he named a condition' of his staying 'that he accepted'; and while that condition is never specified to the reader, its effect upon Robin is dramatic: 'He released her, as if his desire had suddenly died out [...] it was galling to him, and seemed all wrong.' What could this detumescing precondition be? That he wears a condom? Unlikely, since his presumptiousness is such he has surely come prepared. That their intimacies not proceed to penetrative sex? Or that they sleep together chastely, as friends rather than lovers?

The effect of Larkin's ambiguity is to make us uncertain as to whether or not intercourse takes place; and critics like Alan Brownjohn, Trevor Tolley, Janice Rossen, James Booth, Liz Hedgecock, Conny Engel and Stephen Cooper who blindly assume that it does are rendering determinate a key *aporia* of the text. Booth's emotive description of 'Katherine's despair as she hopelessly submits to Robin's advances' is notably at odds with her cool, controlling behaviour.[26] Ignoring Katherine's precondition not only entails an assumption that sex takes place, with Robin in charge, it also involves suppression of the puns and hints colouring her stream of consciousness. 'Now she could go through with her decision, and be sure that nothing would come of it' (*AGW*, 244). Does this mean: she could sleep with Robin safe in the knowledge their relationship has no future; or, that she can sleep with Robin without fear of pregnancy (perhaps because of an insistence upon use of a prophylactic)? 'He seemed restless and unsatisfied, as she knew he would be' (*AGW*, 246). Is Robin's anticipated unfulfilment the result of her stipulation – proof, perhaps, of her prohibiting intercourse or else limiting it to the manual or the oral? The text as insistently invites us to ask these questions as it withholds the evidence allowing us to conclusively answer them. In short, Larkin's radical ellipsis robs not only the protagonists but also us readers of an assured climax.

To what end? Larkin's calculated indeterminacy subverts the conventional war novel by casting doubt on the sexual prowess its male hero is meant to display at home before demonstrating his military prowess in foreign fields. Through this ellipse a novel which has already debunked the workplace patriarchy of Mr Anstey and the debilitating matriarchy of the Parbury household ends by subverting the martial patriarchy embodied in the uniformed Robin Fennel. Before they succumb to a deep sleep whose restorative, gladdening qualities are oxymoronically couched in a language of 'darkness' and 'icefloes', Robin discloses that Jane's dead daughter had been named after Katherine (*AGW*, 248). This reminder that in some ways

Jane, whose marriage sounds unhappy, was always the Fennel sibling most attuned to Katherine's bracing sensibility, is not a last-minute assertion of 'female' values. The symbolism of the little girl's death from 'a defective heart' works against that idea (*AGW*, 236). If *A Girl in Winter* undermines the conventions of male war fiction, it as forcefully rejects both the women's romance novel with its obligatory 'happy ever after' conclusion and the female friendship novel with its lesbian subtext ('men are the problem, women are the solution'). Katherine has overcome her idealization of Robin, and with it her idealization of a specifically English construction of masculinity, without reaching for an answering idealization in the form of domestic matriarchy (the Parburys) or sisterhood (Jane Fennel). The novel's concluding *aporia* undoes realist concepts of verifiability and authentication, leaving Katherine to quest forward icily undeceived by the snares of such essentialized thinking.

A prevision of the four-act structure

We began this chapter with Richard Palmer's claim that Larkin's prose fiction 'does not remotely telegraph the poetry that would ensue, either in quality or in the specifics of style, tone, choices of form, governing preoccupations and subject matter'.[27] Larkin himself recognized no such demarcation, repeating to one interviewer after another that the strengths and weaknesses of *Jill* and *A Girl in Winter* stemmed from their closeness to poetry. He told Ian Hamilton 'they were over-sized poems'. To Neil Powell he was more expansive: 'I was influenced by the kind of critical attitude that you used to get in *Scrutiny* – the novel as dramatic poem. I certainly saw novels as rather poetic things, perhaps too poetic.' This argument was punched home in interviews with John Haffenden ('I don't think my books were novels, they were more kinds of prose poems'), A.N. Wilson ('they were poems. Long, diffuse poems perhaps') and the *Paris Review* ('A long poem for me would be a novel. In that sense, *A Girl in Winter* is a poem') (*FR*, 24, 32, 49, 114; *RW*, 66).

Larkin was a master at sending commentators accelerating down hermeneutical *culs-de-sac*. In this instance, however, there are grounds for favouring his position over that of proponents of the rupture like Palmer. One such which might be pursued at length concerns the insistent use of *as if*, an unusual variant of the simile which Virginia Woolf had already made great play with in her most 'poetical' novel, *The Waves*:

> As the light increased a bud here and there split asunder and shook out flowers, green veined and quivering, *as if* the effort of opening had set them rocking, and pealing a faint carillon as they beat their frail clappers against their white walls. Everything became softly amorphous, *as if* the china of the plate flowed and the steel of the knife were liquid.[28] (The emphases here and in the sequent four quotations are added.)

This construction is employed on nearly 40 occasions in *A Girl in Winter*, sometimes two or three to a page:

> So far he had stood insipidly upon his party-manners, even when they had been alone, *as if* playing at grown-ups [...] They welcomed her undramatically, even casually, *as if* she had come from the next village [...] Really, he acted *as if* he had long ago made up his mind about her. (*AGW*, 90)

> Above all she felt tired, *as if* that day she had made a journey [...] She knew Merion Street well, so that even though it was as dark *as if* the night had collapsed and was heaped all above it, she knew by counting her steps how far she had to go [...] As usual she slid the key straight into the teeth of the lock, but as she did so she heard a breath intaken very close and near the ground, *as if* an animal were there. (*AGW*, 225)

The locution may then be tracked through Larkin poems, early ('So through that unripe day you bore your head') and late ('MCMXIV'):

> Those long uneven lines
> Standing as patiently
> *As if* they were stretched outside
> The Oval or Villa Park,
> The crowns of hats, the sun
> On moustached archaic faces
> Grinning *as if* it were all
> An August Bank Holiday lark[29] (*CP*, 127; *TCP*, 60)

From there one might go on to validate Larkin's crucial role in the evolution from modernist to postmodernist aesthetics by analysing how this same device or formula is used in 'Line with Atoll and Idol', a typically audacious poem by postmodern maestro Peter Didsbury:

> *As if* were being drawn a thin black line
> in the air a dozen feet above the sea.
> *As if* it travelled parallel with Ocean,
> but Ocean lay calm in an everywhere shallow bed,
> devoid of ornament,
> and never did wave snap hungrily up at the sky.
> And *as if* that part of the line which moved
> (for always these things are hard to comprehend)
> made headway toward a coast[30]

Similar arguments might be advanced concerning other forms of figuration characterizing both *A Girl in Winter* and the mature poems, including puns, negative qualifiers, split similes and oxymora.

As promised above (p. 23), I shall instead end this chapter with the claim that *A Girl in Winter* prefigures the classic four-act structure with closing reversal of the major poems. This model was perfected over many years, with much trial and error, poems like 'March Past', 'Places, Loved Ones', 'Reference Back' and 'Send No Money' experimenting with a slightly simpler tripartite format. 'Places, Loved Ones' provides a particularly clear illustration as each stage in the argument has a single stanza allocated to it: *verse one*, I have never found either the place which or the person who commanded my devotion; *verse two*, but wishing to be swept off one's feet may be a way of absolving oneself of responsibility when things go wrong ('I was powerless to resist'); *verse three*, on the other hand, to have missed out on such an overwhelming experience carries its own potential for self-delusion, the temptation being to hide a sense of failure by pretending to have willed what one merely settled for (*CP*, 99; *TCP*, 29).

This matrix may readily be related to *A Girl in Winter*, the present time of the novel being interrupted by a lengthy flashback in a manner that yields a tripartite formation emphatically drawn to the reader's attention by a combination of intervening blank pages with the capitalized subheadings 'PART ONE', 'PART TWO' and 'PART THREE'. A good deal of the novel's business, narrative and thematic, may be mapped onto the template as in Table 1.1. This model also has the virtue of foregrounding that indebtedness to modernist prototypes like *Kangaroo* and *Light in August* which Tolley would deny. Thus the third column, specifying the 'Year', renders visible the prolepsis inevitably entailed to the flashback; for as Part Two jumps *back* six years from Part One, so Part Three jumps *forward* six years from Part Two.

What this grid fails to render visible is a sustained *resistance* to valorized notions of the feminine appealed to by 'sympathetic' critics like Cooper and Booth. Hence, the former greatly simplifies the novel's analysis of sexual politics by demonizing the men: Anstey, something of a stuffed shirt, is described by Cooper as a 'tyrant manager'; Mr Fennel, gentlest of father figures, he presents as 'a tyrannical patriarch'; while the indeterminacies of the novel's denouement are exchanged for a tale of female submission to male predation ('Katherine gives in to Robin's sexual demands'). By contrast, the answering grotesquerie of Katherine's female acquaintances is

Table 1.1 The three-part structure

Section	Time	Year	Season	National context	Social context	Relationship
PART ONE	Present	1942	Winter	England at war	Work	The boss The dentist
PART TWO	Past	1936	Summer	England at peace	Home	Robin Fennel Jane Fennel
PART THREE	Present	1942	Winter	England at war	Work	The boss Robin Fennel

systematically repressed as a prelude to declaring that 'The novel suggests a triumph of the feminine over the masculine.'[31] The reality is very different. Throughout her 1936 stay with the Fennels, Katherine, who 'had so far loved only women and girls', is torn between her infatuation with Robin and an uneasy awareness that Jane may be more of an elective affinity: 'Katherine felt balanced between the two conflicting wills. So far she had given one vote to each' (*AGW*, 127, 122). This dialectic allows the teenage Katherine to rehearse adult choices by exploring the rival attractions of romantic versus companionate affection, heterosexual versus homosexual identification, marriage versus sisterhood. In other words, the brother/sister duality offers her a miniaturized version of the patriarchy/matriarchy dichotomy of her winter of 1942.

Similarly, the trip to the dentist counterpoises Katherine's protectiveness towards Miss Green in the face of the dentist's bullying with the failure of any real communion between the two young women. Katherine volunteers to accompany her 'pathetic and spiteful' looking colleague, cajoles the reluctant patient and tetchy medical practitioner to complete the treatment, takes Miss Green to her flat for post-operative refreshment and recuperation, finally lending her companion the bus fare home because she is too ill to return to work (*AGW*, 28). Katherine then retrieves Miss Green's handbag from Miss Parbury, who had taken it by mistake. Returning to the library after accomplishing this task, Katherine not only finds her lateness exacerbated by the fact that Miss Green has broken her word and reported back ahead of her, she has also been spreading tittle-tattle about Katherine's private life. The force of this betrayal of sisterhood is conveyed in another of the novel's *as if* formulae: 'Katherine felt as if she had suffered a slug to crawl across her' (*AGW*, 214). The horrors of the Parbury household, then, are only the most conspicuous in a series of deflations of essentialized notions of female unity.

We can now see that, as in the mature poems, Larkin presents a deconstructive argument in four stages: first, the establishing of a conventional binary (male/female); second, the demonstration that the antinomies are arranged in a violent hierarchy (Anstey rules his female staff); third, the reversing of that hierarchy (Katherine flouts patriarchal conventions in a variety of contexts); and fourth, the displacement of that reversed hierarchy (in which women are privileged over men) in the disillusioning contacts with Jane Fennel, Miss Green and Veronica Parbury. At the end of this trajectory the reader is confronted, not with an equally monolithic matriarchal mirror-reversal of the patriarchal starting-point, but with a profound realization of the need for new subject positions outside this constrictive either/or. As Katherine earlier advocates intermarriage across national and ethnic lines ('families with a foreign side [...] become much stronger'), so the novel suggests that human subjectivity is too mobile and various to benefit from rigid gender differentiation. *A Girl in Winter* promotes the virtues of heterogeneity, of hybridization, of being released from biological belonging.

Table 1.2   The four-act structure

Act	Larkin's section	Date	Gender context
I	'Part One'	Winter 1942	Adult Katherine under patriarchal rule in the institutional contexts of the library and the dentistry with a subsidiary theme of Miss Green's selfishness.
II	'Part Two'	Summer 1936	Teenage Katherine rehearsing her adult gender alignment through the rival attractions of Robin and Jane Fennel.
III	First half of 'Part Three'	Winter 1942	Adult Katherine's disillusionment with matriarchy as encapsulated in the all-female Parbury household.
IV	Second half of 'Part Three'	Winter 1942	Adult Katherine's alienation from patriarchy in the contexts of work and on the military front (the uniformed Robin Fennel), with a subsidiary theme of Miss Green's betrayal.

Mapping the arc of this deconstructive gender analysis onto the novel's tripartite structure requires some such modification of the earlier grid as in Table 1.2.

By adding a fourth act, *A Girl in Winter* has given a deconstructive turn to the tripartite model inherited from modernism and shifted aesthetics towards a postmodernist practice in which binaries are unfixed, either/ors confounded and anti-essentialist thinking can begin. In the process it has anticipated by five, ten, sometimes 20 years the four-part *schema* of such poetic masterpieces as 'Self's the Man' (with its deconstruction of the husband/bachelor binary), 'Reasons for Attendance' (the social life/the artistic vocation), 'Toads' (employment/unemployment) and 'Dockery and Son' (parenthood/childlessness).

Conclusion

A Girl in Winter is not a masterpiece.[32] One reason for this is the uncertainty with which techniques such as ellipsis are employed. The withholdings or avoidances that so brilliantly problematize stereotypical assumptions on occasion thwart character motivation and strain credulity. In the case of Katherine we have several times remarked the increment of meaning resulting from the *aporia* regarding her origins. For instance, her speaking English better than the British is the more upbraiding for our ignorance of her nationality since it implies that they speak our language better than we do in all the eligible countries – France, Germany, Belgium, Holland, Austria, Luxembourg, Lichtenstein, Switzerland. However, related episodes weaken the text rather than strengthening it. Jane's remark that the Fennel family had speculated that Katherine was Roman Catholic might hint at France as her home country since one would hardly make such a presupposition regarding an intensely Protestant nation like the Dutch, nor even a multi-denominational country like Germany (over 50 million of whose 80 million inhabitants are of Protestant background). Katherine's retort, 'Oh no. I'm not Catholic,' is psychologically implausible in that we are given no explanation for her not supplementing this denial with a corrective – 'Oh no. I'm not Catholic. I'm a Protestant/Jew/atheist/agnostic' (*AGW*, 93). Worse are those occasions when Katherine describes her home: 'I live in a wide street with trees and seats ... The houses are much alike. High, white ... fairly big' (*AGW*, 113). The novel's need to keep her homeland uncertain has rendered her description of it vague to the point of banality.[33]

Yet even if these flaws give it the air of an apprentice piece, rendering it sometimes stilted or pallid – 'constricted', as Martin Amis says – *A Girl in Winter* remains an arresting novelistic anticipation of the key strategies of the verse: radical ellipsis, the four-act structure with closing reversal, deconstructive linguistic tropes, and an anti-essentialist approach to matters of gender, sexuality, nation, race, religion and class.[34] The fact that Larkin scholarship has largely failed to recognize the importance of these techniques to the major poems inevitably leads to an underestimation of this prose rehearsal. That *A Girl in Winter* is at once Larkin's greatest achievement of the 1940s and the most underestimated work in the *oeuvre* demonstrates how few participants in the Larkin debate are willing to undergo (in Sheridan's *mot juste*) the *fatigue* of arriving at an independent judgement.

2
Radical Ekphrasis: 'An Arundel Tomb', 'The Card-Players', 'Lines on a Young Lady's Photograph Album'

The Movement and visual culture

The critical orthodoxy takes it as axiomatic that Movement writers sought to address life direct rather than as filtered through prior art. In the introduction to *Poets of the 1950s* (1955), the first anthology of the Movement generation, D.J. Enright wrote: 'we do need poetry that is *about* something, poetry that is about people – preferably other people'.[1] In his prose contribution to the volume, Larkin put it the other way round – we do not want poetry that is about poetry:

> As a guiding principle I believe that every poem must be its own sole freshly-created universe, and therefore have no belief in 'tradition' or a common myth-kitty or casual allusions in poems to other poems or poets, which last I find unpleasantly like the talk of literary understrappers letting you see they know the right people. A poet's only guide is his own judgement. (*RW*, 79)

Kingsley Amis's position was just as intransigent but was more explicit that the embargo on art about art extended to the visual as much as, if not more than, the literary inheritance: 'nobody wants any more poems about philosophers or paintings or novelists or art galleries or mythology or foreign cities or other poems. At least I hope nobody wants them.'[2] Laurence Lerner summarizes 'the typical Movement poet' who 'emerges from these statements' in the phrase 'the poet as ordinary man'.[3] Alvarez agrees: 'he is just like the man next door – in fact, he probably *is* the man next door'.[4]

The publication of *Lucky Jim* (1954) set a rancorous tone for the debate, Jim Dixon's jibes against 'filthy Mozart' being taken as an article of faith on Amis's part rather than an expression of the protagonist's irritation at the cultural pretension of the fictional Welches. The 'Lucky Jim attitude' was widely condemned, Amis being snobbishly described as a 'Welfare Wodehouse' (*The Sunday Times*), 'the scholarship boy's Stephen Spender'

(*Twentieth Century* magazine) and 'a fish-and-chip Waugh' (*Commonweal*). Larkin was implicated in the same culture wars, a review of *The Less Deceived* in *The Listener* presenting him as one of 'the Lucky Jim poets' – such lines as 'A Grecian statue kicked in the privates' from 'If, My Darling' opening a vein of vandalistic invective that recurs throughout the *oeuvre* ('Books are a load of crap', 'the shit in the shuttered château') (*CP*, 41, 131, 202; *TCP*, 44, 62, 114).

As early as 1957, one of the leading contributors to and theorists of Movement poetry, Donald Davie, was expressing his concern that the group's 'impatience with cultural pretentiousness is turning into impatience with culture'.[5] To this day hostile commentators like Bryan Appleyard castigate 'the cultivatedly philistine sensibilities of the Movement' or insist, in the words of Andrew Duncan, that 'the Movement jettisoned Culture with a shudder'. Even the sympathetic Tolley admits '"Culture" was a bad word for the Movement writers.'[6] Whether they come to praise or blame, these critics all succumb to the Intentionalist Fallacy of supposing that artworks are subservient to the manifestos of their creators. The reality is quite otherwise. As even their titles attest, many Movement poems are directly addressed to or modelled upon pre-existing artworks, commonly paintings or sculptures, and thereby flout the group ideology ('nobody wants any more poems about [...] paintings or [...] art galleries'), refracting raw experience through a recession of visual representations. One thinks of 'The Rokeby Venus' by Robert Conquest; 'Limited Achievement' by Donald Davie; Thom Gunn's 'In Santa Maria del Popolo'; 'The Laughing Hyena, after Hokusai' and 'Home and Colonial: Or, Rousseau's Tropical Storm with Tiger', both by Enright; and, from Elizabeth Jennings, 'Mantegna's Agony in the Garden', 'Michelangelo's First Pietà', 'Caravaggio's Narcissus in Rome' and 'The Nature of Prayer'.

Quite contrary to the blokish persona he sometimes affected, and which was then transfixed by the likes of Germaine Greer (who described him as 'anti-intellectual'), Bryan Appleyard (for whom he is a 'provincial grotesque') or Peter Ackroyd (who dismissed him as 'a foul-mouthed bigot'), Larkin is the most cultured of all Movement writers and possibly the most art-conscious British poet of the mid-century period.[7] Even a preliminary listing of the visual media invoked by his poems would include: painting ('The Card-Players'); sculpture ('An Arundel Tomb'); architecture, ancient ('Church Going') and modern ('The Building'); illuminated manuscripts ('Long Lion Days'); photography ('Lines on a Young Lady's Photograph Album'); posters ('Sunny Prestatyn'); billboard advertisements ('Essential Beauty'); movies ('Born Yesterday', the ending of 'The Whitsun Weddings'); cinema newsreels ('At Grass', 'Faith Healing'); television documentaries ('The Explosion'); and public monuments ('Bridge for the Living'). Moreover, many of these poems situate themselves in relation to previous poems of a similar kind, such as Keats's 'Ode on a Grecian Urn', so that the address to a particular artefact is mediated by awareness of the larger tradition of writerly deference to the visual arts.[8] A brief history of this poetic *ekphrasis* (sometimes Latinized as *ecphrasis*) will help us to calibrate the scale and nature of Larkin's interventions.

The ekphrastic tradition in poetry

The tradition of devoting the part or the whole of a poem to an encounter with visual art is usually said to begin with Homer's account of the shield of Achilles, Hesiod's of the shield of Herakles and dozens of epigrams in the *Greek Anthology*. All of these might be regarded as instances of *notional ekphrasis* in that the visual artworks described are fictional. *Actual ekphrasis*, in which the poem verbally represents a tangible art object which (where it is still extant) readers might visit and independently assess, features prominently in Virgil, Dante, Ariosto, Tasso and Spenser. Both types of ekphrasis riot through post-Renaissance anglophone poetry of the seventeenth (Marvell), eighteenth (Pope, Thomson) and nineteenth centuries (Wordsworth, Keats, Shelley, Byron, Melville, Longfellow, Dante Gabriel Rossetti, Robert Browning, Swinburne). The twentieth century maintained the continuity with notable contributions from Hart Crane (*The Bridge*), William Carlos Williams (*Pictures from Brueghel*), D.H. Lawrence ('Michelangelo'), John Berryman ('Winter Landscape'), Robert Lowell ('For the Union Dead'), Elizabeth Bishop ('Large Bad Picture'), Maurice Rutherford ('The Light of the World, a Holman Hunt print remembered'), Anne Stevenson ('Seven Poems after Francis Bacon'), Douglas Dunn (the sequence *A Line in the Water* with aquatints by Norman Ackroyd), Paul Durcan (*Crazy about Women*), Paul Muldoon ('Paul Klee: They're Biting'), Carol Ann Duffy ('Oppenheim's Cup and Saucer',[9] 'Three Paintings'), Simon Armitage ('Millet: The Gleaners'), Sean O'Brien (*Night Train*, with artwork by Birtley Aris), Grace Nichols ('Weeping Woman'), Jo Shapcott ('Viral Landscape', 'Piss Flower'), Pascale Petit (*What the Water Gave Me*, 52 poems about Frida Kahlo, many of them one-to-one meditations upon individual paintings) and Jackie Kay (with several poems after Degas, Cézanne and Moore in her 2011 collection *Fiere*).

The explosion of ekphrastic verses in the Romantic period – Wordsworth alone wrote 24 such – is intimately connected with the eighteenth-century invention of the public museum. As early as 1619 the Italian Baroque poet Giambattista Marino published a collection of almost five hundred short poems that he called his 'Gallery' (*La Galeria*), all directed to real or imaginary works of art and carefully categorized with regard to subject (portraits, classical mythology, biblical scenes, etc.). In a smaller-scale way, Marvell's 'The Gallery' and Pope's 'To a Lady' use private art collections as extended metaphors or conceits. Long poems chronicling the 'grand tour' also contributed to the growth of the museum mentality, as when James Thomson's *Liberty* (1736) and Byron's *Childe Harold's Pilgrimage* (Canto IV, 1818) offered versified itineraries of such sculptural and architectural wonders as the

Laocoön, the *Apollo* Belvedere, the *Hercules* torso, the *Gladiator* (now known as *The Dying Gaul*), the Coliseum and St Peter's. As for actual museums: 'In 1723, 1749 and 1772', writes Philip Fisher, 'the Vatican collections were opened. The Sloane collection, later called the British Museum, opened in London in 1759. In 1781 in Vienna all court-owned pictures were opened to the public three days a week, and, as a climactic act, the founding of the Louvre was decreed July 27, 1793.'[10] The impact was palpable. The most famous of all poetic meditations on the timeless serenity of visual art – 'Ode on a Grecian Urn' – was made possible by the collections of vases and marbles Keats saw at the British Museum. Within a year of that same institution acquiring them in 1816, Keats wrote a sonnet 'On Seeing the Elgin Marbles'.

With the growth of the public museum there are subtle changes of emphasis within the ekphrastic tradition. Painting gradually replaces sculpture as the favourite art form. Increasing attention is paid to the individual artist, the nature of the medium and the scholarly debate surrounding the chosen artefact. The theme of art's permanence (about which, more anon) is enhanced by the new and expanding culture of restoration and conservation. And poems about *objets d'art* increasingly specify the gallery or museum in which the encounter takes place: think of Shelley's 'On the Medusa of Leonardo da Vinci in the Florentine Gallery'; 'The Municipal Gallery Revisited' by W.B. Yeats; Auden's '*Musée des Beaux Arts*'; Frank O'Hara's 'On Seeing Larry Rivers' *Washington Crossing the Delaware* at the Museum of Modern Art'; and Anthony Hecht's 'At the Frick'. In the New York School one even gets a group of poets whose leading lights (John Ashbery, Kenneth Koch, Frank O'Hara, James Schuyler) all worked in the culture industry, writing for such gallery journals as *Art News* and *Art and Literature*, and in O'Hara's case curating exhibitions for the Museum of Modern Art, New York. Ashbery's 'Self-Portrait in a Convex Mirror', based on a painting of that name by the Italian Mannerist Parmigianino, has with some justice been called 'the most resoundingly ekphrastic poem ever written'.[11]

Ekphrastic meaning, explicit and implicit

In a tradition of such duration there inevitably accrued a repertoire of meanings and techniques, a set of signifying practices – almost, indeed, a 'myth-kitty' – which individual exponents might inherit from past masters and transmit to future ones. The common ground is an acknowledgement of the supremacy of the visual sign in three particulars: its ability to arrest time by spatializing it; the instantaneity and, therefore, universality of its communicability; and its physical longevity. These meanings are especially evident in Renaissance and post-Renaissance responses to newly discovered monuments of classical antiquity. One of the most famous examples is that of the ensemble sculpture of Laocoön and his two sons at the moment when they are fatally entwined by a pair of gigantic serpents. The sculpture

probably dates from the second century BC, was already celebrated by Pliny, and depicts a scene from the Trojan War that also features in Virgil's *Aeneid*. The group carving was rediscovered in 1506 in a vineyard on the Esquiline Hill in Rome and, as well as inspiring visual artists from Michelangelo to Blake, prompted poems by Jacopo Sadoleto, Thomson, Byron and Josiah Gilbert Holland. All praise the anonymous sculptor for so brilliantly arresting the narrative at the moment of maximum terror and pathos. All remark the way in which the piece still speaks immediately to the contemporary viewer's emotions, with no need to 'translate' from ancient to modern as there would be with a written text in a foreign or dead language. (A comparison might be drawn with the global appeal of silent movie stars like Charlie Chaplin and the more limited, balkanized cinema of the sound era in which most films are distributed only within linguistic frontiers.) And all celebrate the fact that the marble *Laocoön* has outlasted by centuries its maker, its intended audience and even the civilization that produced it.

In English poetry the durability of sculpture, the tendency of portrait paintings to long survive their sitters, quickly became a symbol of transcendence, an emblem of artistic immortality. Edmund Waller salutes the 'immortal colours' in a deathless portrait by Van Dyck ('To Van Dyck'); Andrew Marvell tells a painter to depict Lady Castlemaine 'in colours that will hold' ('Last Instructions to a Painter'); John Donne predicts that when he comes back weather-beaten and careworn from his travels, the picture of his youthful face 'shall say what I was' ('Elegie V: His Picture'); Wordsworth salutes the 'calm of blest eternity' in Beaumont's 'Beautiful Picture'; Shelley finds 'everlasting beauty' in the painted face of Medusa; Keats saw the young woman depicted on the Grecian urn as eternally beautiful ('she cannot fade'); and for Byron the Belvedere *Apollo* enshrines 'A ray of immortality'.[12]

This emphasis upon transcendence entails a complex of meanings: the uniqueness of the specified artwork; the concept of art as the expression of individual genius; regard for authenticity of authorship, sometimes with attention to signature and provenance as guarantors of the validity of attribution; and a belief in Platonic essences, the masterpiece often being characterized by its rendering visible of an ideal unmatched by any reality (as in Cicero's account of how Zeuxis painted a perfect Helen by combining features from the five most beautiful virgins of Crotona).

The first three of these meanings are in play in the notionally ekphrastic 'My Last Duchess' by Robert Browning, in which the Duke swiftly authenticates the authorship of the portrait of his late wife –

> That's my last Duchess painted on the wall,
> Looking as if she were alive. I call
> That piece a wonder, now: Frà Pandolf's hands
> Worked busily a day, and there she stands.

– boasting of his ownership of the masterpiece and strictly controlling who sees it ('none puts by / The curtain I have drawn for you, but I').[13] Many Romantic instances of actual ekphrasis foreground the genius of the artist by packing the poem's title with authenticatory information (as in Wordsworth's 'Elegiac Stanzas Suggested by a Picture of Peele Castle, in a Storm, Painted by Sir George Beaumont' or Washington Allston's 'On the Group of the Three Angels Before the Tent of Abraham, by Rafaelle, in the Vatican'). This practice can have unintentionally comic consequences when the unique genius being celebrated is the wrong one. Shelley's 'On the Medusa of Leonardo da Vinci in the Florentine Gallery' lauds a painting no longer attributed to da Vinci; Dante Gabriel Rossetti's 'For Our Lady of the Rocks By Leonardo da Vinci' celebrates the version in the National Gallery, London, now thought to be a copy by the de Predis brothers of the original, which is in the Louvre; while the same poet's 'For A Venetian Pastoral By Giorgione' trumpets a painting now ascribed to Titian!

As for the power of art to present a Platonic ideal more perfect than any reality, Lord Byron unequivocally declared in 1821 that 'sculpture in general [...] is more poetical than nature itself, inasmuch as it represents and bodies forth that ideal beauty and sublimity which is never to be found in actual nature'. This thesis is repeated in *Childe Harold's Pilgrimage* when Byron claims that in the Belvedere *Apollo* 'are exprest / All that *ideal beauty* ever bless'd'.[14] (My emphasis.) Such moments are, then, a compact of transcendentals: the beauty of the human subject depicted is ideal by virtue of exceeding that of any actual person; and by virtue of being immutable, not subject to the temporal processes of decay and death.

We have already said enough to suggest why the time-based art of poetry might defer to the ocular immediacy of painting and sculpture, the visual sign holding out the prospect of an escape from narrative into an eternalized realm of permanent truth. These attractions are the more pronounced in secular societies such as our own, aesthetic transcendence displacing religious transcendence, art providing consolations once sought in church. Consider the eternalizing of the aesthetic in this representative passage from a guide to painting by D. Talbot Rice, influential Professor of Fine Art at the University of Edinburgh, published in 1955 (the year of *The Less Deceived*):

> A great work of art is always great, and it can be appreciated at any age. It is true, I think, to say that if it is great enough it can be appreciated without the aid of any close familiarity with the culture of the age and surroundings in which it was produced [...] it is the universal language of art.

Talbot Rice ends his monograph asserting the quasi-theological superiority of the visual sign over the textual by repeating Leonardo da Vinci's *dare* to anyone who might doubt it: 'Inscribe in any place the name of God, and set opposite to it His image. You will see then which will be held in greater reverence.'[15]

In practice, however, ekphrastic poems rely upon precepts, tropes and techniques implicitly at odds with the genre's prevailing writs of convention. This conflict between explicit and implicit, text and subtext, exposes hermeneutical fissures and ambiguities which – as we shall see – Larkin is able to exploit the better to reinvent tradition. One such cause of contradiction is the way ekphrastic poems explain what led up to the moment arrested in spatial form, the back story, by converting fixed pose and gesture into narrative. Again, those poems that supplement the artwork with imagined dialogue, whether between viewer and object or between depicted characters, inevitably imply a deficiency in the original. In both cases the written word is summoned to envoice what the visual sign silences. What began as writing's prostration before a painting or sculpture swiftly leads to friction between signifying processes, a struggle for mastery, in which the word usurps its subject by speaking for it.

Another cause of confusion which should be remarked concerns the damaged condition in which venerable relics come down to us, for if a poem acknowledges any erosion it immediately sets limits to the claim of artistic immortality. The alternative of refusing to admit any fragmentation does not resolve the contradiction but exacerbates it, sometimes rendering poems laughable, as with Leconte de Lisle's 'Venus de Milo' which devotes ten strophes to the eponymous goddess's timeless beauty without appearing to notice that time has actually disposed of both her arms. One line draws attention to what the poem would suppress by asserting that 'Marmoreal waves are washing your white feet' – 'Un flot marmoréen inonde tes pieds blancs' – virtually obliging the reader to observe that she only has one foot, the left one having been shorn off sometime between her creation in the second century BC and rediscovery on Melos in 1820.

The American poet Emma Lazarus did better by acknowledging in the opening quatrain of her sonnet 'Venus of the Louvre' that this same statue's immortality has to be measured against its historical wear and tear:

> Down the long hall she glistens like a star,
> The foam-born mother of Love, transfixed to stone,
> Yet none the less immortal, breathing on.
> Time's brutal hand hath maimed but could not mar.[16]

But perhaps only Shelley, in his sonnet 'Ozymandias', fully reversed the logic of the ekphrastic tradition by predicating his poem on the perishability, rather than the immutability, of visual art:

> I met a traveller from an antique land
> Who said: Two vast and trunkless legs of stone
> Stand in the desert. Near them, on the sand,
> Half sunk a shattered visage lies, whose frown,

And wrinkled lip, and sneer of cold command,
Tell that its sculptor well those passions read
Which yet survive, stamped on these lifeless things,
The hand that mocked them, and the heart that fed:
And on the pedestal these words appear:
'My name is Ozymandias, king of kings:
Look on my works, ye Mighty, and despair!'
Nothing beside remains. Round the decay
Of that colossal wreck, boundless and bare
The lone and level sands stretch far away.[17]

One critic, James W. Heffernan, has plausibly argued that 'this sonnet manifests what virtually all ekphrasis latently expresses: the poet's ambition to make his words outlast their ostensible subject, to displace visual representation with verbal representation'.[18] However, it might as persuasively be claimed that the inscription on the crumbling monument shows the scribal art to be as subject to time's merciless erosion as the sculptural: the one fragments with the other. Either way, Shelley's desire to expose the hubris of all tyrants yields a rare example of ekphrasis explicitly in the service of impermanence.

The instability of the visual sign: 'An Arundel Tomb'

Larkin's interrogation of the ekphrastic tradition may be summarized with regard to three areas of validation, each of which will be discussed with regard to a different medium: the historical variation of meaning attributed to a single artefact (sculpture); the problematics of identification, authentication and categorization (painting); the challenge to the theory of uniqueness posed by mechanical reproduction (photography). The third of these will provide the bulk of the ensuing argument, the other two being examined in more cursory form as background. Between them, the pertinent poems query, challenge and sometimes overturn key assumptions of the inherited discourse.

Although he would never have theorized it in this way, at the root of Larkin's critique is a sense that the differences between the verbal and the pictorial sign have been exaggerated to the detriment of the word. The central issue is that of the supposed unfixity of the one as compared with the other. In the theories of the founding father of structuralism, the Swiss linguist Ferdinand de Saussure, for example, words draw their meanings, not from the objects referred to, but from their place within the entire linguistic system. That is to say, the connection between the word *dog* and a canine is arbitrary rather than essential. It would not matter if canines were called *cat* provided we had a different word for felines, perhaps dog. Thus dog is dog because it is not cat or mouse or horse (or man or pylon or globe or quark, etc.). If every sign is what it is because it is not all the other signs within the system, meaning is scattered or dispersed along the whole chain of signifiers rather than being a concept tied firmly to the tail of a particular signified. Thus, meaning is never fully present in signs, every word containing the absent presence of all the other words it has to differentiate itself from in order to signify at all.

It is this arbitrary relation of signifier to signified, with its potential for endless slippage across the linguistic code, that the pictorial sign – most notably, the sculptural – is thought to arrest. The anglophone poet who best exemplified this view is Larkin's *bête noire*, the arch-modernist Ezra Pound. As early as 1913, in the essay 'A Few Don'ts By An Imagist', he was advising budding poets to 'Go in fear of abstractions'; advocating instead what his poem *Hugh Selwyn Mauberley* describes as 'the "sculpture" of rhyme'.[19] In *ABC of Reading*, which was published in 1951, just before Larkin wrote the poems we are about to examine, Pound elaborated upon the hegemony of the abstract in Western culture:

> In Europe, if you ask a man to define anything, his definition always moves away from the simple things that he knows perfectly well, it recedes into an unknown region, that is a region of remoter and progressively remoter abstraction.
>
> Thus if you ask him what red is, he says it is a 'colour'.
>
> If you ask him what a colour is, he tells you it is a vibration or a refraction of light, or a division of the spectrum.
>
> And if you ask him what vibration is, he tells you it is a mode of energy, or something of that sort, until you arrive at a modality of being, or non-being, or at any rate you get in beyond your depth, and beyond his depth.

Pound goes on to point out that 'there are two kinds of written language, one based on sound and the other on sight', and to assert that the more a language approaches the pictographic the less susceptible to abstraction:

> the Chinese still use abbreviated pictures AS pictures, that is to say, Chinese ideogram does not try to be the picture of a sound, or to be a written sign recalling a sound, but is still the picture of a thing [...]
>
> Gaudier Brzeska, who was accustomed to looking at the real shape of things, could read a certain amount of Chinese writing without ANY STUDY. He said, 'Of course, you can see it's a horse' (or wing or whatever).

The 'Gaudier Brzeska' referred to is Henri Gaudier-Brzeska, a brilliant young sculptor killed in the First World War. Pound's 1916 memoir of his friend was a major influence on the greatest British sculptor of the century, Henry Moore. It is also pertinent that Larkin's fellow Movementeer, Donald Davie, subtitled a monograph on Pound, *Poet as Sculptor*.

But how does a picture-based language represent a more abstract quality, such as *red*? According to Pound, by putting together 'the abbreviated pictures of ROSE, IRON RUST, CHERRY and FLAMINGO', so that the reader infers the abstract value from pictographic representations of four objects that share it: 'The Chinese "word" or ideogram for red is based on something everyone KNOWS.' As a result, 'a language written in this way simply HAD TO STAY POETIC; simply couldn't help being and staying poetic in a way that a column of English type might very well not stay poetic'.[20]

The basic principle at stake seems self-evident: a depiction of Venus presents the identical physiognomy to all eyes, whereas the *word* Venus varies across linguistic frontiers – even as transliterated into English, one gets Akkadian *Ishtar*, Aramaic *Astarte*, Hebrew *Ashtoreth*, Greek *Aphrodite*, Latin *Venus*, Italian *Venere*, Romanian *Venuše*, Polish *Wenus*, Welsh *Gwener* and so forth. In 'An Arundel Tomb' (*CP*, 110–11; *TCP*, 71–2), however, Larkin not only seeks to unsettle the self-evidence of this stark binary opposition, he uses sculpture, the most physically tangible of all sign systems, to do it. This might seem a perverse claim. The memorability of the poem's last line, 'What will survive of us is love', has caused it to be detached from context and cited in dictionaries of quotations, thereby assuming the axiomatic status of a biblical proverb. This has led to the popular misconception that the poem asserts the permanence of love as embodied in a late medieval tomb upon which the recumbent effigies of an earl and countess have held hands down the centuries. The immutability of love combines with the obduracy of stone in perfect ekphrastic union. This kenning might be supported by reference to the diction of longevity (*in stone, so long, prolong, stationary*) which culminates two-thirds of the way through the poem in an apparently categorical statement: 'Rigidly they // Persisted, linked, through lengths and breadths / Of time.' The somewhat opaque lines – 'And up the paths / The endless altered people came, // Washing at their identity' – might then be parsed, in accord with ekphrastic tradition, as signifying by contrast the mutability of the living who change generation by generation, and even across a single lifetime, their identities fading 'as a bright pattern will fade in many washings' (in the words of *A Girl in Winter*) (*AGW*, 184).

But this is wrong. A second reading confirms that it is the identities of the earl and countess that are washed away, subsequent generations of visitors forgetting the values the tomb was built to honour and reading it in the light of new, alien conventions. Rereading the poem alerts us to the sculpture's susceptibility to being reread: the verbal and the visual signs alike defy self-evidence. Modern viewers experience 'a sharp tender shock' at the intimacy of the handholding, blithely unaware that the monument was raised by an armorial age whose attitude to love was decidedly pre-Romantic. The gesture may just have been the artistic means to an end –

> A sculptor's sweet commissioned grace
> Thrown off in helping to prolong
> The Latin names around the base.

– but twentieth-century eyes, unable to read the Latin, ignorant of baronial culture, mistake the handholding as an earnest of a concept of love that is a thoroughly modern invention. In coming to signify something utterly anachronistic, something that cannot possibly have been intended, the sculpture has deceived the modern sensibility. As the last stanza says, 'Time has transfigured them into / Untruth' – a proposition built up to by repeated punning on the rival meanings of *to lie* ('The earl and countess lie in stone', 'They would not think to lie so long'). So it is that 'The stone fidelity / They hardly meant' proves 'almost true' our wish to believe that 'What will survive of us is love'. Almost, but not quite.[21]

Our poem, then, is finely aware that nothing changes more frequently or more radically than the past, redefined in every present. Even our narrator, who *is* conscious of our modern misunderstanding of the sarcophagus, cannot bridge the chasm between the two eras and provide a definitive reading, finding the monument 'blurred', vague and faintly 'absurd'. This instability of historical values, evinced by our ever-changing attitudes to love, forcibly demonstrates that even if the sculpture is immutable – and the facial erosion suggests otherwise – what it signifies is not. Though not as arbitrary as the relation of Saussure's signifier and signified, the relation of sculpture to meaning is unfixed, inconstant, subject to historical accident.

In 1987 Chichester Institute published *An Arundel Tomb*, a small collection of essays, in a series that includes pamphlets on *The Chichester Roundel*, *The Chichester Reliefs*, *Chichester Tapestries* and *Chichester Misericords*. One might be forgiven for thinking that Larkin's poem was set in Chichester. And, indeed, most commentators begin their analyses of it as Andrew Swarbrick does, in *Out of Reach: The Poetry of Philip Larkin* (1995), with the information that 'Larkin visited the tomb of the Earl of Arundel and his wife in Chichester Cathedral at the end of 1955.'[22] That is to say, their discussions begin with a safe anchorage in place and time, which is exactly what the poem does not provide. 'An Arundel Tomb' not only thwarts ekphrastic tradition by showing that sculptures are highly mutable, in the sense of being subject to a potentially endless variation in interpretation, but also by foregrounding that problematics of identification, authentication and categorization which we shall pursue with regard to painting.

Hence, the poem makes no mention of Chichester, nor of a cathedral. Only one fleeting reference to what may be windows ('Light / Each summer thronged the glass') gives any indication of a habitation, though we are not told of what kind nor whether the tomb lies within or without. The poem's title suggests the location might be the West Sussex town of Arundel, with its historic castle. The consensual critical response is to deny this element of indeterminacy regarding the location (and, therefore, the subject) of the tomb by glossing the title as a reference to the 14th Earl of Arundel and his Countess, as commemorated at Chichester Cathedral. There are two impediments to this identification: who the Chichester effigies represent is a matter of some dispute; and the tomb described in Larkin's poem differs in so many particulars from the Chichester monument that the two can never be conclusively linked.

Thus, there is a degree of uncertainty as to which of the Earls of Arundel and Surrey the Chichester tomb commemorates, a difficulty compounded by the fact that the strongest candidate, the 13th Earl, had more than one wife. As for the discrepancies of visual detail, in the poem it is the earl's left hand that is ungloved to hold that of his countess; at Chichester, the right hand. The poem specifies 'little dogs under their feet' whereas the Chichester tomb has a dog for the countess but a lion for the earl. The poem identifies 'Latin names around the base', but there is no inscription at all on the Chichester monument. The poem makes no mention of restoration, whereas the Chichester tomb was so substantially restored in the Victorian era that it is uncertain whether the handholding dates from the medieval period or the 1840s.[23] Finally, the figures in the poem have been 'stationary [...] through lengths and breadths / Of time', whereas the tomb in question is thought to have been erected in the chapel of Lewes Abbey and subsequently moved to Chichester Cathedral, within which it has occupied several different positions. Whether these discrepancies are ascribed to authorial intention or authorial *inattention*, they are too many and too marked to justify the naive biographical resolution of the Larkin debate.

The problematics of identification: 'The Card-Players'

That Larkin's strategy of guiding the reader through an ekphrastic poem while systematically abnegating all the key elements of the genre was no accident is suggested by the fact that he repeated the exercise in 'The Card-Players' (*CP*, 177; *TCP*, 84). Once again the information with which past authors packed even the titles of their poems is withheld throughout the piece – the name of the visual artist, the particular artefact under discussion, its precise location, the names of those represented therein; and these elisions in turn render deeply problematic those issues of signature, provenance and unique genius upon which are based ekphrastic claims for artistic immortality. The title itself is little help: even if we take it as the name of the painting described, rather than a more generalized indication of the subject depicted, we are confronted as possible sources with works by artists as various as Caravaggio, the Brothers Le Nain, Meissonier, Adam de Coster, Frederick Arthur Bridgman and Toulouse-Lautrec. If we narrow the options by assuming from the Dutch names of the characters depicted that the artist was Dutch or Flemish, the shortlist still includes such candidates as Pieter de Hooch, Adriaen Brouwer, David Teniers the Younger, Theodor Rombouts, Jan Steen, Florent Willems, Lucas van Leyden and Willem Van Herp.

Ever the master of misdirection, Larkin's correspondence yields contradictory signals. More than two decades before penning the poem he returned an art book to the painter Jim Sutton with the words 'Cézanne's Card Players p. 410 – wonderful, this, I think'.[24] To Arthur J. Hobson he wrote, answering a specific query, 'You are quite right in detecting the presence of Brouwer behind "The Card-Players", although I had no particular picture in mind. I should not go quite as far as to say that Brouwer was my favourite painter, but he is the only artist of whose work I have bothered to buy a book of reproductions, and in general I like Dutch low-life painting very much indeed.'[25] To his long-distance companion Monica Jones he sent a colour reproduction of a painting called *The Card Players* by another genre master, the Flemish artist David Teniers the Younger. The message reads: 'Hope you like this! It's about the nearest I could get to anything *I* like – cold outside, warmth & booze & smoke within.'[26]

Each of these candidates has found critical champions: Christopher Fletcher favours the Teniers identification; István Rácz has done most to advance the claims of Cézanne; while James Booth opts for a more inclusive approach that encompasses Bruegel, Teniers, Brouwer and Cézanne. Most contributors to the debate muddy the waters with factual slips and special pleading. Fletcher forbears to mention that the Larkin poem describes only four characters whereas the reproduction sent to Monica Jones sports ten. Booth confusingly refers to David Teniers as Martin Teniers. Rácz and Booth see the Larkin as partaking of the stasis and monumentality of Cézanne's *The Card Players*, thereby underplaying the poem's stress upon verbs, physical actions, bodily functions (spewing, pissing, defecating, belching, snoring, farting, spitting) and time-based processes (such as digestion). Motion, Holdefer and Booth sex as male Larkin's non-gender-specific fourth figure, the better to present the poem as a masculinist relishing of unbuttoned corporeality freed from female sensitivities. This loses the pun on 'the queen of hearts', who might as readily be a woman as a playing card, and loosens the connection to Cézanne, Brouwer and Teniers who often included solo females alongside the grouped men in scenes of this kind. Elsewhere, Palmer presses the candidacy of another Dutch artist – '"The Card Players" has Van Gogh written all over and through it' – casually overlooking the hyphen in Larkin's title and the fact that Van Gogh has no pictures of that name or on that subject.[27]

If we set aside these errors and exaggerations, concentrate exclusively on the three artists Larkin cited in this context, limiting our consideration to those paintings directly alluding to cards – what then? Answer: further frustration. This arises from two irreconcilable facts. First, that Cézanne has not one painting on this theme but five; Brouwer, several dozen; Teniers, dozens more – and more again on the related subjects of smoking, drinking, male camaraderie and cognate forms of gaming (backgammon, dice, skittles). It is clear from the way the same few characters and props recur with slight variations in their disposition that these scenes were turned out to a model: for instance, *Le Bonnet vert*, *Le Bonnet rouge* and *Le Bonnet blanc* by Teniers present the almost identical card-playing tableau, but with the cap hung on the back of a participant's chair changing from green to red to white in successive images. There is, in short, a plethora of originatory candidates to choose from. This brings us to the second fact: not one painting has thus far been identified that matches the particulars of the poem. It would seem that Larkin has deliberately contrived verses that summon a multiplicity of visual images, all of which bear upon his meaning but none of which comprehends it. *Notional ekphrasis* masquerades as *actual ekphrasis*.

This iconographic excess is matched by the literary allusions. The poem is a sonnet which spatchcocks Petrarchan and Shakespearean rhyme schemes only to fracture both with a typographical space between the thirteenth and fourteenth lines rather than between the octave and sestet. In a general way, there may be a debt to a great Larkin favourite, Thomas Hardy, whose admiration for artists like Brouwer, Ostade, Teniers and Douw, led him to subtitle the novel *Under the Greenwood Tree* as *A Rural Painting of the Dutch School*. However, the un-Hardyesque emphasis on bodily functions invokes the scatological novels of the sixteenth-century Frenchman François Rabelais and his twentieth-century Russian explicator Mikhail Bakhtin; though the coarser passages of English writers like Blake may also be in play ('The Old Nobodaddy aloft / Farted & Belch'd & Coughed'). The first half of the last line – 'Rain, wind and fire!' – echoes the title of Turner's magnificent *Rain, Steam and Speed*; though the line's typographical isolation and short exclamatory sentences recall the poetic endings favoured by French Symbolists like Baudelaire and Rimbaud. As the poem proliferates painted progenitors, so it does literary ones, the slipperiness and fecundity of both discourses eluding ekphrastic certitudes to paradoxical effect: this poem about physical embodiment is itself physically unhoused; this poem of obvious and coarse meaning is also a poem of coyness and uncertainty; this poem of the repellently visible is a poem whose own origins are hidden.

'The Card-Players' also assaults ekphrastic orthodoxy by forcibly rejecting Platonism. Where a Keats, Byron, Shelley or Rossetti praises the ideal beauty depicted in classical sculptures and in Renaissance paintings by the likes of Leonardo, Michelangelo or Titian, Larkin honours an anonymous work from a Dutch genre tradition notorious for its vulgar realism. In so doing he set himself against several centuries of received aesthetic opinion. Horace Walpole dismissed the Dutch as 'those drudging Mimics of Nature's most uncomely coarsenesses'. William Hazlitt attacked the poetry of George Crabbe with the words: 'the adept in Dutch interiors, hovels, and pig-sties must find in Mr Crabbe a man after his own heart'. Most scathing was John Ruskin, the greatest art critic of the nineteenth century, who railed against 'the various Van somethings and Back somethings' with their debased obsessions with the 'pleasures of the ale house and the card-table'. The 'effect' of the Dutch landscapists 'on the public mind is so totally evil', he wrote in *Modern Painters* (five volumes, 1843–60), 'that [...] I conceive the best patronage that any monarch could possibly bestow upon the arts, would be to collect the whole body of them into one gallery and burn it to the ground'.[28]

Larkin had a direct acquaintance with this mentality, for as Dutch genre paintings were to Ruskin, so was jazz to the director general of the BBC, Sir John Reith. The latter went so far as to praise the Nazis for banning jazz, his only regret being that 'we should be behind in dealing with this filthy product of modernity'. Throughout Larkin's lifetime his favourite art form was largely excluded from the BBC's 'serious' music channel Radio Three (formerly the Third Programme), as it was from the standard reference guide to music, the *Grove Dictionary*.[29] As someone who 'can live a week without poetry but not a day without jazz', Larkin detested the tendency of cultural elites to reify 'high art' by defining anything more demotic and accessible as 'low'.[30] In melding the high art of poetry with the low art of genre painting, 'The Card-Players' collapses the hierarchical distinction between the two, thereby striking at the Platonic idealism that underpins so much ekphrasis.

So it is that far from denying the vulgarity of its sources or contriving to show that (appearances notwithstanding) their tawdry contents point an elevated moral, the poem takes a childlike delight in transgression. The opening is at once indecent and tipsy –

> Jan van Hogspeuw staggers to the door
> And pisses at the dark.

– Larkin docking a syllable from the initial pentameter so that the line staggers a little in rhythm with the intoxicated Jan. As always, the fascination of his verse turns on the way it encourages and contests dogmatic readings by holding extreme alternatives in tension. This ambivalence is encapsulated in the ribald Dutch surnames, as funny as they are crude: Hogspeuw combines pigs and vomit; Dogstoerd suggests canine defecation; Old Prijck, male impotence. On the one hand the reader is licensed to disapprove on the grounds of the characters' intoxication (Old Prijck to the point where a gale cannot rouse him), inability to control their bodily functions, feckless-ness (frittering their lives away on card games) and corporeal corruption (epitomized by Old Prijck's 'skull face'). On the other, that same reader might relish their abundant food and drink, the camaraderie epitomized by their shared pastime, their uninhibited physicality and a nonchalance in the face of death symbolized by Jan's pissing 'at the dark'. As Steve Eddy has remarked, the phrase 'lamplit cave' might indicate an almost palaeo-lithic primitivism or the enviable cosiness of their shelter; the men may be 'bestial' but they *are* at peace.[31] To extend even this qualified indulgence to Platonic idealism's abjected other is to challenge ekphrastic certitude with ambiguity's liberating unfixity.

The work of art in the age of mechanical reproduction: 'Lines on a Young Lady's Photograph Album'

With 'Lines on a Young Lady's Photograph Album' the argument reaches new levels of complexity (*CP*, 71–2; *TCP*, 27–8). So much so, indeed, that it will be helpful to call upon such cultural theorists as Walter Benjamin, Roland Barthes and Laura Mulvey when attempting to unpack the poem's meaning. Use of these sophisticated theoreticians has the added attraction of highlighting Larkin's much disparaged intellectual profundity, especially as the poem antedates their theories by ten, 20, sometimes 30 years. As we shall see, the title of the poem (for all its old world gallantry) raises to attention a thoroughly modern phenomenon, the family photograph album, which brings with it original approaches to collaborative authorship, narrative construction and anonymity. The poem itself divides into three acts, each with its own theoretical dimension: the first three verses posit that the camera encourages performativity in the human subject and scopophilia, or voyeurism, on the part of the viewer; the middle section appears to apostrophize photography as the *ne plus ultra* of realism while simultaneously undermining that proposition; the third act offers a disquisition on time that shifts our perception of photography from an art of presence to a poignant art of absence. Underlying the entire enterprise is an acceptance of photography as a mechanical medium whose very reproducibility challenges ekphrastic norms. A brief historical excursion will help us fathom the radicalism of Larkin's intervention.

'From today, painting is dead!' So said Paul Delaroche, a French history painter, on first seeing a daguerreotype.[32] Though not as fatal to the existing arts as Delaroche predicted, the second half of the nineteenth century, the era into which Larkin's parents were born, did witness an extraordinary explosion of photographic invention and aesthetic development, with profound implications for ekphrasis. The first photograph was taken, without the intervention of a camera, in 1825. The first cameras were invented in the 1830s, by Daguerre in France and Fox Talbot in England. By 1860, there were nearly 3000 photographic studios in England; a decade later, double the number. In 1888, when Sydney Larkin was four years old, Eastman Kodak produced the box camera ('You Press the Button, We Do the Rest') that stimulated the rise of amateur photography. By 1900, when Sydney was 16 and his future wife Eva Day 14, one in ten people in Britain and the United States owned a camera. The first newspaper photograph was published as early as 1880 and the first photographic supplement in 1896, though it was in 1904 that the British *Daily Mail* became the first paper to regularly print photos. In 1924, two years after Philip Larkin's birth, the Leitz Optical Works in Germany introduced the Leica, the first commercially successful miniature camera taking perforated 35 mm film such as was still in use until the development of digital photography.

The challenge of the camera to painting was immediate and incremental, one genre after another suffering invasion in pace with technological innovation. 'Local colour' painting came under attack in the mid-1840s when Hill and Adamson's callotypes of New Haven fishermen effectively created the category of documentary photography. Military painting reigned supreme during the Napoleonic wars but came under challenge with Roger Fenton's Crimean War photographs; Matthew Brady, Timothy O'Sullivan and Alexander Gardner's portfolios documenting the American Civil War; and, in the Franco-Prussian War of 1870–71, the first action shots (such was the advance in camera shutter speeds). As for portraiture, for so long indispensable to the professional painter's livelihood, by the 1850s Europe's cultural elite went by preference to Nadar's photographic studio in Paris where once they might have sat for an Ingres, Reynolds or Gainsborough – Offenbach, Berlioz, Rossini, Baudelaire, Bakunin, George Sand, Victor Hugo and Sarah Bernhardt all making the change of allegiance. Again, we associate Prince Albert with sentimental portrait paintings by the likes of Winterhalter or Landseer, but when he died prematurely in 1861 a single British company sold 70,000 photographic cards of the Prince within a week. A revolution was in progress.

The established art of poetry largely resisted that revolution. Baudelaire's poems on the etchings of Goya, Callot and Mortimer are rare examples of literary ekphrasis welcoming mechanically reproduced images. Much more typical was Wordsworth who having repeatedly presented painting as a window on the transcendental, as in the 'Peele Castle' poem referred to earlier, balked at the arrival of mass-produced images. His sonnet 'Illustrated Books and Newspapers', written in the year the *Illustrated London News* was launched, adopted a last-man-on-the-ramparts, end-of-civilization-as-we-know-it tone of hysterical oppositionalism:

> A backward movement surely have we here,
> From manhood – back to childhood; for the age –
> Back towards caverned life's first rude career.
> Avaunt this vile abuse of pictured page!
> Must eyes be all in all, the tongue and ear
> Nothing? Heaven keep us from a lower stage![33]

Alarmingly, this opposition has been maintained down the decades and into the new millennium, through successive generations of modernists and postmodernists. In his post-Great War masterpiece, *Hugh Selwyn Mauberley*, Ezra Pound was still contrasting to their disadvantage the new reproducible art forms with the traditional art of marble sculpture:

> The 'age demanded' chiefly a mould in plaster,
> Made with no loss of time,

> A prose kinema, not, not assuredly, alabaster
> Or the 'sculpture' of rhyme.[34]

More than half a century on from Pound, John Ashbery's 'Self-Portrait in a Convex Mirror' echoed in less hysterical mode Wordsworth's nostalgia for the unique work of art:

> Secrets of wash and finish that took a lifetime
> To learn and are reduced to the status of
> Black-and-white illustrations in a book where colourplates
> Are rare. That is, all time
> Reduces to no special time.[35]

Romantic, modernist and postmodernist concur: the age of mechanical reproduction is an era of impoverishment; the present is 'no special time', as Ashbery has it.

The quickest way to grasp the issues at stake – and thereby calibrate Larkin's radicalism in embracing what his poetic peers shunned – is by reference to Walter Benjamin's classic essay 'The Work of Art in the Age of Mechanical Reproduction' (1936).[36] Although 'in principle a work of art has always been reproducible', as in the aforementioned copy by the de Predis brothers of Leonardo's *Madonna of the Rocks*, Benjamin argues that 'mechanical reproduction of a work of art [...] represents something new'. It has ever been the case that 'even the most perfect reproduction of a work of art is lacking in one element: its presence in time and space, its unique existence where it happens to be'. Hence, copies of a classical sculpture are always referred back to the masterwork: 'the presence of the original is the prerequisite to the concept of authenticity'. Benjamin terms the unique authority of the original the 'aura' of the work of art and argues that it is precisely this quality 'which withers in the age of mechanical reproduction'.[37]

This is not just a matter of the twentieth century proving particularly hospitable to work produced in multiples, such as lithographs, silkscreen prints and limited edition sculptures, but that the quintessential new art forms of the era – recorded music, photography and cinema (all major sources of inspiration for Larkin) – dispense altogether with *aura* as Benjamin defines it:

> To an ever greater degree the work of art reproduced becomes the work of art designed for reproducibility. From a photographic negative, for example, one can make any number of prints; to ask for the 'authentic' print makes no sense.[38]

Benjamin demonstrates films to be subject to an equivalent loss of aura regarding the uniqueness, integrity and authenticity of the actor's performance. The fragmented nature of cinematic editing deconstructs the mystique of theatrical performance. Similarly, 'a phonograph record' carries a performance 'into situations which would be out of reach for the original itself': 'The cathedral leaves its locale [...] the choral production [...] resounds in the drawing room.'[39]

According to Benjamin, 'much futile thought had been devoted to the question of whether photography is an art. The primary question – whether the very invention of photography had not transformed the entire nature of art – was not raised.'[40] Two areas of transformation as explicated by Benjamin will further our analysis of Larkin's ekphrasis. The first is the way that photography opens up whole new ways of seeing and, arguably, experiencing human subjectivity:

> With the close-up, space expands; with slow motion, movement is extended. The enlargement of a snapshot does not simply render more precise what in any case was visible, though unclear: it reveals entirely new structural formations of the subject [...] Even if one has a general knowledge of the way people walk, one knows nothing of a person's posture during the fractional second of a stride. The act of reaching for a lighter or a spoon is a familiar routine, yet we hardly know what really goes on between hand and metal, not to mention how this fluctuates with our moods. Here the camera intervenes with the resources of its lowerings and liftings, its interruptions and isolations, its extensions and accelerations, its enlargements and reductions. The camera introduces us to unconscious optics as does psychoanalysis to unconscious impulses.[41]

The second point concerns the politics of mechanical reproduction, though here we can afford to be more succinct as this is an area where Larkin's practice entails issues Benjamin did not anticipate. What he did state with characteristic lucidity was that the new art forms were revolutionary in their capacity to communicate with all strata of society rather than a cultural elite: 'Mechanical reproduction of art changes the reaction of the masses toward art. The reactionary attitude to a Picasso painting changes into the progressive reaction toward a Chaplin movie.'[42] What he grasps less securely than Larkin was that this revolutionary extension of the franchise of art affected production as much as consumption.

The unusual warmth of Larkin's address to photography is apparent not only in such mature achievements as 'Wants', 'Whatever Happened?', 'Afternoons', 'Wild Oats' and 'Lines on a Young Lady's Photograph Album'; but also throughout such 1940s apprentice pieces as 'Autumn', 'Disintegration', 'Poem', 'Femmes Damnées' and 'Behind the Façade'. Between them these poems demonstrate what no earlier poet so fully documented and Benjamin neglected to theorize, the way the advent of cheap camera equipment democratized visual representation. At the most immediate level, these poems testify to the normalization of the photograph and its

ubiquity in modern life: the Rachel Wilson of 'Femmes Damnées' has graduation photographs of herself upon her walls; the narrator of 'Wild Oats' has
'two snaps' in his wallet; the role of Kodak in memorializing holidays is
captured in 'Whatever Happened?'; 'Autumn' imagines the protagonist in
the evening of life surrounded by 'boxes of photographs'; and by the end of
the 1950s the lower-income families of 'Afternoons' possess commemora-
tive albums 'lettered / *Our Wedding*'.

At a deeper level, what is being dramatized is the emergence of ordinary
people into visibility as subjects of representation; their learning to pose
and perform for the camera, to achieve new levels of self-consciousness
and to explore subjectivity in relation to the visual record. And, equally
important, the emergence of ordinary people as producers of art, both as
wielders of hand-held cameras and as editors of their own histories as they
quickly learned to compile family albums, selecting and arranging some
images while suppressing others so as to construct the desired narrative.[43]
As 'Whatever Happened?' puts it:

> 'Perspective brings significance,' we say,
> Unhooding our photometers, and, snap!
> What can't be printed can be thrown away. (*CP*, 74; *TCP*, 34)

The individual image may not falsify, but the process of picture selection
does.[44] This dual emphasis upon the mutability of the self when performing
before a camera and the constructedness of the family album means that,
despite occasional concessions to the opposite persuasion, it is the essential
inauthenticity of the photographic art that is foregrounded. Contrary to pro-
verbial wisdom, the camera *does* lie.

'Lines on a Young Lady's Photograph Album', Act I (lines 1–15)

To prove as much with regard to 'Lines on a Young Lady's Photograph
Album', we must first unhouse the poem from biographical belonging.
Critics routinely parcel out Larkin's love poems to a succession of women
in his life: Eva Larkin, Ruth Bowman, Winifred Arnott, Jane Exall, Monica
Jones, Maeve Brennan, Betty Mackereth. In this chronology, 'Lines' is
invariably ascribed to Larkin's early 1950s infatuation with Winifred Arnott,
such commentators as Motion, Booth, Bradford, Terry, Gilpin, Marsh and
Swarbrick predicating their analyses of it upon an assumption that the
eponymous album is Winifred's own. Thus, Motion's biography captions a
photograph of Winifred swimming with the claim: 'Philip Larkin refers to
this picture in "Lines on a Young Lady's Photograph Album" when he wonders "if you'd spot the theft / Of this one of you bathing".'[45] As we shall see,
there are good reasons for asserting that the narrator is no more Larkin than
the addressee is Winifred: what is immediately apparent is that in making

a direct one-for-one relation between picture and poem, Motion loses the double meaning of the word 'bathing'; the Winifred photograph insists it can only mean *swimming*, but the poem licenses the delicious possibility that it depicts the Young Lady luxuriating in a hot tub!

The point at issue is not whether Larkin's poem drew inspiration from Winifred's photographs – it clearly did; but whether it follows the pattern of 'An Arundel Tomb' and 'The Card-Players' and deviates so far from its sources as to vex, even sever, the connection. The poem's title refers to a single album but Larkin conflated details from at least two collections. Moreover, he freely altered the original scenes, adding to and subtracting from their contents for the sake of a rhyme, to thicken the sexual plot or in the service of the poem's larger purport. The 'reluctant cat' was actually a dog. The 'trilby hat', which has been such a source of comment, does not exist; though there is a photograph of Winifred in a beret. 'Hall's-Distemper boards', advertising panels for cheap household paint, were real enough; however none appears anywhere in the Arnott collections. Nor is there 'a fence' against which the addressee is 'balanced on a bike'. Nor does Winifred accept that she is the 'Young Lady' represented in the poem ('I wasn't "sweet"!') nor that her relationship with the author was that of the narrator and addressee ('I never, ever, *ever* flirted with Philip').[46] 'Lines on a Young Lady's Photograph Album' is more fiction than faction; and if, as so many critics claim, the poem affirms the view that the camera does not lie, it seems an odd strategy indeed to begin by lying about real photographs.

This unhousing of the poem from biographical origins complements a view of human subjectivity, proposed in the opening stanzas, as itself unfixed, endlessly mutable. The Young Lady appears in eight or nine different roles in as many lines: as schoolgirl ('In pigtails, clutching a reluctant cat'); as university student ('a sweet girl-graduate'); as beauty in the bower or, perhaps, gardener ('lifting a heavy-headed rose / Beneath a trellis'); as cross-dresser ('in a trilby hat'); as heterosexual love object ('these disquieting chaps who loll / At ease about your earlier days'); as mature woman whose past images have begun to acquire a period charm ('you / Contract my heart by looking out of date'); as cyclist ('balanced on bike'); and swimmer or, more enticingly, nude at her ablutions ('this one of you bathing'). The most obvious explanation the poem offers for this mutability of self is that of historical progression: 'All your ages / Matt and glossy on the thick black pages!' In effect, one is being invited to imagine the photographs arranged on a temporal axis from childhood through youth to adulthood, a visual *Bildungsroman*: in other words as adhering to the master narrative of the family album genre, *chronology*.

This is a necessary but not an exhaustive explanation: the narrator's description in the poem's first act of the photographic sequence moving 'from pose to pose' suggests an element of theatricality in the portraits, as though the presence of the camera encourages an acting out of imagined selves, selves that would not have been generated before its invention. Something of this is implied in *Camera Lucida* when Roland Barthes admits that 'once I feel myself observed by the lens, everything changes: I constitute myself in the process of "posing", I instantaneously make another body for myself, I transform myself in advance into an image'. He goes on:

> In front of the lens, I am at the same time: the one I think I am, the one I want others to think I am, the one the photographer thinks I am, and the one he makes use of to exhibit his art [...] I do not stop imitating myself, and because of this, each time I am (or let myself be) photographed, I invariably suffer from a sensation of inauthenticity, sometimes of imposture (comparable to certain nightmares).[47]

In Larkin's poem this sense of 'imposture' is endorsed by the way in which some of the 'poses' are differentiated from each other by invoking distinct literary models. This in turn suggests that selfhood is not only mutable and performative but acquired rather than given, a cultural rather than a biological precipitate, something defined by the contingent world of representations, whether in novels, movies or poems. The phrase 'a sweet girl-graduate' is a quotation from a passage of Tennyson's *The Princess* in which the young Lilia longs for the day when Oxford University will have a college for women to rival the exclusively male colleges of that era.[48] Tennyson's phrase was subsequently adopted in the 'New Woman' literature of the late nineteenth century, such as L.T. Meade's novel *A Sweet Girl Graduate* (1894) and Isabella Maud Rittenhouse's memoirs, *Maud* (published in 1939 but written in the 1880s).[49] The Young Lady of Larkin's poem has in the mid-twentieth century fulfilled the educational aspirations of the suffragist generation by successfully completing her university degree. On the other hand, the trilby hat which Winifred Arnott never wore was famously brandished by Lady Brett Ashley, the hard-drinking sexually voracious 'love interest' of Ernest Hemingway's classic novel *The Sun Also Rises* (1926).[50] The use of the word 'Lady' in the poem's title may nod back to Brett's title by marriage to Lord Ashley. Brett is an iconic representative of liberated twenties women, quite unlike a late-Victorian bluestocking: where the latter fought for political and educational equality, Brett stands for woman's right to be as personally permissive as a man – a stance symbolized by her trilby ('She pulled her man's felt hat down and started for the bar').[51]

We can now see that when the narrator says 'From every side you strike at my control', there congregate behind his particular addressee a multiplicity of other women whose protean demands for new subject positions have struck against male constraints. To put it another way, the fragmentation of subjectivity represented by the Young Lady's 'poses', supplemented by the discrepant role models of the literary citations, works to suggest that a woman's identity is so mobile, contradictory and prolific as to elude patriarchal definition. As we have seen, the woman before us is both 'Young' and 'out of date', butch and a 'Lady', intellectual and athletic, an alloy of 1890s bluestocking and 1920s barfly. This profligacy of self-invention is something which it took the cheap, spontaneous, disposable medium of photography to verify; something which the camera unleashed.[52]

If the composite portrait of the Young Lady that emerges from her album demonstrates a mutability of identity impossible to depict before the speed and affordability of the camera, and thereby illustrates Benjamin's thesis that photography enables us to know ourselves in thoroughly new ways, it also summons from the narrator responses just as new, just as performative, and which anticipate several decades of theorization. In particular, the poem dramatizes the constitution of the male gaze as pornographic effected by mass-produced erotica. That the eponymous album seems not to be sexually explicit only serves to demonstrate that pornography is a way of reading as much as a type of material, and a way of reading separable from the intentions of artist or author (in his autobiography Nicholas Monsarrat, author of *The Cruel Sea*, recounts masturbating to the Bible).

The concept of *the male gaze* has been more utilized in relation to cinema than to either literature or still photography, with feminist critics defining the key terms of the debate. The classic text is Laura Mulvey's 'Visual Pleasure and Narrative Cinema' (1975) in which it is argued that

> In a world ordered by sexual imbalance, pleasure in looking has been split between active/male and passive/female. The determining male gaze projects its fantasy on to the female figure which is styled accordingly. In their traditionalist exhibitionist role women are simultaneously to be looked at and displayed, with their appearance coded for strong visual and erotic impact so that they can be said to connote *to-be-looked-at-ness*.

In the typical Hollywood film, Mulvey goes on, the male viewer is able to identify with the hero 'so that the power of the male protagonist as he controls events coincides with the active power of the erotic look, both giving a satisfying sense of omnipotence'.[53] Women are looked at both in the film (by other characters) and in the cinema (by the audience), and the gaze is in the possession of men. Women are to be looked at, not to look, their alienation from the gaze an aspect of their passivization and reification.

In *Looking for the Other: Feminism, Film, and the Imperial Gaze* (1997), E. Ann Kaplan makes a distinction between the gaze and the look:

> I will reserve the term 'look' to connote a process, a relation, while using the word 'gaze' for a one-way subjective vision [...] Looking will connote curiosity about the Other, a wanting to know (which can of course still

be oppressive but does not have to be), while the gaze I take to involve extreme anxiety – an attempt in a sense *not* to know, to deny, in fact.

Moreover, 'the subject bearing the gaze is not interested in the object per se, but consumed with his (sic) own anxieties, which are inevitably intermixed with desire', so that 'process' or interaction is not possible.[54] The constitution of the male gaze as *pornographic* is an under-acknowledged aspect of modernity and one that is crucial to an understanding of this same first act of Larkin's poem. Of course, the depiction of sexual acts can be found throughout history in many countries and civilizations; but much of it was produced in religious contexts, such as those associated with fertility rites, rather than as an adjunct to individual sexual arousal and release. The concept of pornography as understood today did not exist until the Victorian era, the first law prohibiting it being the Obscene Publications Act passed by the British Parliament in 1857, its conceptualization intimately connected to the rise of photography. In the 1840s it was cheaper to hire a prostitute and engage in sexual intercourse than to purchase an erotic photograph of the same woman; by the following decade, the opposite was true. In 1840 there were only 13 photographic studios in Paris; by 1860 there were 400, most including the sale of illicit pornography among their services. The pornographic magazine containing monochrome photographs arrived with the new century, sometimes connected to the cult of naturism (Britain's still extant *Health and Efficiency* magazine started in 1900). The first full-colour mass-circulation pornographic magazine, Hugh Hefner's *Playboy*, was launched in 1953 – the year of our poem. The recency of the phenomenon is evidenced in the recency of the terminology: the word pornography dates to that same inaugural year of 1857; voyeurism to 1924; scopophilia, 1937; pin-up, 1941; under-the-counter, the early 1940s; x-rated, x-certificate, 1950; hardcore, the early 1950s; the abbreviation *porn*, 1962; centrefold, 1966; and softcore, the late 1960s.

The essential displacement of pornography, from person to image, the viewer's stimulation focussed on self rather than other, auto-erotic rather than conjugal, is indicated in the opening lines:

> At last you yielded up the album, which,
> Once open, sent me distracted.

The language of *yielding* and *opening* – with its implications of wooing, submission and penetration (in short, of *intercourse*) – is rendered bathetic by the immediate acknowledgement that it is not the woman, who is present, but her representation that provokes the excitation. The diction is scrupulous: the narrator is *distracted* from the real by the replica. (One is reminded of that moment at the end of *The Great Gatsby* when the eponymous protagonist's father, Mr Gatz, celebrates his murdered son's ascent from rags to riches by flourishing a photograph of the latter's mansion, *in which he stands*: 'I think it was more real to him now than the house itself'.)[55]

That the narrator's response is disproportionate is communicated by suffusing his narration with verbal excess – a piling up of hot-house images, polysemic diction and theatrically lecherous gestures, in a punographic enactment of the pornographic. There is the play on hunger, nutrition and chokingly rich confectionery with its attendant but unstated endearments (Sweetie, Sweetie-pie, Sugar, Honey, Honeybunch) and indelicacies (cheesecake, jelly roll, tart, fig, buttered bun, etc.). At the time of the poem's composition these metaphors of sweetness were the more salivating in that confectionery of all kinds was in short supply thanks to post-war rationing, the minuscule weekly allocation of sugar having been further reduced in 1952. There is the semantic overload of the phrase 'My swivel eye' which encompasses multiple meanings, some mutually exclusive: to *swivel* is to rotate on a pivot, suggesting the narrator's frantic leering from one picture to another; the expression *swivel-eyed* is synonymous with squint-eyed; to be *swivelly* is to be drunk; to *swive* is to copulate; and the *wive* contained within swive means to provide with or take a wife. The juxtaposition of the Young Lady with a cat and in her fur-trimmed graduation robes conjures an obscene pun, the phrase 'furred yourself' hinting at pubic hair and the paired images playing on the word 'pussy' which, according to Partridge's *Dictionary of Historical Slang*, has been a vulgarism for the female genitalia since the seventeenth century. Similarly, the picture of the addressee 'in a trilby hat' adds a Greta Garbo–Marlene Dietrich touch of androgyny, a titillating hint of perversity, that is answered by a distant bisexual commotion in the narrator's emotions ('Faintly disturbing, that, in several ways'). Elsewhere one remarks linguistic play on the rose, in ancient Greece and Rome sacred to Aphrodite and in English poetry a vaginal symbol; on issues of explicitness ('But o, photography [...] will not censor'); and, more coyly, on the mid-century cultural icon of the bathing beauty ('this one of you bathing').

That Larkin is deliberately constructing a stereotype of the lecher the better to explore the dynamics of the pornographic gaze, rather than voicing unmediated autobiographical feeling, should already be evident from the way in which he fabricates the pun on *pussy* by substituting a cat for Winifred's dog.[56] The literary allusions work in a similar way. The description of Lilia as a 'sweet girl-graduate' comes from a young man who condescends to her university aspirations by picturing an all-female college as an object of male voyeurism:

> 'Pretty were the sight
> If our old halls could change their sex, and flaunt
> With prudes for proctors, dowagers for deans,
> And sweet girl-graduates in their golden hair.

[...]
> yet I fear,
> If there were many Lilias in the brood,
> However deep you might embower the nest,
> Some boy would spy it.'

Angered, Lilia counters: 'I would make it death / For any male thing but to peep at us'.[57] That Lilia's response is itself intemperate is suggested by the ancient fable of the Princess which Tennyson's narrator then orates, with its message that sexual equality will be more readily achieved by integration than segregation of the sexes, but her reproof to the patronizing young man remains. By quoting his words without apology or qualification, our poem's narrator is implicated in his embarrassment.

More telling is the replacement of Winifred's chic beret with Lady Brett Ashley's trilby. This not only adds a hint of gender ambiguity to the poem's fictional young woman but by invoking Hemingway's *The Sun Also Rises* casts aspersions upon the narrator's masculinity. That novel is narrated by Jake Barnes who has been emasculated in the First World War ('You [...] have given more than your life', an Italian liaison colonel tells him in hospital) and who now, in the expatriate Paris of the twenties, agonizingly observes the sexual adventures of the woman he loves, unable to command or even partake of her rampant promiscuity.[58] In one disgraceful episode he acts the pander between Brett and her latest 'crush', bullfighter Pedro Romero, humiliatingly arranging for another man to do that which he longs to but cannot. In a single stroke that man's hat adds a sexual *frisson* to the depiction of the Young Lady and a trace of impotence to the depiction of the narrator. The pornographic gaze, our poem suggests, is born of inadequacy rather than virility.

This reading is subsequently endorsed by contrast with a third intertext, C. Day Lewis's poem 'The Album', in which the identical plot, a male narrator discovering his beloved's past by paging through her photograph album, has the opposite outcome:

> I close the book;
> But the past slides out of its leaves to haunt me
> And it seems, wherever I look,
> Phantoms of irreconcilable happiness taunt me.
> Then I see her, petalled in new-blown hours,
> Beside me – 'All you love most there
> Has blossomed again', she murmurs, 'all that you missed there
> Has grown to be yours.'[59]

'The Album' ends with the hero getting the girl. As we shall see, Larkin's poem ends with his masturbatory anti-hero wondering, doubtfully, if he could carry off – not the girl, nor even her album – but a solitary snap!

'Lines on a Young Lady's Photograph Album', Act II (lines 16–26)

At this point, one-third of the way through, the poem switches abruptly from the first to the second short act. The discussion of the pornographic imagination is halted, the narrator apostrophizing photography in terms that seem to confirm the maxim that the camera does not lie:

> But o, photography! as no art is,
> Faithful and disappointing! that records
> Dull days as dull, and hold-it smiles as frauds,
> And will not censor blemishes

For critics like Tolley, these lines are crucial to the definition of 1950s culture as aesthetically realist and philosophically empiricist: 'Nothing that went before [...] quite prepared the reader for "Lines on a Young Lady's Photograph Album". It has been recognized as a typical Movement poem.' Interpreting the passage quoted above as testament to photography's superiority over painting and sculpture, he adds:

> It is the honesty of photography that is praised and the truth that it offers that is valued; while 'art' characteristically of the Movement, is made to come off second-best [...] The culminating praise of photography is that it 'persuades / That this is a real girl in a real place, / In every sense empirically true!' What is praised is again 'truth'; but 'empirically true' recalls the philosophy of Bertrand Russell and G. E. Moore, the fathers of the linguistic analysis that dominated British philosophy, especially at Oxford, in the nineteen-fifties, and where what was 'meaningful' was equated with what was 'empirically verifiable'.[60]

There is, of course, a shard of plausibility in the argument. Behind the narrator's claim that photography 'will not censor blemishes' one catches an echo of the famous 'warts and all' incident in which Oliver Cromwell reproved Peter Lely, who was painting his portrait as Lord Protector:

> Mr Lely, I desire you would use all your skill to paint your picture truly like me, and not flatter me at all; but remark all these roughness, pimples, warts, and everything as you see me. Otherwise, I will never pay a farthing for it.[61]

Lely had been portraitist of Charles I and would later be Charles II's Principal Painter in Ordinary. His entire style was based on the experience that wealthy patrons, royalty above all, commissioned artists to produce an idealized representation. The point of the anecdote is that Cromwell is the exception that proves the rule: portrait painting typically censors blemishes in the interests of idealization. The narrator's point in echoing the anecdote is that with photography, by contrast, the blemishes typically show.

We can deepen our understanding of the issues at stake – and allow Tolley's view a temporary reprieve – with the help of Barthes's exquisite little book on photography, *Camera Lucida*. Barthes observes that not only can other media censor or edit what they depict, they can invent the scene entire: 'Painting can feign reality without having seen it.' By contrast, 'every photograph is a certificate of presence', a ratification of what had actually been placed before the lens, such that 'I can never deny that *the thing had been there*.' Photography became

> possible only on the day when a scientific circumstance (the discovery that silver halogens were sensitive to light) made it possible to recover and print directly the luminous rays emitted by a variously lighted object. The photograph is literally an emanation of the referent. From a real body, which was there, proceed radiations which ultimately touch me, who am here.

For Barthes 'it is Reference, which is the founding order of Photography'.[62]

All then seem agreed: the camera can neither invent nor suppress only ratify, making photography the most truthful of visual media and a fitting objective correlative for the Movement realism inaugurated (Tolley assures us) by 'Lines on a Young Lady's Photograph Album'. As Dion Boucicault has it as early as 1859, in his play *The Octoroon*: 'The apparatus can't lie.'[63] Even if this *is* what verses four and five propose, we need to remember that such are the views of the narrator not the text; and he only makes this declaration in Act II of the poem, by which point his views on photography are already compromised by his pornographic appreciation of it. Besides, those opinions, for all their declarative intensity – and the second act is entirely constituted of exclamations – are more ambiguous than Tolley (that master of the *single entendre*) comprehends. The lines 'But o, photography! as no art is, / Faithful and disappointing!' may indeed signify that this new medium is superior to art by virtue of its greater veracity. In which case, the new technology has simply retrenched the central assumption of the ekphrastic tradition, that of the superiority of the visual to the verbal sign. On the other hand, those same lines may be parsed as an assertion of photography's inability to rise above the literal and achieve artistic freedom. Art's need for a degree of *factitiousness*, fictional elbow room or poetic licence is thwarted by photography's stubborn *facticity* – its inability to swap a beret for a trilby, a dog for a cat. As Larkin said, 'I often feel poems have to have some falsity in them, like yeast, or they won't "rise"' (*LM*, 205). In this interpretation, photography's truthfulness thwarts its status as an art: it is 'disappointing' *because* it is 'faithful'.

What, then, of the climactic assertion of this middle act, that photography's unique 'candour [...] overwhelmingly persuades / That this is a real girl in a real place, // In every sense empirically true!' Surely this is confirmation of Tolley's position that 'Lines on a Young Lady's Photograph Album' categorically asserts the truth of photography? Alas, this reductionist reading misses the central paradox of the passage: that the album does *not* present 'a real girl in a real place' but a depiction thereof, a fraction the size of the reality, two- rather than three-dimensional, in 1953 almost certainly monochrome (though the poem does not specify), constituted of paper and emulsion rather than flesh and blood, as much a token of absence as of presence. Like a mirror, photographs show us where we are not; put us in the presence of events from which we were absent; make us shudder in anticipation of catastrophes that preceded our birth. This is a complication which *Camera Lucida*, having appeared to deny it, affirms in its closing pages:

> Now, in the Photograph, what I posit is not only the absence of the object; it is also, by one and the same movement, on equal terms, the fact that this object has indeed existed and that it has been where I see it [...] The Photograph then becomes a bizarre *medium*, a new form of hallucination: false on the level of perception, true on the level of time.[64]

Absent and present, here and there, then and now, true and false: suddenly Tolley's definitively trustworthy medium, turgid with truth content, basking in its own self-evidence, slips between his fingers. For all the time the 'real girl in a real place, // In every sense empirically true' is *not* the one in the pictures, the one who validates and is validated by photography, but the one the narrator studiously ignores, the one who in the opening clause hands him the album and who, for all we know, may be in his *distracted* presence for the duration of the poem.

In its own very different way, then, the second act as much as the first testifies (in Laura Mulvey's words) to the narrator's 'displaced drives and misrecognised desire'; demonstrates 'that the sexualized image of woman says little or nothing about women's reality, but is symptomatic of male fantasy and anxiety'; and thereby deflects the male gaze back onto itself, 'from woman as spectacle to the psyche that had need of such a spectacle'.[65]

'Lines on a Young Lady's Photograph Album', Act III (lines 27–45)

Our understanding of the psychopathology of the male narrator deepens in the somewhat elongated final act of the poem (four verses compared to previous acts of three and two). However, that insight comes encrypted in an abstract discussion of time to which the poem now turns with an abruptness similar to that of the transition between Acts I and II:

> this is a real girl in a real place,
>
> In every sense empirically true!
> Or is it just *the past*? Those flowers, that gate,
> These misty parks and motors, lacerate
> Simply by being over; you
> Contract my heart by looking out of date.

That language of *laceration* and *heart contraction* is supplemented by references to *crying*, *grief* and *mourning* as though the addressee were dead, the poem an obsequy or exequy, the mood funereal. At one level, this is a simple statement that the photograph album – *any* photograph album – is a repository of past vogues, a graveyard of spent styles. Compare with this passage from *Camera Lucida* in which Barthes contemplates an early photograph of his mother:

> Here, around 1913, is my mother dressed up – hat with a feather, gloves, delicate linen at wrists and throat, her 'chic' belied by the sweetness and simplicity of her expression. [She is] caught in a History (of tastes, fashions, fabrics): my attention is distracted from her by accessories which have perished; for clothing is perishable, it makes a second grave for the beloved being.[66]

But behind both passages lies a profound apprehension of photography's morbid character, its lack of protensity or forward propulsion, the way it 'flows back from presentation to retention'. The moment a photograph is taken it freezes a present and holds it there, suspended in time, like a cryogenized body, no longer alive yet not allowed either to decay and dissolve – a new kind of *undead*. The present captured in a photograph instantly ceases to be the present, but neither is it the past perfect; it is a past present preserved.

Larkin and Barthes are equally good at registering this taxidermal melancholy of the photograph. In Barthes's words: 'The important thing is that the Photograph possesses an evidential force, and that its testimony bears not on the object but on time.'[67] Larkin makes the same point differently: the photograph confronts us with 'a past no one now can share' and if 'we cry' at the resultant sense of 'exclusion' we do so knowing that the emotion is vicarious, 'without a chance of consequence', and therefore a comment on our own mortality rather than on the object portrayed.[68]

Larkin's cunning is to exemplify this theme in the narrator's half-suppressed awareness of the age gap between himself and his Young Lady. The possibility that he is older than the addressee, with manners and values pertaining to an earlier generation, is flagged up in the quaint wording of the title with its calculated echoing of Edwardian and Georgian writers.

The particular model is the Yeats of the 1910s (the title combining integers from the latter's 'Lines written in Dejection', 'To a Young Beauty' and 'To a Young Girl'), just as 'He Hears that his Beloved has become Engaged' which Larkin wrote earlier that same year echoes the Yeats of the 1890s ('He thinks of those who have Spoken Evil of his Beloved', 'He bids his Beloved be at Peace', 'He gives his Beloved certain Rhymes', 'He mourns for the Change that has come upon him and his Beloved'). Hostile critics often cite Larkin's claim to have abandoned the example of Yeats for that of Hardy as proof of his retreat from modernism to earlier, safer poetic models. In the example before us, the very opposite is the case: writing from a decidedly postmodern vantage point, Larkin incorporates Yeatsian allusions as proof, not of the narrator's contemporaneity, but of his old fogeyism.

Of course, the *Young* Lady formula adapted from Yeats automatically implies that he is her elder; for if both were youthful, the matter of age would not arise. Again, his old-world gallantries and pre-war diction ('disquieting chaps who loll [...] Not quite your class, I'd say, dear') – the verbal equivalent of holding the door for the woman to enter first – suggest that the Young Lady is not being addressed by a Young Lad. Indeed, the way the narrator equates a sense of exclusion from her past with uncertainty about her prospects – 'a past that no one now can share, / No matter whose your future' – conveys a queasy awareness that she will never be his. This may explain his falling so voraciously upon her album, as though acknowledging that this is the nearest he will ever get to possessing her. It may also lend a degree of poignancy to his fantasy of stealing the snap of her bathing, as though that token might provide some small consolation.

But this is only half the story: for the subtextual sense that he has missed the boat with her for reasons of age is counterpoised by a matching theme that she, though too much his junior to accept his advances, is no longer the Young Lady of the album. This double-helix on the ageing process may once again be tracked back to the poem's title, the very first word of which is a compound pun: 'Lines' meaning versified lines, the ensuing poem; 'Lines' meaning signs of wear and tear on the album itself, the corollary being that if the portfolio shows marks of age its owner will no longer be the Young Lady represented within it; and, supplementing this last, 'Lines' as in wrinkles sullying that once young demeanour. This is a pun Larkin was still toying with six or seven months later in the poem 'Skin':

> Obedient daily dress,
> You cannot always keep
> That unfakable young surface.
> You must learn your lines – (*CP*, 92; *TCP*, 44)

The instant this scenario is licensed to run, so many hints and innuendos spring forth in support that the reader may suspect the narrator of bitterness – as though, miffed at being perceived as too old by his younger addressee, he cannot desist from reminding her that she is not immune to time's merciless vandalism. To exclaim while contemplating her portraits that photography is unique in not censoring blemishes is to suggest that she sports such Cromwellian disfigurements. To add that the camera only 'shades / A chin as doubled when it is' ungraciously implies that the chin in question is hers. The barbed formulation 'you / Contract my heart by looking out of date' not only suggests that enough time has elapsed since the 'you' of the photograph album was 'Young' for the pictures to have acquired an historical patina, but may also signify that it is her datedness that speaks to his fogeyism, contracting his heart (squeezing it) and contracting his heart (impelling it towards marriage). Even the phrasing of the concluding claim that the album 'holds you [...] / Unvariably lovely there' may mean *there* by contrast with how you now look *here*! The narrator's adoration, however real, bristles with barbs and resentments.

At which juncture, the question might arise: where does this leave the ekphrastic norms with which we began? We have already remarked that this poem's preoccupation with the photographic image, with its infinite potential for replication, strikes at the 'aura' of the artwork, that quality of uniqueness especially prized in ekphrastic tradition. Again, the pictorial dynamics associated with photography's compromised voyeurism may be thought to betray the transported, mystical, upturned gaze of ekphrastic perspectivism ('Painting! Descend on canvas wing, – / and hover o'er my head, Design!').[69] Our discussion of the poem's punning title, with its implication that the photographic album already shows signs of damage, simply confirms what we already know: that being printed on perishable paper, photographs entirely lack that physical durability which makes architectural monuments, sculptures and mural paintings emblems of immortality. The fact that the typical family album is constituted of images by diverse contributors, none of them known to posterity, none of their pictures likely to be reverenced outside an immediate circle of kith and kin, abnegates the ekphrastic emphasis upon the concept of artistic genius. Consequently, 'Lines on a Young Lady's Photograph Album' is entirely devoid of information regarding authorship, signature, provenance and authentication; no names, dates, scholarly debate, nor gallery context; no sense of personal mystique attached to this or that photographer, no appeals to general knowledge about the artist's life such as might attend a poem on painters like Van Gogh (the severed ear, the suicide), Picasso (the wives and mistresses) or Warhol (the 'Factory' entourage, the wigs). Even the eponymous 'Young Lady' is an *anonymous* young lady: no Aphrodite, Helen or Primavera, she. By honouring the addressee's vivacity while resisting the temptation to so idealize her beauty that she is converted into a public figure or symbol of transcendent beauty, the poem captures the camera's revolutionary capacity to represent that overwhelming mass of humanity formerly kept below the parapet of visibility. What the poem finds in her album is what we find in our own – not something exalted and universally admired, but *ourselves made worthy in our anonymity*. That is to say, the complete reverse of ekphrastic *doxa*.

The one ekphrastic principle that *is* upheld may seem to carry extra authority by virtue of coming in the very last lines, as though the previous reversal of norms was just a build-up to a climactic restitution of order. But in a further reversal that regulative ideal is itself punningly dashed, bringing the argument full circle. The ekphrastic norm at issue is that which credits great art with a power to transcend time, granting viewers access to an eternalized realm of emotional and aesthetic truth. Despite having abandoned the idea that photography *is* great art, and despite foregoing any appeal to the Young Lady as the Platonic paragon of beauty – a Venus, *Ewig Weibliche* or 'face that launched a thousand ships' – the poem yet posits that her album 'holds' her 'like a heaven [...] / Unvariably lovely there, / Smaller and clearer as the years go by'. 'Unvariably lovely' plays upon rival meanings: that her youthful beauty does not vary from one pose to another across the pictorial contents; and that her beauty does not fade with the passage of time ('Smaller', yes, but 'clearer'). It is this latter sense of photography's ability to freeze an instant forever that chimes with ekphrastic transcendence, reminding of Wordsworth's 'one brief moment caught from fleeting time'.[70] The words 'It holds you' echo Marvell's insistence that a portraitist use 'colours that will hold'; while the other half of that phrase, 'like a *heaven*', recalls Byron's declaration that in the Belvedere *Apollo*

> are exprest
> All that ideal beauty ever bless'd
> The mind within its most unearthly mood,
> When each conception was a *heavenly* guest –
> A ray of immortality –[71]

(My emphases.)

Yet issuing from a poet as resolutely post-Nietzschean as Larkin, that simile – 'like a heaven' – seems calculated to provoke readerly unease: it might as well read *like a mirage*. When this is followed by 'you lie / Unvariably lovely there', the word *lie* is invested with added emphasis by the terminal juncture, the pause enforced by the line break, as though to draw attention to its double meaning. That which poetry traditionally praises, the artistic illusion that time can be arrested, Larkin's poem punningly denounces: the one ekphrastic norm to have survived the photographic revolution is finally dismissed as a falsehood.[72]

Coda

Writing in 1995, the poet and scholar John Hollander claimed that 'Photographic portraits pose special problems, as do photographic images generally, for poetic ekphrasis. So far, there have not been that many inter-esting examples of such poems by important modern poets.'[73] This might have been true before Larkin's intervention: C. Day Lewis's 'The Album' was one of the few precursors available as a model for 'Lines on a Young Lady's Photograph Album'. After his intervention the situation is transformed: one thinks of poems like Richard Howard's 'Nadar', Douglas Dunn's 'Writing with Light', David Ferry's six poems on photographs by Thomas Eakins, Carol Ann Duffy's 'War Photographer', Jaroslaw Kosciuszko's 'Punctum', Glyn Maxwell's 'My Grandfather at the Pool', Robert Pinsky's 'Photograph' and Grace Nichols's 'To the Curator of the Museum of Baghdad'; or such book-length ventures as Thom Gunn's *Positives* (with photos by his brother Ander), Ted Hughes's *Remains of Elmet* (images by Fay Godwin) or Edwin Morgan's exhilarating *Instamatic Poems*. In most of these cases the photog-raphers are famous and therefore more easily recuperable to the ekphrastic tradition's deference to artistic genius. Larkin remains exceptional in his concentration upon anonymous human subjects depicted by anonymous photographers.

Maggie Humm has reminded us that 'To date there is no "theory" of amateur photography.'[74] As shocking is the lack of conceptualization of the family album genre. Larkin's meditation upon the matter not only marked a huge advance in poetry's address to photography, it was and remains in advance of critical theory. For instance, Barthes's classic *Camera Lucida* is punctuated by handsome reproductions of masterpieces by Nadar, Hine, Stieglitz, Sander, Kertész, Avedon, Mapplethorpe. Not content with this illustrious shortlist, Barthes captions one image: 'Who do you think is the world's greatest photographer?' 'Nadar.'[75] The old ekphrastic quest for transcendent genius is revived for the age of the camera. With the amateur album, by contrast, the concept of artistic exceptionalism is replaced by the concept of the democratically representative. The photographs, by virtue of their very anonymity, invite a reading position more akin to Barthes's cel-ebrated essay on literature, 'The Death of the Author', than to his writings on photography.[76] Indeed, with albums typically assembling snaps from multiple sources, authorship is scattered, dispersed across the paper gal-lery. With amateur photography the author Barthes would have us forget is always already forgotten. Even more resoundingly than 'An Arundel Tomb' and 'The Card-Players', then, 'Lines on a Young Lady's Photograph Album' shatters the author- (or artist-) centred approach of which Larkin was post-humously a conspicuous victim. Hence the folly of reading the poem as a versified autobiographical address to Winifred Arnott. To conflate author and narrator in this way is to miss the point: for the narrator is a bit of an old fogey, but the poem is revolutionary. It revolutionizes ekphrasis.[77]

3
Radical Deterritorialization: 'At Grass', 'March Past', 'Church Going'

Deterritorialization

The term *deterritorialization* derives from Lacanian psychoanalysis and refers to the detaching of Freudian libido from early fixation upon the mother's breast.[1] The concept was given wider application in *Anti-Oedipus* (1977), a profoundly anti-contextual collaboration between Gilles Deleuze and Félix Guattari which identifies all processes of becoming and creativity with a view of identity as detached, mobile and nomadic. In a later work, *Cinema I: The Movement-Image* (1986), Deleuze characteristically proposes that cinema is at its most cinematic not when it is presenting ordered temporal narratives, such as historical epics or costume dramas, but when it frees us from the idea of time as a connected order or sequence, 'deterritorializing' the image from its origins and aspiring to a condition of 'pure affect'.[2] The term deterritorialization has latterly been adopted by anthropologists and social geographers who use it to designate any weakening of ties between culture and place. For example, when an area of the world gains access to the internet it simultaneously gains access to every community already online. At that moment the deterritorializing process begins as the local culture is enveloped by the global community. Some anthropologists present this as a process in which *deterritorialization of the local* is seamlessly conjoined with *reterritorialization by the global*. This terminology is now commonplace in debates about the globalization of culture.

In this chapter I will endeavour to keep all these meanings in play while using the term deterritorialization in its most literal sense to designate Larkin's assault upon geographical origins. This will entail an examination of Larkin's drafting process as a series of deletions, divestings and disinvestments. The examination is not undertaken in the hope of arriving at an originatory moment of authorial revelation, like Tennyson's cry to the spirit of Arthur Hallam, 'wed me', in the manuscripts of *In Memoriam XCIII* – a cry which may anyway have been suppressed by the poet because it was embarrassingly false, rather than embarrassingly true. Instead, we shall focus upon that exquisite ratio in which the abandonment of poetic drafts equates to the abandonment of geographical roots. The poem emerges, like a photograph in a developing tray, by dissolving the sense of place.

To keep the investigation within manageable bounds, I shall concentrate upon the poems Larkin wrote in the period 1950–55 when he was mainly resident in Belfast. Manuscripts will clarify how he systematically wrote Ireland out of the poems while refusing to write England in: *deterritorialization of the margin resists reterritorialization by the centre*, thereby calling the centre-margin model into question. Part of the fun of the game will be to see how critics were wrong-footed by the procedure. It might even be claimed, with only a little exaggeration, that English critics initially constructed Larkin as Irish only for Irish critics to reconstruct him as English. *What the poet deterritorializes, the critics reterritorialize.* In other words, the poems themselves are radically unhoused and it is the critics who assign them a national identity – now this side of the Irish Sea, now that – in accord with what they know, or think they know, about the author's geographical origins.

The English construction of Irish Larkin

Some of the poems Larkin wrote in Belfast appeared in English periodicals and anthologies before being gathered in his first great book, *The Less Deceived* (1955). The editors who gave these poems their first airings perceived them as the work of an Irishman. When the typically Larkinesque pieces 'Deceptions', 'Coming' and 'Wants' were included in the 1953 London anthology *Springtime*, the editors G.S. Fraser and Iain Fletcher, one an expatriate Scot and the other English, described their author as a 'Northern Ireland regional poet'. The anthology classified young British poets under six headings: Academics, Empsonians, Neo-Decadents, Naked Sensitives, Sophisticates and Regionalists. Whereas Larkin's fellow Movementeers – Davie, Amis, Gunn, Wain – are placed in the first two categories, he is put in the last section alongside Scottish poets Sydney Goodsir Smith, Robert Garioch and Tom Scott, all of whom often wrote in Lallans, the language of Lowland Scotland. The editors go on to say that 'Irish poets, like Mr Larkin, though writing in standard English, reflect another regional value, that of rootedness.'[3] Their point, presumably, is that Larkin's indigeneity is no less emphatic than that of the Scots despite his eschewal of the Irish language.

Two other poems that would later be cited as expressive of Larkin's rooted Englishness, 'No Road' and 'Next, Please', were published in a 1955 edition of Alan Brownjohn's magazine *Departure*. According to the 'Notes on Contributors' section of the magazine, Larkin 'was born in Northern Ireland'.[4] By the time of the anthology *Poetry Now* (1956), Fraser had probably realized his mistake, yet still contrives to describe Larkin as 'a chastened Yeats – a Yeats "done over again" in water-colour'[5] ('Preface', 24). This sort of thing provoked derision on the parts of Amis and Larkin. In a letter to

Larkin of 21 January 1953, Kingsley mocked the Lallans of Tom Scott in his description of a reading to launch *Springtime* and was still joking about the 'regionalist' tag in a follow-up letter on 5 May.[6] It might be that early commentators in England were simply misled by Larkin's Irish surname and Belfast address. The fact remains that readers as sensitive as Fraser and Brownjohn – reputable poets as well as critics – found nothing in the poems so incontrovertibly English as to queer their assumption that their author was Irish.

The Irish construction of English Larkin

The Irish construction of English Larkin began in the 1970s and has been dominated by two Ulster poets, Seamus Heaney and Tom Paulin. Their rival views have been influential with English critics of Irish extraction – Neil Corcoran, Stephen Regan, Sean O'Brien, Terry Eagleton – most of whom favour the Paulin approach, though Regan lurches opportunistically from side to side. Both define Larkin as an English nationalist, but what the one affirms the other denounces. Paradoxically, the Catholic Heaney affirms, because his own removal to Eire entails a matching Irish nationalism; while the Protestant Paulin denounces, because his removal to England makes him anxious to project onto others his exacerbated Orange background. (Like the Reverend Ian Paisley, he has made a career out of denouncing.)

Heaney's essay 'Englands of the Mind' (1976) anticipates Tom Nairn's classic study *The Break-Up of Britain* (1977) by setting the work of Ted Hughes, Geoffrey Hill and Philip Larkin in an historical context that is not just post-imperial but post-Union Jack:

> I think that sense of an ending has driven all three of these writers into a kind of piety towards their local origins, has made them look in, rather than up, to England. The loss of imperial power, the failure of economic nerve, the diminished influence of Britain inside Europe, all this has led to a new sense of the shires, a new valuing of the native English experience.[7]

Heaney is at pains to acknowledge that the end of empire returned England to a postcolonial condition akin to that of the colonies it once controlled: 'The poets of the mother culture, I feel, are now possessed of that defensive love of their territory which was once shared only by those poets whom we might call colonial.' Larkin takes his place in Heaney's trinity as 'a poet [...] of composed and tempered English nationalism, and his voice is the not untrue, not unkind voice of post-war England'.[8]

Paulin's essay 'Into the Heart of Englishness' (1990) sees Larkin's nationalism in diametrically opposed terms – discomposed, distempered, untrue, unkind. Larkin is a 'reactionary' who 'loves the unchanging' and who 'is opposed to the historical process', his 'rancid prejudices' expressive of 'a type of terminal Englishness that feels lost and tired and out of date'.[9] Larkin's real theme is national decline, his melancholy lyricism stemming from a deep distaste for contemporary social democracy and a profound nostalgia for the days of empire. When the *Selected Letters* appeared two years later, Paulin was on hand to denounce 'Larkin's racism, misogyny and quasi-fascist views'.[10] He thereby set the tone for Corcoran, O'Brien, Eagleton and James Simmons, all of whom address Larkin as his moral superiors, as though they were *seeing through* his 'great author' status to an ideological inferior within. The ensuing chapter shows Larkin's finely nuanced poems elegantly eluding the vulgar nationalisms of both the Heaney and the Paulin camps. So much the better if it also helps discredit the Paulinites' critical condescension.

The Irish Englishing of 'At Grass'

Shortly before applying for the job at Queen's University, Belfast, Larkin wrote what many regard as his first masterpiece, 'At Grass' (*CP*, 29–30; *TCP*, 45–6). Heaney described this and subsequent Larkin poems as embodiments of an ideal of England sanctified by literary tradition:

> All these moments spring from the deepest strata of Larkin's poetic self, and they are connected with another kind of mood that pervades his work and which could be called elysian: I am thinking in particular of poems like 'At Grass', 'MCMXIV', 'How Distant' and, most recently, 'The Explosion'. To borrow Geoffrey Hill's borrowing from Coleridge, these are visions of 'the old Platonic England', the light in them honeyed by attachment to a dream world that will not be denied because it is at the foundation of the poet's sensibility. It is the light that was on Langland's Malvern, 'in summer season, when soft was the sun', at once local and timeless.[11]

Larkin's adherence to this exclusively English literary nationalism is demonstrated by identifying 'At Grass' with Gray's 'Elegy written in a Country Church-Yard' which he once claimed was his favourite poem:[12]

> 'At Grass' could well be subtitled, 'An Elegy in a Country Paddock'. Behind the trees where the horses shelter there could well rise the spire of Stoke Poges church [...] And when, at the conclusion of the poem, 'the groom and the groom's boy / With bridles in the evening come', their footsteps surely echo the ploughman homeward plodding his weary way.[13]

Gray's mother lived at Stoke Poges. They are both now buried in the church-yard there.

By the time of Stephen Regan's monograph *Philip Larkin* (1992), Heaney's anglicizing tendency had hardened into orthodoxy:

'At Grass' is a quintessentially English poem. Its Englishness is evident not just in its memories of 'Cups and Stakes and Handicaps' and its bright evocation of 'classic' summers, but also in its modified use of the pastoral convention. There are hints of eighteenth-century English pastoralism in the elegiac mood of the poem.[14]

Repeating the argument five years on, in the essay 'Larkin's Reputation', Regan arrives at Stoke Poges a full 21 years after Heaney: 'The subtle melancholy which pervades "At Grass" recalls the eighteenth-century pastoralism of Thomas Gray.'[15] Actually, the poem's pastoral echoes are not confined to Gray. The elate anonymity of Larkin's horses ('they // Have slipped their names, and stand at ease, / Or gallop for what must be joy') owes something to the equating of fulfilment with innomination in Pope's 'The Quiet Life' and to Goldsmith's praise of spontaneity in 'The Deserted Village' (whence Larkin's unusual description of the meadows as 'unmolesting'):

> Spontaneous joys, where Nature has its play,
> The soul adopts, and owes their first-born sway,
> Lightly they frolic o'er the vacant mind,
> Unenvied, unmolested, unconfined.[16]

The same theme recurs in Wordsworth's sonnet 'Written in Very Early Youth' which provided the opening motif of a dimly visible horse cropping grass:

> The horse alone, seen dimly as I pass,
> Is cropping audibly his later meal[17]

Although the Wordsworth was possibly written around 1790, it may date from as late as 1802: in which case, the emphasis upon 'Elegy written in a Country Church-Yard' is too narrowly lodged as to century as well as to author.

Heaney's affirmation of the English nationalism exemplified by 'At Grass' was countered by Paulin and Simmons for whom the identical poem constituted proof of Larkin's imperial sentiments. Paulin's 1990 essay twice accuses the poem of nostalgia for a hazy golden age before the First World War: 'this lack of unity of social being which he mourns in "At Grass" – it exists somewhere in the Edwardian past, an idealised memory against which 1950s England appears dull, pinched, banal and second-rate'.[18] Regan lauds Paulin's 'incisive historical method', blithely unaware that it directly contradicts the Heaney approach he has already endorsed; but, in truth, there is something seriously amiss with Paulin's grasp of history.[19]

The term 'Edwardian' refers to the reign of Edward VII (1901–10). The poem was begun in 1949 and rather precisely refers the reader back 'fifteen years' to 1934. Regan himself quotes the cancelled manuscript draft in which the flashback sequence is dated 'thirty-three and -four'. Paulin's insistence upon the Edwardian era is out by a quarter of a century. Simmons's sneer that 'At Grass' reads like 'a poem by a very talented Georgian' is only a little less anachronistic.[20] As a literary term, 'Georgian' is associated with the five anthologies of *Georgian Poetry* edited by Edward Marsh in the decade before Larkin's birth (1910–22). The poem's description of the 'Squadrons of empty cars' parked at the race-courses is alone sufficient to rule out that decade: only in the early thirties did private automobile ownership flourish in accord with Larkin's account.

Larkin's deterritorialization of 'At Grass'

Irish attempts to English 'At Grass' exhibited not only a weak sense of history, but wilful ignorance of the poetic manuscripts. The holograph drafts of 'At Grass' were reproduced in *Phoenix* magazine in 1973, before any of the foregoing essays were written, and show Larkin patiently erasing anglocentric references. These handwritten pages stop well short of the poem's final form, suggesting that Larkin made the decisive edit after transferring the work-in-progress to the typewriter. This is Trevor Tolley's 'reconstruction' of where the poem was up to at that point of transference:[21]

AT GRASS
[Draft version from Workbook – BM Ad MS 52619]
[The stanzas of the published version are indicated by numbers in the left-hand margin. Changes (other than of punctuation) made in the published version are shown in the right-hand margin.]

1. The eye can hardly pick them out
   From the cold shade they shelter in,
   Till the wind distresses tail and mane;
   Then one crops grass, and moves about,
   The other seeming to look on.
   The sky blows dark with new Spring rain.   /And stands anonymous
                                                              again/

   And now no London newspaper
   Pries round their paddock solitude.
   They are as other horses are.
   Yet, fifteen years ago, both were
   More famous than most men, pursued
   By camera, field-glasses and car.

In City dining-rooms in clubs
And barbers'-shops and billiard halls,
Their flippant names were burrs that stuck
To gossip; and in back-street pubs
Their tinted pictures on the walls
Embodied every earthly luck.

2. Through thirty-three and four, perhaps   /Yet fifteen years ago,
   Two dozen distances sufficed   perhaps/
   To fable them, far afternoons   /faint afternoons/
   Of Cups and Stakes and Handicaps,
   Whereby their names were artificed
   To inlay faded, classic Junes.

3. Silks at the start: against the sky
   Numbers and parasols: outside,
   Squadrons of empty cars, and heat,
   And littered grass; then the long cry
   That hangs unhushed till it subside
   To sports editions in the street.   /To stop press columns

   But money rode them, led them in,
   Curry-combed their croups and flanks;
   Every canter, swerve or sweat
   Money measured; every win
   Was endorsed at different banks.
   Guiltlessly they galloped, yet

   Broke three people in one day,
   The two of them, and every race
   They ran brought small disturbances –
   One pawns his coat, one cannot pay:
   [Strange such seediness to trace]   [Not drafted to
   Back to such splendid energies.   completion]

4. Do memories plague their ears like flies?
   They shake their heads. Dusk brims the shadows.
   Summer by summer all ebbed away.   /all stole away/
   – The starting-gates, the crowds and cries
   All but the unmolesting meadows.
   Almanacked, their names live; they

5. Have slipped their names; and stand at ease
   Or gallop for what must be joy.

No field glasses pursue them home.	/And not a field-glass sees them home/
Stopwatches make no prophecies.	/Or curious stop watch prophesies/
Only the groom, or the groom's boy With bridles in the evening come.	/and the groom's boy/

At this juncture the poem's theme is the place of racehorses in a capitalist economy, with much emphasis on the financial imperatives of the sport ('money rode them'), the benefits to the banking system ('every win / Was endorsed at different banks') and the cost to individual punters ('One pawns his coat, one cannot pay'). In amputating four stanzas from the text Larkin not only suppressed the critique of capitalism, he also deleted the site-specific references. Hence, the mentions of a 'London newspaper' and 'City dining-rooms' in the second and third verses of Tolley's reconstruction were excised. The *Phoenix* facsimile shows comparable passages not included in Tolley's transcription were also subject to deletion. Larkin tries and discards

> Brief, silk-dazzled distances
> At Ascot, Epsom, Newmarket
> Changed them to more than horses

and

> Fifteen years ago, they were
> More famous than most men, pursued
> By cameras, field-glasses and cars,
> Ham-sandwiches, and newspapers:
> On Epsom Downs, at Newmarket

before arriving at the 'Cups and Stakes and Handicaps' of the finished poem, a description sufficiently deterritorialized to apply to Ireland or France as readily as England. Again, the *Phoenix* reproduction shows that the reference to a 'London newspaper' documented by Tolley went through an even more topographically precise version – 'smudged stop-press on Regent Street' – before mutating into the geographically vague 'stop-press columns on the street' of the published poem.[22] These versions show that Larkin went to considerable pains to sever the poem from the geographical certitudes upon which are predicated the nationalistic kennings of both the Heaney and the Paulin camps.

Brown Jack

What, then, of the consensual view that at the tonal and metrical level 'At Grass' is embedded in an exclusively English tradition of elegiac pastoralism? The English critic David Timms appears to support that claim by identifying the metre of 'At Grass' as iambic pentameter, the classic mode of English verse including Gray's 'Elegy'.[23] Tolley goes further, seeing the composition of this poem as the precise moment when Hardy replaced Yeats as Larkin's artistic mentor:

> 'At Grass', completed on 3rd January, 1950, might be seen as the first major mature poem by Larkin; and it brings in a wholly new approach to composition, undoubtedly associated with the abandonment of the inspirational approach to composition associated with his admiration for Yeats, and the discovery, through the influence of Hardy, of the possibility of making poetry out of things that made up his own life.[24]

A master of thinking *inside* the box, Tolley credulously repeats Larkin's cod account of his poetic development as a one-way journey from modernism to realism, from internationalism to nationalism, from Yeats to Hardy.[25] In point of fact, 'At Grass' is not scored in the iambic pentameters of 'Elegy written in a Country Church-Yard' but in the iambic tetrameters, six per verse, of 'The Wild Swans at Coole' by the identical W.B. Yeats. The manuscript reduction of 'At Grass' from nine to five stanzas, which Tolley himself details, fits it perfectly to the Yeats original. Moreover, the structural parallelism is replicated at the thematic level. In both poems a narrator's melancholy at the passage of time is offset by the consolation of contemplating other creatures. In Yeats the objects of observation are 59 swans; in Larkin, two horses. The creatures are presented as emblems of companionability, the swans paddling a lake 'lover by lover'; while in Larkin, one of the horses 'crops grass [...] / – The other seeming to look on'. In both cases, the present time of the poem is interrupted by a flashback of between one and two decades: 19 years in Yeats; 15 in Larkin. The diurnal and seasonal settings carry intimations of mortality: 'The Wild Swans at Coole' takes place in 'October twilight'; 'At Grass' is set at dusk and carries hints of autumn ('cold shade', a distressing 'wind'). As day draws to a close, so does the year. Yet the animals in both poems are undiminished by time: of the swans it is said, 'Their hearts have not grown old'; while the aged horses still 'gallop for what must be joy'.[26]

Further correspondences might be drawn, as when Yeats's 'brimming' water is echoed in the way Larkin has 'Dusk brims the shadows'. However, the relation between the two involved contestation as well as emulation, Larkin using 'At Grass' to distinguish the Yeats he found utile from the one he found inutile. The striking deployment of the archaic 'artificed' to describe the immortal status of the racehorses before they escaped into their physically exuberant private lives reverses the Yeats of 'Sailing to Byzantium' whose narrator would exchange the physical world for one static and eternalized:

> Consume my heart away; sick with desire
> And fastened to a dying animal

It knows not what it is; and gather me
Into the artifice of eternity.[27]

In privileging 'The Wild Swans at Coole' over 'Sailing to Byzantium', Larkin may also be putting some distance between his work and the Joyce of *A Portrait of the Artist as a Young Man* which famously ends: 'Old father, old artificer, stand me now and ever in good stead.' However, Joyce's hero Stephen Dedalus does not, like Yeats, embrace artifice at the expense of this-worldly experience: this same magnificent ending of the novel has him exclaim 'Welcome, O life!'[28] Either way, the poem Tolley sees as a Hardyesque allaying of the Celtic fever is richly infolded with Irish influences.

In 2007 Regan belatedly acknowledged that 'the poet who provided the blueprint for Larkin's shadowy elegy [...] is not Thomas Gray, but W.B. Yeats', cannily neglecting to mention his own previous advocacy of Gray.[29] He also fails to address the question of why the 'quintessentially English poem' of his earlier description adopts an Irish role model. One way we might broach the question he ducks is by considering the incident biographical critics regard as the inception of the poem. Andrew Motion's version is as follows:

On the afternoon of 3 January [1950] he went to the cinema to try and divert himself. Before the main feature started, he watched a short film about a racehorse called Brown Jack, which had been famous before the war. 'It was', [he] remembered later, 'a film about, you know, "Where is Brown Jack now?" Where Brown Jack was now was at grass, quite happy, moving about, no harness, no jockey, nobody shouting the odds, simply cropping the grass and having a gallop when he felt like it.' As Larkin walked home that evening he found the story of the horse had 'for some reason' impressed him 'very strongly', and when he reached his room he wrote about it. The result was the poem 'At Grass'.[30]

This account has informed academic discussions of 'At Grass' up to and including Booth's *Philip Larkin: The Poet's Plight* (2005). Yet there are good grounds for distrusting it. The *Phoenix* magazine facsimile reproduces 12 densely worked pages of drafts of the poem, the last of which is dated 3 January 1950, the very day on which Motion has Larkin witness the cinema newsreel in a matinee screening.[31] The abundance of the holographs, the sudden breakings off and resumptions on a different page, often entailing an entirely different approach, strongly suggest a worrying away at the poem over several days, if not weeks. This seems to indicate, though it does not prove, that Larkin saw the film and commenced the poem *before* 1950. Burnett hazards December 1949 as the more likely date (*TCP*, 696).

The quotations from Larkin which underpin the Motion–Booth account are taken from an interview conducted by Melvyn Bragg for a 1981 *South Bank Show* television special. Larkin recalls that the documentary footage he witnessed more than 30 years earlier was on the 'where are they now' model and that 'Where Brown Jack was now was at grass, quite happy [...] and having a gallop when he felt like it.' This is not true. Brown Jack was dead. Any newsreel film about him screened in 1949 or 1950 would have been an obituary commemorating the passing of what many equestrian experts to this day regard as the greatest racehorse ever. The whiff of mortality many commentators detect in the last stanza may be a trace of this real event, though questions remain as to why (and how successfully) Larkin suppressed Brown Jack's identity and stopped the narrative short of his actual demise.[32]

Before we address those questions, we need to answer the earlier one of why 'At Grass' is more closely modelled on Yeats than on those English poets (from Gray to the Georgians) promoted by Irish commentators. The paradoxical answer may be because Brown Jack was an Irish horse who began his racing career in Ireland before being bought by an English owner. His English stable paired him with Mail Fist, another Irish horse, who acted as pace-maker. This Irish duo dominated English flat racing in the late 1920s and early 1930s, Brown Jack winning the Queen Alexandra Stakes at Ascot on six consecutive occasions culminating in 1934.[33] The celebrated pair stayed together in retirement at Thorpe Lubenham, Leicestershire, until Brown Jack's death in 1948 – Larkin at the time being Assistant Librarian at the University College of Leicester. The work that critics who are Irish or of Irish descent repeatedly define as unambiguously English is modelled upon a famous Irish poem and describes two famous Irish horses.

If Larkin had wanted instant recognition of his ageing hero he could have entitled the poem 'Brown Jack at Grass'. He did not. The poem names neither of the horses nor their country of origin. However, Brown Jack's fame was comparable with that of Fred Perry, who in the same period won Wimbledon three times, or of the African American athlete Jesse Owens, whose triumph at the 1936 Munich Olympics was a symbolic affront to Nazi propaganda: all three have so entered the public consciousness that their exploits remain common knowledge with those born long afterwards. To this day there is an annual Brown Jack Stakes at Ascot; a Brown Jack pub at Wroughton, Wiltshire, where he was stabled; and innumerable thoroughfares around the country named in his honour. The question therefore arises as to whether Larkin's manuscript erasures obliterated the connection with Brown Jack or left clues in the authorized text. The poem's invocation of racing triumphs of 'fifteen years ago', though not as categorical as the deleted reference to 1933 and 1934, might well bring Brown Jack's greatest season to mind. That the legendary status of the horses was established over 'perhaps / Two dozen distances' is also suggestive: Brown Jack scored 25 wins in his career. Talk of 'names' being 'artificed' reminds that a plaque was erected at Ascot commemorating Brown Jack's achievements. Above all, the poem's account of horses paired in fame and in retirement invokes the names of Brown Jack and Mail Fist, the most celebrated such twinning in racing history.

Larkin's deterritorializing drafting process can now be seen to have an odd, possibly unintended symmetry: English place names are erased in a manner which means we cannot be sure, even if we suspect, that the setting is England; and the names of the Irish horses are suppressed even if the Yeatsian (and Joycean) echoes and incompletely erased references to Brown Jack keep the links to Ireland in subliminal play. Whatever this palimpsest offers, with its overlay of citations, some barely legible, it is not the unalloyed Englishness imagined by Irish critics.

A category error

We have already quoted Heaney to the effect that 'At Grass' could be subtitled 'An Elegy in a Country Paddock'. This proposition depends upon a dubious identification of nation and genre. 'At Grass' is equated with the genre of elegy and elegy equated with Englishness in a conflation that is indistinguishable from stereotyping and in other realms might be denounced as racism.[34] Nonetheless, critics as diverse as Paulin, Regan, Booth and Gilroy have joined Heaney in describing 'At Grass' as 'elegiac'. In classical times the word *elegy* was not exclusively funereal, though its etymological origins in the ancient Greek *elegeia*, meaning 'lament', already gave it sorrowful associations. By the time of 'Elegy written in a Country Church-Yard' the term had narrowed to a formal lamentation upon the death of an actual person, often accompanied by a general meditation upon mortality. Hence, in Gray's masterpiece a narrator first surveys the graves of the dead in a country churchyard before contemplating his own death, the poem ending with the epitaph he wishes inscribed on his gravestone. The presiding theme is encapsulated in the line 'The paths of glory lead but to the grave'.

The initial contradiction of critics characterizing as English a poem they identify with a newsreel about an Irish horse is herewith compounded with a greater paradox: for these same commentators classify 'At Grass' as an elegy despite believing Brown Jack was still alive. This is a comic reversal of the equally paradoxical truth: 'At Grass' steadfastly resists the elegiac mode despite the fact that its protagonist had recently died. This resistance may be measured as the gap between the poem's actual title and the one Heaney subtends. As we have seen, the word 'elegy' means (in the definition of the *Concise Oxford Dictionary*) a song of lamentation for the dead; but the term 'at grass', like 'out to grass' and 'out to pasture', does not mean to be dead but to be retired. According to Partridge's *Dictionary of Historical Slang*, the related expression 'to be sent to grass' could mean to be rusticated, to retire or to live in the country. These last two definitions are relevant to Larkin's poem. At its simplest, of course, the title means 'to be engaged in the act of eating', as in the cognate expressions 'at lunch' and 'at dinner' – a meaning foregrounded in the very first sentence ('one crops grass'). In categorizing the poem as elegiac, Larkin's critics have exaggerated its morbidity and minimized its originality: elegies are commonplace; meditations upon retirement, rare.[35]

This manoeuvre is vital to those historicists who parse the poem as an elegy for empire. The evocation of past racing triumphs is combined with the occasional military metaphor – 'Squadrons of empty cars', 'stand at ease' – to suggest that the real theme of the poem (in Blake Morrison's brilliant phrase) is 'post-imperial *tristesse*'. It is true that 'At Grass', like the aptly named 'Triple Time', has a tripartite temporal structure: past, present, future. There is also a plausibility to the claim that being retired, their glory days behind them, the horses personify human apprehensions regarding relinquishing of duties, fading power, intimations of mortality. However, the meaning of the poem depends upon reader recognition that the horses themselves entertain no such fears. 'Do memories plague their ears' regarding past fame? 'They shake their heads' in the negative (they would *nod* their heads in the affirmative), happy to have their celebrity 'Almanacked' in history books while they revel at being 'anonymous again'. Is their present 'dull, pinched, banal and second-rate' as Paulin asserts? On the contrary, they graze, 'stand at ease' or 'gallop for what must be joy' in 'unmolesting meadows'. Being retired does not mean these horses are *out of the running*, but that they run freely, joyously, where once they were molested into running competitively. Yes, but is not the prevailing mood elegiac, the men who come to stable the horses 'in the evening' emblematic agents of death? Possibly. But the marital puns with which the poem closes hold out sweeter associations: groom/bridegroom; bridle/bridal; come/consummate.

The discrepancies are so pronounced, the silencing so resounding, that matrixed as in the manner in Table 3.1 they can make the critics look ridiculous. Tempting though it is to present this grid as proof of wilful misreading, it is truer to the poem's purport to posit that the critics are not so much wrong as one-dimensional, emphasizing the anthropomorphic at the expense of the equine and thereby betraying the subtle dialectics.

'At Grass' does voice our incapacitating sense that retirement (the present) would be preferable to work (the past) did it not carry us nearer to extinction (the future). Yet it simultaneously counters this view with the horses' enviable capacity for living in a continuous present. As Edward Picot has finely observed, *the horses are not immune from time but immune from the fear of it*.[36] By slipping their names and leaving behind the glamour and fuss of the racing spectacle, they have freed themselves from the human world with its attendant dread of mortality. If the poem bespeaks nostalgia for the

Table 3.1   The temporal structure of 'At Grass'

past glory	the horses minimize it	the critics maximize it
present joy	the horses maximize it	the critics minimize it
future extinction	the horses minimize it	the critics maximize it

imperial past, as the Paulinites claim, that is an entirely human propensity challenged and upbraided by the joyousness of the beasts. And if this dialectic, this tension between the two, is brought to bear on the subject of retirement, as desiderated by the poem's title, it surely offers as complex a statement as may be found in our literature of the mixed emotions with which we approach the constraints and the liberations of the later stages of life. This subsuming of the elegiac into a more nuanced address to the neglected subject of retirement is a good example of Larkin's genius for involving poetic genres only to elude them, the slipstreaming of standard taxonomies an index of his imaginative daring.

'March Past'[37]

'At Grass' was written in England before Larkin moved to Belfast but still necessitated radical misreading for Irish critics to render it a testament to English nationalism. One might expect that the poems written after Larkin's removal to Northern Ireland would be more resistant to anglocentric reterritorializing. This is not so. Brief discussion of 'March Past' and more extended analysis of 'Church Going' will demonstrate two hermeneutical strategies commentators used to anglicize these works: first, by identifying Larkin's politics with the ultra-patriotic Orange tendency in Ulster Protestantism; and second, by going into denial that the poem could possibly be written or set anywhere but England.

The agenda for the discussion of 'March Past' (*CP*, 55; *TCP*, 277–8) was set by Paulin, who uses it to embed his critique of Larkin's imperial sentiment in the context of British history: 'In the deep, or not so deep, recesses of Larkin's imagination, there is a rock-solid sense of national glory which reveals itself in "The March Past", a poem about a military band which he wrote in Belfast in 1951.' The poem does not specify that the band is a military one – though that is a reasonable inference; nor what city or country provides the setting; nor what period we are in other than the twentieth century ('Cars' are mentioned in the second line); nor anything of the age, sex, class, religion, race or political affiliations of the narrator. Undeterred, Paulin assumes that the poem takes place in Belfast, presumably because that is where it was composed (on which basis Joyce's *Ulysses* must henceforth be said to take place, not in Dublin as was previously thought, but in Trieste, Zurich and Paris in which it was written), and brazenly conflates author and protagonist: 'The poet' – the poet, note, not the narrator – 'is overcome by a "blind // Astonishing remorse for things now ended".' Having decided, entirely without evidence, that the narrator is a white, male, middle-class Englishman named Philip Larkin, Paulin feels justified in placing the author's private opinions on the same diagnostic plane as those of the protagonist: 'Larkin called himself "one of nature's Orangemen", adopting the mask of an Ulster Protestant, a sort of Belfast Dirk Dogstoerd.'

Paulin concludes by comparing Larkin to Spenser: 'Both are English Protestant royalists whose nationalism was intensified by their experience of Ireland.'[38] As usual, Regan cheers from the sidelines: 'Tom Paulin has given an excellent account of how an early and little-known poem by Larkin, "The March Past", embodies a deeply felt nationalist and imperialist sentiment.'[39] Larkin *did* describe himself as 'one of nature's Orangemen'; but what that means is difficult to fathom since he disowns religious belief ('I'm not someone who's lost faith: I never had it'), literary imperialism ('I cannot *like* any writer who hunts with the pack like Kipling'), patriotic sentiment ('nationalism is the surest mark of mediocrity') or any kind of group mentality ('To me I seem very much an outsider') (*FR*, 56; *LM*, 70, 94; *SL*, 460). Besides, shortly after completing 'March Past' he sent Monica Jones an eyewitness account of an Orange parade that could scarcely be more disgusted:

It reminded me of a parade of the 70,000 Deadly Sins. Take a standard football crowd (soccer), cut a fringed orange anti-macassar in two and hang one round the neck of each man: give him large false orange cuffs and white gloves to emphasise the tawdry ugliness of his blue Sunday suit, & clap a bowler hat on his head – then you have a Lodger ready for marching [...] [C]ertain members ('Sir Knights' or 'Provosts') carry shiny and curiously repellent symbolic swords and axes – not real, but silver-plated. The dominant impression from this endless tramping file of faces was of really-depressing ugliness. Slack, sloppy, sly, drivelling, daft, narrow, knobby, vacant, vicious, vulpine, vulturous – every kind of ugliness was represented not once but tenfold – for you've no idea how *long* it was [...] about 20,000 men in all shambled by, or 280 Lodges. It was a parade of staggering dullness (every face wore the same 'taking-himself-seriously' expression) & stupefying hypocrisy ('Civil and religious liberty' was a catchphrase much repeated, like Ridley and Latimer). Having seen it, I shall *not* see it again. (*LM*, 49)

When Larkin did see another parade, entirely by accident, his thoughts were with the Catholic minority: 'I should think all the roman catholics must pray fervently for rain on these days, the processions must be so irritating' (*LM*, 102). He also wrote a satirical squib lampooning the Reverend Ian Paisley, most strident of Unionists, as more vicious than any tenant of the Vatican:

> See the Pope of Ulster stand,
> Spiked shillelagh in each hand,
> Vowing to uphold the Border,
> Father, Son, and Orange Order. (*TCP*, 310)

Despite these obvious shortcomings, the Paulin position quickly found favour with English critics of Irish descent. Neil Corcoran also presents a Larkin subject to 'the compulsions of nostalgia', the imperialistic militarism of the band described in the poem being entailed to 'a conception of an Englishness as the repository of value and identity for this poet who could find precious little of either anywhere else'. Once again Regan is on hand with the plaudits: 'Corcoran's impressive readings of such poems as "The March Past" suggest the extent to which "Englishness" became a repository of tradition and identity that outweighed all other sources of potential value.'[40] Alas, the poem itself makes no mention of Englishness, Ireland, Ulster, Belfast, Protestantism, the Orange Order, royalty, nationalism or imperialism. It has been thoroughly deterritorialized. Paulin, Corcoran and Regan (professors of English, all) are describing, in some detail and with a deal of political heat, a poem Larkin did not write.

Conversely, they neglect the one he did. None remarks that 'March Past', written in May 1951, is the first of that series of poems in which Larkin experimented with a tripartite structure with closing reversal before going on to perfect the four-act model as described in Chapter 1 (see Table 3.2).

Table 3.2 Larkin's three-act structure

	'March Past'
Act I: Thesis	The march interrupted the light afternoon. Cars stopped dead, children began to run,
Jolly street scene interrupted by a 'bullying' marching band.	As out of the street-shadow into the sun
	Discipline strode, music bullying aside The credulous, prettily-coloured crowd, Evoking an over-confident, over-loud
	Holiday where the flags lisped and beckoned, And all was focused, larger than we reckoned, Into a consequence of thirty seconds.
Act II: Antithesis	The stamp and dash of surface sound cut short Memory, intention, thought;
The marching band awakens nostalgia for past glories.	The vague heart sharpened to a candid court
	Where exercised a sudden flock of visions: Pure meetings, pure separations, Honeycombs of heroic apparitions,
	Until the crowd closed in behind. Then music drooped. And what came back to mind Was not its previous habit, but a blind
	Astonishing remorse for things now ended That of themselves were also rich and splendid But, unsupported, broke, and were not mended –
Act III: Reversal	Astonishing, for such things should be deep, Rarely exhumable, not in a sleep
Nostalgia should not be so easily awoken.	So light they can awake and occupy An absent mind when any march goes by.

Though less effective than the four-act versions, the three-act series inaugurated by 'March Past' and mainly dating from the first half of the 1950s already applies to major issues a deconstructive approach that is analytically sophisticated and ideologically profound. Hence, in Act I of 'March Past', verses 1–3 of the poem, a jolly street scene is interrupted by a marching band in a manner sufficiently threatening to send the children running. Descriptors like 'dead', 'Discipline', 'bullying' and 'over-confident' lend credence to the speculation that this is a military parade. In Act II, verses 4–7, the argument shifts to an impressionistic but compelling statement of nostalgia for past glory, the adjective 'heroic' suggesting combat and, perhaps, conquest. This section ends with a rousing statement of

> blind
>
> Astonishing remorse for things now ended
> That of themselves were also rich and splendid
> But, unsupported, broke, and were not mended –

A lesser poet would have ended 'March Past' at this juncture – which is, indeed, where Paulin and Corcoran conclude their expositions. However, this is a false ending, overstated so as to be more effectively reversed in the enlarged strophe (four lines instead of three) which constitutes the last act:

> Astonishing, for such things should be deep,
> Rarely exhumable, not in a sleep
> So light they can awake and occupy
> An absent mind when any march goes by.

This quite clearly proposes the opposite of what Paulin, Corcoran and Regan contend: the nostalgia for the heroic of Act II 'should be' – but, unfortunately, is not – too 'deep' for easy exhumation; militarism is a 'light' sleeper, empty heads (heads, as the last line puts it, from which the 'mind' is 'absent') becoming bellicose when 'any' old 'march goes by'.

Although this reversal may initially come as a surprise, it has been fully prepared for, fully earned. It is there in the punning title, 'March Past', with its implication that marches belong to the past (a meaning more apparent perhaps in Larkin's typescript version, 'March past', which Burnett has 'regularized' in *The Complete Poems*). It is also there in the poem's emphatic aaa // bbb // ccc rhyme scheme, so unvaried by Larkin's standards, so obviously designed to suggest regimented lines goose-stepping down the page in neat stanzaic platoons. The conclusion is also prepared for in Act II when the 'stamp and dash' of the band is said to 'cut short / Memory, intention, thought' – proleptic of the last line's empty heads – or when regret for a lost heroic past is described as 'blind'. Really, the poem goes to considerable lengths to condemn the militarism Paulin and Corcoran claim it favours. But like theatre reviewers who leave in the interval between Acts II and III of, say, *The Importance of Being Earnest*, and who therefore write accounts of the play that omit Jack Worthing's discovery that he is really Ernest Moncrieff and eligible to marry Gwendolen Fairfax, the pair of them scandalously suppress Larkin's third act climax. The effects of this bowdlerism might be indicated with a little of the historical contextualization that Paulin, Corcoran and Regan claim to trade in. For two months before the poem was composed, Kingsley Amis wrote to Larkin applauding the Labour government for resisting the mounting American pressure for military involvement in the Korean crisis:

> It looks now as if the filthy bomb-drunk Yanks are having two fingers extended to them from Britain's bunched fist so much that they won't be able to have their lovely war. Anybody over here now who is not pro-Chink wants his arse filled with celluloid and a match applied to his arse-hairs.[41]

With the world poised on the brink of nuclear Armageddon, the poem's anti-militarist message seems remarkably timely. Indeed, exactly nine months earlier a North Korean army with full Russian support crossed the 38th parallel into South Korea. The next day, 27 June 1950, President Truman announced that US air and naval forces would be sent to support South Korea. The allies who less than five years previously had triumphantly marched against fascism were now marching against each other. 'March Past' does not locate itself in a precise historical moment and it would be a critical violence to suggest otherwise. The fact remains that as the ink dried upon the page world events took a turn that made the poem's anti-war message sadly relevant. And having released the poem from the Belfast incident that prompted it, Larkin had given this message universal applicability: *deterritorializing of the national facilitates reterritorializing by the global*. It would be gratifying if once in a while Larkin's Paulinite critics would acknowledge such presciently eirenical aspects of his art.

It is also worth remarking that as a non-combatant Larkin might have dramatized his pacifist testimony in a self-righteous way by adopting a 'them and us' narrative strategy – possibly on the intemperate, tub-thumping model of Amis's letter. Instead, he implicates the narrator in the militarism the poem condemns as if to demonstrate that all must guard against these aggressive propensities that all are subject to. This narrative humility is one of many subtleties in 'March Past', yet Larkin chose not to publish it. While he can hardly be credited with anticipating the critical barbarism of a Paulin or Corcoran, he perhaps foresaw that the poem's very nicety made it susceptible to vulgar misreading. He was certainly under no illusions about the quality of academic analysis. As he remarked to Ian Hamilton: 'There is nothing like writing poems for realizing how low the level of critical understanding is; maybe the average reader can understand what I say, but the above-average often can't' (*FR*, 25).[42]

'Church Going', photography and the hermit of Hull

Of all the poems Larkin wrote in Ireland, the one that features most prominently in the critical construction of his Englishness is 'Church Going' (*CP*, 97–8; *TCP*, 35–7). In 'Englands of the Mind', Seamus Heaney includes it in his list of representative national scenes: 'the rituals of show Saturdays and race-meetings and seaside outings, of church-going and marriages at Whitsun'.[43] This list was augmented down the decades but church decline was still there, 20 years later, in John Whitehead's *Hardy to Larkin: Seven English Poets* (1995):

> Taken together his poems may be compared to a picture gallery illustrating the social history of England in the latter part of the twentieth century. It is all there: the high streets and the suburbs, hotels and bed-sits, the empty church and the recreation ground, weddings and race-meetings, train journeys and hospitals, agricultural shows and pit disasters, ports and the seaside, music and advertisements, girls.[44]

Quite why the enumerated items are constitutive of Englishness remains something of a mystery: declining church attendances, seaside outings, suburbs, pit disasters, advertisements and girls were features of my native Wales – as, surely, of many Western nations.

Other critics anglicized 'Church Going' by seeing it as the very embodiment of the Movement. For Alvarez, this was entirely regrettable: English national values of decency and politeness are mirrored in the well-bred lines of the Movement aesthetic; and polite lines do not make for great poems:

> The pieties of the Movement were as predictable as the politics of the thirties poets. They are summed up at the beginning of Philip Larkin's 'Church-going' [sic]:
>
> Hatless, I take off
> My cycle-clips in awkward reverence.

This, in concentrated form, is the image of the post-war Welfare State Englishman: shabby and not concerned with his appearance; poor – he has a bike, not a car; gauche but full of agnostic piety; underfed, underpaid, overtaxed, hopeless, bored, wry [...] The upper-middle class, or Tory, ideal – presented in its pure crystalline form by John Betjeman – may have given way to the predominantly lower-middle class, or Labour, ideal of the Movement [...] but the concept of gentility reigns supreme.[45]

Blake Morrison puts the same case for the defence rather than the prosecution: '"Church Going" *does* observe the best principles of the Movement programme,' the poem testifying to 'the persistence of both the English Church and an English poetic tradition'.[46]

This use of 'Church Going' in the consolidation as English of the poet once perceived as Irish was intimately connected to two processes: the dissemination of Larkin's photographic likeness, whether in still photographs or motion pictures; and the anchoring of his Englishness in the port of Hull. The first image to facilitate this process was that of Larkin in Spring Bank Cemetery, Hull, which appeared on the cover of the Listen Records LP of him reading *The Less Deceived*. Jean Hartley has acknowledged that she and her husband chose that photograph because 'the Cemetery would have some link with "Church Going", one of the book's strongest and most celebrated poems'.[47] The strategy worked, critics like Philip Gardner, in his essay 'The Wintry Drum' (1968), spotting the connection between the Hull cemetery and Larkin's poem:

> Larkin's poetic persona was that of the ordinary, rather unsuccessful, man equipped with a wry, out-of-the-ordinary awareness of his limitations. This persona was emphasised by the photograph of Larkin on the sleeve of his recording of his poems (issued by The Marvell Press in 1958): as if in illustration of 'Church Going', the poet stands in a grass-grown cemetery, wearing an old mackintosh and cycle-clips and propping up a pushbike, and gazes glumly at stone angels and monumental masonry.[48]

Of course, the connection was spurious: 'Church Going' was completed on 28 July 1954 and Larkin did not move to Hull until 12 March 1955. Not only is any suggestion that the poem was about Spring Bank Cemetery anachronistic, but that romantically overgrown graveyard has no church.

Even more influential was *Down Cemetery Road*, the BBC *Monitor* documentary televised on 15 December 1964. Although it presented Larkin in a variety of contexts (from the Hull Fish Dock to the Brynmor Jones Library) and in relation to seven poems (from 'Wants' to 'Toads Revisited'), a good deal of footage bore directly or indirectly upon 'Church Going'.[49] There is a sequence set in that same Spring Bank Cemetery, which Larkin described as 'the most beautiful spot in Hull'. Then there are three sequences which accompany a reading of the poem by John Betjeman: Larkin cycling to and from a church (or churches); Larkin inspecting the interior of an intact church, all fitments ready for the next service; Larkin picking his way through an abandoned church, derelict and graffitied.

With only two television networks available at the time, the programme had extraordinary penetration, carrying into the homes of a sizeable proportion of British citizens the visual equation of 'reclusive' poet and 'remote' city: 'You can just see Hull, where Philip Larkin lives,' says Betjeman at the start of the programme, pointing two miles across the River Humber from the safety of the south bank. This geographical distancing was always a media figment, as Alan Bennett observed, with characteristic wit:

> Then there is Larkin the Hermit of Hull. Schweitzer in the Congo did not derive more moral credit than Larkin did for living in Hull. No matter that of the four places he spent most of his life – Hull, Coventry, Leicester and Belfast – Hull is probably the most pleasant; or that poets are not and never have been creatures of the capital: to the newspapers, as Motion says, remoteness is synonymous with integrity. But Hull isn't even particularly remote. Ted Hughes, living in Devon, is further from London (as the crow flies, of course) than Larkin ever was.[50]

Besides, the intercutting of the sequences enumerated above permitted different readings of 'Church Going' in relation to different facets of Hull. Richard Bradford's emphasis falls emphatically upon the derelict church which he credits the film's director Patrick Garland with deploying against Alvarez's accusation of gentility:

> Larkin in one memorable sequence appears to have stepped out of Alvarez's article as the bald, slim, bespectacled man, clad in a very ordinary mackintosh who does indeed ride a bike and at one point enters a church and removes his bicycle clips. Alvarez's case might easily have been proven by this had Garland not cleverly altered the panorama, making sure that the church is derelict and sinister in aspect and that the entire landscape through which his camera follows Larkin is quite the opposite of, as Alvarez puts it, 'Larkin's [...] elegant and unpretentious [...] nostalgic recreation of the English scene'. In the film the sheer ugliness of Hull and its suburbs is almost celebrated. The heavily industrialized landscape of the north of the city, bisected by open drains, gives way to the gloomy, untended Sculcoates Cemetery; via television the fish docks do not smell, but the expression on Larkin's face indicates their level of foulness.[51]

The Bradford version: Larkin as hermit of Hull; Hull as misprint for Hell.

Bryan Appleyard, Geoffrey Thurley and Alun R. Jones veer to the opposite pole, that represented by the overgrown Spring Bank Cemetery, the *plein air* cycling, the intact church:

> 'Church Going', published in 1955 in the collection *The Less Deceived* is the Movement poem *par excellence*. The poet wanders into a country church,

his persona of the provincial hick intact [...] In the long term this became associated with a certain view of the whole of British culture as isolated, limited in ambition and of little interest to the rest of the world. Even the idea of wandering into parish churches has a Little England quality about it. Indeed, this made it an exemplary activity to inspire Larkin's poem.[52]

The Appleyard version: Hull as Hicksville, a provincial citadel from whence the poet 'wanders' into an English rural past.

No matter their differences regarding which England Hull epitomizes, all these critics see Larkin as parochially anglocentric and all conflate his photographic portraits with his literary narrators. Like fragments of the holy cross, the bike, mackintosh and cycle-clips are hailed as physical manifestations of English nationalism – though none of them is of English invention.[53] The church in the poem is specifically located midst 'suburb scrub': neither Bradford's 'heavily industrialized landscape', keyed to the long-demolished Sculcoates church in the *Monitor* film, nor Appleyard's 'country church', closer to the footage of the intact church and the leafy cemetery, fits this description. Indeed, the well-maintained church of *Down Cemetery Road* is actually Holy Trinity, in Barton upon Humber, in Tennyson's county of Lincolnshire, and has nothing whatsoever to do with Kingston upon Hull or Larkin's beloved East Riding of Yorkshire.[54]

The reason these commentaries were so skewed to the poem was knowable in advance. For as Larkin explained on a BBC Radio broadcast on 3 July 1964, nearly six months before the *Monitor* film was televised, 'Church Going' was not only written in Belfast but was inspired by an Irish scene:

One Sunday afternoon in Ireland when I had cycled out into the country I came across a ruined church, the first I had seen. It made a deep impression on me. I had seen plenty of bombed churches, but never one that had simply fallen into disuse, and for a few minutes I felt the decline of Christianity in our century as tangibly as gooseflesh. The poem I subsequently wrote [is] called 'Church Going'. (*FR*, 83)

When Larkin repeated this account in a 1981 interview, John Haffenden commented: *'It's not clear in the poem that you began with a ruined church.'* Larkin replied: 'No, it wasn't in the poem' (*FR*, 56). A glance at the drafting process will allow us to see how Larkin embarrassed the more credulous *Monitor*-watchers by writing the Irish origins out of 'Church Going' without writing English ones in.

'Church Going' and deterritorialization

The drafting of 'Church Going' was arduous. Larkin began work on the piece on 24 April 1954 and by 10 May was telling Patsy Strang that he hoped it would 'be finished tonight' (*SL*, 227). In reality, he laboured on for a fortnight before scrawling 'abandoned 25/5/54' on a manuscript that had now reached 21 pages. Two months later he resumed work on the poem and after an additional eight pages of trial and error, each misdirection heavily scored through, he completed the holograph copy on 28 July. Further changes were made at the typescript stage and again after publication in *The Spectator*. Burnett gives 24 November 1955 as the date of completion (*TCP*, 698).

One of the reasons the process was so protracted was that Larkin interpreted the Irish experience as prophetic of what would happen in England. To Haffenden, in public interview, he repeated the categorical statement that the poem 'came from the first time I saw a ruined church in Northern Ireland, and I'd never seen a ruined church before – discarded. It shocked me' (*FR*, 56). But in a private letter to Patsy he claimed that it 'arose from reading an appeal made by the Archbishop of Canterbury about 14 months ago for money, without which he said about 200 churches were in imminent danger of ruin' (*SL*, 244). As that letter is dated 18 June 1955, the Archbishop's speech coincided with the conception of 'Church Going'. Burnett points out that a cutting from the *Church Times*, 7 May 1954, headed 'Save Our Churches week', and kept by Larkin, actually quoted the Archbishop as saying that 'over *two thousand* must be helped at once' if they are to be saved from decay and ruin (*TCP*, 369–70) (my emphasis).

Larkin's difficulty was in deciding whether to have the church ruination actual, as in Northern Ireland, or imminent, as in the Primate's appeal. The manuscript begins by describing abandoned buildings – 'discarded', as he said to Haffenden – only to deviate dramatically to the other side of the Irish Sea:

> How strange, these abandoned buildings!
> Why am I brought repeatedly up and down
> What brings me time and again into your silences
> Up and down England?[55]

Is he, for a moment, contemplating an England in which the predicted two hundred churches have already suffered abandonment?

Even after the manuscript settles upon a single church, and one whose dereliction is foreseeable but not actual, the drafts occasionally revert to the Irish scene of devastation:

> doorless arches weedy floors and arches faintly reek
> Like an abandoned earth of something lost, dispersed
> Already, psychic cruse, your walls crack
> Already the walls are broken, ebbingly
> The frail cruse walls helplessly leak

Towards the end of July, the poem nearing completion, one last image of dilapidation pops up, like the return of a repressed memory:

> marriage and birth,
> And death and thoughts of these – for which was built
> This special shelter; and for thoughts on time,
> On being born indigenous to earth
> Though promised faithfully a tearless clime,
> Though if it had, the walls would not be down.

Yet this struggle to contain the originatory Irish episode, to stop it dictating the poem's terms, is complemented by the equal but opposite struggle to hold at bay an English identity whose churchy associations easily become nostalgic, sentimental, twee. We have already seen how the word 'England' appeared on the first page of drafting only to be immediately crossed out as error. Similarly, the following lines, with their English surnames, have an anglocentric homeliness that invited – and received – swift cancellation:

> Power of one sort or other will persist
> Beyond Flower rota: Mrs Page, Mrs Croome

Deleting to the left of him, deleting to the right, Larkin steers the poem's purport between the Scylla and Charybdis of Ireland and England, devastation and tweeness. The poem deterritorializes its Ulster origins while resisting reterritorialization by England.[56]

Something similar obtains with regard to metre and diction. The spacious stanzas allow for a stately sequencing of argument that is modelled on Yeats's large verse paragraph. True, Yeats favoured an eight-line rather than the nine-line stanza of 'Church Going'; nor does he utilize the ababcadcd rhyme scheme (the sixth line open to variation) employed by Larkin. Nevertheless, 'Church Going''s seven verses of nine iambic pentameters apiece, 63 lines in all, is very close to the eight verses of eight iambic pentameters of Yeats's 'Among School Children', which totals 64 lines. The latter poem may also have provided the archaic 'blent' of Larkin's last stanza ('A serious house on serious earth it is, / In whose blent air all our compulsions meet'), the Yeatsian persona fondly recalling of a youthful *amour*: 'it seemed that our two natures blent'.[57] However, just when the poem's prosody seems to incline to an Irish model, it invokes a countervailing English source, as if to demonstrate its freedom from conscription to either side. Blake Morrison sees a precedent for the 'Bored, uninformed' but finally 'serious' narrator of 'Church Going' in the abstracted, daydreaming boy of 'Afternoon Service in Mellstock' by Thomas Hardy.[58] At a more particulate level, the unusual diction of 'Church Going' sometimes draws upon Hardy's idiolect. The aforementioned 'blent' of 'Among School Children' also crops up in Hardy's 'A Wasted Illness', 'In a Museum' and 'The Maid of Keinton Mandeville'. The oft-remarked 'pyx' of stanza three has a precursor in Hardy's 'The Lost Pyx' ('the Pyx has gone / Of the Blessed Sacrament').[59] The 'accoutred' of the penultimate stanza has a precedent in *Tess of the d'Urbervilles*.[60] While 'In the Old Theatre, Fiesole' meditates upon a ruined building as emblematic of the fall of the Roman Empire much as 'Church Going' meditates upon an empty building as an earnest of the decline of Christianity. Hardy's narrator recounts a young girl showing 'an ancient coin / That bore the image of Constantine':

> As with one half blind
> Whom common simples cure, her act flashed home
> In that mute moment to my opened mind
> The power, the pride, the reach of perished Rome.[61]

Similarly, Larkin's narrator, 'wondering [...] / When churches fall completely out of use / What we shall turn them into', asks himself

> will dubious women come
> To make their children touch a particular stone;
> Pick simples for a cancer [...]?

This melding of Yeatsian and Hardyesque influences, if that is what they are, blends Irish and English in a complex alloy that is both and neither. The national certitudes encouraged by LP photograph and TV film are collapsed by a text whose doubled territorialization is also a double deterritorializing.

An Irish sixpence

This double deletion of geographical markers leaves stranded and exposed, like an amoeba upon a slide, the phrase 'an Irish sixpence' – the three most hotly contested words in Larkin's *oeuvre*. We shall briefly review a dozen evaluations of the phrase, some of them mutually exclusive, but all predicated upon just such national assumptions as Larkin was at pains to deny. The standard view was that the donating of a foreign coin in an English collecting box was a gesture of some contempt for religious belief, for Christianity, perhaps for the Anglican Church in particular. Charles Tomlinson, disdainful of such schoolboy humour, regarded the gesture as one of Larkin's 'naughty jokes', transgressive but infantile.[62] This early consensus was countered by critics like David Timms and Roger Day who brought in biographical evidence of Larkin's sojourn in Belfast to query the assumption that the church was in England:

> The Irish sixpence the speaker drops into the collection box in 'Church Going' has occasioned some misunderstanding. It is suggested that the

coin has absolutely no value for the speaker, and its contribution is a way of cocking a snook at the Church, and at religion. But if we happen to know that the poem was written in Ireland, and that Larkin lived there for four years, we can see that this is not necessarily so.[63]

It is not self-evident why residence in Ulster renders less cynical the donating of an 'Irish' coin, nor do our critics explain. This oversight has allowed Laurence Lerner and (as here) Stephen Cooper to make forcible interventions:

The reference to the 'Irish sixpence' has caused considerable speculation. It is likely that Larkin was referring to the Eire sixpence which was in circulation between 1928 and 1969 in The Republic of Ireland. The coin was slightly larger than its GB counterpart and bore the Irish harp and bloodhound on its sides. As no Northern Irish sixpence – as distinct from the standard British 'tanner' – was ever minted, Larkin can't have been thinking of any regional variant of the mainland sixpence. The speaker's gesture of donating the Irish sixpence is, therefore, a cynical one. Larkin's comment suggests that the poem is based on a trip to a church in Northern Ireland but the donation of the Eire sixpence would not have been legal tender anywhere in the United Kingdom.[64]

David Punter agrees, adding that 'Irish coinage is not accepted in the UK (though UK coinage, prior to the advent of the euro, was accepted in the Republic of Ireland), hence it is here symbolic of worthless money.'[65] However, the Lerner–Cooper–Punter position has itself been challenged by Brownjohn and Tolley, who correctly point out that Irish coinage *was* 'accepted currency in Northern Ireland, where the poem was written'.[66]

With so much disputation, so little concord, it is not surprising that one or two commentators have identified these three words as a flaw in the poem, a failure of transparency. The clearest statement of this position was offered 40 years ago by Thwaite:

'Church Going' is not a perfect poem, though a fine one, and it is not Larkin's best [...] That Irish sixpence, for example – many readers don't know whether they are supposed to laugh here or not (many do in any case); but if the ruined church which started the poem off was in Ireland, as Larkin in a broadcast said it was, wouldn't it make a difference? Does he mean to demonstrate the sort of unthinking piety that agnostics hold to out of habit, or is he chalking up another mild self-revelatory bit of schoolboyish japing, as in the mouthing of 'Here endeth' from the lectern? (What Larkin intends of *that* performance comes out very clearly in his Marvell Press recording.) One doesn't know, and in a poem so specific that is a flaw.[67]

For all their differences, most of the foregoing pundits proceed as though the church was ascertainably in England. Even those who acknowledge that it might be in Ireland ignore the implications thereof. Hence, the England–Ireland dichotomy is discussed, if at all, without consideration of the distinctions entailed – whether between political systems (constitutional monarchy versus republicanism) or between Christian denominations (Protestant versus Catholic). The stark truth is we are told neither the nationality nor the religious affiliation of either narrator or church. Instead, we are presented with a limited plurality of interpretative options, each of which conveys a subtle variation of theological and political weighting, and all of them part of the poem's purport. Here are a few of them.

If the poem is set in England and the church is Protestant, the donating of an Irish sixpence may be a gesture of contempt, indifference or flippancy from a narrator who is clearly not religious. However, if that same narrator carries Irish coinage because he is from the Republic or of Irish ancestry that same gesture combines religious unbelief with a hint of political disaffiliation from the UK. If that Irish narrator was brought up a Catholic, though now an unbeliever, the donation may register a degree of denominational as well as political dissidence. These same possibilities are much exacerbated if we follow Larkin's claim that the church was in Northern Ireland. Although Irish coinage was legal tender in Ulster, so that the donation is not financially invalid, the gesture carries strongly Republican implications, the more so if the church is Protestant. If the church is Catholic (and the references to pyx, rood-screens, organ-pipes and myrrh are sufficiently high church to keep that possibility in play) such a choice of coin might still suggest an identification with the persecuted minority despite the narrator's personal loss of faith.

It may seem that consideration of the poem being set in the Republic is invalidated by that very word 'Irish' which raised the issue in the first place. Surely, if the church is in Eire that degree of specificity would be redundant (if I asked a fellow resident of the UK to lend me a fiver I would not feel it necessary to stipulate that it be a British one). Yet once again *what we do not know licenses meaningful speculations*. If the church is in Eire but the narrator English (during his Belfast years Larkin often forayed into the Republic, regularly taking Sunday lunch in Dublin), donating an Irish sixpence might convey empathy with the host society despite his religious scepticism. This option is underlined by the fact that UK currency was acceptable in the Republic at the time, the narrator's choice of coin symbolizing a choice between his country of origin and his country of adoption.

Morrison has helpfully pointed out that the donating of the sixpence has a literary precedent in George Orwell's *Coming Up for Air* (1939) in which the protagonist George Bowling enjoys a return to his old parish church only to find himself cornered by the vicar:

> He said good evening and promptly started on the usual line of talk – was I interested in architecture, remarkable old building this, foundations go

back to Saxon times and so on and so forth [...] As soon as I decently could I dropped sixpence in the Church expenses box and bunked.[68]

However, this very English source is matched by Irish poet Louis MacNeice's 'In the Cathedral', the narrator of which makes a similar donation ('I give six-pence').[69] Besides, Orwell has established that both the church and the pro-tagonist of his novel are English; and we can assume the sixpence is British because he has not felt the need to tell us otherwise. All three elements – church, protagonist, coin – are brought into national alignment. Larkin does the exact opposite. Had he retained Orwell's Englishing of the first two while Irishing the sixpence, the donation would be cynical in the manner assumed by Tomlinson and Cooper. Alternatively, he could have arrived at that meaning without Englishing church or protagonist simply by designat-ing the coin 'foreign'. To specify the nationality of the coin and not of the other two elements is to license – indeed, to generate – speculations (such as those rehearsed above) which can neither be confirmed nor terminated. *The territorializing of the sixpence highlights by contrast the deterritorializing of every-thing else.* To what end? So as to bring the poem's address to nationality to the same crisis point as its address to theology: the site demarcated by neither God nor flag, the site of unverifiability, of questions rather than answers.

A serious house[70]

'It has always been well liked', Larkin said of 'Church Going'. 'I think this is because it is about religion, and has a serious air that conceals the fact that its tone and argument are entirely secular.'[71] They certainly are! For the way the poem proceeds is by having the narrator put himself through just such a catechism regarding the role of the Church as readers are put to trying to assign a nationality.

Pondering the future use of churches, the possibilities considered are: that a few cathedrals be kept on show while the rest are abandoned to sheep pens or the like; that they be avoided as unlucky places; conversely, that they attract the superstitious who come to touch particular stones for luck, to gather herbal cures ('simples') or to spot ghosts; and, finally, that nature be allowed to reclaim them. These four options may be read as alternatives or as succes-sive stages in the Church's demise. As for the question of who will be 'the very last' visitor to the site, the narrator's speculations are: the antiquarian scholar; the collector with an eye for valuable antiques; the 'Christmas-addict' in love with church ceremonial; or 'my representative, // Bored, uninformed' yet ready to acknowledge 'A serious house on serious earth it is'. Although the interrogation concludes with the narrator elaborating upon the viewpoint of 'my representative', this answer (however persuasive) is not demonstrably 'correct', the original question not being subject to verification.

God is entirely absent from these deliberations, his death or abscondence so complete as not to merit comment. The word 'God' only crops up once, in a throwaway colloquialism ('God knows how long'). Jesus puts in an appearance at the drafting stage, presumably in the form of a stained-glass window or crucifix, but is instantly ejected ('Catching sight / Of Christ, I turn in some embarrassment'). The clause 'When churches fall completely out of use' is unflinching in its acceptance that Christianity is moribund. The line 'But superstition, like belief, must die' is equally adamant that the miasma of the cultish which lingers round the sites of dead religions will evaporate in its turn. Indeed, it is God's absence ('Once I am sure there's nothing going on / I step inside') that creates the 'unignorable silence' which it 'pleases' the narrator 'to stand in'. What he finds this special silence fit for is thought, not prayer; reason, not belief; philosophy, not theology; inquisition, not revelation. As the poem's title punningly forewarns, his church going yields a meditation on the inevitability of the church going.

The narrator expresses only one regret at this momentous collapse, and even this is secular rather than religious: namely, that it will disperse to separate buildings and separate discourses the key events of human life – birth, marriage, death – which the church brought under one roof, one dispensation. His is a nostalgia for the unified life narrative of Christianity, not for the pre-Nietzschean religious credulity that facilitated it.[72] So why does the narrator think that even projected forward into a state of ruination the church will still draw visitors?

> someone will forever be surprising
> A hunger in himself to be more serious,
> And gravitating with it to this ground,
> Which, he once heard, was proper to grow wise in,
> If only that so many dead lie round.

The institution which formerly assured us of our immortality henceforth confronts us with our mortality, not least because of *its* mortality. Everything that lives, dies; and there is no site more 'proper' for the getting of this wisdom than a graveyard dedicated to a defunct deity.

Once God is removed as transcendental guarantor, all essentializing discourses, including that of nationalism ('God Save the Queen'), lose legitimacy and assume their place in the panoply of competing relativisms. It is a pretty paradox that this poem which has patriotism deconstructed by the reader and theology by the narrator is routinely used to attribute to Larkin an English identity dependent upon both. Even those who recognize the poem's irreligion find themselves describing it in quasi-religious terms, as when Corcoran sees it as an expression of 'the social religion of an enduring Englishness'; or Regan claims that

> 'Church Going' embodies what Marwick calls 'secular Anglicanism': it concedes that 'belief must die' and yet it cannot relinquish the spirit of tradition that the Church of England represents.

Others are more evangelical. J.R. Watson identifies in 'Church Going' 'deeply felt longings for sacred time and sacred space'. R.N. Parkinson feels that 'The whole tone of the poem expresses doubts about the validity of atheism.' Terry Whalen detects 'an oddly religious glow' in the narrator's 'agnostic humanism'. Patrick Garland runs 'the risk of appearing sentimental' in claiming to descry a 'form of surreptitious belief' beneath the surface scepticism. And always the assumption that the building described is (in Janice Rossen's words) 'an old *Anglican* church' licenses the answering assumption that the setting is England.[73] (My emphasis.) Our critics have reterritorialized what Larkin deterritorialized by disinterring the deity he presumed dead and buried.

Coda

Thwaite's edition of the *Collected Poems* (1988) includes 46 poems written during Larkin's Belfast sojourn. Many of them incorporate Irishisms after the manner of 'At Grass' and 'Church Going': the Yeatsian titles 'He Hears that his Beloved has become Engaged' and 'Lines on a Young Lady's Photograph Album'; the rewriting of Yeats's 'A Prayer for my Daughter' in 'Born Yesterday'; the echoes of Joyce's *Portrait of the Artist* in 'Unfinished Poem' and *Ulysses* in 'Negative Indicative'; and, almost as conspicuous as the 'Irish sixpence', the 'blarney' of 'Toads'. Yet when 20 of these poems were included alongside 'At Grass' in *The Less Deceived*, commentators suppressed the Celtic connection under the sovereign order of Saxonry. As recently as 2001, Regan was describing the volume as the epitome of Little Englandism:

> The creation of a self-effacing, 'modest' discourse and a self-deprecating, ironic person is immediately apparent in the poems of *The Less Deceived*; so too is a distrust of large, idealistic gestures and a preference for English provincial settings over those of 'abroad'.[74]

Over the years critics of violently opposed opinion have concurred: Larkin's 'collected work would fit happily under the title *Englanders*' (Heaney); 'Larkin offers the patriotism of the rooted' (Grubb); 'We recognize in Larkin's poems the seasons of present-day England, but we recognize also the seasons of the English soul' (Davie); 'He was extremely English, as his poetry reveals' (Levi); 'He was a poet of England' (Bennett); 'Although he mischievously played up his Little Englandism, he was in truth the genuine article' (Eagleton).[75]

The present chapter has sought to problematize this consensus by exploring Larkin's use of Ireland to articulate estrangement from England. That this stratagem was already a part of his practice before his removal to Belfast, as witnessed in 'At Grass', confirms its role as signifier of unhousedness rather than of love for the Emerald Isle: *bilocation imports dislocation rather than relocation.* The Anglo-Irish blendings and nullifications vary from poem to poem while sharing the general tendency towards deterritorialization. As we have seen, these exilic nuances were lost to sight as commentators reterritorialized the poems in the desire to secure their author's national identity. We have also remarked how Larkin's ideological nimbleness wrong-footed his exegetes at every turn. Hence, those critics who site 'March Past' in Belfast, on no better grounds than that it was written there, as insistently site 'Church Going' in England despite its having been penned in the very same city. The biographicalist assumption that poems passively mirror the locales in which they are written – the hermeneutical equivalent of flat-earth cosmology – collapses under the weight of its internal contradictions. The collapse of this orthodoxy affords an ideal opportunity for enhanced appreciation of a particular form of ellipsis pertaining to geographical origins that was begun in *A Girl in Winter* and perfected in the Belfast poems. Ladies and Gentlemen, in place of the obdurately English poet of the critical consensus, I offer you Philip Larkin, master of deterritorialization.

4
Radical De-essentialism: 'The Whitsun Weddings'

> in one person many people
>
> – Shakespeare, *Richard II*

A monstrance against the sexing of texts

Seventy per cent of English novels published in the last three decades of the eighteenth century were anonymous; in the first three decades of the nineteenth century, almost 50 per cent. In the Victorian period there was a vogue for female authors to publish under male pseudonyms. 'The object', wrote Mary Ann Evans under the name George Eliot, 'was to get the book judged on its own merits, and not prejudged as the work of a woman.'[1] The result of these preoccupations with anonymous and pseudonymous authorship was an era of such extreme gender confusion as ought to serve as a permanent monstrance against the sexing of texts. When Emily Brontë published *Wuthering Heights* (1847) under the pseudonym Ellis Bell, a name chosen (according to her sister Charlotte) on account of its sexual indeterminacy, most reviewers assumed it to be the work of a man and interpreted it accordingly. Conversely, Tennyson's anonymous elegy for his friend Arthur Hallam, 'In Memoriam', won praise as having 'evidently come from the full heart of the widow of a military man'.[2] George Eliot's *Scenes of Clerical Life* was widely believed to have been written by a country parson. On the other hand, some reviewers attributed to Eliot, whose gender identity had by then been revealed, the novel *Far from the Madding Crowd*, which Thomas Hardy contributed for anonymous serialization in the *Cornhill* magazine. Arnold Bennett threw the George Eliot model into reverse, writing prolifically for Victorian and Edwardian women's periodicals under such *noms de plume* as Gwendolyn, Barbara, Ada, Cecile and Sal Volatile. As Carol Ohmann has remarked, 'there is a considerable correlation between what readers assume or know the sex of the writer to be and what they actually see, or neglect to see, in "his" or her work'.[3]

This warning from recent literary history notwithstanding, Larkin's admirers and detractors conspire to conduct the debate in unashamedly biographical terms. The overwhelming majority of the poems tell one nothing about the gender, race, class or nationality of either their narrators or their addressees, but both the poet's champions and his denigrators fill in the missing information by jumping to the conclusion that the protagonist is always and only a white, male, middle-class Englishman named Philip Larkin.

The present chapter mounts an assault upon biographicalism by exposing the narratological violence it visits upon a Larkin masterpiece, 'The Whitsun Weddings'. The text-centred methodology employed involves three levels of intertextuality: early Larkin writings rehearsive of or directly transposed into 'The Whitsun Weddings'; works by other authors cited or alluded to in the poem; and subsequent works, often by leading postmodernist practitioners, that in modelling themselves upon 'The Whitsun Weddings' tease out areas of possibility nascent within it. What I hope to demonstrate by this text-centred hermeneutics is that the use of ellipsis in *A Girl in Winter* to withhold Katherine Lind's nationality, ethnicity, religion and class is here extended to encompass the narrator's sex and gender. The conception of selfhood embedded in the poem's narrator is protean, inclusive and responsive in a manner that eludes those identitarian certitudes used by prosecutorial biographicalists to arraign Larkin for sexism, classism, racism and xenophobia.

The Whitsun train journey that never was

To turn to 'The Whitsun Weddings' is to validate Carol Ohmann's point in terms of class and nationality as well as gender, Larkin's commentators knowing much more about the narrator than the poem does (*CP*, 114–16; *TCP*, 56–8). All agree with Timms that the perceiving subject is a 'man'. From that basic assumption rival exegetes are able to construct an identikit picture: 'he' is 'a solitary' (Curtis); 'lonely' (Carey); 'locked away in his very own train-compartment' (Wiemann); a 'bachelor' (Lerner); a 'librarian' (Tolley); a 'poet' (Swarbrick); 'a creature of long-established habits' (Marsh); an 'intellectual' (Regan); reading a 'book' (Whitehead); a 'commuter' (Kuby); planning to spend 'a week-end in London' (Tolley); 'middle-class' (Morrison); and travelling from Lincolnshire (Kuby) or Hull (everyone else). As the poem does not vouchsafe a single one of these details, some of which are demonstrably false (Lolette Kuby twice describes the journey as taking place on 'Whitsunday' when the opening sentence categorically specifies Saturday), we deduce that all these explicators are tailoring the poem to preconceptions about the author.[4]

The shared predicate that, in Tolley's words, 'the "I" is clearly Larkin' allows hostile commentators to invest the narrator with supposed authorial prejudices. Regan finds 'The Whitsun Weddings' plagued by 'class consciousness'; Gilbert Phelps detects 'a distinct touch of hauteur' about the way 'Larkin puts a distance between [...] himself' and 'the comical goings-on of the lower orders'; while for Corcoran the poem is expressive of an ideology 'in which class is supposed to have no part, but in which in fact it sets the entire tone of poetic address'.[5] For Paulin the poem is a compact of 'élitist distaste for British mass society', 'misogyny' and wounded English nationalism. The train journey to London is a journey 'into the unknown heart [...] of Englishness': 'Most daringly, the "sense of falling" in "The Whitsun Weddings" becomes an "arrow-shower" like the clothyard arrows in Olivier's film of *Henry V*. The poem summons both the play's patriotism and that of the film (it was made during the Second World War).' The connection between this 'terminal Englishness that feels lost and tired and out of date' and the young couples embarking upon married life 'is made through the idea of power and its loss', the feelings of assent to the newly-weds being undercut by 'sceptical assertions of male autonomy' and nostalgia for 'that greatness [...] which a now-drab island once gave to the world'.[6]

Larkin's admirers and detractors might alike defend their author-centred preconceptions by pointing to those recordings and interviews in which the poet described the inception of the poem in purely autobiographical and documentary terms. On the Marvell Press LP of *The Whitsun Weddings* (1965) he said that the only work the poem entailed was in 'recreating the whole experience which came all at once'; adding, 'I knew it could be a poem if only I could be fortunate enough to transcribe it.' He repeated this passively stenographic conceit in his interview with John Haffenden:

> It was just the transcription of a very happy afternoon. I didn't change a thing, it was just there to be written down [...] You couldn't be on that train without feeling the young lives all starting off, and that just for a moment you were touching them. Doncaster, Retford, Grantham, Newark, Peterborough, and at every station more wedding parties. It was wonderful, a marvellous afternoon. It only needed writing down. Anybody could have done it. (*FR*, 57)

In the *South Bank Show* interview with Melvyn Bragg, as transcribed by Andrew Motion, Larkin was emphatic that the poem was prompted by a single, unique event; that the train journey was from Hull to London; and that the authenticity of the detailing was vouchsafed by the fact that the original occasion was indelibly etched in his memory:

> I hadn't realized that, of course, this was the train that all the wedding couples would get on and go to London for their honeymoon. It was an eye-opener to me [...] I suppose the train stopped at about four, five, six stations between Hull and London and there was a sense of gathering

emotional momentum. Every time you stopped fresh emotion climbed aboard. And finally between Peterborough and London when you hurtle on, you felt the whole thing was being aimed like a bullet – at the heart of things, you know. All this fresh, open life. Incredible experience. I've never forgotten it.[7]

This is the authorized version of events and has misled commentators ever since. Motion confidently declares: 'The poem had first begun to take shape during a journey from Hull to London on Whit Saturday, 1955.' Bradford goes one better, specifying the precise date of the Christian festivity: 'The Whitsun Weddings' was 'inspired by a train journey from Hull to London on 28 May 1955, the Saturday of the Whitsun weekend'.[8] As recently as 24 May 2009 the poets Paul Farley and Kate Clanchy repeated the mantra on their BBC Radio 3 programme *Children of the Whitsun Weddings*, from where it was picked up in the *Wikipedia* entry on the poem. No doubt thousands of GCSE and A-level pupils are even now downloading it into their essays as unimpeachable truth. As Archie Burnett is the first to point out, there is strong evidence to suggest that the journey was not in May, not at Whit, and not to London (*TCP*, 411).

Though they are contradictory and error-prone, two statements from Larkin's last years help to thicken the plot. In an interview with the *Paris Review* (1982) he said:

I was looking at 'The Whitsun Weddings' just the other day, and found that I began it sometime in the summer of 1957. After three pages, I dropped it for another poem that in fact was finished but never published. I picked it up again, in March 1958, and worked on it till October, when it was finished. But when I look at the diary I was keeping at the time, I see that the kind of incident it describes happened in July 1955! So in all, it took over three years [...] I did write slowly, partly because you're finding out what to say as well as how to say it, and that takes time. (*RW*, 75)

The admission that the poem required 'over three years' to complete works against the earlier *doxa* that the subject was gifted to the poet 'all at once' and 'only needed writing down'. In a letter to Monica Jones dated 18 October 1958, Larkin complained:

I have spent all evening trying to finish this poem: I've never known anything resist me so! [...] It's called 'The Whitsun Weddings', unless I can think of anything better. I have just hammered it to *an* end, but really out of sheer desperation to see this fiendish 8th verse in some kind of order. Verses 7 and 8 have taken since about the beginning of August. (*LM*, 240)

The letter forcibly conveys the emotional stress ('sheer desperation') and endurance (a month and a half on the last two verses) required to drive the poem through to a conclusion.

Even more destructive of the authorized version is Larkin's introduction to his reading of 'The Whitsun Weddings' on the Faber cassette *Douglas Dunn and Philip Larkin* (1984):

> remembering the genesis of poems is always a tricky business. For years I believed that I wrote 'The Whitsun Weddings' over about three months in the summer of 1957, after going down to London to see some friends who had just got married. But when I came to look it up I found that although I'd begun it in 1957, I'd dropped it after three pages, and didn't pick it up again until March 1958, finishing it in the following October. Not only that, but a diary I kept at the time makes it clear that the actual journey took place in 1955, not at Whitsun, and so far from going on to London to see friends, I got off the train at Grantham and took a bus to the Midlands to see my family.[9]

The 'diary' Larkin was keeping at the time was destroyed at his death in accord with his wishes. What evidence does survive verifies the July date and the Grantham destination for one 1955 journey but also pulls back into the same time frame that second rail trip 'to London to see some friends who had just got married'.

Hence, on 3 August 1955 Larkin wrote to Monica enthusiastically recounting a visit to his mother's home in Loughborough which involved a train journey from Hull to Grantham:

> I went home on Saturday, 1.30 to Grantham – a lovely run, the scorched land misty with heat, like a kind of *bloom* of heat – and at every station, Goole, Doncaster, Retford, Newark, importunate wedding parties, gawky and vociferous, seeing off couples to London. (*LM*, 170)

Thwaite's footnote observes: 'This appears to be the germ of what became "The Whitsun Weddings"' (*LM*, 173). From the itinerary described in the letter the outward journey took place on Saturday 30 July, Larkin returning to Hull on 2 August. It is diverting to note that critics like Tolley and Regan accept that July point of genesis without appearing to notice that to do so is to scotch the connection with Whit! The historian David Kynaston offers a convincing reason why the initiatory journey was never likely to have taken place on 28 May: 'As for Whit Saturday that year, it was on the eve of a national strike, and it is temperamentally unlikely that Larkin would have taken the risk, not knowing how he was going to get back.'[10]

The second trip was to visit the recently married Patsy and Richard Murphy (Larkin's Faber reminiscence garbles the year). His thank-you letter of

17 August 1955 allows one to date the outward leg to Saturday 13 August (*SL*, 248–50). If the Grantham trip furnished the poem with the wedding parties, this one provided the London destination and the gathering momentum of the 'fifty minutes' from the unnamed last stop of Peterborough ('Free at last'!) through to Kings Cross. It may also have provided a psychological motive for any sexual ambivalence regarding the newly-weds and their soon to be consummated marriages: after all, Larkin had been Patsy's lover until only a few months before she met Murphy. Indeed, Thwaite gives the dates of their affair, the most sexually rewarding of Larkin's life, as 1952–55 (*LM*, 454).[11]

According to biographer Richard Bradford – not a reliable witness – Larkin did make Whit Saturday train trips from Hull to Grantham, in 1957 and 1958.[12] Larkin started the poem shortly after the first of these, breaking off to write 'Letter to a Friend about Girls'. He resumed work on 'The Whitsun Weddings' in March 1958, any repeat journey in May possibly being undertaken, at least in part, as a research trip, a calculated quest for such anthropological detail as might facilitate completion of his recalcitrant masterpiece.

To sum up: the first journey was not at Whit and not to London; the second was to London but not at Whit; the third and fourth, if they happened at all, were at Whit but not to London. There is no single moment of origination, no actual journey that combines the Whit timing with the London destination. The poem's travelogue is a fabrication, a composite of diverse experiences, literary borrowings and imagination. The author's claims that he did not change a thing are false. His repeated assertion that the originatory experience was 'unforgettable' is rendered farcical by the fact that he cannot remember from one interview to the next in what year, on what day and to which destination he travelled. His claim that 'it just needed writing down' is belied by the protracted effort of composition ('I've never known anything resist me so!'). Finally, his throwaway remark that 'Anybody could have done it' is preposterous: like Yeats's 'Easter 1916', Eliot's 'Prufrock', Auden's 'In Memory of W.B. Yeats' or Plath's 'Daddy', 'The Whitsun Weddings' is an inimitable product of a unique twentieth-century sensibility.

Constructing the narrator: first-level intertextuality

In the previous paragraph it was proposed that the poem's travelogue was a fabrication; the corollary is that *in the process of constructing the narrative, Larkin constructs the narrator*. One reason the drafting process was so protracted was Larkin's willingness to try out different options. Sometimes this entailed minor alterations to the narrator's observations: like Winifred Arnott's dog transmogrified into the 'reluctant cat' of 'Lines on a Young Lady's Photograph Album', the 'short-shadowed cattle' of 'The Whitsun

Weddings' began life as 'sheep [...] scattered with their shadows'. However, other drafts credited the narrator with a vastly expanded temporal knowledge of the newly-weds, encompassing their diverse pasts ('Some had lived far apart, some side by side') and futures:

> Some meant what they had promised but would lapse
> One pair within a week would set up home
> Beneath the half-lit sea, in seventy years
> Another pair would meet the press, perhaps
> Describe their wedding day[13]

The claim that '[i]t was just the transcription of a very happy afternoon' hardly squares with a proleptic leap of 'seventy years' to 2025 (if we use those 1955 train journeys as the year of the poem's setting). Clearly, this prophetic narrator is not Larkin who, had he lived, would have been 103 years of age!

Perhaps to steady himself in the dizzying throes of composition, Larkin summoned into the emerging text images, tropes and turns of phrase deployed in his earlier writings. As observed in Chapter 1, significant scenic details of 'The Whitsun Weddings' were anticipated by *A Girl in Winter* (see Table 4.1). This novel was written in 1944–46, a full decade before the earliest of the mid-1950s train journeys under discussion, and the unfolding panorama used by hostile commentators as proof of the misogyny and anglocentrism of the poem's narrator earlier found expression as the heightened observations of a teenage girl visiting these shores from north-west Europe. The ease with which Katherine Lind's perceptions from a novelistic journey made in 1936 are decanted into a poem written and set in the 1950s poses major problems for author-centred critics, not just regarding the mythical mid-1950s point of origin, but also the narrator's sex and nationality. As the poem nowhere stipulates otherwise, the possibility must at least be entertained that the narrator of 'The Whitsun Weddings' is female or foreign or both.

But there is more! For if key details of 'The Whitsun Weddings' are anticipated by Katherine's train and car-window observations in *A Girl in Winter*, others are as surely recycled from Larkin's first novel, *Jill* (1946) (see Table 4.2). This time the protagonist is a young Englishman going up to Oxford University, much as the author had done. However, Larkin was born in Warwickshire, his creation John Kemp in Lancashire. Larkin was from a prosperous bourgeois background, Kemp from an impoverished working-class one. Kemp can only afford to attend university because he has won a scholarship, whereas Larkin's attendance at Oxford was paid for by his father. Kemp is the only boy from his school ever to go to Oxford, travelling there alone and frightened; King Henry VIII, Coventry, specialized in getting its pupils into Oxford, Larkin travelling in the company of one of his closest school

Table 4.1 'The Whitsun Weddings' and *A Girl in Winter*

	'The Whitsun Weddings'	*A Girl in Winter*
Verse 1	That Whitsun, I was late getting away: Not till about One-twenty on the sunlit Saturday Did my three-quarters-empty train pull out, All windows down, all cushions hot, all sense Of being in a hurry gone. We ran Behind the backs of houses, crossed a street Of blinding windscreens, smelt the fish-dock; thence The river's level drifting breadth began, Where sky and Lincolnshire and water meet.	No-one else got into their compartment and after a while the train started (75) It was intensely hot (78) There was no end of the cars. They streamed in both directions [...] she looked into the driving mirror above the windscreen (80–1)
Verse 2	All afternoon, through the tall heat that slept For miles inland, A slow and stopping curve southwards we kept. Wide farms went by, short-shadowed cattle, and Canals with floatings of industrial froth; A hothouse flashed uniquely: hedges dipped And rose: and now and then a smell of grass Displaced the reek of buttoned carriage-cloth Until the next town, new and nondescript, Approached with acres of dismantled cars.	At length when afternoon had become late afternoon (81) a row of cottages, a church on rising ground, the slant of a field (80) [...] a wide field that sloped down to the river [...] A few cattle stood in the shade of trees (98) there were innumerable hoardings, empty petrol drums and broken fences lying wastefully about. (80)
Verse 3	At first, I didn't notice what a noise The weddings made Each station that we stopped at: sun destroys The interest of what's happening in the shade, And down the long cool platforms whoops and skirls I took for porters larking with the mails, And went on reading. Once we started, though, We passed them, grinning and pomaded, girls In parodies of fashion, heels and veils, All posed irresolutely, watching us go,	the continued brilliance of the sun (81) The porters and customs officials (73)

(continued)

Verse 4
As if out on the end of an event
  Waving goodbye
To something that survived it. Struck, I leant
More promptly out next time, more curiously,
And saw it all again in different terms:
The fathers with broad belts under their suits
And seamy foreheads; mothers loud and fat;
An uncle shouting smut; and then the perms,
The nylon gloves and jewellery-substitutes,
The lemons, mauves, and olive-ochres that

Verse 5
Marked off the girls unreally from the rest.
  Yes, from cafés
And banquet-halls up yards, and bunting-dressed
Coach-party annexes, the wedding-days
Were coming to an end. All down the line
Fresh couples climbed aboard: the rest stood round;
The last confetti and advice were thrown,
And, as we moved, each face seemed to define
Just what it saw departing: children frowned
At something dull; fathers had never known

Verse 6
Success so huge and wholly farcical;
  The women shared
The secret like a happy funeral;
While girls, gripping their handbags tighter, stared
At a religious wounding. Free at last,
And loaded with the sum of all they saw,
We hurried towards London, shuffling gouts of steam.
Now fields were building-plots, and poplars cast
Long shadows over major roads, and for
Some fifty minutes, that in time would seem

they were on the edge of London. (78)
a small lawn edged by poplar trees, where two
striped deckchairs lay empty in the sun. (82)

Table 4.1 Continued

	'The Whitsun Weddings'	A *Girl in Winter*
Verse 7	Just long enough to settle hats and say *I nearly died,* A dozen marriages got under way. They watched the landscape, sitting side by side – An Odeon went past, a cooling tower, And someone running up to bowl – and none Thought of the others they would never meet Or how their lives would all contain this hour. I thought of London spread out in the sun, Its postal districts packed like squares of wheat:	Occasionally she saw white figures standing at a game of cricket. (80)
Verse 8	There we were aimed. And as we raced across Bright knots of rail Past standing Pullmans, walls of blackened moss Came close, and it was nearly done, this frail Travelling coincidence; and what it held Stood ready to be loosed with all the power That being changed can give. We slowed again, And as the tightened brakes took hold, there swelled A sense of falling, like an arrow-shower Sent out of sight, somewhere becoming rain.	

Table 4.2 'The Whitsun Weddings' and *Jill*

	'The Whitsun Weddings'	Jill
Verse 1	That Whitsun, I was late getting away: Not till about One-twenty on the sunlit Saturday Did my three-quarters-empty train pull out, All windows down, all cushions hot, all sense Of being in a hurry gone. We ran Behind the backs of houses, crossed a street Of blinding windscreens, smelt the fish-dock; thence The river's level drifting breadth began, Where sky and Lincolnshire and water meet.	past coalyards, railway sidings, the backs of houses and gardens (193) the flashing windscreens of cars (97)
Verse 2	All afternoon, through the tall heat that slept For miles inland, A slow and stopping curve southwards we kept. Wide farms went by, short-shadowed cattle, and Canals with floatings of industrial froth; A hothouse flashed uniquely: hedges dipped And rose: and now and then a smell of grass Displaced the reek of buttoned carriage-cloth Until the next town, new and nondescript, Approached with acres of dismantled cars.	When they were clear of the gasometers, the wagons and blackened bridges of Banbury, he looked out over the fields, noticing the clumps of trees that sped by, whose dying leaves each had an individual colour, from palest ochre to nearly purple, so that each tree stood out distinctly as in Spring. The hedges were still green, but the leaves of the convolvuli threaded through them (21) he made his way to the canal [...] disfigured at times by scum (193) It was a third-class carriage, and the crimson seats smelt of dust and engines and tobacco, but the air was warm. (21)

(continued)

Table 4.2   Continued

	'The Whitsun Weddings'	Jill
Verse 3	At first, I didn't notice what a noise The weddings made Each station that we stopped at: sun destroys The interest of what's happening in the shade, And down the long cool platforms whoops and skirls I took for porters larking with the mails, And went on reading. Once we started, though, We passed them, grinning and pomaded, girls In parodies of fashion, heels and veils, All posed irresolutely, watching us go,	From the end of the train came a banging as porters threw luggage in and out of the van (220) a young man was arguing with a porter (24) He tried to read. (22)
Verse 4	As if out on the end of an event Waving goodbye To something that survived it. Struck, I leant More promptly out next time, more curiously, And saw it all again in different terms: The fathers with broad belts under their suits And seamy foreheads; mothers loud and fat; An uncle shouting smut; and then the perms, The nylon gloves and jewellery-substitutes, The lemons, mauves, and olive-ochres that	
Verse 5	Marked off the girls unreally from the rest. Yes, from cafés And banquet-halls up yards, and bunting-dressed Coach-party annexes, the wedding-days Were coming to an end. All down the line Fresh couples climbed aboard: the rest stood round; The last confetti and advice were thrown, And, as we moved, each face seemed to define Just what it saw departing: children frowned At something dull; fathers had never known	

And as if the train knew his destination was near it seemed to quicken speed, plunging on with a regular pattern of beats. He looked from the window and saw a man with a gun entering a field, two horses by a gate, and presently the railway line was joined by a canal, and rows of houses appeared. He got to his feet and stared at the approaching city across allotments, back-gardens and piles of coal covered with fallen leaves. Red brick walls glowed with a dull warmth that he would have admired at another time. (23)

For one curious transient second he thought he knew how a bride feels on the morning of her wedding. (195)

He felt extraordinary power over them all, thinking that although he was not the best of them, he was the only one who realized their collective excellence. (104)

The train clattered by iron bridges, cabbages and a factory painted with huge white letters he did not bother to read; smoke dirtied the sky; the train swung violently over set after set of points. A signal-box. Their speed seemed to increase, as they swept towards the station round a long curve of line through much rolling-stock [...] Then the eaves of the platform, hollow shouting, the faces slowing down as he dragged down his heavy suitcase from the rack, the shuddering halt and escape of steam. (24)

Verse 6

Success so huge and wholly farcical;
The women shared
The secret like a happy funeral;
While girls, gripping their handbags tighter, stared
At a religious wounding. Free at last,
And loaded with the sum of all they saw,
We hurried towards London, shuffling gouts of steam.
Now fields were building-plots, and poplars cast
Long shadows over major roads, and for
Some fifty minutes, that in time would seem

Verse 7

Just long enough to settle hats and say
I nearly died,
A dozen marriages got under way.
They watched the landscape, sitting side by side
– An Odeon went past, a cooling tower,
And someone running up to bowl – and none
Thought of the others they would never meet
Or how their lives would all contain this hour.
I thought of London spread out in the sun,
Its postal districts packed like squares of wheat:

Verse 8

There we were aimed. And as we raced across
Bright knots of rail
Past standing Pullmans, walls of blackened moss
Came close, and it was nearly done, this frail
Travelling coincidence; and what it held
Stood ready to be loosed with all the power
That being changed can give. We slowed again,
And as the tightened brakes took hold, there swelled
A sense of falling, like an arrow-shower
Sent out of sight, somewhere becoming rain.

friends, Noel Hughes, who was to attend the same college. As Larkin empha-sized in 'A Conversation with Neil Powell':

> I was not poor, I liked the chap I shared rooms with, and I didn't make up a fantasy about a younger sister. Similarly, in *A Girl in Winter* [...] I wasn't a girl and I wasn't foreign. (*FR*, 33)

No more than Katherine Lind is John Kemp a cipher for Philip Larkin.[14]

Jill depicts Kemp's Michaelmas term at Oxford as an almost continuous sequence of humiliations at the hands of wealthier contemporaries. His mother advises him to avoid the toffs and make friends with those 'of his own standing', but on arrival at the university Kemp is painfully aware that even 'the college porter is better dressed' than he (*J*, 25). Kemp's answer is to live vicariously through his more sophisticated and *louche* room-mate, Christopher Warner, and Christopher's public school cronies: 'he did not expect to be included in the talk, but it seemed a great privilege simply to be allowed to listen to them as they talked casually'. John's pitiful gratitude for the slightest gesture of friendliness is recorded in uncompromisingly class-conscious terms: 'When he looked at them, he felt like a waiter in an expensive restaurant. Their friendliness to him was like the tips they would give a waiter' (*J*, 60). At times the pronominal fluctuations between singular and plural, first and third person, register Kemp's anxiety as to whether or not he has been subsumed into the collective 'we' and his painful recogni-tion that he has not: 'He was acutely conscious of being referred to in the third person.' At other times, he is mercilessly satirized for his provincial, northern, working-class roots:

> 'I went to Huddlesford.'
> 'Why?'
> 'I live there, that's why.'
> 'Do people live there?' inquired Patrick with an air of surprise. 'I thought it was a music-hall fiction.' (*J*, 32, 221)

That this tale of working-class immiseration shadows sizeable passages of 'The Whitsun Weddings' problematizes the standard criticism that the lat-ter articulates middle-class disdain for the 'comical goings-on of the lower orders'.

If we ask on what basis the testimonies of two such discrepant characters as John Kemp and Katherine Lind can possibly be amalgamated to construct the poem's narrative, we strike at another predicate of biographical criticism – for the answer is *outsiderdom*. We have already observed how Katherine's enigmatic refugee status maximizes her alienation: not only does she not fit in among the English in the present time of the novel, but we never discover where she did belong in the past. John Kemp is likewise doubly distanced from indigeneity, his very name emphasizing deracination by invoking the protagonist of Robert Graves's folk masque *John Kemp's Wager* (1925). Graves's ballad opera is set in an early eighteenth-century pre-industrial Merry England. The eponymous hero is a descendant of William Kemp, the comic actor and dancer who performed in plays by Shakespeare and Jonson before famously Morris dancing from London to Norwich, his written account of the feat being published as *Kemps Nine Daies Wonder*. In the play, John is the embodiment of village virtues: he sings folk songs, makes hobby-horses, earns his living as a wood carver, performs St George in a local show, engages in Morris dancing and defeats all-comers in inter-village fisticuffs. In short, he exemplifies belonging. The John Kemp of *Jill* has already suffered a symbolic expulsion from Eden with the industrial revolution reducing his class to an anonymous proletariat. Now we witness John's humiliation as he attempts to rise into a higher social stratum: he is rebuffed by contemporaries at Oxford and (unlike his Gravesian namesake) he fails to win the girl.

As we saw in the last chapter, innumerable critics have concurred in the view that Larkin (in Seamus Heaney's words) is 'a poet [...] of composed and tempered English nationalism'. Even our cursory examination of the passages cannibalized from his own novels suggests, to the contrary, that the narrative of 'The Whitsun Weddings' will be marked by gender ambiguity, class displacement and a sense of incomplete belonging. Moreover, the substantial recyclings from Larkin's prose fictions are complemented by numerous fleeting borrowings from his poetic back catalogue. Tolley has already noted that the association of 'postal districts' with fertility, coupledom and the unloosing of flighted love at the climax of 'The Whitsun Weddings' was rehearsed in an unfinished Larkin poem from early 1951. The poem in question, 'Two by two in February air', contains the lines 'Unloose the little loves to fly in pairs / About the postal districts'.[15] Similarly, 'Deceptions' (1950) anticipates in the phrase 'All the unhurried day' the wording of several lines from the opening verses of 'The Whitsun Weddings' ('all sense / Of being in a hurry gone'; 'All afternoon, through the tall heat') (*CP*, 32; *TCP*, 41). As early as 1942, the poem 'Leave' sports an uncle shouting smut ('Uncle Joe's humour / Approaching the dirty') (*TCP*, 207). While the protagonist's sense that what the weddings dramatize is the capacity for transformation within our determinate lives ('with all the power / That being changed can give') was anticipated in 'New Year Poem' (1940): 'make me remember, who am always inclined to forget, / That there is always a changing at the root' (*CP*, 255; *TCP*, 187). Elsewhere, one might remark the innumerable poems that predicate their narrative arc upon a train journey. 'The local snivels through the fields' (1951) already presents the central motif of a detached narrator seated amidst interacting fellow passengers:

> I sit between felt-hatted mums
> Whose weekly day-excursion yields

> Baby-sized parcels, bags of plums,
> And bones of gossip good to clack
> Past all the seven stations back. (*CP*, 59; *TCP*, 292)

'Like the train's beat' (1943–44) offers carriage-window glimpses of an alternating panorama of urban ('The train runs on through wilderness / Of cities') and rural ('English oaks / Flash past the windows'). That the narrator's attention is transfixed by a 'Polish airgirl in the corner seat' has led some commentators to link this poem with *A Girl in Winter*, which was begun shortly thereafter, and to speculate that Katherine Lind might herself be exiled from Poland (*CP*, 288; *TCP*, 11).

We have now enumerated in a list that is far from exhaustive eight Larkin works that rehearse aspects of 'The Whitsun Weddings' and all of which predate, sometimes by as much as 15 years, the 1955 train journey he liked to claim had gifted him 'the whole experience [...] all at once'.

Constructing the narrator: second-level intertextuality

In *Larkin, Ideology and Critical Violence* I proposed that 'The Whitsun Weddings' not only adopted the citational method of Eliot's *The Waste Land* but made that work a principal source of allusion.[16] I shall now adapt that argument to a different end – that of showing how it inevitably yields a model of subjectivity as discontinuous, syncretic, heterogeneous. In a central passage of *The Waste Land* the narrator manifests as both male and female:

> I Tiresias, though blind, throbbing between two lives,
> Old man with wrinkled female breasts
> [...]
> I Tiresias, old man with wrinkled dugs
> Perceived the scene, and foretold the rest[17]

Eliot's footnote explains:

> Tiresias, although a mere spectator and not indeed a 'character', is yet the most important personage in the poem, uniting all the rest. Just as the one-eyed merchant, seller of currants, melts into the Phoenician Sailor, and the latter is not wholly distinct from Ferdinand Prince of Naples, so all the women are one woman, and the two sexes meet in Tiresias. What Tiresias *sees*, in fact, is the substance of the poem.[18]

In Greek myth Tiresias was a Theban man transformed into a woman for seven years. Called upon to settle a dispute between Zeus (Latin Jupiter or Jove) and Hera (Juno) as to whether men or women take most pleasure in sex, he having experienced both, Tiresias declared for women in a ratio of nine to one. Hera punished him with blindness for adjudicating against her: Zeus rewarded him with long life (hence the Eliotic wrinkling) and foresight for adjudicating in his favour. This figure of the *blind seer* was deployed in the works of Victorians like Tennyson and Swinburne and modernists like Pound and Apollinaire, though Eliot is unusual in rendering Tiresias simultaneously (rather than sequentially) male and female. In running a parallel with *The Waste Land*, 'The Whitsun Weddings' is reinforcing the gender ambiguity of a narrative that, as we have seen, melds the perceptions of John Kemp and Katherine Lind.

What, then, are the parallels? Both poems begin with departures from the north, Eliot's 'I read, much of the night, and go south in winter' becoming Larkin's 'slow and stopping curve southwards'. Both travel from heat and drought, with much play on the way shadows contract and lengthen in accord with the angle of the sun, to hints of regenerative rain. Both describe major rivers, Eliot's 'Sweet Thames, run softly, till I end my song' being a quotation from Edmund Spenser's 'Prothalamion', a poem written, like 'The Whitsun Weddings', to celebrate a multiple marriage. Both poems complicate these wholesome riverine images with descriptions of industrial waterways, Eliot's seedy urban pastoral ('I was fishing in the dull canal / On a winter evening round behind the gashouse') being closely paralleled in Larkin's description of 'Canals with floatings of industrial froth'. Both move towards a close with references to towers, London and polluted walls (*The Waste Land* describes 'a blackened wall', 'The Whitsun Weddings' has 'walls of blackened moss'). Both end with the prospect of sexual regeneration – the restoration to potency of the Fisher King in *The Waste Land*, the consummation of the marriages in 'The Whitsun Weddings' – alike symbolized by the yoking of the word 'rain' to a present participle (Eliot's 'Bringing rain', Larkin's 'becoming rain'). Add the paralleling of word and phrase (Larkin's 'girls' marked off 'unreally from the rest' invoking the 'Unreal city' motif in *The Waste Land*; or Eliot's 'She [...] nearly died of young George' becoming '*I nearly died*' in 'The Whitsun Weddings') and the analogies become pronounced enough to be expressive.

Technically, also, the two poems are more akin than has been noted, in that both incorporate literary allusions along the way before climaxing in a kaleidoscopic tessellation of citations. Hence, in addition to the running parallel with *The Waste Land*, 'The Whitsun Weddings' orchestrates an army of echoes some of which effectively prick out, as though upon a map, the poem's geographical itinerary. The end of the first stanza

> The river's level drifting breadth began,
> Where sky and Lincolnshire and water meet.

invokes the opening of 'The Lady of Shalott':

> On either side the river lie
> Long fields of barley and of rye,
> That clothe the wold and meet the sky.[19]

all very appropriate as the train passes the river Humber into Tennyson's county of Lincoln. The frame-by-frame succession of carriage-window views, some urban, some rural, culminating at the end of stanza three with the startling sight of the 'girls' from the wedding parties, may have been modelled on Hardy's 'Faint Heart in a Railway Train':

> At nine in the morning there passed a church,
> At ten there passed me by the sea,
> At twelve a town of smoke and smirch,
> At two a forest of oak and birch,
> And, then, on a platform, she[20]

If Terry Whalen is right to detect a kinship between the central stanzas of 'The Whitsun Weddings' and the marriage of Anna and Will Brangwen in D.H. Lawrence's *The Rainbow* – both feature uncles making sexual innuendoes – then the train's progress might plausibly be located in the Midlands.[21] Barbara Everett has strengthened this connection by detecting an influence from 'In the Train', 'a pleasant though unremarkable little poem' by the late Vivian de Sola Pinto, Professor of English in Lawrence's home city of Nottingham and editor of his *Complete Poems*, which begins –

> I am in a long train gliding through England,
> Gliding past green fields and gentle grey willows,
> Past huge dark elms and meadows full of buttercups,
> And old farms dreaming among mossy apple trees.
>
> Now we are in a dingy town of small ugly houses
> And tin advertisements of cocoa and Sunlight Soap,
> Now we are in a dreary station built of coffee-coloured wood
> Where barmaids in black stand in empty Refreshment Rooms,
> And shabby old women sit on benches with suitcases.

In Everett's opinion, the central conceit of the train journey together with specific images ('Sunshine flashes on canals', 'In the murky Midlands where meadows grow more colourless') formed a fund of suggestion for Larkin's much greater opus.[22]

As already noted, '*I nearly died*' in stanza seven parallels 'She [...] nearly died' in *The Waste Land*; now we can add that both may share a common source in 'Laugh! I thought I should 'ave died' from Albert Chevalier's music-hall hit 'Wot Cher' or 'Knocked 'em in the Old Kent Road' (the cockney accent of which signifies that we have now reached the outskirts of London). In the penultimate stanza the clause 'An Odeon went past' invokes 'An Odeon flashes fire' from Betjeman's 'The Metropolitan Railway', another apposite allusion since that poem too links London, trains and marriage; while London's 'postal districts packed like squares of wheat' derives from Auden's 'As I Walked Out One Evening':

> As I walked out one evening,
> Walking down Bristol Street,
> The crowds upon the pavement
> Were fields of harvest wheat.[23]

Larkin told his publisher, Jean Hartley, that the arrow-shower simile in the last stanza was inspired by a scene in Laurence Olivier's film of *Henry V* (1944), permitting those who so wish – Paulin included – to link the patriotic fervour of the English defeat of the French at Agincourt to the wartime context in which the film was made and seen by Larkin.[24] However, such expressions as 'There we were aimed', 'it was nearly done', the 'frail / Travelling coincidence' and 'sitting side by side' are altogether closer to the following passage from *The Waves*, young Larkin's favourite Virginia Woolf novel:

> 'How fair, how strange,' said Bernard, 'glittering, many-pointed and many-domed London lies before me under mist. Guarded by gasometers, by factory chimneys, she lies sleeping as we approach [...] But we are aimed at her [...] The early train from the north is hurled at her like a missile [...]
> 'Meanwhile as I stand looking from the train window, I feel strangely, persuasively, that because of my great happiness (being engaged to be married) I am become part of this speed, this missile hurled at the city [...] I do not want the connexion which has bound us together sitting opposite each other all night long to be broken [...] Our community in the rushing train, sitting together with only one wish, to arrive at Euston, was very welcome. But behold! It is over. We have attained our desire. We have drawn up at the platform.'[25]

In the final sentence of the poem, Larkin's narrator describes the arrows 'Sent out of sight', not knowing where they will land but knowing they must land 'somewhere'. This recalls 'The Arrow and the Song' by Longfellow:

> I shot an arrow in the air,
> It fell to earth, I know not where.[26]

Longfellow had already suggested the title of Larkin's 'Under a splendid chestnut tree' and later supplied the *Hiawatha* metre of 'The Explosion'. However, as Andrew Motion remarked, 'Larkin's arrows serve Cupid's purpose, not Mars'.'[27] The deathly arrows of Agincourt are transmuted into William Blake's 'arrows of desire'. This list of citations might readily be multiplied. We have already said enough to demonstrate that, far from being generically pure, the text of 'The Whitsun Weddings' is a hybrid which freely appropriates constituent granules from plays, films, novels, ballads, schoolroom classics, canonical masterpieces, music-hall songs and hardcore modernist epics. Far from being insistently English, the narrative 'voice' is a transatlantic medley encompassing contributions from Brits (Blake), Americans (Longfellow), Americans who became naturalized British citizens (Eliot) and Englishmen who became naturalized Americans (Auden). Far from being repressively masculinist, the narrative welcomes on an equal basis intertexts from gay men (Auden), bisexual women (Woolf), the sexually tepid (Eliot, Hardy) and the sexually feverish (Lawrence). The previous section of this chapter proposed that Larkin's citings of his own back-catalogue are so heterogeneous as to constitute a polymorphously perverse narrator. We can now add that Larkin's citings of other writers powerfully endorse this view – to the point where 'The Whitsun Weddings' may be said to project a model of selfhood as endlessly mutable.

One way we can test this hypothesis is by examining four tiny excerpts from the narrative, representative textemes[28] that constitute the larger text, so as to calibrate the polysemic details and extraordinarily subtle shifts of register that moment by moment change our sense of who the narrator is.

'porters larking with the mails'

This seemingly transparent clause may be parsed in at least five ways. It may be read 'innocently' as a description of railway porters fooling with the mailbags on the station platforms. It may be read as a homoerotic pun, porters larking with the *males*. Such an interpretation might license the speculation that the narrator's distance from marriage, however sympathetically inclined, is informed by homosexual feeling. The same seven-syllable unit may be scanned as an authorial private joke of heterosexual temper. Peter Sheldon, Sub-Librarian to Larkin at the University of Hull's Brynmor Jones Library, explains:

> A shared joke (oh yes, there were some) between him and his staff in the early days of The New Library, now the East Building, was that a certain store room was known as 'Miss Porter's Room', Miss Porter being a generously endowed student whom he had professed to lust after and proposed to install in this room. On at least two occasions he told me that this passion was enshrined in 'The Whitsun Weddings':

> > And down the long cool platforms whoops and skirls
> > I took for porters larking with the mails.

Porter ... Larkin ...
A whimsical little memorial, and I never knew why he wanted me to
know it was there.[29]

This predacious heterosexuality is implicitly critiqued by the simultaneous
invocation of Tennyson's anti-patriarchal poem 'Godiva', which begins:

> I waited for the train at Coventry,
> I hung with grooms and porters on the bridge[30]

Though Tennyson's narrator is not sexed, the poem is resolutely woman-
centred, with Lady Godiva's husband Earl Leofric arraigned for cruelty and
Peeping Tom for voyeurism. Coventry was Larkin's home city, of course, and
he had already leaned on the Tennyson when writing his anti-roots masterpiece 'I Remember, I Remember'.

Finally, poet Paul Muldoon has pursued an Eliotic reading of Larkin's lines
by referring the 'porters' to 'Mrs Porter and her daughter' in *The Waste Land*:

> The sound of horns and motors, which shall bring
> Sweeney to Mrs Porter in the spring.
> O the moon shone bright on Mrs Porter
> And on her daughter
> They wash their feet in soda water.[31]

The Eliot passage in turn derives from a scurrilous ballad, popular with
Australian troops in the First World War, concerning the role of a Cairo
brothel-keeper and her prostitute daughter in spreading venereal disease.

The 'innocent' interpretation yields a non-gender-specific narrator, as
plausibly female as male; the 'gay' interpretation yields a male homosexual;
the private joke yields a narrator as mouthpiece for the author as hammy
heterosexual; the Tennyson echo yields a narrator sensitive to women's
rights, perhaps a heterosexual woman; while Muldoon's Eliotic reading
yields a heterosexual male, possibly antipodean, whose knowingness regarding the sex trade carries an undertone of gynophobia.

'The nylon gloves and jewellery-substitutes'

This is John Whitehead's paraphrase of the description of the wedding
guests in stanzas four and five: 'fathers wearing broad belts and *unaccus-
tomed* suits, fat mothers *weeping unashamedly, youths with smarmed-down
hair*'.[32] The emphases are mine and indicate details Whitehead has invented.
The additions I wish to dwell upon concern the men, beginning with those
fathers with their broad belts. In an earlier draft this line read 'The fathers
with their workmen's belts under their suits'.[33] This version categorically
identifies the fathers as working class, strongly implies that they are too

poor to have smart belts to go with their wedding outfits and thereby offers some validation to Whitehead's guess that they rarely have cause to wear suits. However, this degree of class explicitness was clearly not what Larkin wanted, the substitution of 'broad belts' for 'workmen's belts' permitting the counter possibility that they are actually wearing cummerbunds. The ambiguity in the wording creates ambiguity in the precise class placement (the difference, say, between proletarian and petit bourgeois), though either way we are clearly dealing with lower-income families.

In his account of the 'youths with smarmed-down hair', Whitehead, a male critic, is (presumably unwittingly) making good the poem's deficit in male representation. Only the parental generation gets a mention, the fathers and the uncle shouting smut: the bridegroom, the best man, any brothers of bride or groom, the male cousins (sons of that foul-mouthed uncle), the groom's mates, the boyfriends of the bridesmaids, the page-boys ... none of these standard presences at a wedding is represented anywhere in the poem. By contrast, their female equivalents, 'the girls', feature significantly in stanzas three, four, five and six. This passage has no equivalent in *Jill* or *A Girl in Winter* (as Tables 4.1 and 4.2 demonstrate), the asymmetrical representation of the sexes being especially created for this particular narrative. What does this gender bias in the depiction suggest about the gender of the narrator? Does the fixation upon the young women take the form of the appraising, voyeuristic gaze of a captivated male – we know from 'Lines on a Young Lady's Photograph Album' how well Larkin can handle such a theme? Or does it suggest, to the contrary, sympathetic identification by a member of the same sex? Even today, could most men spot from a train window the substitution of nylon for silk, a fake from a real jewel, or recognize the colour 'olive-ochre'? As the principal targets of the fashion industry, women are likely to be conscious of the way society uses clothes and accessories to construct 'femininity'. Simone de Beauvoir famously began volume two of *Le Deuxième Sexe* (1949):

> One is not born, but rather becomes, a woman. No biological, psychological, or economic fate determines the figure that the human female presents in society; it is civilization as a whole that produces this creature [...] which is described as feminine.[34]

Two decades earlier, Virginia Woolf's novel *Orlando* (1928) had this to say on the role of costume in the production of gender identity:

> there is much to support the view that it is clothes that wear us and not we them; we may make them take the mould of arm or breast, but they mould our hearts, our brains, our tongues to their liking [...] Different though the sexes are, they intermix. In every human being a vacillation from one sex to the other takes place, and often it is only the clothes that keep the male or female likeness.[35]

Is this what our narrator means by claiming that their clothes mark off the girls 'unreally'? If so, might the narrator (like Woolf, like de Beauvoir) be female? And if that is even vaguely possible, might the touch of satire in the depictions of the wedding parties be as plausibly attributed to proto-feminist scepticism as to the authorial class condescension identified by Paulin, Regan and Phelps?

'Free at last'

Larkin boldly declared 'I can live a week without poetry but not a day without jazz.' It is therefore not surprising that his own writings are as suffused with jazz allusions as with references to poetry or painting. The half-line 'But not for me' which opens the last stanza of 'Reasons for Attendance' is the title of a 1930 song by George Gershwin. The affirmative exhortation 'Oh, play that thing!' in the poem 'For Sidney Bechet' has many possible sources, the most likely being the 1923 cut of 'Dippermouth Blues' by King Oliver's Creole Jazz Band and its rising star Louis Armstrong. The title 'Love Again' tellingly recalls the Frederick Hollander–Sammy Lerner song 'Falling in Love Again', an ode to helpless promiscuity made famous by Marlene Dietrich in the movie *The Blue Angel* and subsequently recorded by Billie Holiday. The American scholar B.J. Leggett has convincingly argued that the opening of 'Aubade' – 'I work all day, and get half-drunk at night' – begins by echoing many a classic blues (as when Lonnie Johnson begins 'I work all day for you, until the sun go down').[36] And in the sixth strophe of 'The Whitsun Weddings' we have this:

> Free at last,
> And loaded with the sum of all they saw,
> We hurried towards London

In 1958, when the poem was completed, perhaps only Larkin's fellow jazz buffs and some members of the black community would have caught the echo of the African American spiritual 'I Thank God I'm Free at Las'. Five years later the citation became world famous when Dr Martin Luther King invoked the same source at the climax of his 'I have a dream' speech in Washington DC, on 28 August 1963:

> when we allow freedom to ring [...] from every village and every hamlet, from every state and every city, we will be able to speed up that day when all of God's children – black men and white men, Jews and Gentiles, Protestants and Catholics, will be able to join hands and sing in the words of the old Negro spiritual: 'Free at last! Free at last! Thank God Almighty, we're free at last!'[37]

At which point the reader has been licensed to speculate whether the narrator might be an American visitor to these shores, and not necessarily a white one.

'someone running up to bowl'

Table 4.1 correlates Katherine Lind's train and car-window observations and the train-window sightings of 'The Whitsun Weddings'. However, some of the parallels involve an intervening text by another author. Kingsley Amis read *A Girl in Winter* before writing *Lucky Jim*, and Katherine's glimpse of 'white figures standing at a game of cricket' informs the scene where Jim Dixon 'switched his attention to the other side of the road, where a cricket match was being played and the bowler was just running up to bowl'.[38] Larkin read *Lucky Jim* many times (as unofficial editorial advisor) before writing 'The Whitsun Weddings', and his brilliant cinematic freeze-frame of a cricket match – 'someone running up to bowl' – lifts four of its five words from the Amis. Larkin influences Amis influences Larkin, the non-gender-specific narrator of the poem melding the perceptions of Jim and Katherine, male and female, a Lancastrian in South Wales and a European in the south of England. Sexes, classes, countries, cultures and continents meet and dissolve in the space of seven syllables. Eliot at his most nuanced did not work citation more deftly than this.

The four textemes analysed total 19 words. There are 552 other words in the poem which might be subjected to similar scrutiny. We have put under the microscope one-thirtieth of the poem, yet have already seen how four tiny digits generate a multiplicity of sometimes mutually exclusive characterizations of the narrator: as authorial mouthpiece, gay man, hammy heterosexual, macho gynophobe, middle-class snob, proto-feminist, jazz fan, transatlantic observer, African American, English academic in Wales, continental teenage girl. This remarkable narratological mobility is an under-appreciated aspect of Larkin's literary greatness, and one of the ways in which he far exceeds poets who in other regards might be his equals (Robert Lowell, say, or Ted Hughes). Certainly, our model of multiple selfhood – infinitely subtle, infinitely various – is entirely at odds with the monolithic stereotype of Larkin as male, bourgeois, English, white and Tory. Either Larkin was not like that or he is not the narrator. Or both.

Constructing the narrator: third-level intertextuality

Lisa Jardine is the most distinguished academic to subscribe to that monolithic stereotype, seeing Larkin as the embodiment of a spent national ideology. The 'cultural frame within which Larkin writes' is 'one which takes racism and sexism for granted as crucially part of the British national heritage'. As self-elected spokesperson for a more enlightened multicultural society, Professor Jardine finds little need to include Larkin in the syllabus: 'Actually, we don't tend to teach Larkin much now in my Department of English. The Little Englandism he celebrates sits uneasily within our revised curriculum, which seeks to give all of our students, regardless of background, race or creed, a voice within British culture.' The sole pedagogical value of studying these texts is to teach students 'to see through the even texture of Larkin's verse, to the parochial beliefs which lie behind them'.[39]

Jardine is a cultural historian: the past is her profession; yet her attitude to recent history, as exemplified in the Larkin case, is massively condescending. She approaches the greatest poetic *oeuvre* of the age like a bacteriologist isolating a virus. What a contrast, what a relief, to turn to Larkin's literary heirs, younger writers from across the spectrum of class, race, sex, gender and religion, who offer confirmation from the multicultural future – our multicultural present – of his continuing relevance and efficacy. Hence, Gavin Ewart's 'The Larkin Automatic Car Wash' replicates the metre, rhyme scheme and stanza count of 'The Whitsun Weddings' only to replace Larkin's detached observer with a family man ferrying 'Six teenagers' by car. Andrew Motion's elegy 'This is your subject speaking' occasionally echoes 'The Whitsun Weddings' as the author retraces by car Larkin's bicycle rides in east Yorkshire.[40] Julian Barnes made glancing references to 'The Whitsun Weddings' in his debut novel *Metroland* (1980); but in his fifth novel and second masterpiece, *A History of the World in 10½ Chapters* (1989), takes further the poem's decentring of bride and groom:

> In a wedding photograph, the interesting faces are not those of the bride and groom, but of the encircling guests: the bride's younger sister (will it happen to me, the tremendous thing?), the groom's elder brother (will she let him down like that bitch did me?), the bride's mother (how it takes me back), the groom's father (if the lad knew what I know now – if only *I*'d known what I know now), the priest (strange how even the tongue-tied are moved to eloquence by these ancient vows), the scowling adolescent (what do they want to get *married* for?), and so on. The central couple are in a profoundly abnormal state; yet try telling them that.[41]

In the brilliantly satirical *Solar* (2010), titled after another Larkin poem, Ian McEwan sustains over 14 pages a discontinuous running parallel between the narrator of 'The Whitsun Weddings' and his own protagonist, Nobel Prize-winning physicist Michael Beard. The scrupulous attention Larkin's narrator lavishes upon the human and topographical spectacle seems engaged and generous compared to Beard's egocentricity and self-indulgence. McEwan has drawn the parallel so as to show up by contrast his character's moral and emotional vacuity.[42]

Of course, Jardine might rejoin that since all of these writers – Ewart, Motion, Barnes, McEwan – are, like Larkin, white middle-class men, they by no means represent the inclusive society she was speaking for. But then our list is far from complete. Larkin's supposed class constraints were breached as early as 1986 when Peter Reading's *Stet* deliberately invoked 'The Whitsun Weddings'

> A cooling tower, scrap cars bashed into cubes,
> a preternaturally mauve canal.

before going on to suggest that in Mrs Thatcher's England of mass unemployment and industrial deregulation, the working class is so culturally impoverished as to only be fit for cannon-fodder:

> Slight, acned raw cadets who may well be
> spatchcocked in Ulster or some bloody fool
> flag-waving bunkum like the Falklands do

The uncle shouting smut has been replaced by a generation of young men whose sexism is an index of ignorance of their true position in the world:

> One
> pustular soldier of the Queen pretends
> to grapple with an imaginary huge
> phallus – his fellow-warriors are seized
> with mirthful paroxysms. They all have spots
> (compulsorily shaved, not left to heal)
> and all read comics.[43]

An altogether more sympathetic foray into working-class territory is provided by Maurice Rutherford's 'The Autumn Outings'. Like the Ewart, this poem exactly replicates the form of 'The Whitsun Weddings' only to apply the template to the subject of business closures and redundancy slips:

> That autumn, I was quick getting away:
>   only about
> one-twenty on the rain-drenched Wednesday
> I locked the premises and motored out,
> all staff sent home, all workshop plant closed down,
> all sense of any kind of business gone

It might be thought that Rutherford's identification with the unemployed ('some will get by and others go to bits') and rage against the Tory government of the day amounts to a critique of Larkin's private prejudices, disclosed earlier that year by posthumous publication of the *Selected Letters* (1992). This would make 'The Autumn Outings' a cunning turning of the structure of 'The Whitsun Weddings' against its creator. However, the magnificent ending of Rutherford's poem –

> In brass-lined boardrooms up and down the land
> > deep in regret
> a million more redundancies get planned,
> while chairmen's hiked-up salaries are set,
> and Urban Councils chase arrears in rents.
> Wideboys, insider-dealers, some M.P.s
> grow richer by a second home in Spain,
> a custom-plated white Mercedes-Benz,
> that new portfolio. True-blue disease.
> The spores of loss, somewhere becoming gain.[44]

closely resembles these lines from Larkin's 'Going, Going':

> On the Business Page, a score
>
> Of spectacled grins approve
> Some takeover bid that entails
> Five per cent profit (and ten
> Per cent more in the estuaries): move
> Your works to the unspoilt dales
> (Grey area grants)! (*CP*, 189; *TCP*, 83)

'Going, Going' was commissioned by the Conservative government for an HMSO document on the environment but proved so little to their liking that they expurgated it before publication. The passage quoted above, with its suggestion that big business rapacity and government folly were combining to ravage the countryside, was found particularly objectionable and excised in its entirety. Larkin wrote to friends protesting this Tory censorship ('It makes my flesh creep': *SL*, 459) and the offending passages were defiantly restored when two years later he included the poem in *High Windows*. Perhaps Larkin and Rutherford are closer ideological kin than might at first appear, fully paid-up members of the Republic of Letters, and the structural mimicry of 'The Autumn Outings' more affectionate than parodic.

If Reading and Rutherford demonstrate the applicability to working-class subjects of the Larkin model, thereby honouring the John Kemp narrative that lies just below the surface of 'The Whitsun Weddings', various women writers have articulated the submerged feminine registers in the text. Elizabeth Jennings shifted the parameters of both gender and religion by centring 'Whitsun Sacrament' in the troubled consciousness of a young Catholic woman. The Welsh poet Sheenagh Pugh comparably shifts the boundaries of gender and nationality. Her poem 'Small Changes' begins:

> The train I'm on is well late already,
> crawling behind a slow local freight,
> with an endless scrapyard filling the window.

Each of these lines is shadowed by an equivalent in 'The Whitsun Weddings': *line 1*, 'That Whitsun, I was late getting away'; *line 2*, 'A slow and stopping curve southwards we kept'; *line 3*, 'acres of dismantled cars'.[45] Similarly, the black British poet Grace Nichols begins her poem 'Outward from Hull' with echoes of the first verse of 'The Whitsun Weddings':

> The gulls of Hull
> the train pulling out –
> a metallic snake
> along the estuary
> leaving behind
> the forceful ghost
> of Wilberforce
> the confluence
> of the Hull and Humber.
> Brough, Selby, Doncaster.[46]

One might even catch an echo in that enumeration of train stations of the lists Larkin gave in interviews about his poem ('Doncaster, Retford, Grantham, Newark, Peterborough, and at every station more wedding parties'). A more sustained parallel may be found in Beryl Bainbridge's novel *Sweet William* (1975). The protagonist Ann, unmarried but pregnant, takes a train from Euston to Liverpool (though she only gets as far as Crewe) to join the man she wrongly thinks is the father of her child, and her carriage-window observations repeatedly draw upon those of Larkin's narrator:

> She was travelling through an area of devastation, a rubbish tip of piebald fields filled with falling barns of rusty tin, chicken coops, lumpy cows lying down under a pale sky [...] What a mess it was, the countryside, fractured and torn, threaded with abandoned canals, tyres floating along the thick green water – caravans, ruined cars [...]
>
> Gardens slid past the window – allotments, fences made of doors, shacks of corrugated iron, potting sheds, greenhouses with smashed panes of glass [...]
>
> She looked out of the window. There were poplars along the horizon and pale fields of green grass. Gone in a flash, replaced by buildings and blackened walls.[47]

Perusing Jennings, Pugh, Nichols and Bainbridge, it is difficult not to recall how some of the substance of 'The Whitsun Weddings' was initially attributed to Katherine Lind.

Perhaps the most striking antidote to the Jardine position is provided by the title poem of Tariq Latif's third collection, *The Punjabi Weddings* (2007). Like Ewart and Rutherford, Latif models his poem directly upon 'The Whitsun Weddings': the iambic pentameters offset by a short second line, the big ten-line verse paragraphs (though only five stanzas compared to the original eight), the ababcdecde rhyme scheme, the marital theme – a parallelism flagged up in the title. This by-now-familiar repertoire is here applied to the unfamiliar subject of a wedding in the Anglo-Punjabi community:

> The cars parked outside the reception hall
>   range from recent
> models of BMW to old Vauxhalls.
> Inside, the marriage rites for the decent
> groom and bride takes place in separate rooms.
> The bride is adorned in a crimson and
> gold sari. A *dupata* hides her face.

No more than the Larkin is this an entirely admiring account: the strict separation of the sexes documented in these opening lines moves swiftly to an acknowledgement that this is an arranged marriage and then on to the social ostracism, perhaps worse, visited upon those who try to leaven the strict sexual code with more liberal Western values:

> The secret lovers,
> fearful of being found, leave in a hurry.
>
> No-one speaks of the indelible stains
>   of dishonour.
> Instead the family goes to great pains
> to track them down or pretend the flower
> of their lives never existed.[48]

This may not be the kind of ethnic uplift Jardine favours but proves Latif a true poet – one attracted to the Larkin model precisely because it melds scepticism and celebration, an admixture of doubt and affirmation.

As Jardine also insists that her students 'belong to a generation whose face is turned towards the new Europe, and for whom comfortable British insularity holds no romance', we might supplement the foregoing examples from multi-racial Britain with, say, Dutch composer Lowell Dijkstra's 1996 choral setting of 'The Whitsun Weddings'.[49] However, we have done enough to demonstrate that today's writers from across the postmodernist, post-feminist, postcolonial spectrum find in Larkin's protagonist a flexible mould

that allows them to put this infinitely malleable model to new narratological uses: as paterfamilias (Ewart); young male poet (Motion); sophisticated
cultural analyst (Barnes); megalomaniacal academic (McEwan); dismayed
anthropologist of Thatcherism (Reading); working-class sympathizer
(Rutherford); adolescent Catholic girl (Jennings); Welsh woman (Pugh);
black woman (Nichols); unmarried mother-to-be (Bainbridge); member of
the Anglo-Asian community (Latif).[50] It is also relevant that many of these
artists (like the fictional Katherine Lind and John Kemp) are exiles, outsiders
and displaced persons: Pugh filters her Welsh identity through an English
language mediated by her training in Russian and German;[51] Nichols was
born in Guyana and came to England in her twenties; the Dutch composer
Dijkstra was Canadian born but taken as a child to the Netherlands; Latif
was born in a village outside Lahore, Pakistan, before becoming an English
poet based in Manchester, and now lives in the Scottish Highlands. It is
as if Larkin's poem, even as it describes a condition of national belonging,
addresses itself to those who, like the poem's narrator, can only observe
such indigeneity from outside – or, at best, with one foot inside the culture,
one out. In modelling works upon it, these diverse authors render explicit
meanings that are implicit in 'The Whitsun Weddings' but which are utterly
ignored by Jardine.

Sexualizing Pentecost

We have now established at three different levels of intertextuality that the
narration of 'The Whitsun Weddings' is characterized by multiplicity and
heterogeneity: the duetting of John Kemp and Katherine Lind at level one;
the Eliotic medley of level two; the multicultural chorus of level three. This
orchestral approach to identity yields a narrator so populous as to invite
identification by readers from all meridians; and this, in turn, has important
consequences for the poem's meaning. Certainly, it renders deeply problematic Corcoran's claim that the issue of 'class [...] sets the entire tone of poetic
address', the narrative being far too polyphonic to answer to a monological
reading. This same narratival richness requires us to re-examine the possible causes for any condescension to the wedding parties, paying particular attention to the way in which the satirical gap between observer and
observed narrows across the poem's trajectory. Something altogether more
flexible is entailed than the rigid battle lines of class warfare. Finally, we
need to establish a connexion between these identitarian complexities and
the poem's relentless stripping of both the Whit festivity and the marriage
service of their Christian associations.

To take the last point first: uniquely for Larkin, 'The Whitsun Weddings'
flags up in both title and opening line a temporal connection to a major
religious festivity. Whitsun falls on the seventh Sunday after Easter and is
celebrated in the Christian calendar as the day of Pentecost when the Holy

Spirit descended upon the disciples of Jesus in Jerusalem empowering them to speak in tongues. Outside England, the symbolic colour of Pentecost is red, emblematizing joy and the fire of the Holy Spirit as recounted in Acts 2:3–4: 'And there appeared unto them cloven tongues like as of fire, and it sat upon each of them. And they were all filled with the Holy Ghost, and began to speak with other tongues, as the Spirit gave them utterance.' However, Pentecost is the most popular day for baptism throughout the Church and in England this led to the alternative name of White Sunday, or Whitsunday, after the special white garments worn by the newly baptized. There is no certain evidence of the baptism of infants in the early Church and the ancient baptismal liturgies are all intended for adults. It was the growing fashion for child baptism that created a need for the subsequent rite of confirmation, usually at adolescence, so as to verify the transformational relation to God established before the initiate was properly conscious.[52] With this development the baptismal associations of Whit were doubled, Pentecost becoming a favourite day for the confirmation of youths.

The most arresting feature of this exposition of the Christian festivity invoked by the title and first line is its irrelevance to a reading of the ensuing poem. Such tantalizing details as invite theological exegesis are so skewed to the named festivity as to frustrate expectation. There may be an echo in the fifth line of the poem – 'All windows down, all cushions hot' – of the last line of Milton's masterpiece, *Samson Agonistes*, 'And calm of mind, all passion spent'. However, the story of Samson is distinctly Old Testament and not at all Christian, let alone Pentecostal. There may be something stigmatic in the description of the 'girls' staring 'At a religious wounding', but by invoking the crucifixion this connotes Easter rather than Pentecost. Similarly, the reference to 'A dozen marriages' can hardly be said to invoke the disciples receiving the Holy Spirit since by Whit the treacherous Judas Iscariot had hanged himself, reducing their number to 11. The 'lemons, mauves, and olive-ochres' of the girls' costumes are far indeed from Pentecostal red, the cricketer 'running up to bowl' the closest we get to Pentecostal white.

The question that really needs addressing is this: why did Larkin set his fictional train journey at Whit when the poem resolutely declines to exploit the religious associations of the occasion?[53] One possible answer: so as to render unavoidable its secularizing and sexualizing of religious discourse and thereby mount a critique of the Christian revivalism of the modernist recidivist, T.S. Eliot, whose citational method Larkin appropriates. The Eliot poems invoked for contestation are *The Waste Land* and *Four Quartets*. The former is, in part, an account of the emotional and spiritual bankruptcy of Western culture in the aftermath of the First World War. In this composite metaphysical allegory, sexual malaise is a recurrent symbol of spiritual impoverishment: from the aristocratic woman of 'A Game of Chess', possibly at commode, whose opulent surroundings have as their centrepiece a painting of a rape; via the garrulous cockneys in the pub with their rotten teeth ('You have them all out, Lil, and get a nice set') and their abortions ('It's them pills I took, to bring it off, she said'); to 'the young man carbuncular' of 'The Fire Sermon', who takes his sexual pleasures without regard for those of his partner ('His vanity requires no response, / And makes a welcome of indifference'). The poem ends with the voice of the thunder issuing spiritual commands ('Datta. Dayadhvam. Damyata.') and the symbolic arrival of a baptismal drench ('a flash of lightning. Then a damp gust / Bringing rain').

A fuller account of the mystical renewal Eliot was groping towards came 20 years later with 'Little Gidding', the splendid closing movement of *Four Quartets*. The name is taken from a village in Huntingdonshire where in 1626 one Nicholas Ferrar established a devotional Christian community. As Helen Gardner says, this Quartet 'celebrates the eternal Pentecost, the perpetual descent of the Dove in tongues of fire'; adding that 'in the mystical sense the subject is the Holy Spirit, the gift of the risen and ascended Lord'.[54] Punning audaciously on the *Luftwaffe* planes he witnessed while on fire watch during the London blitz, Eliot presents the descent of the Holy Spirit as a terrible fire, at once purgatorial and Pentecostal, which redeems us from the satanic fire of those debased passions enumerated in *The Waste Land*:

> The dove descending breaks the air
> With flame of incandescent terror
> Of which the tongues declare
> The one discharge from sin and error.
> The only hope, or else despair
>   Lies in the choice of pyre or pyre –
>   To be redeemed from fire by fire.[55]

This is the ideology Larkin challenges in 'The Whitsun Weddings' by using one of his modernist heroes, D.H. Lawrence, to supplant another, T.S. Eliot.

'To me, Lawrence is what Shakespeare was to Keats,' Larkin wrote. 'In my opinion he is the greatest writer of the century, and in many things the greatest writer of all times' (*SL*, 101). These superlatives were tempered over the years by Larkin's growing regard for writers like Hardy; but as he acknowledged to his fellow devotee, Jim Sutton, 'no one who has really thrilled to Lawrence can ever give him up' (*SL*, 154). As late as 1980, Larkin opened an exhibition organized by the University of Nottingham to commemorate the fiftieth anniversary of his predecessor's death, and even purchased a T-shirt emblazoned with a portrait of Lawrence which he wore when mowing the lawn.[56] Larkin always believed that 'poetry & sex are very closely connected' (*SL*, 6), and his high regard for Lawrence had much to do with the latter's Captain Cook role in the literary mapping of uncharted oceans of human sexuality. One index of this is the prominence Larkin gave to *Lady Chatterley's Lover*, of which Lawrence said: 'I always labour at the same thing, to make the sex relation valid and precious instead of shameful. And this novel is the furthest I've gone. To me it is beautiful and tender as the naked self.'[57] Larkin's letters to Sutton are punctuated with praise for the novel: 'If one knocks out all his books except "S & L" [*Sons and Lovers*] and "Lady Ch" [*Lady Chatterley's Lover*] he is still England's greatest writer' (*SL*, 32). 'Yours till Lady C. is read out in churches' (*SL*, 57). 'I have just read a little Lady C. to check that quotation, and by jays! any man who says a word against it needs his teeth knocking down his throat' (*SL*, 54). In 1948 he bought a signed first edition of *Lady Chatterley's Lover*, and when in 1960 he organized an exhibition in the Brynmor Jones Library to celebrate Penguin Books' victory in the obscenity trial that followed publication of an unexpurgated version of the novel, Larkin proudly added this copy to the display (*SL*, 150).

Of course, Larkin's most celebrated allusion to Lawrence comes in the poem 'Annus Mirabilis' in which the *Chatterley* trial assumes heraldic status as harbinger of sixties sexual liberalization:

> Sexual intercourse began
> In nineteen sixty-three
> (Which was rather late for me) –
> Between the end of the *Chatterley* ban
> And the Beatles' first LP. (*CP*, 167; *TCP*, 90)

However, it might be claimed that *Lady Chatterley* has a more sustained, if submerged, presence in 'The Whitsun Weddings'. Connie Chatterley's meditation upon the way the new urban-industrial economy is superimposed upon an older agrarian one –

> This is history. One England blots out another. The mines had made the halls wealthy. Now they were blotting them out, as they had already blotted out the cottages. The industrial England blots out the agricultural England. One meaning blots out another. The new England blots out the old England.[58]

may lie behind the poem's brilliant synoptic account of a displaced rural geography residually visible in the contours of the metropolis: 'Now fields were building-plots, and poplars cast / Long shadows over major roads [...] // I thought of London spread out in the sun, / Its postal districts packed like squares of wheat'. The possibility that the oxymoronic 'religious wounding' refers less to Christ's stigmata than to the act of sexual penetration, an interpretation encouraged by the train's ejaculatory 'gouts of steam' and the glimpse of a phallic 'cooling tower', forges a link with Connie's sacramental response to being 'pierced again with piercing thrills of sensuality':[59]

> She yielded with a quiver that was like death, she went all open to him [...]
> She quivered again at the potent inexorable entry inside her, so strange

and terrible. It might come with the thrust of a sword in her softly-opened body, and that would be death. She clung in a sudden anguish of terror. But it came with a strange slow thrust of peace, the dark thrust of peace and a ponderous, primordial tenderness.[60]

The remarkable *swell/fall* conjunction of the poem's close ('there swelled / A sense of falling') also has parallels in the novel, as when Connie experiences her lover's tumescence ('she felt the soft bud of him within her [...] swelling and swelling') and postcoital detumescence ('She could feel him ebbing away, ebbing away').[61]

Although *Lady Chatterley* is written in the third person, not the first, most of the novel is filtered through the consciousness of Connie. However, her lover is allocated some important speeches, the occasional spot of interiority, and the long letter with which the novel closes. It is in this last that the gamekeeper, Oliver Mellors, describes to Connie how the sexual love between them has caused him to redefine the meaning of Whit Sunday:

I believe in the little flame between us [...] It's my Pentecost, the forked flame between me and you. The old Pentecost isn't quite right. Me and God is a bit uppish, somehow. But the little forked flame between me and you: there you are! That's what I abide by [...] My soul softly flaps in the little Pentecost flame with you, like the peace of fucking. We fucked a flame into being.[62]

If Larkin's eroticized narration derives from Lady Chatterley, the Whit connection derives from her lover, so that once again the narrator is a compound of male and female.[63] The important point is not that Larkin is directly alluding to Lawrence, though he might be, but that they alike equate Pentecostalism with sexual consummation. In this, they are both at the opposite pole to Eliot, stripping Whit of its religious associations in order to suggest that sexual union has a consecration of its own requiring no theological blessing.

That the anticipation of sexual intercourse is not passively observed but draws the narrator into an excited identification with the newly-weds is communicated through the poem's prosody and diction. The metrical structure of 'The Whitsun Weddings' is modelled on Keats's 'Ode to a Nightingale': there is the identical span of eight stanzas; the shared rhyme scheme, ababcdecde; and the same use of a ten-line verse in which nine iambic pentameters are diversified by a short line (a trimeter in Keats, a dimeter in the Larkin).[64] However, Larkin shifts Keats's abbreviated line from eighth to second place in the stanza. This seemingly slight modification of the inherited verse form, typical of Larkin's non-reverential approach to the canon, has two important effects. The poem explicitly states

> All afternoon, through the tall heat that slept
> For miles inland,
> A slow and stopping curve southwards we kept.

As Thwaite excellently observes: 'each ten-line stanza of "The Whitsun Weddings" seems caught on the pivot of the short four-syllable second line, pushing it forward on to the next smooth run'.[65] The placing of the dimeter early in each stanza enacts the interruptive motion of the 'slow and stopping' train journey.

At the same time, the modified stanza is one of a number of prosodic effects employed to simulate the rhythm of sexual intercourse. The stately pentameters irregularly halted by dimeters, stanza breaks and caesuras, mime a luxuriously extended act of sex. Like the snare drum's *ostinato* in *Bolero*, this analeptic rhythm runs through the poem's eight verses though (unlike Ravel) on an accelerating tempo. The descriptive language complements the sense of mounting excitement, from the erotically charged but leisurely diction of the opening verses ('All windows down, all cushions hot, all sense / Of being in a hurry gone [...] All afternoon [...] slow and stopping [...] dipped / And rose') via the pent breathlessness of the last four stanzas ('coming [...] loaded [...] We hurried [...] spread out [...] we raced [...] Came close [...] nearly done [...] it held [...] ready to be loosed') to the dramatic sense of checking and launching in the final lines, like javelin-throwers abruptly arresting their run-up at the demarcated line in order to propel the missile forward ('We slowed [...] tightened [...] swelling [...] falling [...] arrow-shower [...] rain'). That rain shower is more orgasmic than baptismal, more ejaculatory than Eucharistic. And even if the oxymoronic *swelling* and *falling* seems penile rather than clitoral, the poem's climax is protected against phallocentrism by the answering hint of vaginal contractions in the *loosed–tightened* antithesis. The bridal train trip has resolved itself into an anticipation of the moment of consummation, a celebration not of marriage but of coition. Any undercurrent of diminuendo at the end, of postcoital *tristesse*, emblematized by the 'sense of falling' and the onset of rain – in England as much a symbol of *ennui* as fertility – works against idealism. Where Eliot's Pentecostalism holds prospect of eternal salvation, Larkin's holds prospect of sexual release but uncertain marital harmony. As Larkin wrote in a late review: 'I wonder if I am alone in finding the notion of conventional love poetry a little dated at present. After all, it's the orgasm we are interested in now' (*FR*, 274).[66] As we shall see, it is the narrator's identification with the newly-weds' imminent acts of copulation that forms the bridge between observer and observed, Self and Other, which critics like Corcoran would deny.

A tale of transformation

Remembering Eliot's condescension to the author of *Lady Chatterley* ('had Lawrence been sent to a public school and taken honours at a university he would not have been a jot the less ignorant'), class-based exegetes might rejoin that Larkin's depiction of the wedding parties is only a little less patronizing than the depiction of the pub denizens of *The Waste Land*.[67] There is certainly no disputing the lower-income origins of the wedding parties. Indeed, the reason so many marriages coincided with the Feast of Pentecost was fiscal rather than spiritual: the anomalous British tax laws of the 1950s granted a married man's tax allowance for the previous year to couples who got married by a deadline shortly after Whit. The fact that Whit Monday was a public holiday (relocated in 1967 to the last Monday in May) made the long weekend a popular choice for couples anxious to qualify for tax exemption – that time is running out for the present year is encapsulated in the clause 'the wedding-days / Were coming to an end'. The narrator's observation that 'the girls' wear 'nylon gloves and jewellery-substitutes', so often cited as proof of Larkin's middle-class condescension, is actually rather a delicate statement of an economic reality, that the rush to meet the tax deadline was most conspicuous in lower-income groups for whom every penny counts (and who go off on honeymoon by public transport). Larkin brings together Pentecost and the tax factor in a mix Eliot might have used to disdain the present. Larkin does the opposite, using any residue of the sacred to endorse the secular which displaces it.

As for the narrator's bourgeois judgementalism, this is unverifiable, critics like Regan, Phelps, Smith and Corcoran attributing to snobbery attitudes that may instead be indicators of sexual, gender, racial, ethnic or religious difference. The line 'none / Thought of the others they would never meet' is repeatedly cited as an expression of class superiority. It *may* be a false note – how does the narrator know what the other passengers are thinking? – though the primary meaning is obvious: that being unaccompanied the narrator is free to comprehend the whole scene in a manner not true of the participants, the marital partners having eyes only for each other. Besides, as we saw in Table 4.2, the passage in question was anticipated 13 years earlier in this sentence from *Jill*: 'He felt extraordinary power over them all, thinking that although he was not the best of them, he was the only one who realized their collective excellence.' As John Kemp attains from a position of social *inferiority* a comparably enhanced perspective to that of our narrator, the crucial determinant is not the angle of class elevation but the degree of outsiderdom – the need to be sufficiently *a part of* the scene to understand its workings and sufficiently *apart from* the scene to take its measure.

Similarly, the pronominal fluctuations we identified in Kemp's free indirect speech, an uncertainty as to when his grammar school 'I' is subsumed in the public school 'we', are replicated in 'The Whitsun Weddings': *stanza one*, I–my–we; *stanza two*, we; *stanza three*, I–we–I–we–we–us; *stanza four*, I; *stanza five*, we; *stanza six*, they–we; *stanza seven*, I–they–they–their; *stanza eight*, we–we–we. Is this not the precise lexical register of any person caught with one foot inside the culture and the other foot outside? Perhaps the nearest equivalent in *A Girl in Winter* is that moment when Katherine has been told by Robin that 'you're almost one of the family' and will shortly be told by Mrs Fennel that 'England won't be a foreign country to you any longer' (*AGW*, 158, 161) only for Jack Stormalong to turn up and remind her of the limits of her assimilability:

> He took it for granted that he was at home there: he embarked on long anecdotes, sipping at the wine, and after each sip redirecting his discourse to a different person. Only he never said anything to Katherine. When they brought her into the conversation he forced himself to take notice of her, blinking his cold blue eyes once or twice. It was not quite as if they had introduced the maid into the discussion, but all the same he seemed disconcerted. (*AGW*, 160)

Where John on grounds of his lower-class status is sometimes reduced to feeling like a waiter receiving a tip, Katherine on grounds of gender and nationality is reduced to feeling a little like a maid. Once again Larkin's emphasis is less upon the reasons for detachment than the enlarged perspectives it affords. The consistent message, that *outsiders see us more wholly than we see ourselves*, is as routinely suppressed by Larkin's critics as it is affirmed by his literary heirs from across the multicultural spectrum.

Concede this and the core meaning of the poem pivots from an expression of authorial scorn to a conscious calibration of the adjustable gap between insiders and outsiders and between inner and outer selves. The one person whose subjectivity we enter, the narrator, remains more enigmatic than those we observe from outside. This is as it should be: people are easier to categorize, easier to collapse into their roles, when we do not know them. (This perception was anticipated in *A Girl in Winter*, Katherine regretting her glimpse into Anstey's private life as it made it less easy to hate him.) If the narrator brings a hint of sarcasm to the 'loud' mothers, the smutty uncles or the 'girls / In parodies of fashion', it is the pantomime parts that are ridiculed not the actors temporarily performing them (about whom we are told next to nothing). Conversely, our inability to definitively assign the narrator's identity a sex, race, class or religion despite our access to and dependence upon it proves that the deeper reaches of our subjectivities are not defined by such determinants. The apparent chasm between observer and observed bespeaks the Woolfian truth that the stereotypical postures and habiliments of our outward conformity mask seething inner complexities.

Hence, the other characters do not act out prescribed roles because they are intellectual or social inferiors of the narrator but because they are participants in a marital ritual that, like all rites, requires performers to know and keep to the script.[68] The poem begins just as the couples relinquish the sameness of their ritual roles, with their identical responses ('Do you take this man to be your lawful wedded husband?' 'I do.'), and move towards differentiation. Any stereotyping is therefore reserved for the wedding parties who in one last ritual act wave the couples off on honeymoon. The newly-weds themselves have come from different places ('All down the line / Fresh couples climbed aboard'); have no sense of kinship ('none / Thought of the others'); and go off to such discrepant lives that their paths will not recross ('they would never meet'). Their sameness is momentary, 'this frail / Travelling coincidence'.

Our verse travelogue occupies the interim between the public ceremonial recently concluded and the private intimacy yet to come. As the poem's emotional centre of gravity moves from the aftermath of the one to an anticipation of the other, the narrator's position shifts from detachment to identification. We have already remarked how the early emphasis on 'I' and 'my' yields to a run of stanzas in which singular pronouns contend with plural, exclusive plurals (they, their) with inclusive (we, us), until by the last stanza the narrator's outsiderdom has been dissolved and 'we' predominates. This pronominal mutation is complemented by a narrative that, far from being omniscient, is subject to repeated double-takes and rethinks in a species of perceptual relativity. The narrator readily admits that 'At first, I didn't notice what a noise / The weddings made', misreading the 'whoops and skirls' as evidence of the high spirits of the porters. Discovering the mistake –

> I leant
> More promptly out next time, more curiously,
> And saw it all again in different terms

Observation becomes a self-monitoring, self-correcting process, every increase of definition in the visualization of the scene being a mark of the narrator's increasing engagement with the participants. If they accidently share each other's honeymoon journey, the narrator shares it too. The wedding guests they see 'Waving goodbye' from station platforms, the narrator also sees. If they all travel to London, so does the narrator. If 'their lives would all contain this hour', so would the narrator's life. What they witness from the carriage windows the narrator bears witness to:

> They watched the landscape, sitting side by side
> – An Odeon went past, a cooling tower,
> And someone running up to bowl

A narrative perspective which began by looking *at* the newly-weds now looks *with* them, reporting *for* them (the nearest the poem comes to a

Pentecostal gift of tongues). Whether a bachelor observing the newly married; a gay or lesbian observing heterosexuals; a bourgeois surprised by the emotional candour of a lower class; an ethnic outsider observing indigenous social customs; a celibate stirred by the honeymooners' imminent consummations; or a bespectacled Hull librarian travelling to London to meet his lover's latest husband, the narrator too is transformed, however momentarily, by 'all the power / That being changed can give'.

Conclusion

Hostile commentators routinely conflate Larkin with the one-dimensional protagonists of his poems of masculine excess even when the narrator's unlovely views are the very opposite of everything he stood for ('Books are a load of crap'). By contrast, very little attention has been paid to the extraordinary technical resource with which a poem like 'The Whitsun Weddings' de-essentializes narration as a vital step towards dramatizing the inwardness of the Other. Every self possesses the potential to understand, identify with or even *be* all other selves: in the words of the Roman playwright Terence, 'Homo sum; humani nil a me alienum puto' ('I am a man; I consider nothing human foreign to me').[69] If this is true, then we are all multiple personalities who suppress our universality in the pursuit of a chosen role in life and who periodically need reminding that *in each of us there is all of us*. The poem celebrates just such a moment, the narrator being reminded that it takes all sorts to make a self; that we discover in ourselves what others hide from us; and we recognize in others what we hide from ourselves. The reader comes to see that the outflow of feeling to the fellow passengers makes them an objective correlative to the narrator's own inner populousness. The poem's imaginary journey from Hull to London is also a progress from social division (Self and Other, observer and observed, outsiders and insiders) to an affirmation of our common humanity.

5
Radical Laughter: 'This Be The Verse'

Introduction

In his late writings and lectures on perjury, the French philosopher Jacques Derrida collapses the binary opposition between two classical tropes – 'the figure of the *acolyte*, which accompanies' and 'its negative, the *anacoluthon*, which does not accompany'. The term *acolyte* can be used as a synonym for *disciple* or *amanuensis*: 'according to both etymology and usage, the acolyte accompanies with an eye to following and assisting'. By contrast, *anacoluthon*, literally 'lacking sequence' in ancient Greek, is a rhetorical figure in which a sentence begun in one way continues or ends in another ('You know what I – but let's forget it!'). In seeking to demonstrate the interdependence of two terms, one of which means *to follow* and the other *to not follow*, Derrida describes his own relation to his 'masters' Freud and Heidegger as 'a relation of fidelity and betrayal; and I betray them because I want to be true to them'.[1]

The paradox Derrida identifies is this: to follow in the footsteps of a person one admires for originality is to betray that originality by being a replica rather than a prototype, an emulator where the role model was an instigator. To truly follow an original master one must still commit an act of betrayal, overthrowing his or her example in order to be comparably *sui generis*. Either way, one's pledge of loyalty, one's vow to follow, is simultaneously an act of perjury, a refusal to follow: 'So that may be the paradox in the twin concepts of *acoluthia* and anacoluthon. You have to betray in order to be truthful.'[2] Philip Larkin's vaunted admiration for the poetry of Thomas Hardy involves just this sort of complexity, this fidelity and betrayal.

Larkin and Hardy

To accuse Larkin of betraying Hardy may seem perverse when his essays offer such unqualified support against all critical detractors:

> Perhaps the oddest thing about contemporary Hardy criticism [...] is the way in which its mediocre perpetrators consider themselves justified in

patronizing Hardy's poems. Weber, for instance, makes very merry with the early poems [...] Morrell, too, parrots the usual stuff about 'the number of Hardy's poems meriting serious attention is not large in relation to the bulk of his collected verse'. To these two gentlemen (and also to Samuel Hynes, author of *The Pattern of Hardy's Poetry*) may I trumpet the assurance that one reader at least would not wish Hardy's *Collected Poems* a single page shorter, and regards it as many times over the best body of poetic work this century has to show? (*RW*, 173–4)

Larkin's editing of *The Oxford Book of Twentieth-Century English Verse* (1973) was widely regarded as an act of homage to the old master. The dismay with which the volume was greeted – Donald Davie described himself 'reeling aghast from page after page' – arose from the widespread perception that modernists had been demoted, cosmopolites expelled to facilitate a return of the native, and Hardy promoted above his station.[3] A chorus of commentators pointed out that where Eliot was allocated only 9 poems, Hardy got 27, Kipling 13, Betjeman 12, Graves 11, Edward Thomas 9, Housman and De la Mare 8 apiece.

As we shall see in a moment, this widespread perception was grossly distorted: the immediate point to register is that by allocating Hardy many more poems than anyone else in an apparently anti-modernist context, Larkin unintentionally ensured that their names would thereafter be linked as agents of reaction. In the very year of the anthology, Davie's monograph *Thomas Hardy and British Poetry* proposed that 'Hardy's engaging modesty and his decent liberalism represented a crucial selling short of the poetic vocation, for himself and for his successors.' Larkin, too, as principal successor, 'sells off a great deal of the inherited estate' to offer a 'poetry of lowered sights and patiently diminished expectations'.[4] Fifteen years later, introducing 'Some Younger Poets' in *The New British Poetry, 1968–88*, Ken Edwards bemoaned the fact that 'no longer does the establishment revile modernism in poetry; it simply ignores it. The models to follow once again are Hardy and Larkin.'[5] This orthodoxy was still being peddled in 2004 when Randall Stevenson declared in *The Last of England?*: 'Hardy's wan wistfulness and brooding regret for the past added to his appeal for Movement writers, often [...] backward-looking in theme as well as style.'[6]

One way we might broach the unfairness of the foregoing is by reminding ourselves of the 40-year-old status quo at the time of Larkin's anthological intervention. In his polemical study *New Bearings in English Poetry* (1932), the influential Cambridge critic F.R. Leavis found only Hopkins, Eliot and Pound worthy of individual chapters. Four years later, in *The Faber Book of Modern Verse* (1936), Michael Roberts declared the triumph of Hopkins, Yeats, Pound, Eliot, Stevens, Hart Crane, Auden and Dylan Thomas. Equally great but less obviously experimental poets like Hardy, Housman, Kipling, Edward Thomas and Frost were expunged from the record. When Donald

Hall revised the anthology in 1965 he added poets old (William Carlos Williams, Hugh MacDiarmid, David Jones) and new (Charles Olson, John Berryman, Robert Lowell, Thom Gunn, Ted Hughes, Sylvia Plath, Geoffrey Hill) but maintained the embargo on Hardy, Frost, Edward Thomas and company. In his introduction Hall fretfully wondered 'Should I omit Philip Larkin because he is not "modern"?'[7]

On the face of it, Larkin's Oxford anthology was an attempt to redress the balance by presenting modernism as a foreign import that temporarily derailed an older, more metrically regular, more *English* tradition which extended back into the previous century and which was subsequently revived by the likes of John Betjeman ('the first thing to realize about Betjeman as a writer of verse is that he is a poet for whom the modern poetic revolution has simply not taken place'). In an interview with Thwaite a decade after its publication, Larkin explained that his research for the anthology was consciously undertaken with just this agenda:

> I had in mind a notion that there might have been what I'll call, for want of a better phrase, an English tradition coming from the nineteenth century with people like Hardy, which was interrupted by the Great War, when many English poets were killed off, and partly by the really tremendous impact of Yeats, whom I think of as Celtic, and Eliot, whom I think of as American. And I wondered whether, if one looked for them, there hadn't been some quite good poems which had become unfashionable which had never been dug up again and looked at. I certainly had this in mind when reading. (*FR*, 96)

Had Larkin succeeded in this plan, Hardy might have appeared as captain of the home team in the battle against the international brigade; but as Larkin candidly admitted in the same interview with Thwaite, not only did the 'English line' fail to provide the hoped-for neglected masterpieces, its deficiencies obliged him to acknowledge, once and for all, the superiority of the modernists: 'the worst thing about the Georgians as a class was, I am afraid, what has been said by so many people: that their language was stale. It was Eliot and Yeats, and perhaps even Pound, who sharpened up the language' (*FR*, 97). If we return to the anthology with this reluctant admission in mind and count not the poems but the pages, the actual space allocated, these are the poets best represented in the anthology: Eliot with 29 pages; Hardy and Auden with 24 each; Yeats, 21; Kipling, 19; Betjeman, 18; Basil Bunting, 11; Dylan Thomas, 10 and a half; Lawrence, 10; MacNeice, 9. Who would guess from the reception of anti-Movement, pro-modernist jeers and catcalls that this was a volume which gave pride of place to Eliot; which forced Hardy into the company of Eliot, Yeats and Auden as the only four poets to merit over 20 pages apiece; and which allocated a second-generation modernist like Bunting more space than Housman and Edward Thomas combined?

Larkin's recognition that the native tradition had gone 'stale' and that any revival of it must benefit from the achievements of the modernists in sharpening up the poetic medium greatly complicates his relation to Hardy, obliging him to both use and abuse, honour and desecrate his hero's *oeuvre*. Only Jean Hartley has acknowledged this element of vandalism on Larkin's part and its fixation upon obscene diction. In her memoir *Philip Larkin, the Marvell Press and Me*, Jean recounts a trip she and her husband George made with the poet shortly after they had published his first great book, *The Less Deceived*:

> On the way back Philip entertained us with shockingly ribald parodies of great poets. One of his best was a version of Hardy's 'Afterwards' which listed all sorts of dubious activities and retained the punchline 'He was a man who used to notice such things'.[8]

Jean later remarked that 'Such recitals were accompanied by appropriate lewd and lascivious facial expressions.'[9] It is possible that the Hardy parody was not Larkin's own but a recycling of the one Kingsley Amis sent him a decade earlier:

> When the Gents' has received my last consignment of turds,
> And they piss in the bogs where an odour of vomit clings,
> Will they say, as they scan the wall for dirty words,
> 'He was a man who used to notice such things'?
>
> When the village idiot sits on the farmyard gate,
> And croons to himself in the failing evening light,
> Will he say, as he idly begins to masturbate,
> 'To him this must have been a familiar sight'?
>
> In June, when a couple of schoolboys, arm in arm,
> Pass on their way to some sodomy on the lawn,
> One may say, 'He strove that such innocent creatures
>   should come to no harm,
> But he could do little to them, and now he is gone.'
>
> When a young lady lies on the green in her underwear,
> With a young chap pulling her knickers below her knees,
> Will she say, as he starts to rip off her brassiere,
> 'He was one who had an eye for such mysteries'?
>
> Will they say, when two schoolgirls are sucking each other's cunts,
> And their bottoms vibrate as if they were mounted on springs,
> And the air is filled with squelchings and high-pitched grunts,
> 'He hears it not now, but used to notice such things'?[10]

However, we know that Larkin was himself capable of the Rabelaisian excess entailed to such acts of literary vandalism. As a teenage student at Oxford he sent Jim Sutton 'the latest work of the brilliant new Post-Masturbationist Poet Shaggerybox McPhallus', a parody of Keats's 'La Belle Dame Sans Merci' intoning 'And this is why I shag alone / Ere half my creeping days are done' (*TCP*, 195). Two decades later, Andrew Motion notes, Larkin and his long-term, long-distance companion Monica Jones

> began systematically defacing a copy of Iris Murdoch's novel *The Flight from the Enchanter* (1956), taking it in turns to interpolate salacious remarks and corrupt the text. Many apparently innocent sentences are merely underlined ('Today it seemed likely to be especially hard'). Many more are altered ('Her lips were parted and he had never seen her eyes so wide open' becomes 'Her legs were parted and he had never seen her cunt so wide open'). Many of the numbered chapter-headings are changed ('Ten' is assimilated into 'I Fuck My STENographer'). Even the list of books by the same author is changed to include 'UNDER THE NETther Garments'. They continued this precise but childishly naughty game for years, doodling through long evenings and wet weekends, and finally producing a bizarrely sustained performance: nearly 300 pages, every one altered to create a stream of filth, farce and clumping ironies.[11]

As Larkin fell out of love with Keats and Murdoch but not Hardy, the motivations for defacement must differ. Identifying what there is in Hardy's work, especially the poetry, that invited such ribald satire will help us distinguish Larkin's practice from his and set the agenda for the present chapter.

Cultural Tourette's

Although Hardy began writing poems as early as 1865, before becoming a novelist, he only devoted himself wholeheartedly to verse after abandoning prose fiction in 1897. As he did not die until 1928, his poetic *oeuvre* is preponderantly twentieth century. For all the modernity of his attitudes and ideas, that long Victorian apprenticeship is palpable in his poetic registers, the decorum governing permissible and impermissible utterance. Indeed, it might be claimed that Hardy's inability to shake off Victorian prudery and repression – entirely understandable when one remembers he was in his sixties when in 1901 the Queen died – creates intolerable pressures in his prosody and diction. The result is a socially constituted equivalent to the neuropsychiatric disorder known as Tourette's syndrome. This condition is characterized by multiple physical (motor) and vocal (phonic) tics, the best known of which is the exclamation of obscene words or socially inappropriate and derogatory remarks (coprolalia). Whatever their forms, these tics 'occur intermittently and unpredictably out of a background of normal motor activity' and have the appearance of 'normal behaviours gone wrong'. Erratic, involuntary and repetitive, they share features with obsessive-compulsive disorder.[12]

In Hardy's case the linguistic disorder strongly resembles coprolalia, the prevailing decorum of the *Collected Poems* being spasmodically interrupted by profanities regarding all manner of bodily functions, sexual acts and repressed desires. Individual cases might be explained as innocent poems having debased meanings imposed upon them by a later, coarser society or by a subsequent lexical shift as when the word *gay* took on a homosexual meaning. Other obscenities might be harnessed to the specific poem's purport in a manner that may be construed as complementary, even if entirely unintentional. But most instances are disruptive rather than harmonious, 'normal behaviours gone wrong'. Their effect is to subject poem after poem, whether grave or occasional, personal or imaginative, to a chorus of sniggers.

The concept of authorial intentionality is of limited utility in explicating these textual eruptions. The voyeurism of 'The Bride-Night Fire' must be deliberate in that the poem was published in several versions of varying degrees of explicitness according to context. 'Her form in these cold mildewed tatters he views' finally mutated into

> Her cwold little figure half-naked he views
> Played about by the frolicsome breeze,
> Her light-tripping totties[13]

Cwold is risible; *totties*, fatal. However deliberate, the result is uncomfortably akin to the gloriously smutty ditties of Kenneth Williams's mock folk singer Rambling Syd Rumpo.[14] The diction may be intentional, the laughter it elicits is not. Something similar happens in a poem as considerable as 'After a Journey' when Hardy changed 'And the unseen waters' soliloquies awe me' to 'And the unseen waters' ejaculations awe me'.[15] The prevailing mood of romantic retrospection permits a hint of the erotic, but the sexual associations of the word *ejaculation* seem far too thickly spermatic for the context. Was the innuendo intended but misjudged? Or is this a case of textual Tourette's?

Other cases seem entirely gratuitous. In combination, they range across a polymorphously perverse spectrum: female orgasm ('In the Night She Came'); male orgasm ('And consummation comes, and jars two hemispheres'); heterosexual coupling –

> She quickened her feet, and met him where
> They had predesigned:
> And they clasped, and mounted

– masturbation ('I lay in my bed and fiddled'); heterosexual manual sex ('She to Him': 'I grasp thy amplitudes'); homosexual coupling ('I lay me down / Upon the heated sod'); homosexual nostalgia ('Who now remembers Almack's balls [...] Who now remembers gay Cremone?'); exhibitionism –

> You were all of a sudden gone
> Before I had thought thereon,
> Or noticed your trunks were down.

– bestiality ('I mounted a steed'); and necrophilia ('Soon would be growing / Green blades from her mound').[16]

Once this irregular eruption of innuendo is admitted its effects are everywhere observable, totally innocuous lines lending themselves to the leering delivery of a Benny Hill sketch: 'I felt her tether'; the 'sedges were horny'; 'Gone is she, scorning my bough!' 'Last Words to a Dumb Friend' is an elegy for a pet cat:

> Housemate, I can think you still
> Bounding to the window-sill,
> Over which I vaguely see
> Your small mound beneath the tree[17]

The mound that elsewhere inappropriately puns on the female sex organ, the *mons veneris*, here inappositely puns on a pile of feline excrement. The bathos is entirely destructive.

The words *ejaculation, come, sod, balls, totties, mound* and *trunks* had acquired scurrilous meanings well before Hardy penned the poems in question. Even the word *gay* had a decidedly salacious history, as explained in John Ayto's dictionary of *Twentieth Century Words*:

> The adjective had been used to mean 'sexually dissolute' since the 17th century, and by the early 19th century it was being applied to people earning a living by prostitution. It is possible that male prostitutes catering to homosexual men provided the conduit through which it passed from 'living by prostitution' to 'homosexual'. Another element in the equation may be *gaycat*, US hobos' slang for a tramp's companion, usually a young boy, and often his catamite; this is first recorded about the turn of the 20th century, but its origins are unknown. An earlier clue still is a reported 1868 song called 'The Gay Young Clerk in the Dry Goods Store' by the US female impersonator Will S. Hays.[18]

Poets are usually credited with an extreme sensitivity to the resonances of words. Hardy's apparent ineptness regarding sexual innuendo cannot be simply wished away. It needs to be acknowledged and explained. The author is of little help here, with his blanket denials of responsibility and transferral of blame to the readership: 'How strange that one may write a book without knowing what one puts into it – or rather, the reader reads into it'; and, in response to adverse reviews of *Jude the Obscure*, 'What foul cess-pits some men's minds must be, and what a Night-cart would be required to empty them.'[19]

The only way to salvage such lexical disjunction for the concept of authorial intentionality is by invoking a two-tier model of the mind as in the psychoanalytical distinction between *ego* and *id*. Those Latinate terms were introduced by Freud's English translator James Strachey. In Freud's homely German the conscious is given as 'the I' (*das ich*) and the unconscious as 'the not-I' (*das nicht-ich*).[20] This schizophrenic model of the mind in which the intentions of the conscious self are subverted from within by another self of whose agendas one is (by definition) unconscious, might then be applied to the two lexical regimes of Hardy's conflicted poetry. The psychoanalytical concept of *parapraxis*, first systematically explored in Freud's *The Psychopathology of Everyday Life* (1901), might be pressed into service here. This is the concept popularly known as 'the Freudian slip', though Freud no more used that term than he did *parapraxis*, Strachey's Hellenic translation of the German word for 'misperformance'. Freud explained the concept as follows:

> In the same way that psychoanalysis makes use of dream interpretation, it also profits by the study of the numerous little slips and mistakes which people make – symptomatic actions, as they are called [...] I have pointed out that these phenomena are not accidental, that they have a meaning and can be interpreted, and that one is justified in inferring from them the presence of restrained or repressed intentions.[21]

Biographical essentialists might encapsulate this analysis in the formula that Hardy is a deeply repressed man whose seething unconscious motivations manifest themselves in uncontrolled and therefore inutile outblurts and eructations.

My own preference is for a text-centred alternative to this author-centred formula – one that depends less on unverifiable guesses about Hardy's unconscious mind and more on the ascertainable truth that his poetry was produced in the violent historical transition from one regulative regime to another. A Victorian textual economy, with its inherent linguistic and libidinal repressions, struggles to contain an emerging modernist economy with a more transgressive approach to every regulative ideal. For instance, the attempt to use *ejaculation* in its exclamatory sense, as though one could simply repress its equally common usage as 'an emission of sperm', was not confined to Hardy. The same unintentional obscenity riots through such nineteenth-century novels as Charles Dickens's *Oliver Twist*, where the narrator reports that 'The cook and housemaid simultaneously ejaculated', or Charles Reade's *The Cloister and the Hearth*, where we learn that 'Gerald's eloquence was confined to ejaculating and gazing', or George Meredith's *Diana of the Crossways*, where 'Sir Lukin ejaculated on the merits of Diana Warwick'. When Ford Madox Ford uses the word several times in a passage of salacious dialogue from his 1924 classic *Some Do Not* ... the effect is of a modernist knowingness entirely lacking from Hardy, Dickens or Reade:

> 'If Budapest's the place for girls you say it is, old pal, with the Turkish baths and all, we'll paint the old town red all right next month', and he winked at Tietjens [...] 'Not [...] that I don't love my old woman. She's all right. And then there's Gertie. 'Ot stuff, but the real thing. But I say a man wants ...' He ejaculated, 'Oh!'[22]

Larkin's occasional writings support the view that what we are discussing is a cultural pathology rather than an authorial neurosis, a discursive unconscious that evidences in texts by diverse authors of unlike temperaments – thereby suggesting that all are victims of a larger socio-sexual oppression. His reviews of Victorian, Edwardian and Georgian writers like Tennyson, Fitzgerald, Housman and Owen repeatedly refer the emotionally obscure in their works to sexual impulses consciously or unconsciously repressed. Larkin named Christina Rossetti alongside Hardy as one of his 12 poetic 'exemplars' (*RW*, 86). Her most famous poem, 'Goblin Market', has often passed as a children's poem; yet the modern reader is struck by a sexuality the more intense for being hidden from its devout and virginal author. Larkin is also surprisingly hospitable to Rebecca Patterson's claim that the 'cryptic explosiveness' of Emily Dickinson's poetry derives from submerged lesbian proclivities (*RW*, 193). Housman's enigmatic love lyrics are clearly historically specific: his love for Moses Jackson 'was not only unrequited but criminal' (*FR*, 341). Larkin is also undeceived by heterosexual philanderers like H.G. Wells whose message of a Free Love 'by which the nineteenth-century taboos and restrictions and restraints on relations between men and women were to be wiped out' was dependent upon 'the most Victorian of concepts, the wife required to be chaste, supportive and tolerant of the husband's infidelities' (*FR*, 354). The sexual and verbal garrulity of the one is predicated upon the silencing of the other. The expression/repression, manifest/latent model has not been overthrown, simply reconfigured. Larkin's answer, as we shall see, was to adopt a policy of 'better blatant than latent'. By making explicit, even graphic, the improprieties of Hardy's poems, Larkin makes the latter's unintended laughter purposive; the reader laughs *with* the poem rather than *at* it.

Larkin, Hardy and intertextuality

To propose that Larkin in some way *rewrites* Hardy is to go against a critical consensus which defines both as anti-modernist by virtue of their eschewal of citation. W.E. Williams introduced his *Thomas Hardy: A Selection of Poems* (1960) by defining Hardy's *oeuvre* as uniquely free from influence or echo:

> One of the favourite occupations of a certain kind of scholar is to detect 'influences' revealed by a writer's work, to ferret out the clues which show how and where he assimilated other styles into his own. As C. Day Lewis has so aptly said: 'Influence-spotters don't have a very happy time with him'. Hardy's poems, like his novels, derive from his own nature, experience, and integrity, and it is this characteristic which makes his testimony so personal and so moving.[23]

As we have seen, Tolley is equally adamant that 'there is little use of intertextuality (conscious or unconscious) in Larkin's work: the reference to other literatures as a dimension of understanding [...] was anathema to him'. Less adamantine critics maintain the Tolley position as applied to Larkin's relation to Hardy. S.W. Dawson's essay 'On Re-Reading *The Less Deceived*' beautifully conveys the elusive but recurrent echoes of the Metaphysicals in such early Larkin masterpieces as 'Lines on a Young Lady's Photograph Album', only to conclude:

> Hardy was the writer whom, as novelist and poet, Larkin most admired, and it is easy to see why. The confrontation of undramatic suffering, the refusal of facile consolation, the determination as a poet to be himself without concern for literary fashion, these and many other qualities constitute a link between them. Yet, speaking for myself, and as an admirer of Hardy's poetry in particular, I can never hear Hardy behind Larkin's lines, as I can Donne or Marvell.[24]

Hardy is not allusive, say Williams and Day Lewis. Larkin is not allusive, says Tolley. Even if Larkin *is* allusive, says Dawson, he does not allude to Hardy.

This is an orthodoxy that in the present writer's opinion cannot withstand so much as a glance at the contents pages of the two poets, their respective titles suggesting musical as well as temperamental affinity. Consider Hardy's 'Prologue' (Larkin's 'Prologue'), 'First Sight of Her and After' ('First Sight'), 'On a Midsummer's Eve' ('Midsummer Night'), 'Memory and I' ('I Remember, I Remember'), 'Going and Staying' ('Arrivals, Departures'), 'The Going' ('Going'), 'On the Departure Platform' ('One man walking a deserted platform'), 'At the Railway Station, Upway' ('Autobiography at an Air-Station'), 'Departure' ('Poetry of Departures'), 'She, I, and They' ('Mother, Summer, I'), 'Winter Night in Woodland' ('Winter Nocturne'), 'The Man Who Forgot' ('Forget What Did'), 'He Resolves to Say No More' ('The Poet's Last Poem') and 'Epilogue' ('Epilogue').

As with the titles, so with the poems, the whole or a significant portion of many Larkin pieces invoking a Hardy prototype in a one-for-one relation. The first two verses of 'In Sherborne Abbey' lurk behind the arras of 'An Arundel Tomb'. 'Skin' is shadowed by Hardy's 'I Look Into My Glass' ('I look into my glass, / And view my wasting skin'). 'The Oxen', which Larkin included in his Oxford anthology, underwrites the close of 'Climbing the hill within the deafening wind'. As many commentators have remarked, the celebrated ending of 'Toads Revisited' ('Give me your arm, old toad; / Help me down Cemetery Road') is modelled on the first of Hardy's 1866 'She, to Him' sequence ('Will you not grant to old affection's claim / The hand of friendship down Life's sunless hill?') – a poem Larkin included in his anthology and roundly praised in interview. Elsewhere, 'The Selfsame Song' meditates on birds in a manner akin to Larkin's 'The Trees', the last line of which ('Begin afresh, afresh, afresh') was anticipated by Hardy's 'Song to an Old Burden' ('Shall I then joy anew, anew, anew').[25]

However adaptive, most of these parallels are affirmative; more a case of fidelity than betrayal – though even here there is an element of Derridean perjury in Larkin's repeated citing of a poet he praises for avoiding citation. If Larkin's obscenities are read against Hardy's parapraxes, on the other hand, the candour of the modern may be seen as a reproach to Victorian cultural Tourette's. The accidental testicular pun of 'Almack's balls' becomes the 'tuberous cock and balls' of 'Sunny Prestatyn'.[26] Hardy's 'totties' becomes Larkin's 'tits' ('Next, Please'). The presumably unintended masturbation motif of 'In the Small Hours' ('I lay in my bed and fiddled') translates into the blatant 'wanking at ten past three' of Larkin's 'Love Again'. The implied intercourse of 'The Dame of Athenhall' ('they clasped, and mounted') is replaced by the utterly explicit opening of 'High Windows' ('he's fucking her and she's / Taking pills or wearing a diaphragm'). The bathetic excrementalism of 'Last Words to a Dumb Friend' becomes the sustained conceit of 'The Life with a Hole in it', from the title's invocation of the advertising slogan for polo mints, a popular digestive, to the line 'the shit in the shuttered château' with its mock declension of a defecatory verb (shit-shut-shat). While the unintentionally comical undressing of 'Without Ceremony' ('your trunks were down') is rendered inept by Larkin's squib 'Administration' with its frankly salacious manager's-eye-view that the 'girls I tell to pull their socks up / Are those whose pants I most want to pull down'. In his hands, twentieth-century obscenity is the nineteenth century's cultural unconscious made manifest.

Larkin's theory of humour

One of the problems with the immediately foregoing argument is that it appears to endorse a sharp distinction between those serious poems in which Larkin cites Hardy approvingly and those coarsely comical poems in which Larkin's resort to obscenity can be read as a reproach to Hardy's fumbled self-censorship. Not only does this sharp demarcation misrepresent the intermesh of fidelity and betrayal in all Larkin's Hardy allusions, it also makes for a separation of gravity and levity which is the very negation of his aesthetic. The undermining of binary oppositions was central to Larkin's project and he used his essays, reviews and interviews to adumbrate the proposition that humour was not an escape from seriousness but a means of attaining it. Reviewing *The New Oxford Book of Light Verse* (1978), edited by his friend Kingsley Amis, Larkin, on precisely these grounds, compared it unfavourably with its 1938 predecessor selected by W.H. Auden. Quoting the following from Auden's introduction –

> Light verse can be serious. It has only come to mean vers de société, triolets, smoke-room limericks, because, under the social conditions that produced the Romantic Revival, and which have persisted, more or less, ever since, it has only been in trivial matters that poets have felt in sufficient intimacy with their audience to be able to forget themselves and their singing-robes.

– Larkin comments: 'A poetic situation made up of singing-robes on the one hand and A.A. Milne on the other [...] was plainly intolerable to him, and the original *Oxford Book of Light Verse* set out to undermine such a stultifying dichotomy once for all' (*FR*, 277–8). After lambasting his friend for deliberately reviving this very dichotomy, Larkin demonstrates his contempt for the meretricious jokiness of his selections:

> even Amis cannot reconcile me to the Victorian habit of doing a joke to death, as in Hood's 'Faithless Nelly Gray' (puns), 'Mr and Mrs Vite's Journey' (obsolete Cockney trick of pronouncing w as v), and 'Hans Breitmann's Barty' (Dutchmen talking funny). Then there are Thackeray's excruciating 'Little Billee', Stevenson's pointless 'Not I', and other painful reminders of what we have long outgrown [...] it is really altogether too late in the day to be asked to find them amusing. (*FR*, 280)

Though it has never been properly acknowledged as such, this review article has claims to be a major statement of Larkin's aesthetic.

Elsewhere this theoretical position was supplemented by praise for those who demonstrate that there are levels of seriousness which only humour can attain: William Barnes (who is praised for eliciting the response 'I laughed and cried by turns'); Ogden Nash (one of 'those humorists who make you laugh at things not because they are funny but because laughing at them makes it easier to stand them – which is, I suppose, the same as calling him a sort of honorary serious writer after all'); Stevie Smith ('the silliness was part of the seriousness'); John Betjeman ('He is rather like the fool that speaks the truth through jokes'); and Amis himself (his style 'will exasperate only those who cannot see when a poem is being funny and serious simultaneously') (*RW*, 149, 135, 155; *FR*, 29, 162).

Larkin also painstakingly reminded interlocutors of the indivisibility of laughter and gravity in his own work. When the *Observer* interviewer Miriam Gross asked if the 'unhappiness' of Larkin's poetry 'is really a fair impression of the way you see life', he instantly corrected: 'Actually, I like to think of myself as quite funny, and I hope this comes through in my writing' (*RW*, 47). Conversely, when John Haffenden asked if 'Naturally the Foundation will Bear Your Expenses' is 'just a funny poem in which the speaker is the butt of the joke', Larkin rejoined: 'It's both funny and serious. The speaker's a shit. That's always serious' (*FR*, 58).

Despite his patient exposition of this approach, critics have largely conspired to ignore the humour in the interests of presenting Larkin as the High Priest of Miserabilism.[27] Eric Homberger dubbed him 'the saddest heart in the post-war supermarket'. Stan Smith deplored his 'Housmanish world-weariness'. While Terry Eagleton opened his *J'accuse* television programme by declaring that 'few poets of his stature have been so remorselessly concerned to negate rather than affirm, diminish rather than enhance'. (Christopher Hitchens marvellously quipped: 'I had not before understood that Professor Eagleton believed in poetry as uplift.')[28] One can only surmise that none of these commentators has attended such theatrical presentations of Larkin's works as those starring Alan Bates, Patrick Garland, Alan Bennett, Oliver Ford Davies or Tom Courtenay – occasions on which a sense of tragic grandeur is accompanied by incessant laughter – like Aeschylus crossed with Eric Morecambe. Indeed, it might be claimed, with only a little exaggeration, that Larkin pursues the potential for *a light verse that is not light* to the point where the Aristotelian distinction between tragedy and comedy is collapsed. (Even within classical theory, we remember, Plato ends *The Symposium* with Aristophanes and Socrates speculating that comedy and tragedy had common origins.)

As so often, it is Eliot who most closely approximates the Larkin position: writing of Marvell and the Metaphysical poets he detected an 'alliance of levity and seriousness (by which the seriousness is intensified)'.[29] Larkin's levity sometimes takes the forms Eliot admired in the Metaphysicals: wit, word play, satire, irony. However, he was also adept at drollery, self-deprecation, comedy of manners and scatology. The particular mode of humour I wish to explore here is that which induces an involuntary sneeze of derisive laughter, a paroxysm of deconstructive contempt. In Larkin's practice this is intimately connected to his use of obscenity.

This conjunction is not unique to Larkin. In Freudian theory the joke and the obscenity are alike aggressive venting mechanisms which facilitate the expression of repressed anti-social impulses and behaviours. Although the relief afforded the audient by a joke takes the form of laughter while the relief afforded by an obscenity is experienced as shock, both permit psychic release by allowing the unconscious a momentary jailbreak from conscious taboos. At the point of release, both express an anarchistic desire to transcend restraint, to revel in the spontaneous, to flout authorities which restrain creativity – in short, to negate the prevailing moral order. Both, therefore, have considerable potential for being deployed in works of literature antagonistic to hegemonic cultural values. This may be particularly so where the prevailing order is patriarchal. Freud speaks of the comic as a sudden regaining of 'the lost laughter of childhood' and obscenity as an infantile response to the necessary inhibitions of adulthood. The risk in both cases is that their 'liberating' function comes at the price of a regression to the pre-Oedipal. As we shall now see, Larkin uses the de-inhibitive energies of profane humour to a darker purpose: not to revert to a puerile world of 'fun' as, say, in the slapstick comedies of the Keystone Kops, the Marx Brothers, Laurel and Hardy, Abbott and Costello, the Three Stooges or Mel Brooks; but to oblige the reader to confront realities the dominant 'grown-up' culture palliates or denies.[30] For him, ideals are greater enemies of truth than lies; a paroxysm of scoffing laughter the perfect antidote.

'This Be The Verse': Stevenson and Hardy

It is a token of Larkin's admiration that he sometimes used a Hardy allusion to modify, challenge or overturn a citation from another author incorporated earlier in the same poem. Sir Philip Sidney's *Astrophel and Stella* supplies the title of 'Sad Steps'. Initially Larkin follows his illustrious predecessor in apostrophizing the moon as romantic symbol only to then deflate this tradition in the spirit of Hardy's 'Shut Out That Moon' and 'I Looked Up From My Writing'. Similarly, 'The Mower' invokes four poems of that name by Marvell but draws its tone and substance from the third verse of Hardy's 'Afterwards'. The same obtains with our specimen poem, 'This Be The Verse', which plucks its title from Robert Louis Stevenson's 'Requiem' only to savagely undercut that sentimental elegy with lines modelled on Hardy's 'Epitaph for a Pessimist' (*CP*, 180; *TCP*, 88).[31] In all such cases, Hardy's manner and music are administered as 'correctives' to the more inflated rhetoric of earlier masters. At the same time, this fidelity involves betrayal, the incorporation of Hardy allusions in poems conducted through a contention of citations, a tessellation of disjunct quotes, having much more in common with modernist aesthetics than with the values Larkin attributed to his own and to Hardy's works ('Poems don't come from other poems, they come from being oneself in life' (*FR*, 54)).

In the first stanza of Stevenson's 'Requiem' the narrator issues instructions for his epitaph, while in the italicized lines of the second he quotes what was then engraved on his headstone:

> Under the wide and starry sky
>   Dig the grave and let me lie:
> Glad did I live and gladly die,
>   And I laid me down with a will.

> This be the verse you grave for me:
> *Here he lies where he long'd to be;*
> *Home is the sailor, home from the sea,*
> *And the hunter home from the hill.*[32]

The word 'home' is used three times in those three incised lines, suggesting a return to origins after the peregrinations of life (most evident in the sailor motif). This may denote a literal return to the cradle of the family, a going back to *homefolks* in the ancestral *homestead*. However, the fact that there is no mention of kith or kin and that the narrator asks to be buried 'Under the wide and starry sky' rather than in the family plot may work against this idea (without cancelling it). Alternatively, the repetition of 'home' may carry ethnic, regional or patriotic associations, signifying a return to one's *home ground* or national *homeland*. Equally, the wording of the opening verse may suggest a return to Mother Nature, an acceptance of death as a vital part of the natural life cycle. The line 'Glad did I live and gladly die' may point a moral: that those who embrace life's delights are more readily reconciled to mortality; to live well is to die well. This hint of moral earnestness may in turn suggest that the narrator's insouciance is underwritten by religious conviction: perhaps the glad acceptance of death betokens a *homecoming* to God, a return to the bosom of Abraham. Certainly, by the time of the poem's composition the word *requiem*, signifying a Catholic mass for the repose of the souls of the dead, had been so popularized by the musical settings of Mozart, Berlioz, Verdi, Brahms, Fauré and Dvořák that a cosmopolitan artist like Stevenson could hardly be using the title innocently. The clincher is the grammatical resort to the past tense: the entire poem is spoken posthumously, the narrator looking back on his life and his death from an afterlife of some vivacity. It is this cluster of ideas pertaining to family, nation, ethnicity, God and eternity, all crystallized around the concept of belonging, or *at-homeness*, that Larkin invokes in his title, 'This Be The Verse', and then explodes via the agency of Hardy.

The generic link between the Stevenson and Hardy intertexts is that both are epitaphs with a shared address to the meaning of death. The Hardy allusion comes in the last stanza of 'This Be The Verse', which appears to equate the desire for self-extinction with an eschewal of reproduction –

> Man hands on misery to man.
> It deepens like a coastal shelf.
> Get out as early as you can,
> And don't have any kids yourself.

in a manner modelled on 'Epitaph for Pessimist':

> I'm Smith of Stoke, aged sixty odd,
> I've lived without a dame

> From youth-time on; and would to God
> My dad had done the same.[33]

The Hardy is a perfect foil for the Stevenson, the comically exaggerated pessimism of the one versus the relentless optimism of the other. Where Stevenson repeats the word 'home', punning on derivatives like *homecoming*, *homestead* and *homeland*, Hardy approximates the post-Freudian view that home is not one's refuge from the ills of the world but the place where one first experiences them. This difference might be encapsulated in the dramatically opposed meanings of the word *homesickness*: in Stevenson's poem, a profound nostalgia for origins; in the Hardy, a nausea at the very thought of one's original habitation (leading directly to Larkin's 'We all hate home' (*CP*, 85; *TCP*, 39)).

Undergirding the dichotomy between optimism and pessimism, belonging and alienation, is the deeper religious schism. Stevenson's narrator lived a happy life and died a happy death in the fond expectation, subsequently fulfilled, of a glad afterlife. Hardy's narrator, by contrast, has led a sunless existence with no prospect of anything better in what remains of his time on earth and no expectation of redemption beyond the grave. His invocation of the deity ('and would to God') reads as a formulaic phrase, like 'God knows how long' in 'Church Going', rather than an earnest of belief; the poem deriving a grim humour from his paradoxical longing for God to save him from God's creation! However curmudgeonly and self-thwarting, Smith of Stoke's comically unremitting pessimism has the effect of making Stevenson's narrator seem spiritually complacent.

Yet the Hardy was insufficient to Larkin's purpose, such that he felt the need to interpose two verses of his own (betrayal as well as fidelity) between the Stevensonian title and the Hardyesque denouement. In the process he makes the argument more explosive by ratcheting up the humour and the obscenity. A possible rationale for this intervention may be found in the character of Smith of Stoke whose world-view seems less a matter of philosophical pessimism than of misanthropy or, more precisely, misogyny. Religiously self-deluding, Stevenson's narrator attains a level of happiness which may well be found preferable to Smith's 'I-wish-I'd-never-been-born' miserabilism. The only clue Smith vouchsafes for his negativity is the hint of gynophobia in his insistent shunning of dames. Larkin was familiar with 'the psychologists' assertion that an obsession with death conceals a fear of sex' (*RW*, 194), though Hardy's diffidence leaves unclear if his is a portrait of a stalled adolescent, a 60-year-old man afraid of the primal drama of sexual intercourse. Either way, the unmentionable subject of sex in Hardy becomes the shockingly blatant opening of the Larkin, perhaps English literature's rudest since Subtle's 'I fart at thee' at the start of Ben Jonson's *The Alchemist* (1610):

> They fuck you up, your mum and dad.
> They may not mean to, but they do.

> They fill you with the faults they had
> And add some extra, just for you.

In shifting the emphasis from Smith's misogyny (the personalized 'dad' paired with the non-relational 'dame' rather than a personalized 'mum') towards a position where both parents are culpable ('They fuck you up, *your mum and dad*'), Larkin completely reorientates the argument. What began as a study in masculine nihilism becomes a devastating assault upon family pieties of the sort that used to be versified in school primers and can still be found in Mother's and Father's Day cards. It is, then, a reply to, or defacement of, some such triteness as the following:

> They buck you up, your mum and dad.
> They do not have to, but they do.
> They give you all the love they had
> And add some extra just for you.

The opening pun on 'They fuck you up', your parents copulate you into existence but also warp your identity, heightened by the obscene linguistic register, is designed to shatter the saccharine ideal in a rictus of laughter. This is a good example of Larkin's humour at its most somatic, the corporeality of the answering guffaw bespeaking repressed corporeal compulsions. Its function is to dissolve pious values in a reflex convulsion, like a projectile vomit or involuntary belch, not to tease out nuanced alternatives. The audient responds in a paroxysm of recognition before the internal censors can step in and edit his or her reaction for political correctness.

Larkin knew exactly what he was doing in conflating the shock induced by an obscenity with the laugh induced by a joke. When an interviewer asked if he used 'bad language' as 'a shock tactic', he replied:

> Yes. I mean, these words are part of the palette. You use them when you want to shock. I don't think I've ever shocked for the sake of shocking. 'They fuck you up' is funny because it's ambiguous. Parents bring about your conception and also bugger you up once you are born. Professional parents in particular don't like that poem. (*FR*, 61)

This mode of humour is a weapon, 'Professional parents' a target.

Unusually for Larkin, 'This Be The Verse' speaks on behalf of the young. As Steve Clark has said, in one of the finest essays ever written on Larkin, 'the poem might be seen as the kids' retort to the elders'.[34] In this context, the obscene diction bespeaks a youthful rebellion against parental constraint. Larkin's comments in a 1982 letter to Judy Egerton may indicate awareness of the special appeal of this poem to the young: '"They fuck you up" will clearly be my Lake Isle of Innisfree. I fully expect to hear it recited by a thousand Girl Guides before I die' (*SL*, 674). This is borne out by the continuing attraction the poem holds for young musicians in the Alternative Rock style. Jim Orwin, the world authority on musical settings of Larkin's works, cites versions by Sneaky Feelin (1988), Anne Clark (1989), MRI (2001), The Circus McGurkus (2003), Desprez (2004), Jamie Paxton (2008), Humpty Dumpty (2008), Edwina Hayes (2010), Kanal (2010), and the Eef van Breen Group (2011); adding that Laura Marling's song 'Tap at My Window', from her best-selling album *Alas I Cannot Swim* (2008), was inspired by the same source.[35] Nonetheless, part of the *frisson* of the poem stems from its political incorrectness regarding children as well as parents. A work whose resounding last line urges 'And don't have any kids yourself' is clearly not in the business of adulating minors. Indeed, the poem posits that each generation of kids is more 'fucked up' than the last as each generation of parents adds 'some extra' to the stock of human 'misery'. We are, then, a world away from a vision of childhood as lost paradise such as Housman presents in *A Shropshire Lad* in quatrains Larkin mockingly echoes:

> Into my heart an air that kills
> From yon far country blows:
> What are those blue remembered hills,
> What spires, what farms are those?
>
> That is the land of lost content,
> I see it shining plain,
> The happy highways where I went
> And cannot come again.[36]

How this feat of simultaneously speaking *for* and *against* 'kids' is accomplished may be explored (with further light shed on the mode of humour entailed) through two poems that respond to 'This Be The Verse' as it responds to Housman, Stevenson and Hardy.

'This Be The Verse': Rumens and Rutherford

In her introduction to the anthology *Answering Back*, Carol Ann Duffy describes Carol Rumens's poem 'This Be The Verse' as a *rebuke* to the Larkin.[37] Its sprightliness notwithstanding, the Rumens represents a betrayal to the sovereign order of niceness and commonsense of all that is riotous, dissident and unruly in humour:

> Not everybody's
> Childhood sucked:
> There are some kiddies
> Not up-fucked.[38]

The inversion of Larkin's 'fucked up' is pleasing, but the removal of the obscenity from the first to the fourth line forewarns that this is an exercise in pusillanimity. By the second stanza the poem has capitulated to the very tweeness ('Most turn out nice') Larkin's scurrilous belly-laughs release us from. The 'Sad non-begetter' of the concluding sentence is another misjudgement: Larkin begot poems far surpassing those of Rumens and titling her poem after his simply invites us to observe the fact.

Much better is Maurice Rutherford's 'This Be The Curse', which grasps what Rumens does not, that the dysfunctionality of domestic relations is the product of pressures having nothing to do with the niceness (or otherwise) of individual family members:

> I fucked them up, my Mum and Dad;
> I didn't mean to, but I did
> by cropping up late, when they'd had
> their seventh and, they'd thought, last kid.[39]

Reversing the relational logic of the original while retaining the shock value of its opening obscenity, Rutherford makes explicit what is implicit in the Larkin (each text provides the other's subtext), that if parents warp their offspring by passing on their own warped conditioning, offspring warp their begetters – by turning them into parents! The urgency of Larkin's last line, 'And don't have any kids yourself', is explained: the only way to break the cycle is to renounce the reproducing of reproduction.

That the poem's transgressive humour is designed to release the reader from pious attitudes to children as much as to parents is confirmed by a letter Larkin sent to Anthony Thwaite enclosing a draft of the work. Larkin offered it as 'a little piece suitable for Ann's next Garden of Verses' (*SL*, 437).[40] Ann Thwaite in this period edited *Allsorts*, an annual of new writing for children. One is reminded of Larkin's placement of the explosive 'Going, Going' in a government *Report on the Human Habitat* or of 'The Life with a Hole in it' in a *Poetry Book Society Christmas Supplement* (what an antidote to Yule Tide bonhomie!). This aspect of the poem's meaning is of a piece with the hilarious child-hating persona the author cultivated in his journalism and interviews. This is the Larkin who could not review a volume of playground ritual and folklore without proposing an annual 'Herod's Eve' festivity 'on which bands of adults might roam the streets and bash hell out of anyone under sixteen found out of doors' (*RW*, 114). Or who championed the liberties of childless existence: 'I've never lived in hideous contact with them, having toast flung about at breakfast and so on. Perhaps worse than toast' (*FR*, 47–8). The comic timing of the pause between these last two sentences is masterly, as is the delivery of the four-word addendum, afterthought and punchline combined (the more effective for not specifying *what* might constitute a missile worse than toast!).

'This Be The Verse': the assault upon origins

Our commentary has thus far concentrated upon the poem's title and the opening and closing stanzas. This eliding of the middle verse fits a widespread perception that it is the weak point of the poem. Having described 'This Be The Verse' as 'perhaps Larkin's most notorious' work, John Carey targets stanza two: '"Fools", and the awkwardly invented epithet "soppy-stern", come across as rather feeble attempts to sound belligerent and contemptuous. Larkin can usually make us share this scorn, but here he fails.'[41] This may be true but the stanza does important work on the poem's behalf by providing vital context for its assault upon personal, familial and religious origins.

I have elsewhere claimed that Larkin's writings systematically engage in a quest for origins whose fruitlessness becomes an evisceration of origins and even of the concept of origination.[42] Typically, an ontological question is posed, the answer to which opens a subsequent question in a potentially endless interrogation. What determines the life we lead? If character does, as Hardy claimed (roping in Novalis for support), then what determines our character? If our parents do, then does their influence work through nature or nurture? If nature, how far back along the genetic chain must we track to find the root of our personality? If nurture, do our parents influence us more through the lives they lead or the ones they fail to lead? And so on. The heroism of this endeavour lies in Larkin's pursuit of this catechism to the point where every false concept of selfhood is unsinewed and we are brought face to face with the existential terror at the heart of the human condition.

Several of Larkin's late poems hint darkly at 'violence / A long way back' (*CP*, 215; *TCP*, 320) warping a narrator's personality in ways that are hard to correct: 'An only life can take so long to climb / Clear of its wrong beginnings, and may never' (*CP*, 208; *TCP*, 115). As we have seen, 'This Be The Verse' begins by laying the blame at the parental door: 'They fuck you up, your mum and dad'. Verse two pulls back, like a naval telescope, to give a wider perspective:

> But they were fucked up in their turn
> By fools in old-style hats and coats,
> Who half the time were soppy-stern
> And half at one another's throats.

As with the parents, so with the grandparents in a potentially infinite ancestral recession.[43] In what is a recurrent trope of Larkin's thinking on the subject, repetition replaces origination at the source of identity construction. And how is this familial pattern replicated, nature or nurture? 'This Be The Verse' suggests nurture: the emphasis is on cultural and behavioural codes – prudish clothing, inconsistent conduct, emotional repression – rather than genetics, DNA or biological determinism.

The repeating of the *fucking up* motif from the first verse may appear lame in a manner corresponding to Carey's strictures. The shock of laughter comes when the second line is added to the first to suggest that in the grand-parental era sexual mores were so priggish that couples kept their clothes on during intercourse: 'they were fucked up [...] / By fools in old-style hats and coats'. If the narrator is of Larkin's generation, the grandparental era is the Victorian, the comical attempt to have sex while remaining dressed encapsulating the libidinal schizophrenia he identified in writers of that time. The same violent discontinuity is there in the 'soppy-stern' oxymoron and the polysemic phrase 'at one another's throats' (viciously? or out of voracious sexual hunger?).

As for the vagueness Carey detects in some of the stanza's diction (fools, old-style, soppy-stern), this might purport that most of us can only picture our families for a generation or two back before everything becomes hazy. If this reading is tenable then at one level the middle verse is corroborating the position more forcefully expressed in the drafts of 'The Winter Palace' and in 'The View' that time annuls memory:

> The view is fine from fifty,
>   Experienced climbers say;
> So, overweight and shifty,
>   I turn to face the way
>   That led me to this day.

> Instead of fields and snowcaps
>   And flowered lanes that twist,
> The track breaks at my toe-caps
>   And drops away in mist.
>   The view does not exist. (*CP*, 195; *TCP*, 321)

At another level the stanza is advancing a counter-theological approach to origins. The Bible is categorical that there is a creator, an act of creation, a precise moment for the creation of man and a known succession of genera-tions through the male line. Thus Genesis, chapter 5:

> This *is* the book of the generations of Adam. In the day that God cre-ated man, in the likeness of God made he him [...] And Adam lived an hundred and thirty years, and begat *a son* in his own likeness, after his image; and called his name Seth: And the days of Adam after he had begotten Seth were eight hundred years [...] And Seth lived an hundred and five years and begat Enos: And Seth lived after he begat Enos eight hundred and seven years [...] And Enos lived ninety years, and begat Cainan [...] And Cainan [...] begat Mahalaleel [...] And Mahalaleel [...] begat Jared [...]

The unbroken lineage extends from Adam through to Solomon in historical times. This not only means that one can read the generations chronologically into the present but, conversely, that one can trace one's ancestry back to the moment of inception, Michelangelo's pointing finger of God. In 1654 Archbishop James Ussher used the Old Testament genealogy to calculate the moment of creation as 6.00 pm on 26 October 4004 BC. Ussher's chronology was particularly influential because from 1701 it was commonly included in editions of the King James Bible. However, his proposed date differed little from the estimates of Jose ben Halafta (3761 BC), the Venerable Bede (3952 BC), Scaliger (3949 BC), Lightfoot (3929 BC), Johannes Kepler (3992 BC) or Sir Isaac Newton (4000 BC).

In this biblical universe the human subject is temporally anchored and orientated. 'This Be The Verse' unmoors us from such certitude by the simple expedient of describing the clothing of the narrator's parents' parents as 'old-style'. Unable to be sartorially specific about the generation before last – no fob watches, plus fours, handlebar moustaches, bustles or corsets – the poem renders farcical the genealogical literalism and indubitability of theological tradition. No doubt Archbishop Ussher had equally vague memories of his own grandparents, yet he dates and times the origin of the universe with the assurance of one who witnessed the event!

The anti-biblical inflections continue into the third stanza, the opening line of which echoes the patriarchalism of Genesis by shifting from the gender-inclusive 'mum and dad' to the generically masculine 'Man hands on [...] to man'. The syntax mimics (in order to subvert) the patrilineal begetting by which Adam hands on to Seth, Seth to Enos. The stanza even adopts the imperious prohibitive tones of the Old Testament God, such as we associate with the Ten Commandments ('Thou shalt not kill. Thou shalt not commit adultery. Thou shalt not steal'), in order to forbid begetting:

> Man hands on misery to man.
> It deepens like a coastal shelf.
> Get out as early as you can,
> And don't have any kids yourself.

In Genesis Adam and Eve are instructed by God, 'Be fruitful, and multiply': Larkin's narrator counters, 'Thou shalt not reproduce.' The counter-theological theme continues with a touch of humour in the contrast between the last stanza's brazen first line and the beautiful simile in the second: 'It deepens like a coastal shelf.' However unexpected, the simile appositely hints at the geological and maritime investigations with which such Victorian scientists as Lyell, Haeckel and Darwin shattered the Ussher chronology with evidence that the earth was millions of years old. By the time Larkin was penning the poem, *Encyclopaedia Britannica* estimated that the earth was formed as much as 6,000,000,000 years ago, the universe 20,000,000,000.

We are now in a better position to understand the reasons for plucking the poem's title from a half-line of Robert Louis Stevenson. The expression 'This Be The Verse' designates the church and chapel practice of citing on wall or pulpit the biblical chapter and verse to be explicated in that day's sermon. Hymn numbers were also displayed. Larkin's strict quatrains with their unusually emphatic rhymes are modelled on those of hymns, the better to parody their values – try reading 'This Be The Verse' against the metrically similar 'All Things Bright and Beautiful'.[44] In effect, the Church's rhetoric is being marshalled to rewrite Christian metaphysics. If the narrator's gloom regarding the human condition approximates the concept of Original Sin, it strips that concept of both its Edenic prelapsarianism and its paradisal redemption.

'This Be The Verse': the assault upon literary origins

Carey claims that with the first two lines of the last stanza the poem's 'register has changed from the vulgar to the bardic'.[45] However, the swipes at Stevenson and Housman suggest a willingness to quarrel with the poetic heritage that might be perceived as *anti-bardic*. Certainly, the comical bluntness of 'Man hands on misery to man' is a reproof to the lachrymose Robbie Burns of 'Man Was Made to Mourn: A Dirge' –

> Many and sharp the num'rous ills
> Inwoven with our frame!
> More pointed still we make ourselves,
> Regret, remorse, and shame!
> And man, whose heav'n-erected face
> The smiles of love adorn, –
> *Man's inhumanity to man*
> Makes countless thousands mourn![46]

and the pious hand-wringing Wordsworth of 'Lines written in Early Spring':

> If this belief from heaven be sent,
> If such be Nature's holy plan,
> Have I not reason to lament
> *What man has made of man*?[47]

(My emphases.) Even Hardy, if not reproved, is found in need of revision. Throughout his career he experimented with terms with which to de-anthropomorphize and de-Christianize God: the Supreme Mover or Movers, the Prime Force or Forces, the President of the Immortals, the Cause of Things, the Immanent Will, King Doom, the Sleep-Worker:

> 'O we are waiting for one called God', said they,
> '(Though by some the Will, or Force, or Laws;
> And, vaguely, by some, the Ultimate Cause)'[48]

The welter of signifiers conveys how belief in God has come unstuck but not, as in Larkin, its total abandonment. As we saw, 'Epitaph for a Pessimist' combines an invocation of God with a non-redemptive philosophy. In adapting that poem for its conclusion, 'This Be The Verse' finds the God concept so redundant as not to merit mention. Hardy's agnosticism becomes Larkin's atheism.

It might be argued that in stripping the residual deism from 'Epitaph for a Pessimist', 'This Be The Verse' intensifies the equation of self-extinction and species extinction. 'Get out as early as you can' may be parsed as an injunction to commit suicide, the last line of the poem urging one to complete the task before one has time to reproduce. However, the 'And' which provides the hinge between these two propositions makes a consideration of reproduction subsequent to a consideration of suicide: 'Get out as early as you can, / And [then] don't have any kids yourself.' That single conjunction renders the suicidal message untenable and replaces it with a liberational one: since parents ruin the first half of your life and children the second, 'Get out [of the parental home] as early as you can' and don't create one of your own. Hardy's pessimism has no sooner been applied with brutal hilarity to Stevensonian nostalgia than it too is punningly countered with a last-minute message of emancipation. The poem is a trumpet blast aimed at bringing down, Jericho-style, the walls of traditional domesticity. As procreation is prohibited but not sex, this might be perceived as a philanderer's charter befitting the biographicalist stereotype of Larkin as a commitment-phobe. Yet even this masculinist interpretation carries a faintly socialist corollary: the poem's lexicon of increase and bequest ('fill you with', 'add some extra', 'Man hands on [...] to man') confounds the production/reproduction equation of bourgeois ideology – as though that line's ur-text reads 'man hands on *capital* to man'; to renounce the biological production of a son and heir is to renounce the need to build an economic empire worth bequeathing. The narrator renounces the Rule of the Father by refusing to become one.[49] If the narrator is female, the injunction to get out takes on a feminist urgency, like Nora quitting the marital home at the end of Ibsen's *A Doll's House* ('that slammed door reverberated across the roof of the world', a contemporary observed).[50]

Burns, Wordsworth, Alexander (author of 'All Things Bright'), Stevenson, Housman, Hardy: if 'This Be The Verse' rebels against parents thematically, so it does literarily.[51] Why this concentration upon nineteenth-century literature in a poem written in 1971? Because the period 1940–60 witnessed the deepest entrenchment of patriarchal values since the Victorian era, often with specific reference to parliamentary Acts of the 1840s and 1850s. This was especially the case with regard to sex, gender and their representation. For most of Larkin's life the official list of banned books included works by Rabelais, Defoe, Balzac, Flaubert (*Madame Bovary*), Maupassant, Céline, Joyce and Sartre. The peak year for the destruction of obscene publications was 1954, 'when an astonishing 167,000 volumes were sent to the guillotine or used to stoke the furnaces of Scotland Yard'. Most persecuted was D.H. Lawrence. The unexpurgated *Lady Chatterley's Lover* was not prosecuted on one occasion, but repeatedly: between 1950 and 1960 alone, 19 different printings were referred to the director of Public Prosecutions; Customs routinely seized copies sent from abroad to private individuals; and in 1955, the year of *The Less Deceived*, a Soho bookseller was imprisoned for selling the novel. The relevance of this to Larkin's practice is that when Penguin was put on trial in October 1960 for publishing *Lady Chatterley* unbowdlerized, prosecuting counsel, empowered by the 1857 Obscene Publications Act, based the case for censorship on a lexicon that included 'fuck', 'cunt', 'balls', 'shit', 'arse', 'cock' and 'piss'. In the same period the Lord Chamberlain, empowered by the Theatres Act of 1843, was deleting 'poof', 'rogered' and 'balls' from Osborne's *The Entertainer* (1957); 'titties' from Orton's *Entertaining Mr Sloane* (1964); and 'fuck all' and 'bugger' from Pinter's *Landscape* (1967).[52]

Following Penguin Books' victory, Larkin's poems are increasingly suffused with pre-Victorian registers of profanity: 'tits', 'crotch', 'cock' and 'balls' in 'Sunny Prestatyn' (*CP*, 149; *TCP*, 64–5); 'shit' in 'The Dance' (*CP*, 156; *TCP*, 306–9); 'fucking' and 'bloody' in 'High Windows' (*CP*, 165; *TCP*, 80); 'piss' in 'Sad Steps' (*CP*, 169; *TCP*, 89); 'fart' and 'bastard' in 'Posterity' (*CP*, 170; *TCP*, 86); 'turd' and 'prick' in 'The Card-Players' (*CP*, 177; *TCP*, 84); 'arselicker' in 'Poem about Oxford' (*CP*, 179; *TCP*, 312–13); 'fuck' and 'fucked' in 'This Be The Verse' (*CP*, 180; *TCP*, 88); 'craps', 'arse', 'bitch' in 'Vers de Société' (*CP*, 181–2; *TCP*, 91); 'sod' in 'The Life with a Hole in it' (*CP*, 202; *TCP*, 114–15); and in 1979, with his last significant poem 'Love Again', 'wanking' and 'cunt' (*CP*, 215; *TCP*, 320).[53] Almost all these obscenities are deployed for comic effect as well as for their shock value. All are wrecking balls with which to demolish that Victorian ideological formation which had so inhibited the poetry of his hero, Hardy.[54] All, therefore, are as liberating as they are destructive.

'This Be The Verse' and deconstructive laughter

Laughter is inherently anti-authoritarian: if you or I slip on a banana-skin, it is moderately amusing; if Prince Charles does, it is hilarious. The successive involuntary snorts of derisive laughter induced by 'This Be The Verse' are not designed to win assent for the narrator's viewpoint but to afford momentary release, as euphoric as it is scurrilous, from the pieties denounced. These include: the sanctification of the family; the adulation of parents; the idealization of children; the patriarchal linking of God and family through the male line; the conviction that adherence to conventional morality is a gateway to a life after death; and the canonization of literary works (from hymns to Housman) sentimentalizing these values. For a poem comprised of only 85 words, 75 of them monosyllabic, 'This Be The Verse' does a deal of damage. The poem is a sum of destructions.

In his delightful article 'Sing-Along with Philip', Doug Porteous inge-
niously encapsulates this aspect of the poem in a list of 'the ten best tunes'
for setting it to.[55] The inclusion on the list of hymns ('Before the Ending
of the Day'), madrigals ('Greensleeves'), anthems ('God Save Our Gracious
Queen') and snatches of classical music (the 'Ode to Joy' from Beethoven's
Ninth Symphony) deftly acknowledges the poem's subversion of the sentiments of polite society. But deeper than the damage 'This Be The Verse'
inflicts upon individual pieties is the assault upon piety itself – piety and its
hypostases: deference, conformity, sanctimony. *No transgression, no cathar-
sis* is the precept. Larkin's profane laughter unleashes this transgressivity
(where Rumens would sedate it) and in rescuing us from the tyranny of the
pious achieves his stated aim of rescuing humour from lightness. His verbal
affront to the pietistical, the priestly, the politically correct, the *bien pen-
sants*, the panacea-peddlers, the moral police, is not undertaken wantonly
but in a serious endeavour to make the world safe from utopianization. 'This
Be The Verse' is a tweet-sized poem of atomic destructiveness detonated by
laughter.

6
Radical Plot Deflation: 'Vers de Société'

> I've always had the idea that a poem is like a fight and that anybody can get into one but it's only an accomplished fighter who can get out of one.
>
> – George Kendrick[1]

Larkin's perfect plots

Larkin is widely seen as a master of traditional poetic structures with a particular genius for the management of lines, verse paragraphing on the model of Yeats, control of narrative suspense and perfect denouements. In the words of Nicholas Jenkins:

> The mandated structure of the typical modern English poem requires that a lyric build towards an epiphanic ending, often image-based, through which, like a sun rising behind clouds, some revelation of a deeper truth emerges. The meanings come in the ends. Larkin in particular is a master of such resounding endings.[2]

Jonathan Raban shares with Jenkins an awareness of the intricate construction of the body of a poem required to provide the setting for the transfiguring climax:

> No literary training was required to see that a vast amount of highly skilled labour had gone into the construction of a Larkin poem. Every last tiny piece was an exact fit. Like a brassbound ship's chronometer, the thing ticked and chimed and kept strict Greenwich time.

Citing the examples of 'The Whitsun Weddings' and 'Ambulances', Raban beautifully shifts metaphors from the mechanical to the transcendent, like someone moving from an account of an aircraft engine to a description of flight, in the attempt to communicate Larkin's expertise 'at the resplendent, transfiguring ending – the ending that sweeps the reader aloft on a rising thermal of grave and formal language'. Raban particularly favours those poems in which 'lift off' is hard to anticipate, 'the narrowness of the triumph – the against-the-odds transcendence of art over life in that last-minute swoop' investing the works with a real sense of existential hazard. As a result, he prizes such late works as 'High Windows', 'The Old Fools', 'The Card-Players', 'This Be The Verse', 'Sad Steps' and 'Vers de Société' whose profane openings ('They fuck you up'; 'Groping back to bed after a piss'; 'In a pig's arse, friend') seemingly provide a flight-deck too bestial for the imagination to get airborne. When 'from these desperate and squalid beginnings, the poems climb, against all likelihood, to heights like the tragic serenity attained at the end of "High Windows"', the triumph is all the more exhilarating: 'Poems don't get much closer to miracles than that.'[3]

Perhaps the subtlest analysis of what Jenkins described as 'Larkin's gift for the decisive, clear-cut ending' is that provided by Christopher Ricks. He closed his review of 'The Whitsun Weddings' with the following words:

> It was John Donne who said that 'the whole frame of the poem is a beating out of a piece of gold, but the last clause is as the impression of the stamp, and that is it that makes it current'. Larkin's effortless accuracy of conclusion ought to keep these lovely poems current.[4]

Ricks expanded upon this review in his contribution to *Larkin at Sixty*, using 'An Arundel Tomb' as evidence. Of the poem's apparently resounding conclusion he says: 'The very last line has the apothegmatic weight of classical art. Yet Larkin combines what in less good poets prove incompatible: the understandings both of classicism and of romanticism.' Whereas Jenkins, Raban and like-minded commentators (David Timms, for example) describe Larkin's endings as a tidal surge carrying all before them, Ricks's model, in which diametrical opposites are held in tension, creates spaces for readerly choice:

> Larkin's last line has at least two different possibilities of intonation. If you lay more weight on 'survive', you hear a classical asseveration – 'What will *survive* of us is love'. Classical because what is meant by the less stressed 'us' is humanity at large, the largest community of all men and women; classical because of the transcending of individuality within commonalty. But [...] the words might be heard with more of their weight and salience devoted to 'us' – 'What will survive of *us* is love'. This would be the weight of romantic apprehension [...] a particular 'us', here and now, moved not just personally but individually.[5]

Yet whatever the latitude for interpretative variety – and, therefore, readerly disputation – the larger point Ricks makes concerns the artistic balance with which these counterpoised forces are brought to harmonious resolution:

> What Larkin achieves is an extraordinary complementarity: a classical pronouncement is protected against a carven coldness by the ghostly presence of an aching counterthrust, a romantic swell of feeling; and the romantic swell is protected against a melting self-solicitude by the bracing counterthrust of a classical impersonality.[6]

Once again, the impression given is that of a narrative arc that achieves perfect closure, Larkin exiting from the poem in a manner that leaves the reader with a satisfied, sometimes exultant, sense of completion.

Jenkins, Raban and Ricks are subtle and responsible critics and there is much in their shared argument that convinces. One cause of restiveness, however, is the ease with which hostile commentators were able to reverse the terms of the argument, damning as vices what our triumvirate perceived as virtues. Randall Stevenson dismissed Larkin's 'tidily conventional [...] forms' as sadly representative of Movement 'conservatism and constraint'. For Stevenson it is the familiarity of the stratagems, 'backward-looking in theme as well as style', that accounts for their accessibility: 'Such poetry proved agreeably easy to teach in schools, congenial and unchallenging to readers and many poets alike, and freed of demanding metaphysics or the formal complexities of modernism.'[7] While I much prefer the former, my own view is that the pro- and anti-Larkin lobbies alike simplify his work by mistaking for *closure* his justly celebrated exit skills. Instead, the poems pull off the extraordinary double-helix of providing a satisfying aesthetic conclusion with a refusal of consolatory endings or plot resolutions. Even 'The Whitsun Weddings', a travelogue with an unusually emphatic embarkation-to-destination itinerary, stops just short of disembarkation, leaving us with an anticipation of arrival, the newly-wed couples being scattered 'somewhere' 'out of sight'. Another masterpiece, 'Mr Bleaney', charts the narrator's identification with the eponymous character only to conclude that when it comes to the deeper questions about him the honest answer is 'I don't know'. As for 'An Arundel Tomb', one cannot help noticing how Ricks exaggerates the 'apothegmatic weight' of the last line, 'What will survive of us is love', by suppressing the undercutting penultimate line's suggestion that it is 'almost' but not quite 'true'. Nor does Ricks observe the devastating pun on the poem's last word, 'love', which in addition to its tender associations means nil or zero, as in the scoring of tennis: What will survive of us is *nothing at all!*

In what follows I wish to suggest that the way in which even Larkin's most resounding endings are, on closer examination, deeply contradictory – resolutions that do not resolve – points towards a neglected aspect of his technical mastery. For Larkin's skills at perfect plots, narrative sequencing and climactic endings are matched by, played off against and subverted by such techniques as anticlimax, fragmentary endings and radical plot deflation. These stratagems place his *oeuvre* squarely in the domain of modernist and postmodernist aesthetics of the kind he is commonly taken to deplore. Behind both one senses precisely the sort of 'demanding metaphysics' Stevenson would deny Larkin: for the impulse to undermine perfect plotting is expressive of an uneasy conviction that reality is not the exemplification of perfected theological design.

The four-act structure

In a 1964 interview with Larkin, Ian Hamilton observed that many of his poems close with a 'kind of built-in or tagged-on comment on themselves' so that 'the whole poem doubles back on itself' at the last minute. 'I hadn't realized I did that sort of thing,' Larkin replied, though he was impressed enough to repeat Hamilton's *aperçu* in a subsequent interview with Neil Powell (*FR*, 23, 31). Shortly after Larkin's death his fellow Hull poet, the absurdly neglected George Kendrick, offered a more precise account of this narrative inversion:

> Larkin is a pessimist on the question of immortality, and on the face of it has denied himself the possibilities of soaring ecstatic lines. But he does it, and if you examine the moments when he does it, what you find is an inbuilt denial. Larkin's terrific trick for me is his ability to believe only the mundane and the death-laden, and then to bring in the inspiring and the immortal – then, with the barest touch, to reverse it. That is really clever.[8]

What poets Hamilton and Kendrick are describing, years in advance of the critical debate, is Larkin's development of a four-act structure with closing reversal.

This model was perfected over many years with much trial and error. A comparatively early success, 'If, My Darling', has a stark but effective two-part argument: the first three verses list the conventional trappings of bachelor existence that cry out for wifely intervention and the next five itemize the unwholesome contents of the male mind which, were they to become known, would swiftly deter such feminine ministrations. 'March Past', 'Places, Loved Ones', 'Reference Back' and 'Send No Money' adopt a more complex tripartite structure similar to that which we attributed to *A Girl in Winter*. However, matters reached a new level of complexity in a succession of masterpieces which included 'Reasons for Attendance', 'Poetry of Departures', 'Toads', 'Self's the Man', 'Toads Revisited', 'Dockery and Son', 'High Windows' and 'Vers de Société'. All of these use a four-act structure with closing reversal in a manner that anticipates by up to 15 years a central mechanism of Derridean deconstruction. As explicated in Chapter 1, such a practice begins by isolating a particular binary; next establishes that the terms are placed in a violent hierarchy, one being privileged over the other (good over bad, man over woman, white over black, etc.); he follows this by reversing the classical opposition; and finally displaces the second term from its new position of superiority, resisting the replacement of one hierarchy with another and effecting a more general displacement of the system. Derrida accepts that binaries are too deeply embedded in the operations of language to be extinguished; instead, he works within the terms of the system so as to breach it. As does Larkin.

That Larkin is fully alive to the role of binaries in the production of meaning is apparent even from the titles of his poems, which can be double-columned as in Table 6.1 in antithetical pairings.

Table 6.1   Larkin's titular binaries

Coming	Going
Arrival	Poetry of Departures
Spring	Autumn
Success Story	To Failure
Here	The Importance of Elsewhere
First Sight	Long Sight in Age
Dublinesque	Poem about Oxford
The horns of the morning	When the night [...]
Aubade	Afternoons
Modesties	Wants
No Road	Bridge for the Living
Morning at Last	How to sleep
Summer Nocturne	Winter Nocturne
I Remember, I Remember	Forget What Did
Days	Night-Music
Mother, Summer, I	Winter
Self's the Man	The Whitsun Weddings
The Winter Palace	Thaw
Nursery Tale	The Old Fools
Continuing to Live	Disintegration
Solar	The moon is full tonight
Born Yesterday	Last Will and Testament
Essential Beauty	Ugly Sister
Strangers	Letter to a Friend [...]
The Dance	Sad Steps
Waiting for breakfast [...]	After-Dinner Remarks
I have started to say	Nothing To Be Said
This is the first thing	Compline
Sinking like sediment through the day	Lift through the breaking day
Reference Back	Posterity
At Grass	Cut Grass

Time and again a poem with a categorical title will be matched elsewhere in the *oeuvre* by another with the equally adamantine but opposed meaning. However, it is the way Larkin instantiates this radical alterity in the fabric of individual poems, licensing binary opposites to confront, challenge and undo each other, that lends his work its deconstructive profundity.

Consider 'Reasons for Attendance' (*CP*, 80; *TCP*, 30) (Table 6.2). This takes the dichotomy between the social life and the life of solitude and quickly sketches in the dominant view that it is the former that holds most of the potentialities that make life worth living: music, dancing, coupledom, love, sex:

Table 6.2 Larkin's four-act structure: binary opposition: the social life v. the artistic vocation

'Reasons for Attendance'	
Act I: The conventional hierarchy *The narrator envies the conviviality of the group.*	The trumpet's voice, loud and authoritative, Draws me a moment to the lighted glass To watch the dancers – all under twenty-five – Shifting intently, face to flushed face, Solemnly on the beat of happiness. – Or so I fancy, sensing the smoke and sweat, The wonderful feel of girls. Why be out here?

Act II: The reversal of the conventional hierarchy
 	
 The narrator asserts the values of the individual against those of the group.
	But then, why be in there? Sex, yes, but
	     what
	 Is sex? Surely, to think the lion's share
	 Of happiness is found by couples – sheer
	
	 Inaccuracy, as far as I'm concerned.
	 What calls me is that lifted, rough-tongued
	     bell
	 (Art, if you like) whose individual sound
	 Insists I too am individual.
	 It speaks; I hear; others may hear as well,

Act III: Equilibrium between binary opposites *The values of individual and group are equal relative to the point of view.*	But not for me, nor I for them; and so With happiness. Therefore I stay outside, Believing this; and they maul to and fro, Believing that; and both are satisfied,
Act IV: Deflation of binary opposites *But they are also equal in their potential for deceit and self-deceit.*	If no one has misjudged himself. Or lied.

> The trumpet's voice, loud and authoritative,
> Draws me a moment to the lighted glass
> To watch the dancers – all under twenty-five –
> Shifting intently, face to flushed face,
> Solemnly on the beat of happiness.

Halfway through the second stanza the reversal of the conventional hierarchy begins, somewhat uncertainly, with the narrator's interrogation: 'why be in there? Sex, yes, but what / Is sex?' One does not have to be 'under twenty-five' to find that line of questioning uncompelling! This is swiftly followed by three more forceful propositions: that coupledom is no guarantor of happiness; that our narrator feels a vocational call to art; and that art speaks from and to human individuality. Of course, this apparently decisive rejoinder contains its own contradictions: many an artist has combined sex with art (think of Rochester, Byron, Picasso, Mae West, Mailer, Madonna); and some arts are more often created and consumed in convivial contexts than in solitude – Larkin's beloved jazz among them. So just when victory seems assured, with the complete reversal of the original proposition, the narrator shifts to a more relativistic stance in which it is admitted that each has chosen correctly according to the point of view:

> I stay outside,
> Believing this; and they maul to and fro,
> Believing that; and both are satisfied

Yet no sooner is this compromise position established than it is undone in a last-minute twist of the sort Hamilton and Kendrick were the first to identify:

> and both are satisfied,
> If no one has misjudged himself. Or lied.

Our narrator belatedly recognizes that the words 'both are satisfied' might as easily read 'dissatisfied'. The poem ends by deflating both sides of the binary opposition and inviting the reader to contemplate the violence of all such either/or choices.

One can already see that the Jenkins–Raban–Ricks model, in which the poem presses at all points against its narrative arc and is resolved in a resounding climax, is more seeming than real. 'Reasons for Attendance' has a threaded-through argument and punchline ending that appear to fit the consensual template; but the effect is deflationary rather than climactic, more deconstructive than constructive. The poem has a powerful ending without a resolution. It finishes, but it does not conclude.

Postmodernist unmaking

Post-structuralism is to postmodernism what structuralism is to modernism. Deconstruction is a central manifestation of post-structuralism and Larkin's anticipation of Derrida's analytical procedures makes the poet a postmodernist *avant la lettre*. This is denied by Steven Connor in his influential monograph *Postmodernist Culture: An Introduction to Theories of the Contemporary* where Larkin is seen as typifying a 1950s 'Little England' rejection of modernism which thwarted progression to the postmodern. Connor disparages

> the movement towards modest realism in British writing of the 1950s and 1960s, typified in the work of Alan Sillitoe, Kingsley Amis and Philip Larkin, writers who refused what seemed to them the high-minded and elitist obscurity of the modernist inheritance and fostered a return to a writing which was lodged in experience rather than form. In theory, at least, such writing would be less closed off and more permeable to 'life'. Although a case is occasionally made for calling such writers postmodernist, most accounts of literary postmodernism would want to insist on some form of critical engagement with modernism rather than a simple turning away from it.[9]

There is a compound irony entailed to this view, for elsewhere in the volume Connor quotes with approval critics like Alan Wilde who attribute to modernism qualities similar to those we have identified in 'Reasons for Attendance'. According to Wilde, modernism responded to the fragmentation of the period – social upheavals like the First World War and the Russian Revolution; intellectual upheavals such as those associated with the names of Nietzsche, Freud and Einstein – by endeavouring to be true to that incoherence while simultaneously transcending it at the aesthetic level. Hence, Wilde sees a radical incoherence in the works of Joyce and Woolf which is not so much 'resolved' or 'unified' as projected in the form of binary conflicts into delimited aesthetic shapes. The modernist sensibility is 'precisely the aesthetic and aestheticizing consciousness unable to solve or resolve the dilemma it posits, except by hovering over it in the sublimity of form'.

Connor quotes this view of modernism as a prelude to asserting that 'disorder fixed in this way into the rictus of the aesthetic only internalizes pressures which are to erupt to the surface with postmodernism'.[10] This analysis of postmodernism can itself be found compatible with our interpretation of Larkin, for the sorts of binary conflict projected in his poems erupt in subsequent poems that answer them in a kind of dissensual call and response. That is to say, the binaries which undo each other in a specific poem are the object of further undoing in a later more drastically conflicted work. And the poem which revisits the already unresolved 'Reasons for Attendance' in a spirit of radical unmaking is 'Vers de Société' (*CP*, 181–2; *TCP*, 91).

'Vers de Société': the title

The poem's business of unmaking begins with the title, which is a French term for a sub-genre of light verse associated with witty, mildly satirical ditties on the topical frivolities of polite society.[11] The category was popular in eighteenth-century France with key practitioners like Charles de Pougens, Abbé de Chaulieu and Titon du Tillet. The mode crossed the Channel with Matthew Prior, notable English exponents including Ambrose Philips, Winthrop Mackworth Praed, Frederick Locker-Lampson, W.S. Gilbert and Austin Dobson. The characteristic note is also sometimes struck by more ambitious poets like Pope, Cowper, Byron and Betjeman. That note is associated with strict metres, a playful and sparkling tone, high finish and complete unseriousness. In Locker-Lampson's words, *vers de société* 'has somewhat the same relation to the poetry of lofty imagination and deep feeling, that [...] Dresden China Shepherds and Shepherdesses [...] bear to the sculpture of Donatello and Michael Angelo'.[12]

The initial shock at the choice of title in part arises from Larkin's cultivated reputation as a hater of Abroad – a xenophobia that sometimes took the specific form of francophobia ('If that chap Laforgue wants me to read him he'd better start writing in English!').[13] As with 'This Be The Verse', written a few weeks before, and 'Aubade', begun three years later, the shock of the polite title is multiplied by the impoliteness of the immediately consequent lines:

> *My wife and I have asked a crowd of craps*
> *To come and waste their time and ours: perhaps*
> *You'd care to join us? In a pig's arse, friend.*

The word craps in the first line (swiftly followed by arse in the third, bitch in the tenth) belongs to a lexicon that by definition lies outside the genre of *vers de société*. That is to say, the opening is designed to disqualify the poem from that category and, therefore, to ironize the title and mock the mode. According to Partridge's *Dictionary of Historical Slang* to 'pig in the arse', or 'to grease a fat sow/pig in the arse', is a late eighteenth- and nineteenth-century obscenity meaning to give money to the rich. Our narrator rebuffs Warlock-Williams's invitation with the insult that the superfluity of 'craps' already in attendance releases him from the duty of acceptance. This initial impression of verbal violence is confirmed by the tone of contempt that prevails throughout the poem (that 'bitch' talking 'drivel', 'that ass' and 'his fool research'), a tone entirely at odds with the gently mocking but always decorous registers of *vers de société*. It is also confirmed by the poem's metrics, which are much more irregular than might be thought. No two stanzas are alike in terms of the distribution of line lengths, the syllable counts ranging from 5 to 11, and the half-line shifting position from fourth line to fifth and back again across the poem's trajectory. Similarly, the rhyming couplets of the first and last stanza (aabbcc) are not maintained in the body of the poem, the second stanza sporting two couplets (abbcca), stanzas three, four and five containing only one couplet apiece and at different points in the verse (lines 3 and 4, 2 and 3, 4 and 5, respectively). These are not the 'tidily conventional' metrics attributed to Larkin by Stevenson and stand in marked contrast to the sprightly fulfilling of metrical norms associated with *vers de société* – a genre which sometimes resorted to strict and demanding French and Italian forms such as the ballade, double ballade, rondeau, sestina and triolet. For Larkin, form is content and the disaggregation of form a deconstructive practice. Poem after poem invokes tradition – often, as here, in the very title – only to then demonstrate how tradition disintegrates under the pressures of modernity.

'Vers de Société' and the unmaking of 'Reasons for Attendance'

Vers de société is verse about the foibles of polite society. In Larkin this becomes something else: a meditation on the merits of the social life, the life lived in company, versus those of the meditative life, the life of solitude. In other words, it is a revisiting of the theme of 'Reasons for Attendance'. Whereas the latter suggests that the narrator's outsiderdom derives from a commitment to art – 'What calls me is that lifted, rough-tongued bell / (Art, if you like)' – 'Vers de Société' does not specify the sort of solitude. There are hints of the religious life (the hermit, the gown and dish, God), the academic life ('that ass' and 'his fool research'), the creative life (reading and writing 'Under a lamp') and a life of nature observation ('the trees [...] darkly swayed', 'the noise of wind', 'the moon thinned / To an air-sharpened blade'). The point, then, is not the particular activity of a particular narrator, *this one*, but rather the spectrum of vocations whose practice is predicated upon a degree of de-socialization.[14] The fact that a range of pursuits is in play strengthens the case for the life of solitude, especially when the ones enumerated – the spiritual life, the scholarly life, the artistic life, the life of a nature worshipper – have an air of nobility about them, each entailing a setting of principle above material reward. This sense of a calling, an apostolic mission, requires a throwing over of the 'they-self' and an answering to a more existentially authentic state of being. As a result, the putative attractions of the social life are presented as the stuff of inauthenticity, the abject surrender of the I-self to the they-self: 'the big wish / Is to have people nice to you'.

Although this critique of sociability as distraction from the proper objects of contemplation, and indeed from a selfhood capable of such attentiveness, continues through the penultimate verse, it starts to unravel in the fourth and fifth stanzas. In the poem's second act (see Table 6.3) the narrator's increasing

Table 6.3 Larkin's four-act structure: binary opposition: the social life v. the solitary life

	'Vers de Société'
Act I *The life of solitude is more* *rewarding than the social life.*	*My wife and I have asked a crowd of craps* *To come and waste their time and ours: perhaps* *You'd care to join us?* In a pig's arse, friend. Day comes to an end. The gas fire breathes, the trees are darkly swayed. And so *Dear Warlock-Williams: I'm afraid –*
	Funny how hard it is to be alone. I could spend half my evenings, if I wanted, Holding a glass of washing sherry, canted Over to catch the drivel of some bitch Who's read nothing but *Which*; Just think of all the spare time that has flown
	Straight into nothingness by being filled With forks and faces, rather than repaid Under a lamp, hearing the noise of wind, And looking out to see the moon thinned To an air-sharpened blade.
Act II *The difficulties of* *maintaining that view* *when no one else* *shares it.*	A life, and yet how sternly it's instilled *All solitude is selfish.* No one now Believes the hermit with his gown and dish Talking to God (who's gone too); the big wish Is to have people nice to you, which means Doing it back somehow. *Virtue is social.* Are, then, these routines
	Playing at goodness, like going to church? Something that bores us, something we don't do well (Asking that ass about his fool research) But try to feel, because, however crudely, It shows us what should be? Too subtle, that. Too decent, too. Oh hell,
Act III *The failures of the solitary life.*	Only the young can be alone freely. The time is shorter now for company, And sitting by a lamp more often brings Not peace, but other things.
Act IV *Capitulation to the majority* *view but on terms that deflate* *the binary opposition.*	Beyond the light stand failure and remorse Whispering *Dear Warlock-Williams: Why, of course –*

resort to casuistries comes to resemble Freudian *disavowal*, the way in which a person undergoing psychoanalysis will simultaneously affirm and deny something – or affirm *by* denying it. Certainly, there is a sense of the narrator's argument running aground in the interrogatives, the complex syntax and, finally, the *aposiopesis* of stanza five ('Too subtle, that. Too decent, too. Oh hell'), preparing the reader for the complete moral collapse in stanza six.

This answerability to 'Reasons for Attendance', in a kind of dialogic engagement with Larkin's back-catalogue, is riddled with contradiction and paradox: for while it might reasonably be claimed that by its close 'Vers de Société' has rebutted the position adopted in the earlier poem, that the life of solitude is superior to the convivial life, it actually begins with the one position and ends with the other, so that what is conveyed is less the vanquishing of one by the other than the way the human subject is torn between the two. It is indicative that the collapse of the case for solitude is presented in poetry, typically a product of solitude! Again, the narrator's eventual decision to attend the social function is entirely unsupported by positive reasoning: the cheap booze ('washing sherry'), the bad conversation ('drivel') and the wretched company ('a crowd of craps', 'some bitch', 'that ass') clearly constitute a waste of one's life ('time [...] flown / Straight into nothingness'). As the contemplative life carries spiritual, scholarly, artistic and naturalist associations, its abandonment for a sociability entirely defined by negatives seems morally unjustifiable and perverse. As early as 1951, 20 years before the poem's composition, Larkin had written to Monica Jones: 'social life is better than private disintegration, but not than private creation' (*LM*, 55).

This moral abjection brings into focus a further round of deliberations, no less paradoxical, no less deconstructive. For if the social life offers no positive reasons for embracing it, the narrator's decision so to do must arise from the negative incentives of contemplation. What these are is the substance of the poem's third act. One is the narrator's crushing awareness that the solitary life no longer yields the hoped-for spiritual or creative rewards:

> sitting by a lamp more often brings
> Not peace, but other things.
> Beyond the light stand failure and remorse

The other is the ageing narrator's enhanced awareness of mortality:

> Only the young can be alone freely.
> The time is shorter now for company

These two vectors interact in ways that generate a range of meanings, all inflected in shades of bleak. Perhaps what is being proposed is that the young are more creative than the old, so that the justifications for rejecting the consolations of company diminish with age. Alternatively, it may be that the young are simply more egotistical than their elders and therefore find it easier to elevate their inner over their outer lives, themselves above others. Either way, the getting of wisdom comes at the price of acknowledging one's waning vocational aspirations. Consequently, the major incentive for accepting a party invitation may be less the joys of human intercourse – our narrator has made short shrift of those – than the chance to escape, if only for an evening, the pained awareness of one's own impotence. Being alone with other people is less vexatious than being alone with oneself. It might further be averred that the narrator's scorn for the other guests is an expression of self-loathing rather than superiority, for to be included on the same invitation list as 'a crowd of craps' can only signify that in the eyes of Warlock-Williams one is another such. The last stanza's bitterness of tone suggests that not only does our narrator recognize as much but, in accepting the poisoned invitation, accepts that personal estimate.

We are now in a position to see that by revisiting the binary opposition addressed in 'Reasons for Attendance' the poem 'Vers de Société' has extinguished those traces of artistic self-importance that survive in the earlier work. This, in turn, makes for significant differences in the models of selfhood projected by these works, as will be explored later in this chapter.

'Vers de Société' and incompletion

For all its radical unmaking, the foregoing analysis might be assimilated to the structural model explicated in Aristotle's *Poetics*. Aristotle identifies *character* and *action* as the essential elements in a story and posits that character must be revealed through action, which is to say through aspects of the plot. Three plot devices are specified: the *harmatia*, the *anagnorisis*, the *peripeteia*. *Harmatia* means a sin or fault which in tragic drama is sometimes identified as the hero's 'fatal flaw'. *Anagnorisis* means 'recognition' or 'realization', this being a moment in the narrative when the truth of the situation is recognized by the protagonist – which in turn means that the moment is often one of *self*-recognition. *Peripeteia* means a 'turn around' or 'reversal' of fortune. In classical tragedy this is usually a fall from high to low estate as circumstances expose the hero's fatal flaw precipitating his downfall.[15]

It is easy enough to map 'Vers de Société' onto the Aristotelian template. The *character* is the narrator and the *action* that of deciding whether or not to accept a party invitation. The *plot* unfolds in Acts I and II, with the narrator expressing a scorn for the sociable life that readers may already feel to be overstated. The moment of *anagnorisis* comes in Act III with the narrator's recognition of this propensity to overstate the case – which, in turn, is a moment of self-recognition regarding personal failures in the contemplative life. The *peripeteia* comes in the devastating last line, with its complete reversal of the poem's opening gambit (Table 6.4). The *harmatia* is that of hubristically

Table 6.4 The Aristotelian template

	'Vers de Société'
Harmatia *The narrator defends the life of* *solitude without realizing the hubris* *of disparaging more sociable types.*	*My wife and I have asked a crowd of craps* *To come and waste their time and ours: perhaps* *You'd care to join us?* In a pig's arse, friend. Day comes to an end. The gas fire breathes, the trees are darkly swayed. And so *Dear Warlock-Williams: I'm afraid –*
	Funny how hard it is to be alone. I could spend half my evenings, if I wanted, Holding a glass of washing sherry, canted Over to catch the drivel of some bitch Who's read nothing but *Which*; Just think of all the spare time that has flown
	Straight into nothingness by being filled With forks and faces, rather than repaid Under a lamp, hearing the noise of wind, And looking out to see the moon thinned To an air-sharpened blade. A life, and yet how sternly it's instilled
	All solitude is selfish. No one now Believes the hermit with his gown and dish Talking to God (who's gone too); the big wish Is to have people nice to you, which means Doing it back somehow. *Virtue is social.* Are, then, these routines
	Playing at goodness, like going to church? Something that bores us, something we don't do well (Asking that ass about his fool research) But try to feel, because, however crudely, It shows us what should be?
Anagnorisis *The moment of realization.*	Too subtle, that. Too decent, too. Oh hell,
	Only the young can be alone freely. The time is shorter now for company, And sitting by a lamp more often brings Not peace, but other things. Beyond the light stand failure and remorse
Peripeteia *Complete reversal of the narrator's* *position.*	Whispering *Dear Warlock-Williams: Why,* *of course –*

thinking one's inner life rich enough to justify despising other people. Where the classical model falls short is this: in ancient Greek tragedies of the sort Aristotle discusses, the tragic hero may be undone but the narrative is not – indeed, the elements identified in the *Poetics* are precisely those that ensure perfection of the artwork; whereas Larkin's sense of the unfulfilment inherent in the modern condition finds expression through fractured narratives, plot deflation and the unsinewing of cathartic teleologies.

Of course, structural disintegration is not the preserve of the postmodernist. The verse narrative – as it were, the novel in verse – which dominated European poetry from Hesiod's *Theogony* to Tennyson's *Idylls of the King*, from Homer's *The Odyssey* to Bridges' *The Testament of Beauty*, taking in Dante, Chaucer, Shakespeare and Milton along the way, had already begun to fragment by the Romantic period. One thinks of such incomplete epics as Byron's *Don Juan*; Wordsworth's *The Recluse* (he got no further than a *Prelude* to it and an *Excursion* from it); Coleridge's *Kubla Khan* and *Christabel*; Keats's *Endymion*, *Hyperion* and *The Fall of Hyperion*.

By the time of the modernists this unlooked-for narrative incompletion came to typify all the arts. Both T.S. Eliot's *The Waste Land* and Hugh MacDiarmid's *A Drunk Man Looks at the Thistle* had to be edited into shape by someone other than the author. Proust revised only four of the seven volumes of *Remembrance of Things Past*. Not one of Kafka's novels was finished; nor was Robert Musil's *The Man Without Qualities*, the work on which his reputation rests. Picasso's *Les Demoiselles d'Avignon*, the first Cubist masterpiece, was never completed. Schoenberg made repeated efforts to finish *Jacob's Ladder* and *Moses and Aron*, succeeding in neither case. Sergei Eisenstein's movie career was littered with wrecks and abortions.

That these were *involuntary* failures, thematically inapposite, may be demonstrated if we return for a moment to the modernist long poem. Pound's *The Cantos* was planned in a hundred instalments as a modern equivalent to *The Divine Comedy*, though with continual cinematic intercutting between what Dante separates into the *Inferno*, *Purgatorio* and *Paradiso*. After 45 years' work and eight hundred pages, having already burst its Dantean limit of one hundred, the poem stammers to a close, in a volume symptomatically entitled *Drafts and Fragments of Cantos CX–CXVII*, with Pound's plangent admission: 'I am not a demigod / I cannot make it cohere.'[16] Similarly, David Jones's *The Anathemata* was published as the first half of a larger work; the second half never materialized (though some splendid building blocks may be found in *The Sleeping Lord and Other Fragments*). William Carlos Williams finished *Paterson* according to plan in four volumes; later, deciding that the poem was incomplete, he added a fifth and final volume; after his death, drafts of a sixth volume were found among his papers.

Larkin writes in full consciousness of Romantic and modernist ambition, its magnificence and its failure. His position is different to theirs not because he avoids their narrative incompletion but because their example has trained him to expect it. One measure of this is the way 'Vers de Société' foregrounds its postmodernity by parading modernist citations, as though candidly cherry-picking a spent culture phase. The entire poem may be read as a compressed updating of Eliot's 'The Love Song of J. Alfred Prufrock' (with Prufrock's 'I have measured out my life with coffee spoons' becoming 'I could spend half my evenings, if I wanted, / Holding a glass of washing sherry'). Larkin himself attributed the expression 'washing sherry' to Dylan Thomas. The gas fire breathing was anticipated in Louis MacNeice's 'Schizophrene'. The 'moon thinned / To an air-sharpened blade' is commonly taken as an allusion to 'My Table', Part III of 'Meditations in Time of Civil War' by W.B. Yeats. The hermit reference invokes a specific passage of *Lady Chatterley's Lover*: 'A man could no longer be private and withdrawn. The world allows no hermits.'[17] The philosopher Nietzsche surely lies behind the account of God's abscondence. And so forth.

A second index of Larkin's aesthetic positioning is his enthusiasm for the inconclusive conclusions practised in the modernist–postmodernist tradition. Of his favourite modernist novelist, D.H. Lawrence, he said: 'I love *Lady Chatterley's Lover*, just because it doesn't come to a happy ending, or any sort of ending: Mellors is like everyone else, he wants to have his end away and then forget about it. It's a very equivocal ending' (*FR*, 53). Late in life he repeated that *'doesn't come to ... any sort of ending'* formula when writing to the young Julian Barnes in praise of his postmodern masterpiece *Flaubert's Parrot* (1984):

> I much enjoyed *F's P*, in fact I read 2/3rds one night, and the rest in bed between 5 & 6 a.m. the next day. Couldn't put it down, as they say. That is the best compliment I can pay [...] As I read on, I kept thinking 'This is going to have to have an awfully good end', and it didn't; it didn't have any sort of end. When I read, finally, the doctor's tragedy, I thought 'But this hasn't anything to do with anything'; and it didn't, and yet it's all part of the same thing, the 'resonance of despair' (who wrote that?), the subtle echoes and repetitions, the stark misery that gets at you through this most unexpected and unlikely framework [...] I enjoyed it immensely. Thank you! (*SL*, 721)[18]

This Penelope's web approach to conclusion, in which stories are not so much completed as brought to their final stage of incompletion, is central to postmodernism. As David Lodge argues, in *The Modes of Modern Writing*:

> Endings, the 'exits' of fictions, are particularly significant in this connection. Instead of the closed ending of the traditional novel, in which mystery is explained and fortunes are settled, and instead of the open ending of the modernist novel [...], we get the multiple ending, the false ending, the mock ending or parody ending.[19]

Lodge cites as canonical exponents of the postmodernist ending Samuel Beckett, Alain Robbe-Grillet, John Fowles, Gabriel Josipovici, John Barth,

Richard Brautigan and B.S. Johnson. In a less showy way, the Larkin of 'Vers de Société' keeps such company, as well as anticipating younger postmodernists like Simon Armitage, David Mitchell and Percival Everett. Indeed, with a little ingenuity this single poem might be seen to incorporate several of Lodge's postmodern endings.

False endings

A favourite postmodernist ploy for undermining linear narratives with their neat plot resolutions is to interrupt their trajectories with periodic false endings. John Fowles ends *The French Lieutenant's Woman* (1969) twice, inviting the reader to determine which is the false one. John Barth floats a whole series of possible endings to the title story of his collection *Lost in the Funhouse* (1968), finally settling on the most inconclusive. Alasdair Gray's *Lanark* (1981) contains two distinct narratives presented out of chronological sequence with an Epilogue part way through. Gray's *The Book of Prefaces* (2000), a 640-page survey of anglophone writing from Anglo-Saxon to the twentieth century conducted entirely through the Introductions, takes Shandyism to a new extreme by offering titillations without climaxes, like an indefinite act of *coitus interruptus*. David Mitchell's dazzling *Cloud Atlas* (2004) wraps one story around another so that the second half of the novel offers six conclusions as the stories successively climax. Having stated that 'I always wanted to write a book that ended with the word Mayonnaise', Richard Brautigan's *Trout Fishing in America* (1967) does so twice, in the penultimate and last chapters; but both are false endings, the former because it does not close the book and the latter because it misspells mayonnaise!

Similar experiments characterize the other arts. Alain Resnais's cinematic masterpiece *Last Year at Marienbad* (1961) opens, in the words of the screenwriter Alain Robbe-Grillet, 'with a romantic, passionate, violent burst of music, the kind used at the end of films with powerfully emotional climaxes'.[20] The Beatles' 'A Day in the Life' on the *Sergeant Pepper* album (1967) has a tripartite structure with such resounding crescendos at the end of each part (especially the first) that they feel like the conclusion of the track. The *Abbey Road* album (1969) went a step further in that allowing the gramophone arm to stay on the disc after the final song revealed a snippet of incomprehensible dialogue which only made sense played backwards on the stylus arm's recoil from bumping the label.

The French film's example of beginning with a false ending perhaps comes closest to an anticipation of 'Vers de Société' whose opening invitation is so crushingly rejected at the end of line three as to seem conclusive:

> *My wife and I have asked a crowd of craps*
> *To come and waste their time and ours: perhaps*
> *You'd care to join us?* In a pig's arse, friend.

Were it not for the five and a half verses visibly subtending, the reader might be forgiven for thinking that what we have here is an epigram or limerick, a scurrilous squib to be expedited in a stanza:

> *My wife and I have asked a crowd of craps*
> *To come and waste their time and ours: perhaps*
> *You'd care to join us?* In a pig's arse, friend.
> Such shits as you need flushing round the bend.

When the poem forgoes the excremental ending flagged up in the first three lines (*craps*, arse), switching register completely –

> Day comes to an end.
> The gas fire breathes, the trees are darkly swayed.

– the contrast highlights that the party invitation and its contemptuous dismissal are a satirical correspondence transacted in the narrator's head. No sooner have we deduced that the dismissal of the invitation was a mock ending than the narrator sets pen to paper as though to commit the rejection in writing: 'And so *Dear Warlock-Williams: I'm afraid* –'. However, instead of concluding the note of apologetic rejection just begun, the second stanza opens a stream of consciousness that defers the ending for five verses. That is to say, the first verse contains two false endings, at lines three and six. As we shall see, there are grounds for claiming that when the much-deferred ending of the entire poem finally arrives it proves equally false.

Textermination

A complete narrative is an arc of plenitude generating a sense of symmetry and fulfilment, like living the biblical three score years and ten. In a Godless universe lives are lived under existential pressure, typically accompanied by a sense of falling short, with death always premature, all of us (in Geoffrey Hill's magnificent words)

> Dragged half-unnerved out of this worldly place,
> Crying to the end 'I have not finished'.[21]

Under such conditions a broken narrative arc may more poignantly enact one's meaning, like a single-span bridge that does not reach the other side.

With the example before them of so many incomplete Romantic and modernist epics, the postmodernists sometimes integrate disintegration with an air of acceptance, even insouciance. John Barth's story 'Title' contrives to end before ending:

> It's about over. Let the denouement be soon and expected, painless if possible, quick at least, above all soon. Now now! How in the world will it ever[22]

Similarly, John Hawkes's novel *Travesty* (1976) features a narrator taking his best friend and his daughter for a suicidal ride in his car with the avowed intent of killing them as well as himself, but the story breaks off before the final crash occurs.

Larkin's texterminations are a deal less playful. The most famous example of snapped-off narrative in his *oeuvre* is that of 'The Dance', a poem he struggled with for a year before abandoning it 'unfinished'. It is worth remarking that even after Larkin decided to abandon the poem he seems to have wobbled as to where the termination should come. Thwaite's 1988 edition of the *Collected Poems* follows the most complete typescript and ends on the word 'understand' after 12 full stanzas. In *Larkin at Work* (1997), Tolley printed a further eight lines of handwritten text, ending three-quarters of the way through the thirteenth stanza on the word 'divisible'. Burnett includes 'The Dance' in *The Complete Poems* (2012) despite its not being complete, but ends after six lines of the thirteenth stanza on the word 'then'. The reader has a choice of incompletions: take your pick! The fact that Larkin did not publish the work may suggest that he thought it unfit to place before the public as a fragment. This might situate the poem closer to Romantic and modernist precursors, with their pained, unwished-for fracturing, than to postmodernism's *expectation* of incompletion. Certainly, he told Maeve Brennan that the poem's incompletion represented 'a great obstacle in my creative life: I shan't write anything until it's out of the way'.[23] If we shift our focus from these three alternative endings to the bridge between the eleventh and twelfth stanzas, a different interpretation is offered:

> I sit and beam
> At everyone, even the weed, and he
> Unfolds some crazy scheme
> He's got for making wine from beetroot, far
>
> Too incoherent to survive the band;
> Then there's a *Which*-fed argument – but why
> Enumerate? (*CP*, 157; *TCP*, 309)

This moment establishes a narrative pattern, which recurs in subsequent poems, whereby a narrator slips into an emotional rant only to interrupt it, usually with an interrogative, usually beginning 'but', before abruptly terminating the poem with a more objective form of commentary. In 'Laboratory Monkeys' ('Ape Experiment Room') two verses about animal experiments build up to an outburst regarding the scientists concerned which is then choked off after the manner of 'The Dance':

> a Ph.D. with a beard
> And nympho wife who –
> But
> There, I was saying (*CP*, 160; *TCP*, 304)

The poem ends four lines later. Likewise with 'Love Again', Larkin's last considerable poem:

> Someone else feeling her breasts and cunt,
> Someone else drowned in that lash-wide stare,
> And me supposed to be ignorant,
> Or find it funny, or not to care,
> Even ... but why put it into words? (*CP*, 215; *TCP*, 320)

This poem stutters to a close seven lines later. Two observations ensue. First, that while Larkin's experiments with incomplete narratives lack the insouciance of Barth, Brautigan or Hawkes, they are frequent enough to indicate a conscious working with narrative truncation. Second, the phrasing of the *aposiopesis* in 'Love Again' – 'why put it into words?' – interrogates language in a way that reminds of yet other poems, such as 'Here' and 'High Windows'. 'Here' may rather seem a candidate for narrative perfection of the kind admired by Jenkins, Raban and Ricks than for the kinds of abruptly terminated storylines presently under consideration; but the way the poem gives out, like the land, with arrival at the coast, 'Facing the sun, *untalkative*, out of reach' (*CP*, 137; *TCP*, 49) makes silence preferable to the welter of words. (My emphasis.) 'High Windows' is closer in structure to 'Love Again': after four verses describing the generational upheavals of the twentieth century, religious and sexual, the narrator attempts a psychic leap from historically contingent freedoms to transcendental ones in a last sentence that straddles a stanza break:

> And immediately

> Rather than words comes the thought of high windows:
> The sun-comprehending glass,
> And beyond it, the deep blue air, that shows
> Nothing, and is nowhere, and is endless. (*CP*, 165; *TCP*, 80)

Once again we sense the impatience with language, 'Rather than words' conveying a frustration with the babble of Babel such as we found in 'The

Dance' ('but why / Enumerate?'), 'Laboratory Monkeys' ('But / There, I was saying'), 'Love Again' ('but why put it into words?') and 'Here' (with its yearning for the 'untalkative'). As before, the moment of *aposiopesis*, the point at which the narrative snaps, signals that the poem will be precipitately concluded within a stanza. And this, it may be averred, is a model shared by 'Vers de Société'.

Reverting to Table 6.3, we might identify the precise point of *aposiopesis* as the moment of transition from the second to the third act, the compression of Acts III and IV into the last stanza, after the leisurely and expansive treatments of Acts I and II, communicating the narrator's sudden rush for the narratological exit. In terms of the Aristotelian model (Table 6.4), the *aposiopesis* demarcates the belatedness of the narrator's *anagnorisis* and the calamitous speed with which the *peripeteia* ensues. As with 'Laboratory Monkeys', 'High Windows' and 'Love Again', the typographical space between the last two stanzas is a visual representation of the *aporia*, the moment of narrative breakdown, forewarning of an abrupt cessation of the story. Like 'The Dance', 'Vers de Société' stumbles on for one more verse only to terminate mid-sentence. The fact that Larkin included 'Vers de Société' in the volume *High Windows* (1974) suggests that this was a more chosen incompletion than characterized 'The Dance', closer to postmodernist than modernist aesthetics. To fully understand why, we need to press our analysis one stage further.

Loop poems

Though truncated, the last sentence of the poem says enough to decisively shift the narrator's position from rejection to acceptance of the party invitation extended by Warlock-Williams. Or does it? Is it not in the nature of an incomplete sentence that one can only guess at the meaning of the omitted words? The fragmented sentence which closes the poem opens the letter of reply: we end with a beginning. If the poem ended '*Dear Warlock-Williams: Why, of course!*' the exclamation mark would be conclusive. The exclamatory emphasis would assure the reader that the narrator has decisively reversed his original position and the terminal punctuation would complete the sentence, bringing the poem to closure. The dash, betokening a mid-sentence breaking off, renders '*Why, of course*' at once emphatic and ambiguous: of course, *what?* Even if, upon reflection, the overwhelming likelihood is that the poem ends with the narrator's letter of acceptance, we are not granted decisive witness to that document. A comparison might be drawn with films like *Butch Cassidy and the Sundance Kid* and *Thelma and Louise* in which a freeze-frame ending just before the deaths of the protagonists grants the audience a psychological reprieve from the inevitable.

There is, however, another possibility to consider – one for which the *locus classicus* is James Joyce's *Finnegans Wake*, that signal text in the transition from modernist to postmodernist aesthetics.[24] Joyce deliberately augmented the deflationary mid-sentence ending of a novel which took him 16 years to write by terminating the text on the most insignificant word he could find:

> In *Ulysses*, to depict the babbling of a woman going to sleep, I had sought to end with the least forceful word I could possibly find. I had found the word 'yes', which is barely pronounced, which denotes acquiescence, self-abandon, relaxation, the end of all resistance. In [*Finnegans Wake*], I've tried to do better if I could. This time, I found the word which is the most slippery, the least accented, the weakest word in English, a word which is not even a word, which is scarcely sounded between the teeth, a breath, a nothing, the article *the*.[25]

This is at once true and false: the novel does terminate with the definite article; but, as Joyce told Harriet Shaw Weaver, it 'ends in the middle of a sentence and begins in the middle of the same sentence'. In other words, the closing half-sentence ('A way a lone a last a loved a long the') may be completed by looping it back to the novel's opening:

> riverrun, past Eve and Adam's, from swerve of shore to bend of bay, brings us by a commodious vicus of recirculation back to Howth Castle and Environs.

Upon finishing the novel, Joyce's 'ideal reader suffering from an ideal insomnia' is invited to immediately recommence the process – a 'recircula- tion' indeed! As Joseph Frank advised, modernist texts cannot be read but only reread.[26]

This textual strategy has been adopted by many canonical postmodernists. At the end of the first chapter of *Slaughterhouse-Five* (1969), Kurt Vonnegut discloses what are to be the final words of the novel. Sure enough, at the end of the tenth and last chapter, there they are again: '*Poo-tee-weet!*' Beryl Bainbridge's 1973 novel *The Dressmaker* ends with the same two sentences with which it began, their meaning changed utterly by what transpires in the interim.[27] Gabriel Josipovici's short story 'Mobius the Stripper' (1974) and Anthony Minghella's 1976 stage adaptation of the same name circle back to where they began in a potentially endless regress. More recently, such masterful films as Quentin Tarantino's *Pulp Fiction* (1994) and Paul Haggis's *Crash* (2005) have worked variants on the technique; as has Simon Armitage in what he refers to as his 'loop poems' (including that early gem, 'You May Turn Over and Begin ...').

It is perfectly possible to read 'Vers de Société' as Larkin's intervention in this continuing tradition of postmodernist circular narratives. The par- allelism of the last lines of the first and final stanzas invites the reader to resist exiting from the poem at the end but straightway circle back and recommence the reading process. To do so is to notice that these apparently opposed responses to the invitation, *no* and *yes*, may both say *no*: '*Dear Warlock-Williams: Why, of course* I shan't be attending your wretched function.' Indeed, if we phrase this rejection more politely the wording of the two responses may be amalgamated in a single reply: '*Dear Warlock-Williams: Why, of course* I would love to attend your splendid function but, alas, I have a prior engagement. And so *Dear Warlock-Williams: I'm afraid –.*' This may always be a secondary undercutting interpretation, like the tennis score reading of 'What will survive of us is love'. Nonetheless, such complications testify to the tenacity and invention with which Larkin's poems resist closure.

The surrogate author

We have now analysed in some depth Larkin's mastery of the four-act structure with closing reversal; the playing off of binary pairs which deconstruct each other across a poem's trajectory; the further unmaking when these undone binaries are reinterrogated in a subsequent poem; and the deployment – sometimes, as here, in combination – of false endings, abrupt terminations and loop structures. We have also had cause to remark a pervading frustration with language which links these deconstructive devices to such ancient grammatical figures as *aposiopesis* so that the poem becomes, not just a discussion or thematization, but an *enactment* of a crisis in representation associated with postmodernism.[28] Behind that linguistic crisis lies a metaphysical crisis: for if the omniscient narration of the classic realist text, the author as God seeing into all characters' lives impartially, is (however tenuously) analogous with a God-centred view of the universe; and if the involuntarily fractured narratives of the modernists, so often accompanied by anguished longing for totalizing certitudes (Fascism, Communism, Christian Revivalism), bespeak the trauma of God's death; then postmodernist deconstructions of character, plot, action and resolution indicate a deep distrust of language's continued powers of representation in the absence of absolutist guarantees, theological or political. Postmodernism's vigilant concern to invalidate the transcendental and metaphysical sees the authority of a text arising from its negation of representation's time-honoured writs of convention.

From a postmodernist perspective, then, an effective cultural practice must implicate itself in what it would undo. In this context, a favourite operational device of Larkin's is the surrogate author, differentiated from himself by writing in another genre, whose fraught attempts at self-expression help the real author dramatize the wider crisis of representation. One thinks of the heteronymic writings of Brunette Coleman; the John Kemp of *Jill*; the publisher's reader of 'Fiction and the Reading Public'; the epistolary protagonist of 'Letter to a Friend about Girls'; the biographer Jake Balokowsky in 'Posterity'; or the schizophrenic letter writer of 'Vers de Société'. These are not straightforward examples of *hypodiegesis*, the embedding of one story inside another, but writings about the process of writing that challenge writing's truth claims. Hence, John Kemp compensates for his feelings of inadequacy by inventing a sister, writing both sides of their correspondence, keeping her diary and drafting a short story in her name, only for the situation to be brought to a crisis by his projection of this literary fantasy upon a real person. John ends the novel in a university sickbed, his physical and mental breakdown mirroring the linguistic breakdown between sign and referent, fiction and reality.

Though necessarily terse by comparison, 'Vers de Société' offers a more systematic analysis. The demotion of solitary vocations like writing in post-Nietzschean culture is deftly alluded to:

> *All solitude is selfish.* No one now
> Believes the hermit with his gown and dish
> Talking to God (who's gone too)

The death of God de-eternalizes time and fractures subjectivity. Larkin was ever mindful that the fundamental difference between youth and age is that the former has in prospect life, the latter death. As he wrote to Patsy Strang, 'The passage of time, and the approach and arrival of death, still seems to me the most unforgettable thing about our existence' (*SL*, 223). This sense is especially acute in 'Vers de Société' as the poem is pitched precisely in that moment, sometimes associated with 'the mid-life crisis', when attitudes and enthusiasms formed in youth ('Only the young can be alone freely') have their validity tested against insurgent intimations of mortality ('The time is shorter now for company'). Who one is changes as time changes and the narrator's interior dialogue between these discrepant dispositions of self constitutes the text. In a very real sense the subject of the poem's multiple undoings is the inconstancy of being and time that Larkin's pundits charge him with abjuring. In both cases the master motif is not fixity but impermanence.

Of course, as Geoffrey Braithwaite[29] might point out, Larkin exercises artistic control as surely as any classic realist master of omniscient narration; but it is control in the service of a very different ethos – that of expressing the difficulties of expression and the limits of the expressible. His surrogate author spends the whole poem trying to compose a brief letter, neither of his attempts getting further than the third word of the opening sentence, his message veering from one extreme (no) to another (yes) – neither extreme fully intended, fully cleaved to. This (our poem seems to say) is the character of representation under the conditions of postmodernity. The eschatological consequences of this aesthetic of incompletion – namely, that death does not complete life but randomly terminates it – is the subject of our next and last chapter. For the moment what I wish to emphasize is Larkin's overlooked genius for radical plot deflation. The acclaimed master of narrative completion is also the unsung master of the narrative shortfall.

7
Radical Citation: 'Aubade'

'And I have read the poets
    Yes, every bloody one:
From Langland up to Shelley
    And from Auden back to Donne.'
– Larkin, 'When we broke up, I walked alone' (*TCP*, 164)

The lyric paradigm

In this chapter my intention is to overthrow the conventional view of Philip
Larkin as lyric poet – or, more truly perhaps, to revolutionize the reading
habits this view has helped to normalize. In the process, I shall claim that
what Edna Longley terms 'the quintessential Larkin lyric' – 'The Trees', say,
or 'Cut Grass' – is not the truest representation of his poetic genius which
is to be found elsewhere, in what we might call the *anti-lyric*, the poem that
situates itself within the lyric tradition the better to eviscerate it.[1] This is an
opinion with which Larkin concurred to judge from his comments on those
much-admired lyrics: 'Bloody awful tripe', he wrote on the manuscript of
'The Trees', while in a letter to Monica Jones he described 'Cut Grass' as
'pointless crap'.[2]

To claim as much is to fly in the face of a critical consensus subscribed
to by most of the leading players in what one might call the Larkinocracy;
and if I use James Booth to exemplify this orthodoxy it is not because he
is its worst exponent but its best. Booth is adamant that 'All Larkin's work
is fundamentally autobiographical', the job of the lyric poet being to affect
the reader's emotions by revealing his own. This task is better fulfilled by
poets who approach experience without philosophical or political preconceptions, their poems responding opportunistically to the random flux of
sensation:

> The great strength of this attitude towards poetry is its fundamental
> authenticity, and the flexibility which it gives to the poet's rhetoric.

Larkin has no programme to fulfil, no Byzantium to seek out, no 'still point of the turning world' to which all his experience must be related. Set loose from such anchorage his imagination can be responsive to every different, contradictory twist of his experience, every new insight, however unprecedented.[3]

This conception of the lyricist as one who responds poetically to the fleeting and inchoate sets a premium upon the rhetorics of inspiration, upon the registering of the spontaneous in a language that feels freshly created for each new occasion: 'He seems to write always with the partly-completed *oeuvre* in mind. He waits for the right time to use a word, will not use it until that time comes, and then, if at all possible, never uses it again.'[4] Booth's claim may be said to carry the endorsement of Larkin's declaration, 'I believe every poem must be its own sole freshly created universe' (*RW*, 70).

Thus far we seem to be confronted by an explication of the lyric that privileges the spontaneous, the inspirational, the epiphanous and the profoundly subjective over the considered, premeditated and objective; but while this is true, it is less than the whole truth because, Booth goes on to explain, this very commitment to the immediate necessarily involves the reduction of the ideological repertoire of the lyric to a few familiar themes:

> Kingsley Amis has aptly called Larkin a 'poet of sensation'. He possesses to an extreme degree the lyric poet's ability to capture life as process, without striving to pin it down or harmonize it into an abstract philosophy – beyond the truisms that youth is sweet, love fades, and death awaits us.[5]

Paradoxically, this very limitation is the key to the lyric's virtue, the condensing of all complexity into a core repertoire of emotional states not only speaking to our common humanity, regardless of time or place, but also holding out the possibility of an exceptional talent giving some of these emotions definitive expression: 'His themes as he defined them in a letter to Patsy Strang of July 1953', Booth continues, 'are the universal commonplaces of lyric poetry': 'I should like to write about 75–100 new poems, all rather better than anything I've ever done before, and dealing with such subjects as Life, Death, Time, Love, and Scenery in such a manner as would render further attention to them by other poets superfluous.'[6] A case of 'What oft was thought but ne'er so well expressed', as Pope has it in *An Essay on Criticism*.

The belief that lyric poetry is characterized by its address to the eternal verities of the human emotions makes Booth impatient with, not to say scornful of, those historicists for whom 'The "realities" with which poetry is concerned are "social and historical"'. There can therefore be no poem about Life, Death, Time, Love or Scenery; only poems about particular working-class, or Victorian, or masculine, or postcolonial versions of Life, Death, Time, Love or Scenery.'[7] For Booth,

> Poetry [...] is not an adjunct to history, and the value of a poem is not dependent on whether it registers any particular socio-political moment. It is a matter only of how beautifully and memorably it embodies thought and feeling in words. Larkin is a poet; what will remain permanently interesting about his work is its poetry. To confound poetry with history is perversely to read for a preferred 'something else', rather than poetry itself.[8]

In short, Larkin's 'poems present lyric universals'; true to their genre, they express feelings that are timeless, trans-historical, permanent.[9]

Problematizing the lyric paradigm

The immediate problem posed by this conception of the lyric, which underwrites so much of the discussion of Larkin's poetry, lies with its apparent ignorance of the genre's tradition.[10] For how the term *lyric* is employed continually shifts across time so that any particular definition, including Booth's own, is always historically specific. The most complete written evidence of early lyric activity is the Egyptian: the Pyramid Texts include specimens of the funeral song (elegy), song of praise to the king (ode), and invocation to the gods (hymn); and tomb inscriptions from the same period include the work songs of shepherds and fishers. None of these is marked by the characteristics Booth attributes to *all* lyrics – an opportunistic record of deeply personal sensation. In ancient Greece too, despite the more personalized lyrics written at Lesbos by Sappho and Alcaeus, the dominant lyric tradition, national in character and epitomized by Pindar, was associated with such formulaic categories as the hymn, paean, dithyramb, processional, dance song, triumph, ode and dirge. In none of these would the private sensations of the author be welcome. It is true that with the rise of the Roman Empire there emerged in Latin a sustained emphasis upon the personalized preoccupations of the author: the observations of Propertius, the *amours* of Catullus, the rustic pleasures of Virgil, the exilic lamentations of Ovid, the love songs of Tibullus, the private asperities of Martial and Juvenal. But, ironically, in introducing a subjective tendency of the kind Booth associates with all lyrics, these Latin poets also added a pronounced emphasis upon the topical – thereby inviting the very historical contextualization Booth sees the lyric as transcending.

If there *is* a feature of the lyric that unifies large tracts of the genre's history it is one Booth does not mention: namely, its peculiar proximity to the origins of all verse in musical expression. Indeed, for several millennia the literal meaning of the term 'lyric', which derives from the Greek word for a lyre, was simply a poem written to be sung. This meaning is preserved in the modern colloquialism of referring to the words of a song as its 'lyrics'. One can see why Booth might wish to mislay this obvious truth, for the only mature piece Larkin definitely wrote to be sung is 'Bridge for the Living', which as a large commissioned 'occasional' poem is the diametrical opposite of what our critic means by the term.[11]

Even this millennial definition is not trans-historical, however, for while the use of 'lyric' as a generic term for any poem which was composed to be sung was largely retained until the Renaissance, the impact of print technology thereafter caused an almost complete divorce between, say, the 'songs' of Shakespeare, Jonson and Campion and the non-musical, scribal texts of Donne, Marvell and Herbert. One small index of the change was a new fascination with the shapes of the text on the page, as in those poems of George Herbert, such as 'Easter-Wings' and 'The Altar', in which the eponymous subjects are typographically depicted. With only a few exceptions, the lyric genre since the Renaissance has remained a textual rather than a musical discipline and the traces of a melodic origin have become largely vestigial. Booth thinks he is placing Larkin in an unchanging millennia-old lyric tradition when he is actually situating him in an exclusively post-Renaissance one. Moreover, Booth's emphasis upon a poetry of sensation, a poetry committed to nothing other than the verbal preservation of authorial emotion, is a decidedly Romantic one. As Laurence Lerner has indicated:

> It was a commonplace of Romantic poetic theory that poetry, especially lyric poetry, is the most direct of human utterances, the unmediated, unevasive expression of the poet's emotion. Keats strove to capture 'the true voice of feeling' in his poems, Wordsworth defined poetry as 'the spontaneous overflow of powerful feelings', and praised Shakespeare's sonnets because in them the poet 'unlocked his heart'; Ruskin defined lyric poetry as 'the expression by the poet of his own feelings'. The reaction against this view in the twentieth century claimed that the poetic speaker is always constructed, that even the most apparently personal lyric has a dramatic speaker distinct from the poet; and as a result it has become common to refer to the 'I' of a poem not as 'Shelley' or 'Yeats' or 'Larkin', but as 'the speaker' or 'the persona'.[12]

Booth appeals to the timeless trans-historical values of the lyric seemingly unaware that his conception of it is specific to a narrow slot of post-Renaissance history, somewhere between the birth of Romanticism and the modern period. Larkin, by contrast, is highly aware of the discontinuities in the lyric inheritance, some of his greatest poems defining themselves against specified segments of that history. Which is also to say that some of Larkin's masterpieces are anti-lyrics which take up residence within the lyric tradition the better to destroy it from within, Trojan Horse style.[13]

Larkin's most nakedly autobiographical lyric

One way we might seek to validate this assertion is by identifying a poem which critics agree is particularly personal, peculiarly *felt*, Larkin at his most nakedly autobiographical. An overwhelming majority of critics – Booth, Kelly, Morrison, Rowe, Leggett, George Hartley, Hope, Pritchard, Motion, Rácz and Bradford included – single out 'Aubade' as a uniquely private and subjective document within the Larkin *oeuvre* (*CP*, 208–9; *TCP*, 115–16). In István Rácz's words: 'His last major poem, "Aubade" (1977), is so personal in tone that it cannot be called either a dramatic monologue or a mask lyric. The agnostic poet struggling with the mystery of death shows himself more openly than ever before.' Even Lerner, who is not much given to the conflation of authors and narrators, makes an exception in this instance: 'The tremendous power of "Aubade" – the last major poem Larkin wrote – springs from the conviction that every word is meant, that we are watching some one who is not performing a part but expressing his deepest feeling.'[14] It is only fair to add that Lerner, here as elsewhere in his perspicacious little book, offers a more nuanced reading than many of his peers, going on to point out literary allusions that show the narration of 'Aubade' to be culturally mediated.

The same holds for M.M. Rowe's 'Larkin's "Aubade"', which is not only the most sustained and rigorous analysis of the poem to date but one of the few articles on the poet which may be said to be indispensable. How much this present essay owes to Rowe will become apparent in the next section of the argument. For the moment what I wish to highlight is the speed with which even the estimable Rowe slips from appearing to claim that the narrator is a kind of Everyman too vaguely delineated to be verifiable as the author – 'The only hints about his life and age that might distinguish him from anybody else are the remark that he gets half drunk at night, and the indication that death is coming "soon"'[15] – to a position where he seems to be asserting the contrary, that the narrator is identifiably Larkin and Larkin alone:

no poet ever felt the difference between a misfortune happening to him, and a misfortune occurring to somebody else, more keenly. Looked at in the third person, and from the point of view of society, a plurality of deaths, like a plurality of births, is part of a natural process. But Larkin is not interested in a plurality of deaths; he is interested in one – his own – which is quite different from all the others [...] In the poem, Larkin is hideously aware that his is an 'only life' and that nothing that happens before it, after it, or to others, is of any account [...] [W]hen he awakes panic-stricken at four in the morning, he *really* assents to the fact of his own death, and in doing this realizes it is quite unlike any of the others. His death will bring the world to an end.[16]

Although Booth does not isolate 'Aubade' for this sort of protracted scrutiny, we can now see that those who do, like the splendid Rowe, predicate their analyses upon a view of the lyric very close to his.[17] 'Aubade' therefore offers a perfect test case for those, such as myself, who wish to demonstrate that biographical readings of Larkin's works repress more than they express; that even his most subjective poems are so saturated with intertextual references as to be inclusive, heterodox, multicultural; and that the strategies of his anti-lyrics are premised upon fractures or discontinuities in a lyric tradition Booth and company see as continuous.

The title, 'Aubade'

One of the many excellences of the Rowe essay is its recognition that the title of Larkin's last masterpiece is not a generalized invocation of the dawn but a deliberate – and, ultimately, adversarial – summoning of a precise chapter of lyric history. Rowe is at pains to point out that what by the end of the fourteenth century became known as an *aubade* had its roots in two older troubadour traditions of the *alba* and the *aube*, which may once have been quite distinct. Beginning in tenth-century Provence, these forms spread to the rest of France, Spain, Portugal, Italy and, somewhat later, Germany. Though not unknown, the *aubade* was less conspicuous in medieval English, some distinguished examples being camouflaged by the fact that they were embedded in larger forms such as the verse narrative and the verse drama. There is an *aubade* secreted in Book III of Chaucer's *Troilus and Criseyde* (lines 1450–70, with some foreplay in lines 1427–42). Shakespeare later did something similar in Act III, Scene V, lines 1–3 of *Romeo and Juliet*, with an *aubade* beginning:

> Wilt thou be gone? It is not yet near day:
> It was the nightingale, and not the lark,
> That pierc'd the fearful hollow of thine ear.

Again, the song 'Hark! Hark! The Lark' from Shakespeare's *Cymbeline* has sometimes been separately published under the title 'Aubade', as in Sir Arthur Quiller-Couch's *Oxford Book of English Verse, 1250–1918*.

So what is an *aubade*? In essence, it is a type of lyric in which (i) a narrator of one sex (ii) sings a love song (iii) to a member of the opposite sex (iv) at dawn (v) in one of two eroticized contexts – either, outside the beloved's window (*Cyrano de Bergerac* style), so that the song is one of sexual longing, or else in the beloved's bed, so that the song becomes a lament that with the new day the lovers must part. Most commonly, the narrator is male; but in some *aubades* a woman addresses her male lover; and in yet others a third party, a watchman or maid, warns the lovers of the approaching dawn. (In Shakespeare's play, the *aubade* involves an exchange between Romeo and

Juliet brought to its conclusion by the intervention of the Nurse.) In those instances where dawn brings separation, this is rarely if ever because the world of work calls but rather because the love is in some way illicit – not infrequently because the woman is already married, the love adulterous.[18]

In the medieval period *aubades* were lyric in the original sense of poems written to be sung. Of over four hundred troubadours whose names are known, many belonged to the feudal nobility, their songs performed by professional minstrels or *jongleurs*, and all their categories of lyric subject to regulative conventions (including the five characteristics enumerated above), making it far from certain that the *amours* described were ever authorially felt and meant in the manner presumed by Booth. What we are witnessing may rather be the playing out in the form of song of larger cultural codes of the medieval period, such as those associated with the concept of Courtly Love.[19]

Having gestured in much of the above, Rowe rather loses track of the genre's history. He categorically states that 'there are no French poems called "aubade" in the nineteenth century'.[20] Taken literally, this may be true; but if so, it is because modern French poets preferred the shortened term *aube*, meaning 'dawn', to *aubade*, or 'dawn song'. This in turn may have been an acknowledgement that their poems were not *songs*, not written to be sung. Hence, Baudelaire has 'L'Aube spirituelle', Rimbaud 'Aube' and, at the end of the century, Comtesse de Noailles has 'Aube sur le Jardin'. Larkin's excellent paraphrase of Baudelaire, 'Femmes Damnées', is itself a queered *aubade* –

> The fire is ash: the early morning sun
> Outlines the patterns on the curtains, drawn
> The night before. The milk's been on the step,
> The *Guardian* in the letter-box, since dawn. (CP, 270; TCP, 117)

– though its 'early morning' setting is not in the French original. The resumption of daily life outside the home which witnessed the lesbian seduction anticipates by 34 years the workaday world that stirs at the end of 'Aubade'.

As for the anglophone *aubade*, Rowe jumps straight to twentieth-century poems of that name by Stevie Smith, Louis MacNeice and William Empson – all known to Larkin and all having begun an ironizing of the title that he would take much further. What Rowe neglects to mention are the significant contributions English poets made to the genre in the centuries after Renaissance print technology had converted the *aubade* from song to text, from a medium received by ear to a medium received by eye. The Metaphysical poets of the seventeenth century worked many a variation on the mode. Marvell's 'To his Coy Mistress' is rather a *carpe diem* poem on the theme of 'love me today for tomorrow we die' than a true *aubade*; but the mid-poem allusion to Phoebus the Sun God racing by ('Times winged

Charriot hurrying near') allows the narrator to close with an *alba*-like entice-
ment to consummate the relationship before dawn:

> Let us roll all our Strength, and all
> Our sweetness, up into one Ball:
> And tear our Pleasures with rough strife,
> Thorough the Iron gates of Life.
> Thus, though we cannot make our Sun
> Stand still, yet we will make him run.[21]

A comparable masterpiece by John Donne, 'The Sun Rising', is more squarely
in the tradition:

> Busy old fool, unruly Sun,
> Why dost thou thus,
> Through windows, and through curtains, call on us?
> Must to thy motions lovers' seasons run?

His 'Break of Day' is an *aubade* spoken by a woman:

> 'Tis true, 'tis day, – what though it be?
> Oh wilt thou therefore rise from me?
> Why should we rise because 'tis light?
> Did we lie down because 'twas night?

While his 'Daybreak', which Larkin will have known from Quiller-Couch's
anthology, encapsulates the mode in a stanza:

> Stay, O sweet and do not rise!
> The light that shines comes from thine eyes;
> The day breaks not it is my heart,
> Because that you and I must part.
> Stay! or else my joys will die
> And perish in their infancy.[22]

Although it goes unmentioned by Rowe, the poetic group which did
most to revive the *aubade* for the modern reader was the Anglo-American
Imagist movement of the early twentieth century – often considered, in
T.S. Eliot's words, '*the point de repère*' for modernist poetry in English.[23] The
very first poem published by the group's leader, Ezra Pound, in a student
magazine of 1905, was entitled 'Belangel Alba'. His first pamphlet of poetry,
A Lume Spento (1908), included several dawn poems. His 1909 collection,
Exultations, included 'Alba Innominato', a translation of an anonymous
aubade that had earlier provided Swinburne with the refrain for his poem 'In
the Orchard' and which would later be retranslated by San Franciscan poet

Kenneth Rexroth. His first critical book, *The Spirit of Romance* (1910), was a study of the pre-Renaissance literature of Latin Europe incorporating his own translations of poems from Provence, Italy, Spain and Portugal. In that volume, Pound claims that all 'Romance literature begins with a Provencal "Alba", supposedly of the Tenth Century'.[24] From there he goes on to consider various *albas*, some anonymous and some by such known troubadours as Giraut de Borneh and Guilhem d'Autpol. In 1914 Pound followed this up with 'Langue D'Oc', a sequence of six poems modelled on troubadour originals, three of which are dawn songs. However, his most exquisite contribution to the genre sees Pound trying, almost successfully, to compress the *aubade* into the 17-syllable format of the Japanese *haiku*, in a perfect exemplification of the Imagist principles of succinctness:

Alba
As cool as the pale wet leaves
        of lily-of-the-valley
She lay beside me in the dawn.[25]

Pound's successor as leader of the movement, Amy Lowell, herself contributed to the tradition in such poems as

Aubade
As I would free the white almond from the green husk
So would I strip your trappings off,
Beloved.
And fingering the smooth and polished kernel
I should see that in my hands glittered a gem beyond counting.[26]

and 'Wakefulness'. Closer in spirit to Larkin's 'Aubade' is the first stanza of John Gould Fletcher's poem 'Dawn', which Amy Lowell included in her 1917 anthology *Some Imagist Poets*:

Above the east horizon,
The great red flower of the dawn
Opens slowly, petal by petal:
The trees emerge from darkness
With ghostly silver leaves,
Dew-powdered.
Now consciousness emerges
Reluctantly out of tides of sleep;
Finding with cold surprise
No strange new thing to match its dreams,
But merely the familiar shapes
Of bedpost, window-pane and wall.[27]

That slow resumption of the familiar shapes of the bedroom bears comparison with the last stanza of the Larkin:

> Slowly light strengthens, and the room takes shape.
> It stands plain as a wardrobe

Though the larger point to be made is not that Imagism provided Larkin with a continuity he wished to extend, the *aubade* form being handed down the generations like a relay baton from the troubadours to the Metaphysicals to the Imagists to him, but rather that it kept in the forefront of contemporary awareness a segment of literary history his own contribution was intended to sabotage.

Larkin's radical ellipsis

This last might seem like an absurd overstatement were it not for the brutal contrast between the title of Larkin's poem, freighted with echoes of a thousand dawns, a thousand romantic trysts, and the immediately consequent lines:

> **Aubade**
> I work all day, and get half-drunk at night.
> Waking at four to soundless dark, I stare.
> In time the curtain-edges will grow light.
> Till then I see what's really always there:
> Unresting death, a whole day nearer now,
> Making all thought impossible but how
> And where and when I shall myself die.

That tiny typographical hiatus between the two is an Offa's Dyke demarcating a frontier between opposed discourses: youth and age; sex and death; south and north; rural and urban; ancient and modern; and, undergirding them all, between the sung poems of the troubadours – light, airy, compact – and Larkin's gruelling written-to-be-read poetics. In short, that space between title and text is a moat between lyric and anti-lyric.

In the dense remorseless stanzas that follow, every one of the five characteristics enumerated above as the means by which we recognize a poem as an *aubade* is systematically eviscerated. Hence, (i) the sex of the narrator is not disclosed, the poem (like so many of Larkin's) being resolutely non-gender-specific; (ii) there is no declaration of love, whether proffered below the beloved's window or from within a shared bed; (iii) indeed, there is no beloved, whether of the opposite or the same sex, no addressee implied or directly summoned into a dialogue; (iv) it is not even morning – 'Waking at four *to soundless dark*' (my emphases) – the poem being set towards the end of the night rather than at the start of day; (v) this redefining of the *aubade* as less a dawn song than an hour-before-dawn song setting the stage for the poem's dark theme, the dispelling of the erotic by a terminal morbidity. Unresting sex has been nullified by 'Unresting death'.

These elisions, these emptyings out of what the term *aubade* means, carry other deletions in their wake. Mark Rowe has persuasively argued that

> A further striking inversion in Larkin's 'Aubade' is its sensory blankness. The traditional aubade, as Larkin knew it, celebrates awakening nature, and the sharpness and precision of the senses [...] Larkin's does not begin with the first stirrings of life, but with soundless dark; he is alone with his thoughts. The lack of sight, sound, and movement, already make him seem partially anaesthetized; they act as a portent and analogue for the oblivion to come.[28]

In other words, the brutal contrast between title and opening is *worked through* the rest of the poem, one association after another of the conventional *aubade* being nullified until the genre has been hollowed out, an empty shell, a husk. To what end? So as to speak the unspeakable. If death is the absence of life, as Larkin's 'Aubade' posits, how does one dramatize a blank? By invoking a genre brimful of life and then erasing it. The use of ellipsis to delete the defining conventions of the form enacts that final ellipse, the ultimate deletion of death.

We can now see that the Larkin poem squares up to the lyric tradition in a way that is doubly discontinuous: not only does 'Aubade' strategically depend for its meaning upon the autonomy of the *aubade* within the larger evolution of the lyric; but is itself looking to terminate the genre – or, at least, to subject it to a revolutionary coup. In negating the *aubade* the better to dramatize the way death negates life, Larkin replaces a set of conventions so antique as to seem farcical – who, really, in Callaghan's England, in the prelude to the Winter of Discontent, spent the chilly dawn hours plucking a lute below a virgin's window? – with an experience everyone knows, the 4.00 am horrors. So familiar is that experience, indeed, that once Larkin had effected his coup it became an object of wonder that no-one had done as much before.[29] The lyric tradition encompasses many poems about death but offers no generic equivalent to the *aubade*, no such regulative ideal as the *funereal alba*. Yet medical evidence suggests that the hour before dawn is an hour of maximum human vulnerability: the hour when the body's temperature is at its lowest; when the blood sugar level dips; the hour of maximum broncho-constriction associated with a multiplicity of disorders, from snoring to asthma attacks; the hour when, according to hospital and residential care-home statistics the mortality rate rises. This is the hour no *aube* memorializes:

> It stands plain as a wardrobe, what we know,
> Have always known, know that we can't escape,
> Yet can't accept. One side will have to go.

In effect, Larkin proposes that the love song 'will have to go' – 'Aubade' seeks the discontinuance of *aubades* – and the place filled with something more magnificent and terrible, the *aube* of our imminent annulment. Dread of the temporary loss of one's beloved is replaced by dread at the permanent loss of that most beloved of all, life itself.

First person plural

Of course, it might be rejoined that while the foregoing proves the lyric tradition to be composed of many parts from some of which Larkin disassociates himself, this does not confound the central proposition – that some lyrics are deeply subjective, that Larkin's are of that kind and none more so than 'Aubade'. Indeed, with a little ingenuity the argument might be reconfigured to claim that it is the very intensity and o.liness of his personal dread of death that causes Larkin to rebel against other parts of the lyric inheritance. In this perspective, accepting that lyrics need not be autobiographical exacerbates the fact that 'Aubade' uniquely is.

In rejecting this view, I want first to clarify the point at issue: this is not whether the author experienced the dread of personal extinction expressed in the poem (he clearly did); but whether the text before us identifies the narrator as Philip Larkin and the fear as exclusively his – or, to the contrary, whether the poem is presided over by an unnamed 'I' who might as readily be me as him, a woman as a man, a black as a white. I say the latter. The critics listed above say the former – and this despite the fact that 'Aubade' ruthlessly excludes any indication of the sex, race, class, profession or physical appearance of the narrator. Larkin could easily have steered readers towards a biographical interpretation by opening with a reference to his job ('The library-desk by day, the booze at night'), even his particular workplace ('The Brynmor Jones by day, the booze by night'), supplementing this with some detail that would intensify the identification of narrator and author (his baldness, perhaps, his deafness or myopia):

> The Brynmor Jones by day, the booze by night.
> Waking at four without my specs, I stare.

But the autobiographical poem is the one Larkin chose not to write. By the second stanza the poem finesses from singular to plural: 'The mind blanks at the glare' rather than '*My* mind blanks at the glare'; followed shortly thereafter by 'The sure extinction that *we* travel to' (my emphasis); and then the all-inclusive generalizations – 'The anaesthetic from which none come round', 'Being brave / Lets no one off the grave'. Really, these are very perverse grammatical registers to employ if seeking to dramatize an exclusive, uniquely personal testimony.

That Larkin had the ability to write first person poems packed with detail specific to that narrator had been demonstrated years before in poems like 'Naturally the Foundation will Bear Your Expenses' (*CP*, 134). There, unlike 'Aubade', every referent is particularized: the narrator's aeroplane (a Comet); his cities of departure and arrival (London and Bombay, respectively); his day of travel (Remembrance Sunday); his profession (academic); the previous outlets for the lecture he is to deliver (Berkeley University, BBC Radio's Third Programme, the publisher Chatto and Windus); and his Indian host (Professor Lal). This is the sort of detail 'Aubade' ruthlessly suppresses in the interests of expanding reader identification. The 'I' of 'Naturally the Foundation' is 'I' to the exclusion of everyone else: the 'I' of 'Aubade' is an 'I' everyone is invited to identify with, a representative 'I', an 'I' on behalf of 'us'.

Intertextuality and narratology

If biographical details are conspicuous by their absence, heterodox allusions are conspicuously present. In the interests of promoting the biographical approach, however, the Larkinocracy systematically suppresses the extensive use of citations. According to Tolley, 'there is little use of intertextuality (conscious or unconscious) in Larkin's work: the reference to other literatures as a dimension of understanding [...] was anathema to him'.[30] Leaving aside the extraordinary claim to be able to discriminate between an author's conscious and unconscious citations, this remains a definitive instance of a critic parroting a poet's propaganda at the expense of the poet's practice. Not only do Larkin's poems show him to be a master of allusion in contradiction of his anti-modernist posturing, but even as he was publicly denouncing intertextuality he was privately tipping off friends about his own citations, not least in 'Aubade'. On 11 January 1974 he wrote to Judy Egerton: 'my life at present resembles that of the French *plongeurs* in *Down & Out in Paris & London* – work all day, drink at night to forget it' (*SL*, 498). Turning to Orwell's documentary novel, or 'faction', one reads:

> Generally from ten to midnight I went into a little *bistro* in our street, an underground place frequented by Arab navvies. It was a bad place for fights, and I sometimes saw bottles thrown, once with fearful effect, but as a rule the Arabs fought among themselves and let Christians alone. *Raki*, the Arab drink, was very cheap, and the *bistro* was open all hours, for the Arabs – lucky men – had the power of working all day and drinking all night.[31]

Tolley's blind denials notwithstanding, the opening line of 'Aubade' is an intertextual reference and one which summons into the first person narration not just the *plongeurs* and scullions of Depression Paris, but specifically those who were Arab migrant workers.

That is just the start. Larkin's friend Robert Conquest remembers the pair of them engaging in 'talk [...] of a Blues version [of 'Aubade'] – the first line coming in perfectly, perhaps the sign of a real "influence"'.[32] B.J. Leggett, the scholar who has most assiduously explored Larkin's indebtedness to the blues, has been unable to locate a definitive source for that 'first line' but has identified such a superfluity of half-echoes as to conclude that the poem deliberately opposes African American folk music to the courtly music of the French title. 'The "official" attitude of the poem will be that of the aubade; its unofficial and operative attitude will be that of the blues.'[33] In this perspective, the aforementioned Offa's Dyke between the poem's title and first line demarcates racial and class boundaries.

Leggett offers convincing evidence for his claim that 'Aubade' is modelled on the classic blues:

Working and drinking are the common properties of the blues, drinking most often as a means of coping with despair [...] [as in] Mississippi John Hurt's 'whiskey straight will drive the blues away' [...] At times working and drinking may be found together as in this Lonnie Johnson stanza that has incorporated the floating blues phrase appropriated by 'Aubade':

> I work all day for you, until the sun go down,
> I work all day for you, from sun up until the sun go down,
> An you take all my money and drink it up,
>   and come home and want to fuss and clown[34]

The temporal location of 'Aubade', he continues, also parallels the blues: 'four o' clock turns out to be the most popular blues time for waking. "It's four o' clock in the morning, and I can't close my eyes". Sunnyland Slim's "Train Time" begins, "it was early one morning, just around four o' clock".'[35] In short, the formal grandeur of 'Aubade' is underwritten by a blues template or 'intertext', the poem's complexities carried by and returnable to the elemental simplicity of that mode after the following manner:

> I work all day, and get half-drunk at night.
> I work all day, and get half-drunk at night.
> In time the curtain edges will grow light.[36]

If Leggett's argument is found compelling, then it qualifies my earlier statement that the 'lyric tradition encompasses many poems about death but offers no generic equivalent to the *aubade*, no such regulative ideal as the *funereal alba*'. Though too repetitive to reward being read separate from musical performance, the blues was the nearest Western culture came to providing that *aube* of death.

I am happy to endorse Leggett's researches and to remark, as he does not, how they further complicate a first person singular narration that already carries an inflection of the French Arabs. To claim that the opening lines are modelled on the blues is to claim that at some level the narration is ascertainably African American. This is precisely what I meant when I earlier asserted that 'even his most subjective poems are so saturated with intertextual references as to be inclusive, heterodox, multicultural'. My only quarrel with Leggett is that he concentrates on blues allusions to the exclusion of the many other citations in Larkin's densely textured mosaic. He does not make the Orwell connection. Nor does he follow John Whitehead in catching an echo of Edward Thomas's 'Rain' in this same opening stanza of 'Aubade':

> Rain, midnight rain, nothing but the wild rain
> On this bleak hut, and solitude, and me
> Remembering again that I shall die[37]

Larkin had earlier selected 'Rain' for his Oxford anthology. As for line five's 'Unresting death', that derives from Siegfried Sassoon's poem 'The Darkness', which begins –

> The room, the darkness, and the bed;
> Quick ticks the clock; sleep comes not nigh:
> A melancholy mind must lie
> With troubling of its wakeful head.[38]

– and ends on the words 'undreaming death'. Invocations of Thomas and Sassoon might license the proposition that the impact of 'Aubade' upon the *aubade* is as devastating as that of the First World War poets upon the heroic: both achieve their special effects by chewing up and spitting out the bones of previous forms of lyric. Biographically inclined critics might also wish to observe that Thomas was an Englishman of Welsh extraction while Sassoon was Anglo-Jewish. Add these ethnicities to Orwell's Parisian Arabs and the African American inflections of the blues, and the result is a compound narrator more protean than Leggett knows.

A more extensive appropriation than any of the foregoing which Larkin again drew to the attention of friends concerns *The Green Man*, a 1969 potboiler by Kingsley Amis. When John Betjeman wrote praising 'Aubade', which had recently appeared in *The Times Literary Supplement*, Larkin's reply of 14 January 1978 made a direct link to the Amis novel:

> Your letter about 'Aubade' gave me tremendous pleasure: it was *extremely* kind of you to write [...] I think it's amazing the way people *don't* seem to worry about death. Of course one ought to be brave, and all that, but it's never been anything but a terrible source of dread to me. Kingsley sees the point: there's a wonderful page about it in *The Green Man*. (SL, 576)

That 'wonderful page'[39] is at the centre of a web of derivations from the novel such as might be double-columned, as in Table 7.1. Whether or not these are intertextual references in the usual sense, literary allusions we are required to notice, citations vital to the full meaning of the new encompassing text, I will leave for the reader to decide. However, there are two observations which I do wish to press. First, that the most extensive quotation from *The Green Man* cited in our grid is excerpted from a speech by Lucy Allington, daughter-in-law of the novel's protagonist. Even if her rationalist opinions are being quoted with a view to negating them, the fact remains that the narration of the poem is subject to infiltration from across gender as well as ethnic lines. The point is not that the narrator is a woman or an Arab or black or Welsh or Jewish. Rather, that the racial and gender promiscuity of such references chafes against mono-cultural readings, unhousing the narrative from autobiographical belonging and legitimizing interpretative diversity. The heterogeneity of the Larkin text undermines the narrative homogeneity imposed upon it by biographical critics.

The second, related observation is that narrators do not construct poems in speech but are constructed by them as text. Any form of citation draws attention to the textuality of the text and the factitiousness of the narrator. We are, then, at the opposite pole from the unmediated self-disclosure of the Booth model, what Terry Kelly (in an essay on this very poem) stupefyingly refers to as 'undiluted lyrical autobiography'.[40] The shocking intensity of 'Aubade' is not the precipitate of raw authorial feeling but of an articulation of feeling through a tessellation of quotes and echoes. And the reason that readers of every persuasion are summoned to identify with that 'I' is precisely because that 'I' is constituted by citations of every persuasion.

A few further examples will serve to validate the point. The general tenor of the opening verses and, more specifically, of such a line as 'Unresting death, a whole day nearer now', owes much to Laforgue's 'Stupeur':

> 'Chaque jour qui s'écoule est un pas vers la Mort!'
>
> Chaque jour est un pas! C'est vrai, pourtant! Folie!
> Et nous allons sans voir, gaspillant notre vie,
> Nous rapprochant toujours cependant du grand trou!
>
> ('Each day going by is a step towards Death!'
>
> Each day is a step! It's true, though! Madness!
> And we go along without seeing, wasting our lives,
> Moving closer always to the big hole!)[41]

Mention of 'the dread / Of dying, and being dead' at the end of the opening stanza invokes 'the dread of something after death' in Hamlet's 'To be or not

Table 7.1 'Aubade' and *The Green Man*

	'Aubade'	*The Green Man*
Stanza 1	Waking at four to soundless dark, I stare. In time the curtain-edges will grow light. Till then I see what's really always there	There was no light at all showing between the curtains and at their edges (104) It had been there all along, of course (34)
Stanza 2	the total emptiness for ever, The sure extinction that we travel to And shall be lost in always. Not to be here, Not to be anywhere, And soon	It was a pretty arresting thought, not being anything, not being anywhere, and yet the world still being here. Simply having everything stopping forever, not just for millions of years [...] It's where we're going to get to sooner or later, and perhaps sooner. (77)
Stanza 3	This is a special way of being afraid No trick dispels. Religion used to try, That vast, moth-eaten musical brocade Created to pretend we never die, And specious stuff that says *No rational being* *Can fear a thing it will not feel*, not seeing That this is what we fear – no sight, no sound, No touch or taste or smell, nothing to think with, Nothing to love or link with,	The fear of death is based on not wanting to consult fact and logic and common sense [...] To start with, death isn't a state [...] And it isn't an event in life. All the pain and anxiety you've been talking about can be very horrible, no doubt, but it all takes place in life [...] I mean you're not going to be hanging about fully conscious observing death happening to you. That might be very bad and frightening, if we could conceive of such a thing. But we can't. Death isn't something we experience. (78)
Stanza 5	all the uncaring Intricate rented world begins to rouse. The sky is white as clay, with no sun. Work has to be done.	Meanwhile there was work (of an unexacting sort) to be done. (71)

to be' speech in Act III, Scene I of Shakespeare's play.[42] 'The good not done' of stanza two pertinently echoes 'The Road Not Taken' by the American poet Robert Frost, a Larkin enthusiasm.[43] The lines 'An only life can take so long to climb / Clear of its wrong beginnings, and may never' rewrite 'The Unwanted' by C. Day Lewis (a poet Larkin ever found good to improve upon):

> Sure, from such warped beginnings
>   Nothing debonair
> Can come?[44]

The last line of the third verse, 'The anaesthetic from which none come round', splices the last line of Randall Jarrell's prose poem '1914' – 'It is the dream from which no one wakes' – which Larkin had already raided for his own commemoration of that year, 'MCMXIV' (the substituting of Roman numerals for the original's Arabic ones simultaneously invoking and revoking the association), with the line 'death was no more than anaesthetic' from Ford Madox Ford's Great War novel *A Man Could Stand Up* (1926).[45] Dylan Thomas's injunction to 'Rage, rage against the dying of the light'[46] underwrites the lines

> Most things may never happen: this one will,
> And realisation of it rages out

Eliot's 'Gerontion' (about which, more anon) is glancingly echoed throughout: consider the following likeness:

> Think
> Neither fear nor courage saves us. ('Gerontion')[47]

> Courage is no good:
> It means not scaring others. Being brave
> Lets no one off the grave.
> Death is no different whined at than withstood. ('Aubade')

The grim 'One side will have to go' of stanza five takes on a sardonic humour by association with the words of Oscar Wilde, dying in the shabby Hotel d'Alsace in Paris: 'My wallpaper and I are fighting a duel to the death. One or the other of us has to go.'[48] At which point our poem has added the utterance of a Irish homosexual to its compound narration. Finally, although not a direct citation, Larkin in his introduction to the Faber cassette recording of 'Aubade' pays general tribute to another author:

> In 1871 Thomas Hardy wrote in his notebook 'Dawn. Lying just after waking. The sad possibilities of the future are more vivid than at any

other time.' I've always found this true. And there came a time when it seemed more sensible to get up and write about it, rather than lie there worrying. The result was this poem, 'Aubade'.[49]

Where the other authors provided specific words and phrases, Hardy – by Larkin's own account – provided the overall theme and inspiration.

Compound allusions

Thus far the citations have come thick and fast but separately; Orwell, the blues, Edward Thomas, Siegfried Sassoon, Kingsley Amis, *Hamlet*, Robert Frost, C. Day Lewis, Randall Jarrell, Dylan Thomas, T.S. Eliot and Oscar Wilde yielding discrete verbal formulae. This is already sufficient to high-light Larkin's extraordinary mobility of invocation, an underestimated facet of his acknowledged genius for shifting language registers. In this section of the argument I wish to draw attention to his unparalleled skill at alluding *in a single phrase* to a multiplicity of prior texts, so that tiny integers are made to carry the impress of huge swathes of literary history.

Two examples will suffice, one of which I will present in summary and the other at greater length. Thus, the double 'nothing' of stanzas two ('nothing more terrible, nothing more true') and three ('nothing to think with, / Nothing to love or link with') is an echo-chamber locution whose resonances might plausibly be thought to include the Bible ('For we brought nothing into this world, and it is certain we can carry nothing out'), Lucretius ('Nothing can be created out of nothing'), *King Lear* ('Nothing will come of nothing'), the Arthur Hugh Clough of *The Bothie of Tober-na-Vuolich* ('A world where nothing is had for nothing') and the Francis Thompson of 'Daisy' ('Nothing begins, and nothing ends, / That is not paid with moan').

The second specimen comes near the close of the third stanza when the narrator is ridiculing

> specious stuff that says *No rational being*
> *Can fear a thing it will not feel,* not seeing
> That this is what we fear – no sight, no sound,
> No touch or taste or smell, nothing to think with,
> Nothing to love or link with

Embedded in these lines is a gleaning from one of the most famous monologues in Shakespeare, Jaques's 'All the world's a stage' speech from *As You Like It* (Act II, Scene VII, 139ff):

> Last scene of all,
> That ends this strange eventful history,
> Is second childishness and mere oblivion,
> Sans teeth, sans eyes, sans taste, sans everything.

Larkin has taken Shakespeare's list of sense impressions and Englished the French negative preceding each one. But he was not the first so to do: Cardinal Newman's pious 'The Dream of Gerontius' (1866) has 'Nor touch, nor taste, nor hearing hast thou now'; while Eliot's 'Gerontion' (1920), whose impress upon 'Aubade' has already been remarked, and which Northrop Frye regarded as a parody of Newman, has

> I have lost my sight, smell, hearing, taste and touch:
> How should I use them for your closer contact?

Two other Larkin favourites retained the French negatives, Edward Fitzgerald in *The Rubaiyat of Omar Khayyam* (1868 edition) –

> Ah, make the most of what we yet may spend,
> Before we too into the Dust descend;
> > Dust into Dust, and under Dust, to lie,
> Sans Wine, sans Song, sans Singer and – sans End!

– and the Virginia Woolf of *Between the Acts* (1941): 'All gone. I'm alone then. Sans niece, sans lover; and sans maid.'[50] As it is impossible to quarantine the Shakespeare from these intervening variations, impossible to prove that Shakespeare was indeed the primary citation, all of these texts are 'in play' when we come to parse the Larkin.

But there is more! For the power of this passage of 'Aubade', as of the anterior texts alluded to, arises from our sense that it takes what was a positive statement and nullifies it with a succession of negatives. To revert to Shakespeare for a moment, we might say that our anguish at Jaques's last line stems from the way we hear below it some such positive 'original' as this from another of his plays, *Troilus and Cressida* (Act I, Scene I, line 56): 'Her eyes, her hair, her cheek, her gait, her voice'. If 'Aubade' carries within its field of reverberation not only Jaques's speech but all the interim variations thereon, so it may be said to encompass *Troilus and Cressida* and its successors too. The grievousness of Larkin's lines derives in part from their negativizing of many tender expressions of love, whether sacred or profane. Examples might include: Ralegh's 'Her face, her tongue, her wit'; the colonial American poet Anne Bradstreet's lovely 'Letter to Her Husband absent upon Publick employment' ('My head, my heart, mine Eyes, my life, nay more'); Cardinal Newman's sermon 'Divine Calls', as quoted in *Apologia Pro Vita Sua* (1864) ('Let us beg and pray Him day by day to reveal Himself to our souls more fully, to quicken our sense, to give us sight and hearing, taste and touch of the world to come'); Hardy's 'He Inadvertently Cures His Love-Pains' ('Her lips, her eyes, her moods, her ways!'); and the delightful Jerome Kern–Herbert Reynolds song 'They Didn't Believe Me' (1914), which Larkin will have known in countless jazz versions by the likes of Ella Fitzgerald, Stan Kenton and Oscar Peterson:

> And when I told them how beautiful you are
> They didn't believe me. They didn't believe me!
> Your lips, your eyes, your cheeks, your hair,
> Are in a class beyond compare.

Further echoes abound in such favourite Larkin moderns as the Llewelyn Powys of *Love and Death* ('I saw, heard, tasted, smelt, and touched with her') and *Skin for Skin* ('an ephemeral existence, in which to see, to smell, to hear, to taste, and to touch'); the Virginia Woolf of *Orlando* ('he had heard her, tasted her, seen her, or all three together'); and the Aldous Huxley of *Brave New World* (who quotes the Troilus speech entire).[51]

We have now identified, in a list that is far from exhaustive, 14 works by ten authors that may be said to have left an impress (sometimes strong, sometimes faint) upon this fragment of a sentence that is a mere ten syllables in length, the equivalent of a single pentametric line or one-fiftieth of 'Aubade'. Perhaps this was what the poet John Mowat meant when he exclaimed that no-one makes words work harder than Larkin does.

Form as citation

The form of 'Aubade' is modelled on that of 'Ode to a Nightingale' by John Keats.[52] Where Keats employs a ten-line stanza with a short eighth line, 'Aubade' has a ten-line stanza with a short ninth line. In both cases, pentametric lines are briefly interrupted by a trimeter (irregular in Larkin's case). As we saw, Larkin had earlier utilized an inverted version of the stanza in 'The Whitsun Weddings', in which the second line is truncated, on this occasion retaining the rhyme scheme of 'Ode to a Nightingale' (ababcdecde) which 'Aubade' deviates from (ababccdeed).

The formal parallel may remind us of the thematic similarities between the two poems. In 'Ode to a Nightingale' as in 'Aubade' the narrator longs for an alcohol that will distract from the age, infirmity and death that overshadow life:

> O for a draught of vintage! That hath been
>   Cool'd a long age in the deep-delved earth,
> Tasting of Flora and the country-green,
>   Dance, and Provençal song, and sun-burnt mirth!
> O for a beaker full of the warm South,
>   Full of the true, the blushful Hippocrene,
>   With beaded bubbles winking at the brim,
>   And purple-stained mouth;

> That I might drink, and leave the world unseen,
> And with thee fade away into the forest dim:
>
> Fade far away, dissolve, and quite forget
> What thou among the leaves hast never known,
> The weariness, the fever, and the fret
> Here where men sit and hear each other groan;
> Where palsy shakes a few, sad, last gray hairs,
> Where youth grows pale, and spectre-thin, and dies;
> Where but to think is to be full of sorrow
> And leaden-eyed despairs

That Larkin should modify the Keats stanza in adopting it is apt, for 'Aubade' also deviates from the philosophy of 'Ode to a Nightingale'. Certainly, the death-wish which was a feature of early Larkin poems like 'Wants' ('Beneath it all, desire of oblivion runs' [*CP*, 42; *TCP*, 32]), and which is so pronounced in Keats –

> many a time
> I have been half in love with easeful Death,
> Call'd him soft names in many a mused rhyme,
> To take into the air my quiet breath;
> Now more than ever seems it rich to die

– is utterly renounced in 'Aubade' ('the dread / Of dying, and being dead'). Likewise, the Keatsian dream of artistic immortality emblematized by the nightingale ('Thou wast not born for death, immortal Bird!') finds no place in the 'total emptiness' and 'sure extinction' of 'Aubade'.

Half invocation, half revocation, 'Aubade' summons the Keats into a dialogue in which Romantic ideology is subjected to the acids of modernity. Nor is that reference to 'Provençal song' in the second verse of 'Nightingale' an irrelevance, Keats affirming the birthplace of the *aubade* which Larkin negates. At the formal level as well as the thematic, 'Aubade''s citations situate it in a relation to the lyric tradition that is adversarial, deconstructive, revolutionary.

Self-citation

While it can never be predicted when and to whom a masterpiece will be granted, it is certain that the artist least likely to botch the opportunity is the one who has prepared linguistic means appropriate to the task. The accounts of such friends as his Belfast colleague Arthur Terry confirm what is anyway obvious, that Larkin was a voracious if unsystematic reader of marked personal preferences and astonishing powers of recall.[53] What biographicalists refer to as his poetic 'voice' is a *bricolage* of textual invocations; *his* not by virtue of being newly minted but by being his amalgam, his orchestration of the repertoire of inherited linguistic formulae. In this sense, his practice as a poet is cognate with his work as a librarian, his editorship of the *Oxford Book of Twentieth Century English Verse*, his role as a jazz critic, a poem like 'Aubade' being a symposium of half-quotes and echoes.

However, before moving the argument to a conclusion, I wish to demonstrate that self-citation is part of the vast rehearsive repertoire of recyclings that make an 'Aubade' possible. That is to say, I wish to invalidate Booth's claim that 'He waits for the right time to use a word, will not use it until that time comes, and then, if at all possible, never uses it again.'[54] It is worth reminding ourselves, by way of context, that throughout his career Larkin had intermittently subjected the *aubade* to grievous bodily harm in a manner anticipative of his late masterpiece. In *A Girl in Winter*, Robin Fennel's enigmatic comment to Katherine Lind, 'And so you rose up to see the dawn', sounds like the fragment of an *aubade*. 'The bottle is drunk out by one', from *The North Ship* (1945), subverts the genre by suggesting that 'commerce' between 'lovers' is done well before dawn and is succeeded by night terrors which, as in 'Aubade', are only alleviated by the stirrings of the workaday world:

> The bottle is drunk out by one;
> At two, the book is shut;
> At three, the lovers lie apart,
> Love and its commerce done;
> And now the luminous watch-hands
> Show after four o'clock,
> Time of night when straying winds
> Trouble the dark.
>
> And I am sick for want of sleep;
> [...]
> I lie and wait for morning, and the birds,
> The first steps going down the unswept street,
> Voices of girls with scarves around their heads. (*CP*, 277; *TCP*, 13)

Thirty-three years later in 'Morning at last: there in the snow' (*CP*, 206), written while 'Aubade' was in progress, Larkin was still at it, beginning an *alba* as though the narrator could not wait for the beloved to leave ('Morning at last'!) and ending with a barbed declaration of love ('What morning woke to will remain, / Whether as happiness or pain'). Such full-scale rehearsals of the *anti-alba* prepare us for the innumerable small-scale rehearsals of diction, phrasing and cadence scattered throughout the *oeuvre*. What follows is but a sample.

Stanza one

Line 2: compare 'soundless dark' with 'soundless damage' in 'An Arundel Tomb' (*CP*, 110; *TCP*, 71)

Line 3: 'In time the curtain-edges will grow light' is previewed in both Larkin's novels: 'watching the light grow round the edges of the shutters' (*J*, 44); 'the backs of houses where light showed round the curtains' (*AGW*, 12)

Lines 5 and 10: 'unresting' and 'afresh' had already appeared, along with the 'tricks' of stanza three, *line 2*, in the poem 'The Trees' – 'Their yearly trick of looking new [...] // Yet still the unresting castles thresh [...] / Begin afresh, afresh, afresh' (*CP*, 166; *TCP*, 76–7). The latter had itself been prepared for in 'Long roots moor summer': 'the green / River-fresh castles of unresting leaf' (*CP*, 96; *TCP*, 288) and in an unpublished poem of 1956, 'castles of unresting leaf' (*LM*, 205)

Line 10: for a trial run at 'hold and horrify' see the 'accuse or horrify' of 'Neurotics' (*CP*, 22; *TCP*, 266)

Stanza two

Lines 1 and 2: 'Not in remorse / – The good not done' echoes 'Remorse for foolish action done' in 'After-Dinner Remarks' (*CP*, 238; *TCP,* 179)

Lines 2 and 3: 'the love not given, time / Torn off unused' reminds of the 'love unused' of 'Compline' (*CP*, 31; *TCP*, 270)

Lines 8 and 9: the 'not ... not' formula of 'Not to be here, / Not to be anywhere' was deployed and redeployed throughout Larkin's career, the following being six of the more prominent examples:

   (i) 'Not here but anywhere', 'Wires' (*CP*, 48; *TCP*, 35)

  (ii) 'not untrue and not unkind', 'Talking in Bed' (*CP*, 129; *TCP*, 61)

 (iii) '*Not you, not here*', 'The Dance' (*CP*, 154; *TCP*, 306)

 (iv) 'Not yet, perhaps not here', 'The Building' (*CP*, 192; *TCP*, 85)

  (v) 'Not knowing how, not hearing who', 'The Old Fools' (*CP*, 196; *TCP*, 81)

 (vi) 'Not at night? / Not when the strangers come?', 'The Old Fools' (*CP*, 197; *TCP*, 82)

Stanza three

Lines 7 and 8: the iambic row of nouns preceded by a negative – 'no sight, no sound, / No touch or taste or smell' – which we have already found to ricochet down the grand canyons of English literature also reverberates in Larkin's back-catalogue:

  (i) 'No dark, no dam, no earth, no grass', 'Take One Home for the Kiddies' (*CP*, 130; *TCP*, 59)

 (ii) 'no son, no wife, / No house or land', 'Dockery and Son' (*CP*, 152; *TCP*, 66)

(iii) 'no cost, / No past, no people else', 'When first we faced' (*CP*, 205; *TCP*, 315)

Lines 8 and 9: 'nothing to think with, / Nothing to love or link with' was trialled on many occasions:

  (i) 'nothing received / Nothing unloaded', 'Night in the plague' (*EPJ*, 338)
  (ii) 'For in the word death / There is nothing to grasp; nothing to catch or claim; / Nothing to adapt the skill of the heart to', 'And the wave sings' (*CP*, 6; *TCP*, 258)
  (iii) 'to some / Means nothing; others it leaves / Nothing to be said', 'Nothing To Be Said' (*CP*, 138; *TCP*, 51)
  (iv) 'for me nothing, / Nothing with', 'Dockery and Son' (*CP*, 153; *TCP*, 66)
  (v) 'nothing more terrible, nothing more true', 'Aubade' (*CP*, 208; *TCP*, 115)
  (vi) 'Where much is picturesque but nothing good, / And nothing can be found', 'Observation' (*CP*, 264; *TCP*, 105)
  (vii) 'Nothing so wild, nothing so glad', 'I see a girl dragged by the wrists' (*CP*, 278; *TCP*, 15)

Stanza four

Line 3: 'That slows each impulse down to indecision' renews

  (i) 'And silently, in words of indecision', 'Long Jump' (*TCP*, 153)
  (ii) 'I dread its indecision', 'I am washed upon a rock' (*CP*, 23; *TCP*, 266)
  (iii) 'Surrounds us with its own decisions – / And yet spend all our life on imprecisions', 'Ignorance' (*CP*, 107; *TCP*, 67)

Line 4: 'Most things may never happen: this one will' perfects the clumsy 'Most things are never meant. / This won't be, most likely' of 'Going, Going' (*CP*, 190; *TCP*, 83)

Stanza five

Line 8: 'The sky is white as clay' improves the 'sky is white' of 'Evening, and I, young' (*TCP*, 188)

Line 9: 'Work has to be done' irresistibly recalls 'Toads' (*CP*, 89; *TCP*, 38–9) and 'Toads Revisited' (*CP*, 148; *TCP*, 55–6), but its closest anticipation comes in *A Girl in Winter* (11): 'People were unwilling to get up [...] Nevertheless, the candles had to be lit [...] the men had to be given their breakfasts and got off to work in the yards. Life had to be carried on'

Line 10: As a number of commentators have already remarked, the 'doctors' of the last line recall the eponymous 'Ambulances' which 'come to rest at any kerb. / All streets in time are visited' (*CP*, 132; *TCP*, 63); though both formulations had been rehearsed, like so much else, in *A Girl in Winter* where 'the baker [...] went from door to door' (78).

This list, like that of allusions to other authors, could be doubled, perhaps trebled.[55] We have already done enough to demonstrate that Booth's picture of Larkin the lyricist, unencumbered by memory, spontaneously emoting to novel sensation, could scarcely be wider of the mark. Not only does this stereotype repress all evidence of Larkin's anti-lyricism, it also misrepresents as untutored a talent defined by enormous reservoirs of craft, tenacity, guile and learning. As the whole of life is, in a sense, a preparation for death, so the whole of English literature, and within it the whole of Larkin's *oeuvre*, is made a preparation for the writing of this great death poem.

'Aubade' and the death of God

In his magnificent 'Preface' to *The Anathemata*, poet-painter David Jones declares that 'The arts abhor any loppings off of meanings or emptyings out, any lessening of the totality of connotation, any loss of recession and thickness through.'[56] With much painting and most drawings, including those of Jones himself, the power of the finished composition depends upon the tracery of superseded moves, the *pentimenti*, still visible beneath the surface and constituting a pictorial memory, an evolutionary record of the process that preceded resolution. Larkin hinted at something similar in his account of Charlie Parker, whose music he affected to deplore as wholeheartedly as the poetry of Jones:

> Listening to Parker, one has the impression of a man who not only could translate his ideas into notes at superhuman speed, but who was simultaneously aware of half a dozen ways of resolving any given musical situation, and could somehow refer to all of them in passing beyond it. (*AWJ*, 30)

Larkin's massive orchestration of imports and self-citations functions in a comparable manner, the allusions being so deft and fleeting as to put the alert reader through a process of deduction regarding origins and meanings that remains a permanent part of the poem's purport.

What concerns us here is that the pace and nimiety of allusion not only facilitates a searching address to mortality but permits the poem, with no explicit paradings of chronology, to locate that address in a precise ideological context. To read Larkin through his depth citations is to scotch two persistent misunderstandings of his work: that it is ignorant of philosophy; and that it is ignorant of history. Proponents of the first proposition include Andrew Duncan (who derides 'his emotional deadness to ideas'), Bryan Appleyard (who deplores 'Larkin's aversion to intellect') and Roger Day (who claims that 'his thinking had a very "English" cast to it in that he seemed uninterested in, perhaps mistrustful of, ideas').[57] Proponents of the second proposition are of two kinds: those like Booth who celebrate

Larkin's a-historicism as proof that the 'poems present lyric universals'; and those like the poets Tom Paulin and Sean O'Brien (twin Salieris to Larkin's Mozart) who castigate it as evidence of right-wing recidivism. 'Larkin's attitude is opposed to the historical process' opines the former while the latter returns that 'Larkin's historical sense [...] leaves the history out in favour of religiose pageantry.'[58]

The allusions 'Aubade' steers by are preponderantly twentieth century: a multiplicity of unnamed blues maestros, First World War poets like Edward Thomas and Siegfried Sassoon, moderns like Hardy, Frost and Eliot, such mid-century masters as Orwell, Dylan Thomas and Randall Jarrell, and contemporaries like Kingsley Amis. The citations the poem incorporates to negate are preponderantly pre-twentieth century: the medieval troubadours, seventeenth-century Metaphysicals, Romantics like Keats, Victorians like Swinburne, and the exquisite Imagists so easily made to seem effete by the enormity of the Great War. To put the case over-schematically, the literary citations in 'Aubade' are organized on a temporal basis, before and after modernity, with the poem emphatically in the latter camp. De-historicizing Larkin, whether for praise or blame, entails denial of his mastery of allusion.

It also involves denial of the recency of the kind of death under discussion. Of course, Booth is right to say that lyric poets have routinely reminded that 'death awaits us', some expressing terror at the thought. More often than not, that was a spiritual terror at the prospect of God's judgement and the possibility of eternal damnation. The eighteenth-century poet William Cowper, a man of great simplicity and gentleness of spirit, experienced a succession of terrible psychological prostrations in one of which a messenger of God appeared before him declaring 'Actum est de te, perii sti' ('It is all up with thee, thou hast already utterly perished'), which left him with the inconsolable conviction that he was already damned, though he knew not for what transgressions. Cowper's modern reputation rests upon a handful of popular lyrics memorializing pet animals. Much more representative, however, are poems like 'Song of Mercy and Judgement' in which reality is a floating of tarmacadam over a fathomless inferno:

> Then what soul-distressing noises
>   Seemed to reach me from below,
> Visionary scenes and voices,
>   Flames of Hell and screams of woe.[59]

'The Dream of Gerontius' by Cardinal Newman, to which we have several times referred, may seem the very opposite of Cowper, with its account of a saved soul leaving the body at death; but Cowper and Newman are alike pre-moderns in their assurance of an afterlife. The modern position negates both in its belief that what death represents is

> total emptiness for ever,
> The sure extinction that we travel to
> And shall be lost in always. Not to be here,
> Not to be anywhere,
> And soon; nothing more terrible, nothing more true.

This post-Nietzschean death is a different death to that of Cowper or Newman, with different horrors and consolations, different conceptions of time, different implications for the conduct of one's life. If an *aubade* is a dawn song, Larkin's 'Aubade' articulates the dawning of a new type of dying, the birth of a new death, a simultaneous morning and mourning.

The utter finality of this conception of death, its lack of susceptibility to redemptive interpretation, makes religious belief seem futile and antique, a species of intellectual fraud:

> This is a special way of being afraid
> No trick dispels. Religion used to try,
> That vast, moth-eaten musical brocade
> Created to pretend we never die

Although Christianity is not singled out for assault, its inclusion in the general demolition of theologies is implicit in our poem's title: for in many an *aubade* erotic desire for a female love object is a metaphor for spiritual adoration of the Blessed Virgin Mary (a trope that receives its apotheosis in the celestial vision of Beatrice at the climax of Dante's *Paradiso*).

The philosophical lucidity of the poem derives entirely from its appalled focus upon the enhanced obliterative power of death in a post-theological context. This necessitates the nullification of every form of false consciousness which might be used to evade the terrible truth. The very syntax of the poem, its sentences inverted so as to foreground negatives, takes on an interrogatory ruthlessness with its 'not that and not that, but *this*' clarifications of meaning:

> The mind blanks at the glare. Not in remorse
> – The good not done, the love not given, time
> Torn off unused – nor wretchedly because
> An only life can take so long to climb
> Clear of its wrong beginnings, and may never;
> But at the total emptiness for ever

This deconstructive lexis is then turned upon a succession of false belief systems, not just religion but Epicureanism, Stoicism and existentialism, each of which is subjected to redefinition, if not total invalidation, from this withering late-millennial vantage-point.

That 'Aubade' could not have been written before the twentieth century is enough to prove that it is historically embedded, and by virtue of its ideas and attitudes – its philosophy, if you will – which are specific to modernity. Indeed, it is no exaggeration to claim that Larkin is more modernist than the modernists: for where an Eliot, Auden or David Jones retreated from the nuclear crisis of modernity, the death of God, into a pre-Nietzschean religiosity; he, like his hero Hardy, kept faith with his lack of faith.

'Aubade' and Epicureanism

The assault upon Epicureanism is as direct, the italicized words in the following passage being close enough to the sayings of Epicurus (341–270 BC) to constitute another citation:

> And specious stuff that says *No rational being*
> *Can fear a thing it will not feel*, not seeing
> That this is what we fear – no sight, no sound,
> No touch or taste or smell, nothing to think with,
> Nothing to love or link with

The term Epicureanism is these days a virtual synonym for hedonism, but Epicurus's philosophy stressed the avoidance of anxiety and pain much more than the pursuit of pleasure. He considered fear of death a principal source of human unhappiness and sought to vanquish that dread with rational argument. Death 'is nothing to us', he claimed, for 'so long as we exist, death is not with us; but when death comes, then we do not exist. It does not concern either the living or the dead.'[60]

As James Warren has recently emphasized, the goal of the epicurean is the condition of *ataraxia*, a state of tranquillity or well-being, free of pain or fear.[61] Once this state has been attained, the duration of one's life ceases to be a cause of vexation; and from this it may reasonably be inferred that the only sense in which an epicurean can die prematurely, and therefore dread death, is to die before achieving *ataraxia*. Such a condition of *incompleteness* is alluded to in 'Aubade' –

> An only life can take so long to climb
> Clear of its wrong beginnings, and may never

But Larkin mentions this in order to sweep it aside as part and parcel of the attempt to rationalize, palliate or deny death's omnicidalism.

The philosophy has attracted adherents down the centuries, from early disciples of Epicurus such as Philodemus to eighteenth-century rationalists like Thomas Jefferson (who in its name scripted the Pursuit of Happiness into *The Declaration of Independence*). Its literary influence has also been profound, from the poetry of Lucretius, Horace and Virgil to the prose of Llewelyn Powys, a particular favourite with Larkin. After 'Aubade' had appeared in the *Times Literary Supplement*, the eminent Cambridge sociologist W.G. Runciman engaged Larkin in a correspondence in which the poet drew particular attention to 'Llewelyn Powys's *Love and Death* an autobiographical novel that ends with death in the first person, quite a *tour de force*' (*SL*, 591). That Larkin admired but could not emulate the insouciance of the tubercular Powys is borne out by the following contrast:

> Montaigne in his essay declares that in the hour of death Nature instructs how best to conduct oneself. Anyhow, my agony was not yet, and as Epicurus and Shakespeare had taught, when once I was dead I certainly would have nothing to fear. (*Love and Death*)

> Unresting death, a whole day nearer now,
> Making all thought impossible but how
> And where and when I shall myself die.
> Arid interrogation: yet the dread
> Of dying, and being dead,
> Flashes afresh to hold and horrify. ('Aubade')

Larkin's insistence that the prospect of dying and of being dead alike induce dread contradicts another passage of *Love and Death*, though admittedly one in which Powys departs from strict Epicureanism:

> For which of the horizontal chrysalises of mortal dust, lying beneath the footworn floor of Salisbury Cathedral, would not eagerly snatch at any evening of life, though such an evening were to include the dread hour of their own death? – Better to be dying, they would say, than dead.[62]

For Powys, only the 'hour of [...] death' is characterized by 'dread' (and if Montaigne is to be believed, not even that); in all other regards life – even in its terminal stages – is to be savoured and enjoyed.

The poem's objections to Epicureanism are of two kinds. First, what it perceives as an *aporia* in the proposition that '*No rational being / Can fear a thing it will not feel*' since the prospect of losing the means to feel is precisely '*what we fear*'. Second, the conviction that the use of logic to address the supreme illogicality of death amounts to an evasion, rather than a dissection, of the terror at the core of the human condition. Epicureanism simply looks away from the nothingness we voyage towards – on the grounds that when we get there we will not exist – and by ignoring the terminus also fails to capture the sensation of helplessness at this remorseless, one-way transit to oblivion. Larkin's insistence upon both the *journey* and the *destination* – 'The sure extinction that we travel to' – stands as a reproach to Epicureanism's too easily won *ataraxia*.[63] This is a philosophy that does not so much explain death as explain it away.

'Aubade' and Stoicism

Larkin's critique of Epicurus takes its place alongside those of such contemporary philosophers as Thomas Nagel, Bernard Williams, Martha Nussbaum, Gisela Striker, Joseph Raz and Fred Feldman. To recognize as much is to again be struck by the absurdity of the proposition that Larkin's themes are historically transcendent. 'Aubade' is not referencing these pre-Christian beliefs as a *timeless* font of wisdom, it is deconstructing them in relation to the collapse of that religion by which they were superseded. The poem's methodology is dependent upon the view that, far from being continuous or immutable, history is discontinuous and divisible into discrete cultural epochs (what Foucault dubs *epistemes*). The same predicates prevail when we turn to the rival philosophy of Stoicism.

The issue arises because a majority of commentators upon 'Aubade' see it as modulating from naked terror in the first three verses, via a somewhat more distanced fourth verse ('And so it stays just on the edge of vision, / A small unfocused blur'), to a stanza five characterized by Stoic resolve ('Work has to be done'). John Whitehead and Mark Rowe agree with Andrew Motion that

> On 27 November, having abandoned the poem at a point when 'Courage' had been dismissed as 'no good' because 'Death is no different whined at than withstood', he added a final verse which is stoic where the previous three had been terrified, and packed it with ordinary objects rather than general assertions.[64]

Richard Palmer goes considerably further, finding the Stoicism all-prevailing, the terror non-existent:

> That brooding personal elegy has a tough stoicism that calms, even cheers; the flinty purposefulness of 'Work has to be done' is not that of a man 'just waiting for the end'. Indeed, the poem is amongst all else remarkable for its *complete absence of horror or terror.*[65]

What makes all these judgements otiose is their apparent ignorance of the fact that from the time of its founder Zeno (335–263 BC) to that of Epictetus (AD 55–135) and Marcus Aurelius (AD 121–80), the main sources of doctrine in its last creative phase, Stoicism was deeply grounded in religious belief. Epictetus defined the philosopher as the missionary of Providence to humanity, enjoining an absolute trust in the Divine Will to be maintained through every misfortune. Thus, Epictetus promotes the attitude that death is not the *losing* of life but the *returning* of it to its Creator. Not surprisingly, Stoicism deeply influenced the fathers of the Christian Church, notably Augustine; while the moving accounts by Tacitus of the deaths of the Stoic martyrs provided a model for Christian martyrologists such as John Foxe. In short, Stoicism is party to that 'Religion' which 'Aubade' has already dismissed as a 'vast, moth-eaten musical brocade' and a 'trick'.

It might be rejoined that the ending of 'Aubade' is stoical in the vernacular sense of courage or fortitude, indifference to pain or fear, rather than in a strict philosophical sense. This is scarcely more convincing. 'Courage', we are told, 'is no good: / It means not scaring others.' Nor does the tone of the last six lines seem appositely resolute. Telephones 'crouch', more like predatory animals *getting ready to spring* than instruments 'getting ready to ring'. Offices are 'locked-up', like prison cells (or 'lock-ups'). The workaday world is described as 'uncaring' and 'rented', as though its only value is financial. The sky is 'white as clay': 'white' already carries morbid associations – to appear ashen, to have a deathly pallor, to look as if one had seen a ghost; white 'as clay' deepens the morbidity as white clay, sometimes known as *clay white*, was used in the past for making death masks. The expression 'Work has to be done' more readily suggests compulsion or grim necessity than personal resolve. Even those harbingers of life, 'Postmen', resemble nothing so much as those harbingers of death, 'doctors', as they 'go from house to house'.

That the poem ends with no display of stoic conviction is vital to its meaning and its method. 'Aubade''s integrity stems from the ruthlessness with which it strips away, one by one, the defences we customarily use to shield ourselves against death's encroachment and would be betrayed by a consolatory ending. So how does the poem achieve an artistically plausible exit without succumbing to a false sense of closure? Leggett provides the right answer:

> The genius of the poem is to round back to its opening blues line for what small defence it offers against the fear of death. One cannot escape it or accept it, but one can be distracted from it [...] How does one cope with a thought that is unacceptable and inescapable? By working all day and getting half drunk at night. It was there from the beginning, the point from which the poem departs and to which it returns.[66]

If the thought of work brings any lessening of the narrator's terror it is because it provides a daytime sedative to complement the night-time sedative of booze, distracting from the 'Unresting death' which is 'really always there'. The narrator's punishing cycle begins again of killing time until killed *by* time.

'Aubade' and existentialism

'Aubade''s thesis that we habitually tranquillize ourselves against the radicalism of the human condition is entirely congruent with existentialism. Many existentialist novels and plays turn upon a crisis in which a somnambulatory protagonist is involuntarily awoken to the discomforting 'truth' about his or her place in the universe: *L'Étranger*, for instance, *Les Mouches* or *La Putain respectueuse*. This is the 'plot' of 'Aubade': waking at 4.00 am, divested of the daytime and night-time sedatives of work and alcohol – stripped, too, of the *personae*, the comforting self-projections that accompany these activities – the narrator confronts the loneliness, imminence and finality of personal annihilation. The poem's consonance with this mid-twentieth-century philosophy once again serves to underline the extent to which it is historically specific.

As one would expect of an intelligence as prodigious as Larkin's, 'Aubade' does not passively replicate theories but adjudicates amongst them, rejecting some, modifying others, to arrive at a post-existentialist position. Certainly, the address to mortality in Sartre and Camus receives little endorsement from the poem. Sartre's position is not dissimilar to that of the Epicureans: namely, that because 'I' and death cannot be in the same place at the same time – when my death arrives then, by definition, 'I' have gone – death cannot be experienced and so is of little concern; it just comes along 'into the bargain', as he says, the final absurdity. This is simply a more up-to-date version of what 'Aubade' dismisses as 'specious stuff that says *No rational being / Can fear a thing it will not feel*'. For Camus, by contrast, mortality produces not despair or resignation but rebellion. 'Human insurrection is a prolonged protest against death.'[67] In embracing one's chosen projects despite the meaninglessness death confers upon them, the human subject embraces life, gives it a value and a meaning, and even achieves a degree of personal nobility. Though not explicitly addressed to Camus, the lines –

> Courage is no good:
> It means not scaring others. Being brave
> Lets no one off the grave.
> Death is no different whined at than withstood

– are at the opposite pole to his ontological heroics. Larkin's emphasis upon the equivalence of courage and cowardice – equivalent, that is, in their irrelevance – has the effect of exposing that hint of the Boy Scout in Camus's ethics, with their whiff of earnestness and derring-do, their proximity to Kipling's 'If'.

Of the existentialist philosophers, Heidegger offers the most sustained account of the meaninglessness of death as constitutive of the meaningfulness of life. Like the Larkin of 'Aubade', he sees death as the most inexorable given of the human condition ('Most things may never happen: this one will', as the poem puts it). Like Larkin, he places less emphasis on dying and being dead than on the effects of living with them in prospect (what he terms, being-toward-death). Like Larkin, he postulates that the prospect of death sets a boundary to the subject's consciousness, inducing a sense of finitude; an apprehension that while time may go on forever, *my* time is running out. Like Larkin, Heidegger proposes that death *individuates* the human subject, snatches a 'me' from the 'they'; for while everyone must die, only I can die the death reserved for me – and, more importantly, live *my* life in anticipation of it. As Heidegger says: 'In a way, it is only in dying that I can say absolutely "I am".'[68] At the same time, both are profoundly aware that death abolishes existence rather than completing it: as Heidegger expresses it, death is 'the possibility of the impossibility of any existence at all'; so that whatever value it has pertains to its intensification of life rather than in itself.[69] Thereafter, they disagree.

As John Macquarrie has noted, the Heideggerian 'moment before death' replaces Kierkegaard's 'moment before God' as that 'in which my past, present and future are gathered into the unity of a resolute self'.[70] A life without the prospect of death would be a life of perpetual postponement; it is precisely the awareness of one's own finitude, that time is scant and death final, that obliges one to take life seriously, to abandon frivolities and *divertissements* and instead make fundamental choices. Only by these means does one discover who one is, for a self is not given ready-made but is the precipitate of authentic decision-taking: if the first thing to do is choose choice, in the long run what is chosen is oneself. Hence, Heidegger counsels against regarding death as an event that comes closer moment by moment, like a train approaching from the distance, insisting that we live in the presence of a death that has already arrived. To do otherwise is to make death an external, passive and distanced phenomenon rather than an interiorized and active participant in the ontological drama.

'Aubade' offers a point-by-point refutation of this redemptive view of death. The opening stanza imagines death approaching from a distance in exactly the terms Heidegger decries: 'Unresting death, a whole day *nearer* now' (my emphasis). Rather than concentrating the mind, as the philosopher vouches, the proximity of death so mesmerizes the narrator that 'all thought' is dispersed which is not morbid:

> Unresting death, a whole day nearer now,
> Making all thought impossible but how
> And where and when I shall myself die.[71]

Far from a consciousness of life's brevity making the narrator resolute and decisive, it 'slows each impulse down to *indecision*' (my emphasis). As for the Heideggerian injunction to face death, this simply cannot be met, the poem explains, because of the way it dazzles and blinds: hence the language of *furnaces* and *Flashes*; of that which can only be observed peripherally, 'just on the edge of vision'; for when one tries to stare death in the eye, 'The mind blanks at the glare'.

Compounding the difficulty of confronting a death one can never be present to is the difficulty in conceptualizing the nothingness it ushers in. The very word 'nothing', like the numerical 'zero' sign, betrays its meaning by occupying the site of emptiness: oblivion, it follows, may be properly sounded only in silences. The best the narrator can do from within the prison-house of language is throw out descriptions and definitions whose very inconsistencies bespeak the conceptual *aporia*. Consider three descriptions:

   (i) the total emptiness for ever
  (ii) The sure extinction that we travel to
        And shall be lost in always.
 (iii) The anaesthetic from which none come round.

The first declares death to be a doorway to unmitigated nothingness. The second presents oblivion as a vast receptacle in which we shall be eternally lost, perhaps in disembodied form. The third suggests an embodied post-mortem state akin to cryogenization. That these propositions do not add up despite being stated so categorically is an earnest of the fact that nothingness defies the categorical. Similar complexities arise with those locutions which seem both to affirm and negate the possibility that oblivion has materiality: does 'Nothing to love or link with' mean that the narrator has not anything to love or, to the contrary, that he loves nothingness? The present purpose is not to pursue such paradoxes but to offer them as further enactments of the difficulty of conceptualizing a death Heidegger would have us embrace.

The *syncretism* of 'Aubade', its deftness of citation, permits the summoning of entire philosophies atomized into piths and gists, rumours and reverberations, and all held in tension by the traumatized emotions of the narrator. The result is an evaluation of thought in relation to emotion, the poem as a crucible of *felt* ideas. Without so much as mentioning them, 'Aubade' invalidates the theories of Sartre and Camus and offers only the most qualified assent to those of Martin Heidegger. If the poem can be said to submit earlier belief systems to a corrosively existential gaze – theology, Courtly Love, Epicureanism, Stoicism – then it may be said to subject existentialism to a like deconstruction. The narrator is an existentialist who has ceased to believe in existentialism.

Conclusion

Those of a theological disposition take pleasure in pointing out that a committed atheist like Richard Dawkins is as much a believer as any Deist. Even if we allow that religious belief and unbelief are alike subject to fundamentalist adherency; and even if we go on to accept that God and nothingness share a degree of unknowability, there remains a world of difference between the two modes of address to reality. For the non-religious, the cosmic process is natural rather than supernatural, physical rather than abstract, terrestrial rather than sidereal; whatever spirit there is informs a body, whatever infinite there is informs the finite, whatever intangibles there are inform the actual, whatever ideal there is informs the real. The vision is entirely this-worldly, not other-worldly. The concept of the sacramental is to be tested against *now* and *here* and *this* – what 'The Old Fools' calls 'the million-petalled flower / Of being here' (*CP*, 196; *TCP*, 81). All of which is also to say that this life is not a rehearsal, *it is all there is.* If one really wants to claim that there is an under-pattern of belief in Larkin's unbelief, it is not to be located in a spurious comparison with religion; but rather in the very historicism that so many critics have denied him. For Larkin, the revolution in thought which we associate with such names as Darwin, Nietzsche and Freud may be moved forward from but not back. Though not consolatory in the usual senses, this is an art that is peculiarly liberating in its throwing over of the zimmer-frames of dogma and credulity, in its commitment to the state of knowledge under the conditions of modernity. In other words, 'Aubade' is a masterpiece which affords a barometric reading of late millennial Western culture as encapsulated in its ideologies of death.

Notes

Introduction: A Textuality that Dare not Speak its Name

1. Although Burke's eschewal of narratology means that his position is almost the opposite of my own, this Introduction (from the title onwards) is greatly indebted to *The Death and Return of the Author: Criticism and Subjectivity in Barthes, Foucault and Derrida* by Séan Burke (Edinburgh University Press, 1998).
2. Andrew Motion, 'On the Plain of Holderness', in *Larkin at Sixty*, ed. Anthony Thwaite (Faber, London, 1982), 68.
3. James Booth, *Philip Larkin: Writer* (Harvester, Hemel Hempstead, 1992), 79, 3.
4. Ibid., 93.
5. Anthony Thwaite, 'The Poetry of Philip Larkin', *Phoenix*, 11/12 (1973–74), 41.
6. Anthony Thwaite, *Poetry Today: A Critical Guide to British Poetry, 1960–1984* (Longman, London, 1985), 43.
7. David Timms, *Philip Larkin* (Oliver & Boyd, Edinburgh, 1973), 68.
8. John Whitehead, *Hardy to Larkin: Seven English Poets* (Hearthstone, Munslow, 1995), 215.
9. Jacques Derrida, *Dissemination*, trans. Barbara Johnson (Athlone, London, 1981), especially the essay 'Plato's Pharmacy'.
10. A.T. Tolley, *Larkin at Work: A Study of Larkin's Mode of Composition as Seen in his Workbooks* (Hull University Press, 1997), 179. Contrast Tolley's plodding literalism about the poet's need to 'be true to what did happen' with Larkin's nimble wit:

    INTERVIEWER: *I think you've said that a writer must write the truth ...*
    LARKIN: I was probably lying. (*FR*, 49)

    Similarly, Joseph Bristow argues that Larkin's 'work and his life proved almost inseparable from one another as his career developed over time [...] Rarely have the personality of the poet and his poetic persona been conflated into one and the same image. Larkin, in this respect, appeared to live up to the ordinariness upon which his reputation as a writer had been built.' 'The Obscenity of Philip Larkin', *Critical Inquiry* (Autumn 1994), 161.
11. Anthony Thwaite, 'The Poetry of Philip Larkin', in *The Survival of Poetry*, ed. Martin Dodsworth (Faber, London, 1970), 47.
12. Even a life as short and emphatic as that of Sylvia Plath has leant itself to wildly discrepant biographies involving mutually exclusive assessments of her marriage: Plath the murder victim of Hughes (Robin Morgan); Plath the proto-feminist and her patriarchal husband (Edward Butscher); Plath the unbearable self-destructive genius and her long-suffering consort, Ted (Anne Stevenson); Sylvia and Ted, star-crossed lovers (Ronald Hayman).
13. Such biographical censorings are perpetuated in encyclopaedias and literary Baedekers. Michael Stapleton's *Cambridge Guide to English Literature* (Cambridge University Press, 1983) has the unenviable distinction of failing to explain why Oscar Wilde was imprisoned, or why E.M. Forster's frankly homoerotic novel *Maurice* was published posthumously. Again, W.H. Auden's marriage to Erika

Mann is mentioned, but not that he was a homosexual who entered the contract to give a refugee from the Nazis (she was the daughter of Thomas Mann) American citizenship.

14. Richard Bradford, *First Boredom, Then Fear* (Peter Owen, London, 2005), 154. Ronald Drinkwater writes, in a letter dated 18 March 1986: 'Probably only a few of the older members of the University will remember that he lived in Cottingham for his first few years in Hull – at first in a four-square house over the garden wall from us – now sadly long-since demolished to make way for a block of flats; subsequently, after a chance meeting in Hallgate with my wife at the time when his landlady was just being admitted to hospital with a terminal illness, in a furnished flat which we had available here where he stayed for a year or so until a university flat in Pearson Park became available. In a note which he subsequently wrote in my son's copy of *The Whitsun Weddings* he said that some of the poems in the volume had been written at [our house] 192 Hallgate. Not unnaturally that set us looking out for actual clues, and the fact that he was living in a family house in a not completely self-contained flat suggested a basis for the contrast between his state and that of the family man, allowing for a certain poetic licence in the account of the family man's pattern of life! This is perhaps borne out by the fact that the name Arnold which he gives to the family man is an anagram of my own name' (unpublished private correspondence).

15. Tolley, *Larkin at Work*, 183.

16. Burke, *Death and Return*, 51.

17. Andrew Motion, *Philip Larkin: A Writer's Life* (Faber, London, 1993), 381.

18. Jean Hartley, *Philip Larkin, the Marvell Press and Me* (Carcanet, Manchester, 1989), 68, 73, 68.

19. A.T. Tolley, 'Letter to the Editors', *About Larkin*, 34 (October 2012), 23.

20. Sean O'Brien, 'The Apprentice Poet', *Sunday Times, Culture* supplement, 2005. James Booth and Janet Brennan, 'Editorial', *About Larkin*, 29 (April 2010), 2. Sean O'Brien, 'A Desolation Foretold', *Times Literary Supplement*, 8 June 2012, 9. Terry Kelly, 'Living with Larkin', *About Larkin*, 33 (April 2012), 15. Terry Kelly, [untitled book review], *About Larkin*, 19 (Spring 2005), 32.

21. In the present writer's opinion, the demerits are threefold. First, the volume is too physically unwieldy and awkward of use to meet the needs of the general reader. It is a scholar's edition. A possible solution would be to persuade Martin Amis to enlarge his excellent *Selected Poems* (Faber, London, 2011) sufficiently to plug the gap. Second, the crowding of poems upon the page is not just unsightly but seriously confusing as to where individual works (especially untitled ones) start and finish. Third, while Professor Burnett claims that 'mere scraps of verse' have been excluded, the volume scours Larkin's private correspondence for just such snippets – one runs, in its entirety, 'Thought you might welcome a dekko / At this pre-distortion El Greco'; and another, 'Walt Whitman / Was certainly no titman / Leaves of Grass / ...'. Ridding a second edition of this unworthy material would help create space for a more pleasing presentation of the valid corpus. On the other hand, the need for Burnett's editorial precision is everywhere apparent. For just as the distortions of biographies are replicated lower down the line in literary Baedekers, so the errors of critics like Tolley are mirrored in school and student guides. Alison Jones's *A Student's Guide to High Windows and the Poetry of Philip Larkin* (Twin Serpents, Oxford, 2009) mangles the titles of some of the same Larkin poems as does he. Jones, we are told, 'is an experienced teacher of English and Media Studies' who 'trained at Oxford University, Warwick University and

recently completed an M.A. in Modern Poetry at Oxford Brookes University. She is currently Head of Department at a school in Oxford'. Despite these impeccable credentials, she misspells such illustrious names as T.S. Eliot, Jean-Paul Sartre, Iris Murdoch (her first name is repeatedly given as Irish), Graham Greene, Doris Lessing, Caryl Churchill and Salman Rushdie. *Krapp's Last Tape* is retitled *Krapp's Last Stand*; Stoppard's *Travesties* becomes *Transvestites*; a dramatist named Arnold has a play called *Wesker Roots*; and Larkin's poem 'Sympathy in White Major' is 'named after a well known jazz tune (Theophile Gautier's "Symphonie en Blanc Majeur")'. Does it matter that a generation of questing minds should be fed such misinformation? Yes. It matters.

22. Clive James, 'Pretending To Be Him', *Times Literary Supplement*, 28 February 2003, 19.
23. James Booth, *Philip Larkin: The Poet's Plight* (Macmillan, Basingstoke, 2005), 121.
24. Booth, *Philip Larkin: Writer*, 183.
25. Ibid., 161; Booth, *Philip Larkin: The Poet's Plight*, 104, 170.
26. Tom Paulin, 'She Did Not Change: Philip Larkin', in *Minotaur: Poetry and the Nation State* (Harvard University Press, Cambridge, MA, 1992), 234.
27. Ibid., 235.
28. Terry Kelly, [untitled book review], *About Larkin*, 15 (April 2003), 29.
29. Kelly, 'Living with Larkin', 15.
30. Motion, *Life*, 287.
31. Ibid., 370.
32. Maeve Brennan, *The Philip Larkin I Knew* (Manchester University Press, 2002), 63.
33. Bradford, *First Boredom, Then Fear*, 229–31.
34. As Thwaite's footnote to the letter observes,'This sounds like "Forget What Did", which was not completed to L[arkin]'s satisfaction until almost twenty years later.' *SL*, 187.
35. Marion Lomax, 'Larkin with Women', in *Larkin with Poetry*, ed. Michael Baron (English Association, Leicester, 1997), 39–40.
36. The 'in life, which is true' formula is adapted from a comment Peter Hall made regarding Vanessa Redgrave, quoted in 'A Life in Parts' by Roy Hattersley, *The Guardian Saturday Review*, 6 May 2000, 6. As for the concept of the author being a creation of the text, see Séan Burke's statement that 'faith in the *oeuvre* is nothing less than faith in the author, or in his signature at least, and the constants and correspondences thereby contracted. In absolutely minimalist terms, the author is that principle which unites the objects – whether collusive or discrete – that gather under his proper name.' Burke, *Death and Return*, 35.
37. Gillian Steinberg, *Philip Larkin and His Audiences* (Macmillan, Basingstoke, 2010), xx.

1 Radical Ellipsis: *A Girl in Winter*

1. John Osborne, *Larkin, Ideology and Critical Violence: A Case of Wrongful Conviction* (Macmillan, Basingstoke, 2008).
2. Richard Palmer, *Such Deliberate Disguises: The Art of Philip Larkin* (Continuum, London, 2008), 71.
3. For more of the same see James Booth, ed., *Trouble at Willow Gables and Other Fictions*, by Philip Larkin (Faber, London, 2002), xl–xli. Even the exhilarating young scholar Gillian Steinberg asserts that 'Larkin's novels, however interesting they are as precursors to his poems, never move beyond relatively standard storytelling to play with identity or to destabilize the role of audience in relation to

speaker as so many of his poems successfully do.' This statement neatly summarizes just what I hope to disprove in the ensuing argument. See Steinberg, *Philip Larkin and His Audiences*, 155.

4. A.T. Tolley, *My Proper Ground: A Study of the Work of Philip Larkin and Its Development* (Edinburgh University Press, 1991), 30.

5. Daniel Snowman provides a slightly different exilic context in the following passage from *The Hitler Emigres: The Cultural Impact on Britain of Refugees from Nazism* (Pimlico, London, 2003), 401: 'Novels containing characters who are refugees from Nazism (or Fascism) include Philip Larkin's *A Girl in Winter*, Angus Wilson's *No Laughing Matter*, Margaret Drabble's *The Radiant Way* and Iris Murdoch's *Under the Net*.' It is worth remarking Larkin's personal warmth towards refugees of his acquaintance. According to Motion, 'some sort of near-paternal love' developed between Larkin and J.J. Graneek, Librarian at Queen's University, Belfast. Graneek was 'the son of Russian parents who had fled a pogrom' and was politically 'quite left-wing'. *Life*, 201. Again, Larkin told Judy Egerton that the sculptor Willi Soukup 'has the charm and instinctive tolerant agreeableness of the refugee'. *SL*, 305. Soukop was born in Vienna of an Austrian mother and Czech father but found refuge in England in 1934. This same sense of deracination comes through in the resemblances between Larkin's titles and those of exilic moderns: 'Arrival' (Edward Brathwaite, *The Arrivants*); 'Coming' and 'Going' (Samuel Beckett, *Come and Go*); 'Strangers' (Albert Camus, *The Stranger*); 'Arrivals, Departures' (Arthur Koestler, *Arrival and Departure*); 'The Importance of Elsewhere' (Amos Oz, *Elsewhere, Perhaps*). As for the religiosity of his literary parents, Larkin described Graham Greene (or 'Grum Grin') as a genuine talent 'spoilt & I don't mean marred – by an entire lack of proportion concerning religious matters'. *LM*, 62.

6. Susan Sontag, *Styles of Radical Will* (Secker & Warburg, London, 1969), 157.

7. T.S. Eliot, 'Preface to *Anabasis*', in *Selected Prose of T.S. Eliot*, ed. Frank Kermode (Faber, London, 1975), 77.

8. Bertolt Brecht, 'Indirect Impact of the Epic Theatre', in *Brecht on Theatre: The Development of an Aesthetic*, trans. John Willett (Eyre-Methuen, London, 1964), 57–8.

9. Osborne, *Larkin, Ideology and Critical Violence*, 57.

10. T.S. Eliot, *The Complete Poems and Plays* (Faber, London, 1969), 13.

11. Ibid., 14.

12. Tolley, *My Proper Ground*, 13, 43; 21, 31.

13. Lolette Kuby, *An Uncommon Poet for the Common Man: A Study of Philip Larkin's Poetry* (Mouton, The Hague and Paris, 1974), 7; *Larousse Dictionary of Literary Characters*, ed. Rosemary Goring (Larousse, Edinburgh, 1994), 431; *Chambers Dictionary of Literary Characters*, ed. Una McGovern (Chambers Harrap, Edinburgh, 2004), 390; Paulin, 'She Did Not Change', 242; Motion, *Life*, 160; Nicholas Marsh, *Philip Larkin: The Poems* (Macmillan, Basingstoke, 2007), 172; Carol Rumens, 'Distance and Difference in *A Girl in Winter*', *About Larkin*, 29 (April 2010), 7–12; Birte Wiemann, 'Larkin's Englishness: A German Perspective', *About Larkin*, 29 (April 2010), 25–7. In his critical monograph *Philip Larkin* (Methuen, London, 1982, 57) Motion claims that 'her home [...] has been invaded by the British', though I can find no evidence for this in the novel, only to compound the muddle when in *Philip Larkin: A Writer's Life* he added that Katherine's homeland was 'in middle Europe', no such country having experienced British invasion by 1942. In sharp contrast to the false certitudes of these prominent members of the Larkinocracy, Laurence Lerner's overlooked booklet *Philip Larkin* (Northcote

House and the British Council, Plymouth, 1997) only has space for two paragraphs on *A Girl in Winter* but still finds time to remark the use of modernist ellipsis: 'Less obvious, but more important, is the influence of Virginia Woolf, whose novels are pioneering works of modernism in the way they neglect the external events that traditionally provide a plot, in order to explore beneath the surface of what is said and done. Omission is central to the method of *A Girl in Winter*: [...] there [are] striking omissions in the plot – we are never told what country Katherine is from (no actual country quite fits), or how she came to be in England during the war' (p. 8). Lerner's perceptive link to Woolf brings to mind that brilliant reference in her novel *Orlando* to 'the cardinal labour of composition, which is excision' (Triad/Panther, Frogmore, 1977, 45). I am indebted to Toni Silver for the Larousse citation and a variety of stylistic improvements to the text.

14. Booth, *Philip Larkin: Writer*, 56.

15. Stephen Cooper, *Philip Larkin: Subversive Writer* (Sussex Academic Press, Brighton, 2004).

16. That Larkin is the greatest exponent of ellipsis in contemporary British poetry, often employing it to complicate issues of national and geographical belonging in a way foreshadowed in *A Girl in Winter*, has gone largely unremarked by his explicators – most of whom wad the *aporia* with biographical data in the interests of presenting him as the epitome of unalloyed Englishness. In truth, not only was he happy to draw inspiration from all over the British Isles, he characteristically deleted (or else multiplied) the site-specific references so as to widen still further the franchise of identification. A specimen case is provided by 'Livings' III which critics invariably refer to as a poem about Oxford, presumably because Larkin had been a student there. Thus Timms declares (with Marsh and Palmer offering recent endorsements) that the poem 'is spoken by a young Oxford don – a reference to "the wood from Snape" indicates that the setting is Oxford rather than Cambridge'. However, there are two Snapes, one in Suffolk and the other North Yorkshire, neither of them anywhere near Oxford. Similarly, the 'sizar' of the third verse is a form of bursaried scholar formerly found in Cambridge University and Trinity College, Dublin, but never in Oxford. By refusing to accept these indeterminacies in the texts, Larkin's critics have converted him from what he is, the greatest poet of doubt and ambiguity since Hardy, into a poet of certitude, often to the point of bigotry. See Timms, *Philip Larkin*, 127; Marsh, *Philip Larkin: The Poems*, 92; Palmer, *Such Deliberate Disguises*, xx.

17. Katherine's *grandfather* is the silversmith, not her father as Motion claims, *Philip Larkin*, 57.

18. Rumens, 'Distance and Difference', 10.

19. The Belgian holiday is cursorily mentioned in Motion, *Life*, 27. I am grateful to Jim Orwin for allowing me access to his copies of *The Coventrian*.

20. Alan Brownjohn, 'Novels into Poems', in *Larkin at Sixty*, ed. Anthony Thwaite (Faber, London, 1982), 119.

21. Any hope that the persecutions faced by German Jews since Hitler's accession to power in 1933 were random and unrepresentative evaporated with the Nuremberg Laws of 15 September 1935 which institutionalized anti-Semitism in the legal definition of citizenship of the Nazi state. As this development was recorded in suitably horrified terms in the British and American press, Robin would not have had to look far to be apprised of the unfolding calamity. Young Larkin, by contrast, reacted against his father's fascist sympathies by putting a Star of David alongside his signature in wartime letters to his pal Jim Sutton and incorporating this 'Jewish

badge' in his designs for a bookplate (see the reproduction in *About Larkin*, 12 (October 2001), 26). Shortly before, on 1 September 1941, Reinhard Heydrich as a prelude to genocide made compulsory the wearing of a yellow Star of David by all Jews unfortunate enough to be trapped in Nazi territories. In his interesting though speculative radio play, *Philip and Sydney* (broadcast on BBC Radio 4 on 11 June 2010), the dramatist Alan Pollock suggested that legendary jazz trumpeter Louis Armstrong prompted Larkin's adoption of the Star of David. Abandoned by his father, Armstrong was virtually adopted by a Lithuanian-Jewish immigrant family, the Karnofskys (or Karmofskys), who helped him purchase his first cornet. For the rest of his life Armstrong wore a Star of David around his neck in honour of his surrogate family and also wrote a memoir of the relationship in which he equated persecution of the Jews with persecution of African Americans. The biographer who first made these disclosures was Gary Giddins, *Satchmo* (1988; reprinted, Da Capo, New York, 1998), see especially chapter three. The memoir is included in *Louis Armstrong in His Own Words: Selected Writings*, ed. Thomas Brothers (Oxford University Press, 1999). Larkin's adoption of the Star of David therefore amounts to a siding with Jews and African Americans in a moment of terrible crisis.

22. Palmer's claim that 'No reason is given' for Jane's marriage to Jack, rendering it 'farcically improbable', wilfully ignores this extensive evidence of her desire to travel; though his assertion that 'Jack Stormalong is as absurd as his name' is a sentiment to which every bosom returns an echo. *Such Deliberate Disguises*, 73.

23. The anagrammatic dimension of Anstey's name permits a punning link to the Nazis who by 1942, the present time of the novel, were popularly referred to by the British as the Nasties. (An anti-propaganda film released in that year, *General Adolf Takes Over*, consisted of German newsreels doctored for humorous effect. Hitler and his goose-stepping armies become 'the Nasties' and are edited so as to appear to be skipping and sashaying to the tune of 'The Lambeth Walk'.) The function of the pun may be to apostrophize Anstey as a 'little Hitler', a man who is too *small* for his boots. There may be a subliminal reactivation of the pun towards the novel's close, Anstey deflating when Katherine challenges everything he stands for: job security ('I'll leave now. How soon can I leave?'); patriarchal bluster ('Oh, shut up with your advice, shut up [...] You bore me stiff with such things.'); and browbeaten women ('your silly Veronica Parbury'). Katherine's verbal assault 'exploded like a depth-charge. He sat in his chair as stiffly as a corporal who has been told to remain seated by a field-marshal' (*AGW*, 210–11). When Hitler claimed the German Chancellorship in August 1932, his demand was rejected by the President of the Weimar Republic, Field Marshal Hindenburg, who contemptuously referred to him as 'that Austrian Corporal'.

24. For an analysis of the use of this pun in six of Larkin's mature poems see Osborne, *Larkin, Ideology and Critical Violence*, 126–9.

25. Larkin's preferred title, *The Kingdom of Winter*, pertinently equates male rule with the chilliest season of the year. When his editor at Faber, Alan Pringle, queried the title, Larkin replied: 'I have remembered a title I thought of soon after starting to write [the book]: *A Girl in Winter* – which [...] does conjure up a more precise image than the present one does' (Motion, *Life*, 144). The precision lies not only in the acknowledgement that a young woman is at the centre of the text but also in the way the new title hints at that thinking in the gap between binaries that was to become such a feature of the Larkin project. Hence, *A Girl in Winter* rather than *A Girl in Spring* or *An Old Woman in Winter*; just as his first great verse collection was neither *The Deceived* nor *The Undeceived* but *The Less Deceived*.

Comparisons might be drawn with individual Larkin poems like 'Autumn has caught us in our summer wear', 'An April Sunday brings the snow' and 'Love Songs in Age'; and with such modernist precursors as Eliot's *The Waste Land* (beginning, 'April is the cruellest month') and William Carlos Williams's 'The Widow's Lament in Springtime'.

26. For two decades Booth has adumbrated the view that sex takes place with Robin in control: see *Philip Larkin: Writer*, 55; 'Lyricism, Englishness and Postcoloniality', in *Larkin with Poetry*, ed. Michael Baron (English Association, Leicester, 1997), 21; and *Philip Larkin: The Poet's Plight*, 59–60. Representative statements include, from the first of these, 'Her delicate idyll is shattered and at the end of the novel, beaten down by the day's disasters, she submits wearily to his sexual demands'; and from the last, 'sex with Robin freezes Katherine's summer dream into an icy vision of winter'. That critics like Booth and Cooper should rob Katherine of agency in order then to feel sorry for her involves the same unlovely mix of political correctness and female victimology as Cooper brings to the analysis of poems like 'Wedding-Wind'. Anxious to present the female protagonist thereof as victim rather than celebrant, Cooper 14 times in three pages refers to her as a 'girl' when no indication is given of her age, certainly none emphasizing youth. Purporting to take the woman's side, Cooper unwittingly infantilizes her (*Philip Larkin: Subversive Writer*, 110–13). Cooper's reading of the wind of the poem's title as a metaphor for patriarchal oppression is also at odds with Larkin's own as expressed in a letter to Monica Jones: 'I am quite pleased with the to me successful use of the floods & the wind as fulfillment & joy' (*LM*, 25). As we have seen, however, Larkin's *ex cathedra* comments are not an infallible guide!

27. Palmer, *Such Deliberate Disguises*, 71.

28. Virginia Woolf, *The Waves* (Triad/Panther, Frogmore, 1977), 20.

29. The double 'as if' of 'MCMXIV' is also deployed in 'Dublinesque': 'There is an air of great friendliness, / *As if* they were honouring / One they were fond of [...] // [...] A voice is heard singing / Of Kitty, or Katy, / *As if* the name meant once / All love, all beauty.' (*CP*, 178; *TCP*, 87). (My emphases.)

30. Peter Didsbury, *Scenes from a Long Sleep: New and Collected Poems* (Bloodaxe, Tarset, 2003), 83. For the role of the 'as if' in deconstructionism see Jacques Derrida, *Without Alibi*, trans. and ed. Peggy Kamuf (Stanford University Press, 2002), especially the essay 'Typewriter Ribbon: Limited Ink (2)', 71–160.

31. Cooper, *Philip Larkin: Subversive Writer*, 174, 70, 66, 62.

32. John Bayley has broken ranks with his peers and claimed it such in *The Uses of Division* (Chatto & Windus, London, 1976), 174.

33. Worse still is the depiction of Stormalong. Jack has to represent the experience of empire vivaciously enough for Jane to see in him her longed-for passport to 'abroad', yet superficially enough for us to see that he will make a poor choice of husband. The novel gets the balance wrong. His clichéd Indian adventures are simply unconvincing; what should be his inadequacy becomes the novel's.

34. See Philip Larkin, *Poems*, selected and introduced by Martin Amis (Faber, London, 2011), xv.

2   Radical Ekphrasis: 'An Arundel Tomb', 'The Card-Players', 'Lines on a Young Lady's Photograph Album'

1. D.J. Enright, ed., *Poets of the 1950s: An Anthology of New English Verse* (Kenkyusho, Tokyo, 1955), 103.

2. Ibid., 17–18.
3. Lerner, *Philip Larkin*, 44.
4. A. Alvarez, 'The New Poetry, or Beyond the Gentility Principle', in *The New Poetry* (Penguin, Harmondsworth, 1962), 21.
5. Donald Davie, *The Poet in the Imaginary Museum*, ed. Barry Alpert (Carcanet, Manchester, 1977).
6. Bryan Appleyard, *The Pleasures of Peace: Art and Imagination in Post-war Britain* (Faber, London, 1989), 96; Andrew Duncan, *The Failure of Conservatism in Modern British Poetry* (Salt, Cambridge, 2003), 53; Tolley, *My Proper Ground*, 65.
7. Germaine Greer, 'A Very British Misery', *Guardian*, 14 October 1988, 27; Bryan Appleyard, 'The Dreary Laureate of our Provincialism', *Independent*, 18 March 1993, 27; Peter Ackroyd, 'Poet Hands on Misery to Man', *Times*, 1 April 1993, 35.
8. John Gilroy detects such a connection with 'An Arundel Tomb': 'A Keatsian oxymoron, "sharp tender shock" alerts us to Keats' presence later in the poem where the tomb, like the *Grecian Urn* of the Ode, gives rise to reflection on beauty, truth and the passing of time. The Ode's "O Attic shape, fair attitude" is echoed in Larkin's "Only an attitude remains", although his concern is less with a reciprocity between beauty and truth than it is to do with issues surrounding truth itself.' Gilroy, *Philip Larkin: Selected Poems* (HEB, Penrith, 2009), 65.
9. This poem may be found in Duffy's first collection, *Standing Female Nude* (Anvil, London, 1985), the title poem of which contributes to a fascinating development in woman-centred ekphrasis. Like Vuyelwa Carlin's 'The Life Model' and Maggie Hannan's 'Life Model', 'Standing Female Nude' envoices the anonymous women who have posed down the decades for male artworks on grandiose themes. The American poet Kathleen Rooney has written a memoir of her modelling career, *Live Nude Girl: My Life as an Object* (Arkansas University Press, Fayetteville, 2009). The naked muse answers back.
10. Cited by James W. Heffernan, *Museum of Words: The Poetics of Ekphrasis from Homer to Ashbery* (University of Chicago Press, 1993), 212.
11. Ibid., 171.
12. Ibid., 92, 133.
13. Robert Browning, *Poems of Robert Browning*, ed. Sir Humphrey Milford (Oxford University Press, 1959), 171–2.
14. Lord Byron, *The Works of Lord Byron*, ed. Rowland Prothero, vol. 5 (John Murray, London, 1898–1904), 549. Lord Byron, *Childe Harold's Pilgrimage*, Canto XLXII, in *Poetical Works*, ed. Frederick Page and John Jump (Oxford University Press, 1987), 248.
15. D. Talbot Rice, *Teach Yourself to Study Art* (English Universities Press, London, 1955), 156, 163.
16. Leconte de Lisle and Emma Lazarus, cited by John Hollander, *The Gazer's Spirit: Poems Speaking to Silent Works of Art* (University of Chicago Press, 1995), 171–4, 176.
17. P.B. Shelley, *Shelley*, selected by Kathleen Raine (Poet to Poet, Penguin, Harmondsworth, 1978), 53.
18. Heffernan, *Museum of Words*, 118.
19. Ezra Pound, 'A Few Don'ts By An Imagist', in *Modern Poets on Modern Poetry*, ed. James Scully (Fontana, London and Glasgow, 1966), 31; *Hugh Selwyn Mauberley*, in *Selected Poems, 1908–1959* (Faber, London, 1975), 99.
20. Ezra Pound, *ABC of Reading* (Faber, London, 1951), 19–22.
21. Larkin's comment on the manuscript is even more sceptical than the poem, almost scathing in its dismissiveness: 'Love isn't stronger than death because statues hold hands for 600 years.' Motion, *Life*, 274.

22. Andrew Swarbrick, *Out of Reach: The Poetry of Philip Larkin* (Macmillan, Basingstoke, 1995), 11. Palmer is equally categorical: 'All Larkin devotees know that [...]' "The Arundel Tomb" [sic] sculpture in Chichester Cathedral [...] inspired the 1956 poem which closes *The Whitsun Weddings*.' See *Such Deliberate Disguises*, 162.

23. Charles Crocker, verger of Chichester Cathedral at the time of the Victorian restoration of the tomb, wrote a poem in praise of the restorer which, surfeited with facts, devoid of profundity, is the very opposite of Larkin's:

> Thanks, Richardson! whose renovating hand
> Guided by talent, skill and taste refined
> Hath given to the eye of cultured mind
> The relic of a bygone age to stand
> In all its pristine beauty

This quotation, like much of the historical information about the sarcophagus, is drawn from *An Arundel Tomb* by Paul Foster, Trevor Brighton and Patrick Garland (Otter Memorial Papers, Chichester, 1987). Larkin's artistic distance from the actual tomb, the sense that it is only needed as a kind of flight-deck from which to get the imagination airborne, is captured in a letter to Monica Jones regarding the making of the *Monitor* television documentary about his poetry: 'The TV men are after the Arundel Tomb in Chichester – I hope to God it's there & I didn't dream it. They want to know if it's free-standing, or against a wall. I hope all my descriptions are accurate – jointed armour, stiffened pleat, little dogs. I'm quite likely to have invented them' (*LM*, 334).

24. Unpublished letter from Larkin to Jim Sutton cited by István Rácz, 'Space in Larkin and Cézanne', *Hungarian Journal of English and American Studies*, 9, 2 (2003), 122.

25. Unpublished letter from Larkin to Jim Sutton, Archives of the Brynmor Jones Library, Hull DPL (2) (12/15/9).

26. The card and caption are reproduced in 'Revealingly Yours, Philip Larkin', in Christopher Fletcher, *Sunday Times, Culture* supplement, 11 May 2008, 14. In this context, my eagle-eyed friend Jim Orwin writes (private correspondence, 24 November 2009): 'I keep thinking about Larkin's Christmas card poem reprinted in the journal *About Larkin*, volume 20, which begins "Apples on a Christmas Tree!" How often did he write comments inside about the pictures on the front of cards he sent people? And how often did he choose cards with pictures of recognized works of art on the front? I have one Christmas card he sent to a colleague which has three angelic looking Christmas carollers on the front. Inside he's written "Staff of the librarian's office?".' At the very least, as Orwin suggests, these quips and ditties are further proof of Larkin's responsiveness to visual culture of all kinds.

27. Rácz, 'Space in Larkin and Cézanne'.

28. Ruth Bernard Yeazell, *Art of the Everyday: Dutch Painting and the Realist Novel* (Princeton University Press, 2008), 24–8.

29. The splendid *Grove Dictionary of Jazz* appeared three years after Larkin's death. Reith cited by Jackie Kay, 'Admirable Hornblower', *Observer Review*, 29 November 1998, 14. Martin Bormann, Hitler's confidential secretary, wrote to his wife Gerda in February 1945: 'A victory for Bolshevism and Americanism would mean not only the extermination of our race but also the destruction of everything that its culture and civilization has created. Instead of the Meistersinger we should see

jazz triumphant.' Max Hastings, 'The Wages of Loyalty', *Sunday Times, Culture* supplement, 19 August 2011, 32.

30. J. Horder, 'Poet on the 8.15', Interview with Philip Larkin, *Guardian*, 20 May 1965, 9.
31. Steve Eddy, *Philip Larkin: High Windows* (York Press, London, 2007), 28.
32. Marina Vaizey, *The Artist as Photographer* (Sidgwick & Jackson, London, 1982), 9.
33. William Wordsworth, *Poetical Works*, ed. Thomas Hutchinson and Ernest de Selincourt (Oxford University Press, 1988), 383.
34. Pound, *Selected Poems, 1908–1959*, 99.
35. John Ashbery, *Self-Portrait in a Convex Mirror* (Penguin, Harmondsworth, 1976), 79.
36. Walter Benjamin, 'The Work of Art in the Age of Mechanical Reproduction', in *Illuminations*, ed. Hannah Arendt (Collins, London and Glasgow, 1973), 219–53.
37. Ibid., 220–3.
38. Ibid., 226.
39. Ibid., 222–3.
40. Ibid., 229.
41. Ibid., 238–9.
42. Ibid., 236.
43. Such collections were first compiled in the 1840s, from whence dates usage of the term *album* in this context. However, the practice of collecting photographic images, including *cartes-de-visite*, only became widespread in the 1890s. By the twenties and thirties, the Larkins were busily documenting their various outings and forays, including their trips to Germany: in effect, Philip Larkin belonged to the first generation to grow up with the portable camera, the snapshot and the family album already in place. The earliest of his own albums is one he improvised from a notebook, the images kept in position by small diagonal slits in the pages, and commemorates his student days at Oxford. A combination of group shots and solo portraits, some taken by Larkin and others by friends, this little collection shows him grappling with those issues of editing, collaborative 'authorship' and chronology that characterize the album genre. Of the five subsequent volumes he selected from his own photographs, the most beautiful is the 'blue album' from the 1960s, by which time he was a most accomplished photographer. The collection memorializes such East Riding villages as Yokefleet, Laxton, Faxfleet, Kilpin and Broomfleet, their locations specified by the prominent inclusion of name signs (the very opposite of his poetic practice of eliding topographical particularity in the interests of universalization). Exquisitely composed in a striking square format, these scenes are redolent of a disappearing England of cottages and cowslip, the absence of visible proof of human occupancy combining with proliferant foliage to suggest a world that might easily be reclaimed by nature.
44. Larkin well understood the importance of picture selection. Prematurely bald, gangling, afflicted early by a stammer and late by deafness, he grew up physically ill at ease and 'thoroughly out of love with my own appearance'. This acute self-consciousness made him anxious to control the dissemination of his likeness. Surviving contact sheets suggest that he could be relaxed enough with professional photographers to permit portraits from all angles and in varied poses. However, he would be ruthless in the selection process, complaining bitterly if images he had banned subsequently appeared in print; as when he wrote to Fay Godwin in 1983 claiming to be 'horrified' at the release of an image that made him look like 'the Boston Strangler'. When Godwin protested her innocence, he admitted the fault lay not with her photograph but with 'my sagging face, an egg sculpted in lard, with goggles on – depressing, depressing, depressing'. He

also made the following stipulations regarding further portrait sessions: 'I now have three conditions that photographers must promise to observe in what they print (I am not bald, I have only one chin, my waist is concave), and this means that about the only picture of me now available is full-face head-and-shoulders, chin up, in dark shade. If you feel your genius could flourish under such circumstances, let me know' (*SL*, xxvi, 704).

The other means by which Larkin sought control of his public likeness was through self-portraiture, often involving a delayed-action shutter. Even photographs attributed to others – such as Monica Jones's iconic picture of him beside the Cross of St George or Maeve Brennan's equally spectacular portrait of him leaning against a gigantic piece of driftwood – have clearly been choreographed by the 'sitter'.

45. Motion, *Life*, plate 33.
46. Winifred Dawson, letter to the present writer, 18 May 2004; Booth, *Philip Larkin: The Poet's Plight*, 71. Another of the poems ascribed to Winifred's inspiration, 'Maiden Name', asserts that with the marital change of surname 'you cannot be / Semantically the same as that young beauty' from before the marriage (*CP*, 101; *TCP*, 33). The expression 'young beauty' echoes the 'Young Lady' of the present poem, both deriving from Yeats's 'To a Young Beauty'. More pertinently, the manuscript shows Larkin experimenting with the phrase 'you cannot be' in such a way as to retain a secret, punning connection to Winifred: 'you are not she' ('you Arnott she'). His decision to erase even this oblique connection to his original source of inspiration is indicative of his mature practice as a poet. See Bradford, *First Boredom, Then Fear*, 102.
47. Roland Barthes, *Camera Lucida: Reflections on Photography*, trans. Richard Howard (Fontana, London, 1984), 13.
48. Girton College, Cambridge, founded in 1869, was the first women's college; though it was not until 1948 that Cambridge University granted full membership to women. Dean Burgon of Chichester Cathedral, addressing the academic women of Oxford in 1884, declared: 'Inferior to us God made you, and our inferiors to the end of time you will remain.' See Jane Robinson, *Bluestockings: The Remarkable Story of the First Women to Fight for an Education* (Viking, London, 2009).
49. I am indebted for these connections to a talk by Diccon Rogers, 'Stolen from the Local Girls' School: The New Girl, "Brunette Coleman" and "Lines on a Young Lady's Photograph Album"', Larkin in Context conference, Hull, 29 June 2002.
50. Hemingway was still alive at the time of the poem's composition and publication.
51. Ernest Hemingway, *The Sun Also Rises* (Pan, London, 1951), 23.
52. When in 1918 the American photographer Alfred Stieglitz fell in love with the painter Georgia O'Keeffe, he began a compulsive process of taking her likeness that eventually ran to over five hundred images and constitutes one of the greatest composite portraits on record. As in Larkin's poem, however, the series accrues not so as to finally entrap O'Keeffe's identity but to demonstrate its fugitive, protean, potentially infinite variability.
53. Laura Mulvey, *Visual and Other Pleasures* (Macmillan, Basingstoke, 1989), 19–20.
54. Cited by Jeremy Hawthorn, *A Concise Glossary of Contemporary Literary Theory* (Arnold, London, 1998), 94.
55. F. Scott Fitzgerald, *The Great Gatsby* (Penguin, Harmondsworth, 1979), 179. Larkin had been reading the novel a couple of years before composing the poem: see *LM*, 36.

56. Toni Silver advises that Larkin's manoeuvre 'is redolent of Manet's painting *Olympia* (1863) which pastiches Titian's *Venus d'Urbino* (1538), but instead of the portrait of a well-born lady produced to flatter her husband, here we have a high class courtesan who returns that male gaze steadily, confrontationally and without shame or apology [...] Olympia covers her sex not coyly, but assertively, because it is hers to give. There is no hint of pubic hair beneath the hand, but the cat with staring eyes and raised tail provides the missing fur. Titian's painting, like others of the genre, depicts a sleeping dog, signifying fidelity, but the displaced pussy is saying something else entirely' (unpublished private correspondence).

57. Alfred, Lord Tennyson, *The Poems*, ed. Christopher Ricks (Longman, London, 1969), 747.

58. Hemingway, *The Sun Also Rises*, 25–6.

59. C. Day Lewis, *The Complete Poems* (Sinclair-Stevenson, London, 1992), 317.

60. Tolley, *My Proper Ground*, 69–70. Tolley repeats these sentiments in a later monograph, *Larkin at Work*: '"Lines on a Young Lady's Photograph Album" [...] may be regarded as the first of Larkin's "Movement" poems'; 'the poem is a stylistic breakthrough for Larkin' (59, 60). In the same work, Tolley lamely declares: 'I believe finding voyeuristic undertones' in the poem 'is misguided' (66).

61. Oliver Cromwell quoted by Horace Walpole, *Anecdotes of Painting in England*, ed. R.N. Wornum, vol. 2 (Bickers, London, 1888), 94.

62. Barthes, *Camera Lucida*, 76, 87, 76, 80, 77. Compare with Susan Sontag's claim that a photograph 'is not only an image [...] an interpretation of the real, it is also a trace, something directly stencilled off the real, like a footprint or a death mask'. *On Photography* (Penguin, Harmondsworth, 1979), 154.

63. Dion Boucicault, *Plays*, ed. Peter Thomson (Cambridge University Press, 1984), 163.

64. Barthes, *Camera Lucida*, 115. Compare Sontag: 'A photograph is both a pseudo-presence and a token of absence.' *On Photography*, 16.

65. Mulvey, *Visual and Other Pleasures*, xiii–xiv.

66. Barthes, *Camera Lucida*, 64.

67. Ibid., 90, 88–9.

68. Compare with this passage from *LM*, 109: 'Anything more than 20 years back begins to breathe a luminous fascination for me: it starts my imagination working. Why? Because it *is* past, I suppose, & leaves me free to get to work on it.'

69. Joseph Rodman Drake, 'The National Painting', a poem in praise of John Trumbell's famous canvas, *The Declaration of Independence*. Quoted in Hollander, *The Gazer's Spirit*, 129.

70. Wordsworth, *Poetical Works*, 200.

71. Byron, *Poetical Works*, 248.

72. As though for the benefit of the obtuse, Larkin six years later repeated the pun in another fine poem, 'Afternoons':

> And the albums, lettered
> *Our Wedding*, lying
> Near the television (*CP*, 121; *TCP*, 71)

At one level the meaning is literal and innocent, but the pun on the word *lying* raises darker, more compelling alternatives. How many family albums impartially document rows, sexual frustration, infidelity, despair, divorce? Those are the photographs we do not take or else suppress so as to compile the consoling fiction that the wedding ceremony we put our trust in has yielded the promised happy ever after.

73. Hollander, *The Gazer's Spirit*, 115.

74. Maggie Humm, *Snapshots of Bloomsbury: The Private Lives of Virginia Woolf and Vanessa Bell* (Tate Publishing, London, 2006), viii.

75. Barthes, *Camera Lucida*, 68.

76. Roland Barthes, 'The Death of the Author', in *Image – Music – Text*, ed. and trans. Stephen Heath (Fontana, London, 1984), 142–8.

77. Despite its seemingly nationalistic title, David Kennedy's stimulating monograph *The Ekphrastic Encounter in Contemporary British Poetry and Elsewhere* (Ashgate, Farnham, 2012) entirely neglects Larkin's contributions while honouring those of his American contemporaries Frank O'Hara and John Ashbery. Larkin does not even get a mention in the chapter devoted to 'Poems about Photographs' (147–55).

3 Radical Deterritorialization: 'At Grass', 'March Past', 'Church Going'

1. It is well known that Larkin's diaries were destroyed in accordance with the terms of his will. Less well known is the survival of the diary covers which he had plastered with quotes from favourite writers like Wilde, Hardy, Corvo, Proust, Lawrence, Yeats, Joyce, Flann O'Brien, de Montherlant and, as here, Ernest Hemingway: 'No writer worth a damn is a national writer or a New England writer or a writer of the frontier or a writer of the Renaissance or a Brazilian writer. Any writer worth a damn is just a writer. That is the hard league to play in. The ball is standard, the ball parks vary somewhat, but they are all good. There are no bad bounces. Alibis don't count. Go out and do your stuff. You can't do it? Then don't take refuge in the fact that you are a local boy or rummy, or pant or crawl back into somebody's womb, or have the con or the old râle. You can do it or you can't do it in that league I am speaking of.' See 'Portrait of Mister Papa', by Malcolm Cowley, *Life* magazine, 10 January 1949, 101. I am grateful to Jim Orwin for helping me identify this quotation which, in its way, is a perfect statement of the Larkin approach to deterritorialization.

2. Gilles Deleuze, *Cinema 1: The Movement-Image*, trans. H. Tomlinson and B. Habberjan (University of Minnesota Press, Minneapolis, 1986), 96.

3. G.S. Fraser and I. Fletcher, eds, *Springtime: An Anthology of Young Poets and Writers* (Owen, London, 1953), 12.

4. Alan Brownjohn, ed., *Departure* (Departure, Oxford, 1955), 20.

5. G.S. Fraser, ed., *Poetry Now* (Faber, London, 1956), 24.

6. Kingsley Amis, *The Letters of Kingsley Amis*, ed. Zachary Leader (HarperCollins, London, 2000), 309, 319. Larkin himself described Tom Scott as a 'haggis-fed clown'. *LM*, 210.

7. Seamus Heaney, 'Englands of the Mind', in *Preoccupations* (Faber, London, 1980), 169.

8. Ibid., 150–1, 167.

9. Paulin, 'She Did Not Change', 234, 244.

10. Tom Paulin, Letter, *Times Literary Supplement*, 6 November 1992, 15.

11. Seamus Heaney, 'The Main of Light', in *Larkin at Sixty*, ed. Anthony Thwaite (Faber, London, 1982), 137.

12. See Andrew Motion, 'This is Your Subject Speaking', in *Natural Causes* (Chatto & Windus, London, 1987), 54.

13. Heaney, 'Englands of the Mind', 166.
14. Stephen Regan, *Philip Larkin: The Critics Debate* (Macmillan, Basingstoke, 1992), 82.
15. Stephen Regan, 'Larkin's Reputation', in *Larkin with Poetry*, ed. Michael Baron (English Association, Leicester, 1997), 60.
16. Oliver Goldsmith, *The Poems*, ed. Austin Dobson (Dent, London, 1883), 40.
17. Wordsworth, *Poetical Works*, 1.
18. Paulin, 'She Did Not Change', 237.
19. Stephen Regan, ed., *Philip Larkin: Contemporary Critical Essays* (Macmillan, Basingstoke, 1997), 177.
20. James Simmons, 'The Trouble with Larkin', in *Philip Larkin: A Tribute*, ed. George Hartley (Marvell, London, 1988), 234.
21. Tolley, *Larkin at Work*, 25–6.
22. Philip Larkin, 'Worksheets of "At Grass"', *Phoenix*, 11/12, 91–102.
23. Timms, *Philip Larkin*, 74.
24. Tolley, *Larkin at Work*, 19.
25. Janice Rossen concurs: '"At Grass" marks a definite turning point in its finely crafted style and lyricism which combine with Hardyesque plainness of diction and reverence for nature.' *Philip Larkin: His Life's Work* (Harvester, Hemel Hempstead, 1989), 17.
26. W.B. Yeats, *The Collected Poems* (Macmillan, London, 1965), 147.
27. Ibid., 218.
28. Joyce, *A Portrait of the Artist as a Young Man* (Penguin, Harmondsworth, 1970), 253.
29. Stephen Regan, 'Philip Larkin: A Late Modern Poet', in *The Cambridge Companion to Twentieth Century English Poetry*, ed. Neil Corcoran (Cambridge University Press, 2007), 152.
30. Motion, *Life*, 188.
31. According to Tolley, '"At Grass" was occasioned by seeing a *television* documentary' (my emphasis), but this is most unlikely. Television transmissions were suspended during the war years, only resuming on 7 June 1946, with the result that at the end of that year ownership stood at a meagre 6000 sets. It is true that at the time of the poem's completion ownership had shot up to 3 million sets, though that still represents a small proportion of the population. Larkin did not purchase a television until 1979, 30 years later (*SL*, 596). Tolley, *Larkin at Work*, 19.
32. An anonymous correspondent of the *Times Educational Supplement*, 13 July 1956, records Larkin dating his Brown Jack experience to 'one evening in 1948'. That date would explain why Larkin describes the newsreel showing Brown Jack still alive. This does not alter the fact that the horse had died before 'At Grass' was written and that the poem omits this knowledge. Nor does it explain why Larkin gave an entirely different date in his interview with Melvyn Bragg. See Peter Ferguson, 'Philip Larkin's XX Poems', in *Philip Larkin: A Tribute*, ed. George Hartley (Marvell, London, 1988), 156. The anonymous correspondent later revealed his identity as John Shakespeare and discussed the experience of interviewing Larkin in 'A Few Suggestions', *Times Literary Supplement*, 3 April 2009, 12–15.
33. Some of this information was drawn from the biography by R.C. Lyle, *Brown Jack* (Putnam, London, 1934), a volume bequeathed to me by the late Edwin Tarling, a jazz saxophonist, poet, graphic artist and magazine editor described by Larkin as 'many-talented Ted'.
34. Larkin, by contrast, refused to *naturalize* as intrinsically 'African' the blues music he loved: 'The Negro did not have the blues because he was naturally melancholy. He had them because he was cheated and bullied and starved' (*AWJ*, 87).

35. These lines from 'The Deserted Village' briefly touch on the joys of retirement:

> O blest retirement, friend to life's decline,
> Retreats from care, that never must be mine,
> How happy he who crowns in shades like these,
> A youth of labour with an age of ease

However, Goldsmith's poem is a pastoral elegy in a way that 'At Grass' is not, and this sentiment is quickly subsumed in the overarching lament for the eponymous abandoned village. Goldsmith, *The Poems*, 34–5.

36. Edward Picot, *Outcasts from Eden: Ideas of Landscape in British Poetry since 1945* (Liverpool University Press, 1997), 75.

37. For Burnett's explanation for amending what Thwaite published as 'The March Past' to 'March Past' see *TCP*, 602.

38. Paulin, 'She Did Not Change', 234.

39. Regan, *Philip Larkin: Contemporary Critical Essays*, 161.

40. Neil Corcoran, *English Poetry since 1940* (Longman, London, 1993), 92. Regan, *Philip Larkin: Contemporary Critical Essays*, 16; repeated in 'Larkin's Reputation', 58. Motion has also claimed that Larkin was 'demonstrating his burgeoning Orange sympathies in "The March Past"' (*Life*, 210); and even the admirable Steve Clark has reterritorialized the poem as Larkin's 'reflections on an Orangeman's parade in Belfast' ('"The lost displays": Larkin and Empire', in *New Larkins for Old*, ed. James Booth (Macmillan, Basingstoke, 2000), 167). Larkin made known his distaste for such vulgar biographicalism in a letter composed shortly after 'March Past' and published in *The Listener*, 15 October 1953: 'Sir, I am sorry to find your reviewer (*The Listener* October 1) suggesting that the Hand and Flower Press books "would be even more useful if somewhere they included brief accounts of their authors." Why would they? This potted-biography convention ("educated at Winchester and New College, married with two children, is at present working with a firm of publishers"; "educated at Mansfield Grammar School and Oxford, now works for the British Council in Sweden"; "no education, sleeps in disused railway coach, lives by poaching and blackmailing relatives") began as a fairly harmless gimmick, but by now has become so widespread and farcical that each new example seems a parody of the whole genre. All a reader has a right to be told is what other work a writer has published; the author who supplies more can be suspected of vanity, the reader who expects more of illegitimate curiosity – or else of that well-known attitude, tell me who it's by and I'll tell you if it's any good. Yours, etc, Philip Larkin.' *About Larkin*, 31 (April 2011), 4. Larkin liked to pretend that his critical position was completely untheorized but this letter is not only compatible with but almost certainly indebted to such passages as the following from I.A. Richards, *Practical Criticism* (1929; reprinted Routledge & Kegan Paul, London, 1964), 13: 'There cannot be much doubt that when we know we are reading Milton or Shelley, a great deal of our approval and admiration is being accorded not to the poetry but to an idol. Conversely, if we did not know that we were reading Ella Wheeler Wilcox, much of our amusement or patronising condescension might easily be absent. Far more than we like to admit, we take a hint for our response from the poet's reputation.'

In the few pages of his Wellington diary that survive, the young Larkin was already saying, apropos of writing a regular column telling library subscribers of the new acquisitions: 'I should like to say how *good* some books are, as opposed to psycho-analyzing the authors.' I am grateful to Don Lee of the Philip Larkin Society for bringing these scraps to my attention.

41. Amis, *The Letters of Kingsley Amis*, 252. Larkin shared Amis's worries about American militarism. That these concerns intensified when Truman was replaced by Eisenhower is apparent in the letter he wrote to Monica Jones on 5 November 1952: 'With the 9 a.m. news has come the news of Eisenhower's victory – I *knew* he'd do it. The era of American generosity is at an end. With a military man in charge we are one move nearer the next war [...] it confirms my forecast that U.S.A. is tired of trying to be civilised, & is due for a period of barbarity' (*LM*, 90–1).

42. This statement probably carries an echo of Richards, *Practical Criticism*: 'First must come the difficulty of *making out the plain sense* of poetry. The most disturbing and impressive fact brought out by this experiment is that a large proportion of average-to-good (and in some cases, certainly, devoted) readers of poetry frequently and repeatedly *fail to understand it*, both as a statement and as an expression.' (p. 13)

43. Heaney, 'Englands of the Mind', 151.

44. Whitehead, *Hardy to Larkin*, 235.

45. Alvarez, *The New Poetry*, 24–5.

46. Blake Morrison, *The Movement: English Poetry and Fiction of the 1950s* (Methuen, London, 1980), 237.

47. Hartley, *Philip Larkin, the Marvell Press and Me*, 97.

48. Philip Gardner, 'The Wintry Drum' (1968) reprinted *Phoenix*, 11/12 (1973–74), 27. Warren Hope describes the emergence of 'an identifiable character or persona that eventually merged in the public mind with Philip Larkin, the librarian at the University of Hull. This persona was most fully elaborated in "Church Going".' However, one's confidence in his judgement – or his ability to count – is not strengthened by his immediately going on to describe the poem as 'built of ten-line stanzas'! *A Student Guide to Philip Larkin* (Greenwich Exchange, Holywood, 1997), 5.

49. 'Here', 'The Large Cool Store', 'Study of Reading Habits', 'Toads Revisited', 'Wants' and 'Church Going' are read in their entirety. John Betjeman recites an excerpt from 'Ambulances', misquoting it in the process.

50. Alan Bennett, *Writing Home* (Faber, London, 1994), 367.

51. Bradford, *First Boredom, Then Fear*, 203–4.

52. Appleyard, *The Pleasures of Peace*, 102–4.

53. That Larkin more than a decade earlier began *Trouble at Willow Gables* (1943) with a description of the local postman as 'a slightly-ridiculous figure in cycle-clips' is one index of the reductiveness of the consensual equation of the poet with the protagonist of 'Church Going' (*TWG*, 6–7).

54. See 'Coincidences: Some Successful Detective Work South of the River' by Amber Allcroft, *About Larkin*, 21 (Summer 2006), 36. I am grateful to Jim Orwin for drawing this article to my attention.

55. Tolley, *Larkin at Work*, 75–84.

56. Larkin praised Belfast, where 'Church Going' was written, as 'a good place to be schizophrenic in'. See Shakespeare, 'A Few Suggestions', 14.

57. Yeats, 'Among School Children', in *Collected Poems*, 243.

58. Morrison, *The Movement*, 231.

59. Thomas Hardy, *The Complete Poems*, ed. James Gibson (Macmillan, London, 1981), 152, 430, 564. Two years after 'Church Going' was published in *The Less Deceived*, Ted Hughes included the word 'blent' in his fine poem 'Thrushes'.

60. Thomas Hardy, *Tess of the d'Urbervilles* (Macmillan Papermac, London, 1966), 315.
61. Hardy, *Complete Poems*, 102.
62. Charles Tomlinson, 'Poetry Today', in *Pelican Guide to English Literature*, vol. 7: *The Modern Age*, ed. Boris Ford (Penguin, Harmondsworth, 1961), 471.
63. Timms, *Philip Larkin*, 67.
64. Cooper, *Philip Larkin: Subversive Writer*, 143.
65. David Punter, *Philip Larkin: The Whitsun Weddings and Selected Poems* (York Press, London, 2003), 21. Steinberg likewise describes the 'Irish sixpence' as 'a worthless coin', *Philip Larkin and His Audiences*, 126.
66. Alan Brownjohn, *Philip Larkin* (British Council/Longman, Harlow, 1975), 12; Tolley, *My Proper Ground*, 80–1. I put the following questions to the poet David Wheatley: was UK currency acceptable in the Irish Republic at this time; and, second, was Republican currency acceptable in Ulster? To the first question he replied: 'I quote a text message from my dad (b. 1945, in the emphatically non-border county of Wicklow): "Sterling was used all the time. It was common to get both notes and coins in shops when receiving change. You would have as many sterling coins as Irish ones in your pocket, right up to the 1970s."' To the second question David replied by quoting another fine poet, Ciaran Carson: 'Southern currency, both notes and coins, were indeed commercially acceptable all over the North in the 1950s, and I think the converse must have been true. I remember my father pointing out to me the more elegant design of Southern coinage. Animals, from wren for farthing to horse for half-crown, were to be preferred to a crowned head. Sterling and the Southern punt were on par.' Thanks to all three for setting the Larkin debate straight.
67. Thwaite, 'The Poetry of Philip Larkin, *Phoenix*, 11/12, 53.
68. Morrison, *The Movement*, 234.
69. MacNeice quoted in *TCP*, 372.
70. Jim Orwin emailed (26 July 2012) to say that *Arkham Asylum*, 'the Batman graphic novel by Grant Morrison (illustrated by Dave McKean)', is subtitled *A Serious House on Serious Earth*. As Jim suggests, this is 'another tangential Larkin influence'.
71. Thwaite, 'The Poetry of Philip Larkin', *Phoenix*, 11/12, 52.
72. Larkin's wording here – 'it held unspilt / So long and equably what since is found / Only in separation – marriage, and birth, / And death, and thoughts of these' – may be indebted to the autobiography of Henry Green, *Pack My Bag*: 'the Church [...] seeks to share in all those few moments when we stand alone, at birth, in marriage, and at death'. Quoted by John Updike in his 'Introduction' to Henry Green, *Loving, Living, Party Going* (Picador, London, 1978), 9–10.
73. Corcoran, *English Poetry since 1940*, 93; Regan, *Philip Larkin: The Critics Debate*, 87; J.R. Watson, 'The Other Larkin', *Critical Quarterly*, 17, 4 (1975), 354; R.N. Parkinson, 'To Keep Our Metaphysics Warm: A Study of "Church Going"', *Critical Survey*, 5 (1971), 224–33; T. Whalen, *Philip Larkin and English Poetry* (Macmillan, Basingstoke, 1986), 17; Patrick Garland, 'An Enormous Yes: A Memoir of the Poet', in *An Arundel Tomb*, by Paul Foster, Trevor Brighton and Patrick Garland (Otter Memorial Papers, Chichester, 1996), 24–5; Rossen, *Philip Larkin: His Life's Work*, 45. 'Church Going' echoes several of Betjeman's churchy poems, including 'Sunday Afternoon Service in St. Enodoc Church, Cornwall', 'A Lincolnshire Church' and 'Church of England thoughts occasioned by hearing the bells of Magdalen Tower from the Botanic Garden, Oxford on St. Mary Magdalen's Day'. However, as these lines from the latter

demonstrate, Betjeman conflates Church and state in a manner that Larkin unsinews:

> A Church of England sound, it tells
> Of 'moderate' worship, God and State.
> Where matins congregations go
> Conservative and good and slow
> To elevations of the plate.

This poem was collected in *A Few Late Chrysanthemums*, which was published in 1954, the year in which 'Church Going' was composed. John Betjeman, *Collected Poems*, ed. Earl of Birkenhead (John Murray, London, 1958), 194.

74. Stephen Regan, 'The Movement', in *A Companion to Twentieth-Century Poetry*, ed. Neil Roberts (Blackwell, Oxford, 2001), 217.
75. Heaney, 'The Main of Light', 135; Frederick Grubb, 'Dragons', *Phoenix*, 11/12 (1973–74), 134; Davie, *Thomas Hardy and British Poetry*, 64; Peter Levi, 'The English Wisdom of a Master Poet', in *An Enormous Yes: In Memoriam Philip Larkin (1922– 1985)*, ed. Harry Chambers (Peterloo Poets, Calstock, 1986), 33; Alan Bennett, *Untold Stories* (Faber, London, 2005), 540; Terry Eagleton, 'Larkin: A Left View', *About Larkin*, 9 (April 2000), 6.

4 Radical De-essentialism: 'The Whitsun Weddings'

1. K.K. Ruthven, *Feminist Literary Studies: An Introduction* (Cambridge University Press, 1984), 109.
2. For a comprehensive study of the subject see John Mullan, *Anonymity: A Secret History of English Literature* (Faber, London, 2007).
3. Ruthven, *Feminist Literary Studies*, 110.
4. Anthony Curtis, 'Larkin's Oxford', in *Philip Larkin: The Man and his Work*, ed. Dale Salwak (Macmillan, Basingstoke, 1989), 9; John Carey, 'The Two Philip Larkins', in *New Larkins for Old: Critical Essays*, ed. James Booth (Macmillan, Basingstoke, 2000), 56; Wiemann, 'Larkin's Englishness', 26; Lerner, *Philip Larkin*, 23; Tolley, *My Proper Ground*, 95; Andrew Swarbrick, *'The Less Deceived' and 'The Whitsun Weddings'* (Macmillan, Basingstoke, 1986), 50; Marsh, *Philip Larkin: The Poems*, 72; Regan, *Philip Larkin: The Critics Debate*, 115; Whitehead, *Hardy to Larkin*, 230; Kuby, *An Uncommon Poet*, 120–2; Morrison, *The Movement*, 258; Kuby, *An Uncommon Poet*, 121.
5. Tolley, *My Proper Ground*, 95; Regan, *Philip Larkin: The Critics Debate*, 116; Gilbert Phelps, 'Literature and Drama', in *The Cambridge Guide to the Arts in Britain*, vol. 9: *Since the Second World War*, ed. Boris Ford (Cambridge University Press, 1988), 213; Corcoran, *English Poetry since 1940*, 94.
6. Paulin, 'She Did Not Change', 237–50.
7. Motion, *Life*, 287–8. Burnett quotes the same passage from Motion, *TCP*, 411. However, my tenacious *companiero* Jim Orwin has checked the Larkin edition of the *South Bank Show* and been unable to locate the quotation (private correspondence, 23 June 2013). Presumably the words come from a transcript of footage that wound up on the cutting-room floor.
8. Motion, *Life*, 287; Bradford, *First Boredom, Then Fear*, 157.
9. I am grateful to Jim Orwin for bringing this statement to my attention. The transcription is his.

10. David Kynaston, *Family Britain, 1951–57* (Bloomsbury, London, 2009), 734.
11. However, elsewhere in the same volume Thwaite more plausibly says 'L[arkin]'s affair with Patsy Strang went on intermittently between June 1952 and the autumn of 1954.' *LM*, 185.
12. Bradford, *First Boredom, Then Fear*, 157.
13. Tolley, *Larkin at Work*, 95.
14. Bruce Montgomery put it the other way round, saying of Larkin: 'that massive, affable, pipe-smoking undergraduate was no Kemp'. Edmund Crispin, 'An Oxford Group', *Spectator*, 17 April 1964, 525.
15. Tolley, *Larkin at Work*, 96.
16. Osborne, *Larkin, Ideology and Critical Violence*, 57–63.
17. Eliot, *Complete Poems and Plays*, 68.
18. Ibid., 78.
19. Tennyson, *The Poems*, 355.
20. Hardy, *Complete Poems*, 566.
21. Whalen, *Philip Larkin and English Poetry*, 60–1.
22. Barbara Everett, 'Art and Larkin', in *Philip Larkin: The Man and his Work*, ed. Dale Salwak (Macmillan, London, 1989), 135, 136.
23. W.H. Auden, *Collected Shorter Poems, 1927–1957* (Faber, London, 1966), 85.
24. Hartley, *Philip Larkin, the Marvell Press and Me*, 119; Paulin, 'She Did Not Change', 235.
25. Woolf, *The Waves*, 74–5.
26. Henry Wadsworth Longfellow, *The Works of Henry Wadsworth Longfellow* (Wordsworth, Ware, 1994), 135.
27. Motion, *Life*, 288.
28. I use the term *texteme* to mean, if not the smallest intelligible unit of a text, then isolable units of sense, often smaller than a clause or sentence, and out of which the larger text is constituted – as it were, the *tesserae* that constitute the larger mosaic. Compare *narreme* (the smallest significant unit in narrative); *mytheme* (Claude Lévi-Strauss's term for the smallest comprehensible unit of myth); *styleme* (the smallest independent unit on the stylistic plane); *sememe* (Umberto Eco's coinage for the smallest independent semiotic unit); and *ideologeme* (Fredric Jameson's term for 'the smallest intelligible unit of the [...] antagonistic [...] discourses of social classes') – all by analogy with the well-established linguistic term *phoneme* (the smallest intelligible unit of significant sound in a language). My use of texteme emphasizes the textuality of the text but is in other regards similar to Roland Barthes's *lexie* (in the English translation, *lexia*). In *S/Z* a lexie is a minimal unit of reading, a passage which has an isolable effect on the reader which can be distinguished from the effect of other passages. My thinking in this area was much clarified by Hawthorn's *A Concise Glossary of Contemporary Literary Theory*.
29. Peter Sheldon in 'Philip Larkin: Seven Verbal Snapshots', ed. Jane E. Thomas, *Bête Noire*, 5 (1988), 89.
30. Tennyson, *The Poems*, 732.
31. Paul Muldoon, 'This Be The Verse', *New York Times Sunday Book Review*, 22 April 2012, 1. Eliot, *Complete Poems and Plays*, 67.
32. Whitehead, *Hardy to Larkin*, 230.
33. Tolley, *Larkin at Work*, 93.
34. Simone de Beauvoir, *The Second Sex*, trans. H.M. Parshley (New English Library, London, 1970), 9.
35. Woolf, *Orlando*, 117–18.

36. B.J. Leggett, *Larkin's Blues: Jazz, Popular Music and Poetry* (Louisiana State University Press, Baton Rouge, 1999), 47.
37. Martin Luther King, 'I have a dream', in *The Penguin Book of Historic Speeches*, ed. Brian MacArthur (Viking, London, 1995), 491.
38. Kingsley Amis, *Lucky Jim* (1954; Penguin, Harmondsworth, 1962), 177.
39. Lisa Jardine, 'Saxon Violence', *The Guardian*, Section 2, 8 December 1992, 4.
40. Gavin Ewart, *The Collected Ewart, 1933–1980* (Hutchinson, London, 1980), 254–6. Andrew Motion, 'This is Your Subject Speaking', in *Natural Causes* (Chatto & Windus, London, 1987), 49–57.
41. Julian Barnes, *A History of the World in 10½ Chapters* (Picador, London, 1990), 239.
42. Ian McEwan, *Solar* (Jonathan Cape, London, 2010), 112–26. *Solar* may also be read as a homage to Kingsley Amis's *One Fat Englishman* (1963), a much more brilliantly disagreeable book than *Lucky Jim* (1954).
43. Peter Reading, *Stet* (Secker & Warburg, London, 1986), n.p.
44. Maurice Rutherford, *Love Is a Four-Letter World* (Peterloo, Calstock, 1994), 59–61. The next chapter quotes another of Rutherford's verse responses to Larkin's poems. These responses have been conveniently gathered in an excellent pamphlet, *Flip Side to Philip Larkin* (Shoestring Press, Nottingham, 2012).
45. Elizabeth Jennings, *Collected Poems, 1953–1985* (Carcanet, Manchester, 1986), 118. Sheenagh Pugh, *Sing for the Taxman* (Seren, Bridgend, 1993), 20.
46. Grace Nichols, *Picasso, I Want My Face Back* (Bloodaxe, Tarsent, 2009), 30.
47. Beryl Bainbridge, *Sweet William* (Duckworth, London, 1975), 121, 123, 124.
48. Tariq Latif, *The Punjabi Weddings* (Arc, Todmorden, 2007), 51–2.
49. I am grateful to Jim Orwin for bringing Dijkstra's work to my attention.
50. 'Outward from Hull' is placed in the 'Framing the Landscape' section of Nichols's collection *Picasso, I Want My Face Back*. The poem's references to Wilberforce and to 'black roots' hint at the racing of the narrator, but it is the larger sectional discussion of Guyanese artists expatriated to Europe (most notably the painter Aubrey Williams) that legitimizes speculation about the gender and ethnicity of the protagonist. Although the Sheenagh Pugh poem describes marking creative writing scripts of the sort she receives as a tutor at the University of Glamorgan, the identifying of the protagonist as a 'Welsh woman' is less secure, *Sing for the Taxman* experimenting with a considerable diversity of narrators.
51. One poem is symptomatically subtitled: 'my 1989 English version of Simon Dach's 1651 German translation from the Latin of Carolus Malapertius of Antwerp, 1616'. *Sing for the Taxman*, 61.
52. Larkin marked the distinction between the two in his interview with John Haffenden: 'I was baptized – in Coventry Cathedral, oddly enough: the old one – but not confirmed' (*FR*, 56).
53. A question we have not addressed is this: if the original train journey did not take place at Whit, how come Larkin witnessed 'at every station, Goole, Doncaster, Retford, Newark, importunate wedding parties, gawky and vociferous, seeing off couples to London'? A possible explanation lies in the so-called *Factory Fortnight* or *Industrial Holiday Fortnight* in accord with which whole sectors of the industrial economy of the 1950s and 1960s took a co-ordinated summer break in the last week of July and the first week of August. This accords with the probable date of Larkin's journey to Grantham, 30 July 1955. Though not as popular as the Whit weekend, working-class couples timed their weddings to this agreed holiday so as not to require unpaid honeymoon leave. The poem shifts the dates for strategic reasons, but the financial imperatives are constant.

54. Helen Gardner, *The Art of T.S. Eliot* (Faber, London, 1968), 182.
55. Eliot, *Complete Poems and Plays*, 196.
56. Motion, *Life*, 483.
57. *The Letters of D.H. Lawrence*, ed. James T. Boulton and Margaret H. Boulton, with Gerald Lacy, vol. VI (Cambridge University Press, 1991), 29.
58. D.H. Lawrence, *Lady Chatterley's Lover* (Penguin, Harmondsworth, 1960), 163.
59. Ibid., 258.
60. Ibid., 181. These words are echoed in Larkin's letter to Monica of 23 January 1963 in the context of a discussion of anal intercourse: 'this piercing, rather awful sensuality'. *LM*, 292.
61. Lawrence, *Lady Chatterley's Lover*, 139, 179.
62. Ibid., 316.
63. 'It is fatal', Virginia Woolf wrote in 1929, 'to be a man or woman pure and simple; one must be woman-manly or man-womanly'. Woolf, *A Room of One's Own* (Triad/Panther, Frogmore, 1978), 99. Compare with the following remarks drawn from Larkin's letters to Monica Jones: 'Homosexuality is surely much more like heterosexuality than it's like anything else, don't you think?' (*LM*, 145). 'It seems more to me that what we have is a kind of homosexual relation, disguised' (*LM*, 235). 'I seem entirely lacking in that *desire to impose oneself* that is such a feature of masculine behaviour' (*LM*, 236).
64. 'Ode to a Nightingale' is not the only Keats poem invoked. Larkin's description of how from the train window 'hedges dipped / And rose' echoes Keats's account of a boat bobbing in a stream in Book I of *Endymion* (1818): 'And soon it lightly dipt, and rose, and sank, / And dipt again'. *Keats: Poetical Works*, ed. H.W. Garrod (Oxford University Press, 1970), 65.
65. Thwaite, 'The Poetry of Philip Larkin', *Phoenix*, 11/12, 48.
66. An unpublished Larkin quatrain puts this view more harshly:

> To shoot your spunk into a girl
> Is life's unquestioned crown
> But leading up to it is not
> And nor is leading down.

I am grateful to Alan Brownjohn for bringing this poem to my attention. My wording 'The bridal train trip has resolved itself into an anticipation of the moment of consummation' is an attempt to give a less phallic emphasis to John Bayley's observation that 'the bridal train trip has resolved itself into an image of erection, penetration, fertility'. Bayley, 'Larkin's Short Story Poems', in *Philip Larkin: A Tribute*, ed. George Hartley (Marvell, London, 1988), 282.
67. F.R. Leavis, *D.H. Lawrence/Novelist* (1955; Penguin, Harmondsworth, 1964), 6 (quoting *The Criterion*, July 1931). 'The Whitsun Weddings' may be said to side with Leavis who in this period was conducting a public quarrel with Eliot over his disparagement of Lawrence.
68. This passage is indebted to two essays, '"The Importance of Being Elsewhere", or "No Man is an Ireland": Self, Selves and Social Consensus in the Poetry of Philip Larkin' by John Goodby, *Critical Survey*, 1, 2 (1989), 131–8; and Peter Hollindale, 'The Long Perspectives', in *Critical Essays on Philip Larkin: The Poems*, ed. Linda Cookson and Bryan Loughrey (Longman, London, 1989), 50–61 – though both conflate author and narrator in ways that in my opinion impede full development of their arguments.

69. Terence, *The Self-Tormentor (Heauton Timoroumenos)*, ed. and trans. A.J. Brothers (Aris and Phillips, Warminster, 1988), 48.

5   Radical Laughter: 'This Be The Verse'

1. Derrida, *Without Alibi*, 181, 182; Jacques Derrida, 'Following Theory', in *Life.After. Theory*, ed. Michael Payne and John Schad (Continuum, London, 2003), 9.
2. Derrida, 'Following Theory', in Payne and Schad, eds, *Life.After.Theory*, 11.
3. Donald Davie, 'Larkin's Choice', *The Listener*, 29 March 1973, 420.
4. Donald Davie, *Thomas Hardy and British Poetry* (Routledge & Kegan Paul, London, 1973), 40, 71.
5. Ken Edwards, 'Some Younger Poets', in *The New British Poetry, 1968–88*, ed. Gillian Allnutt, Fred d'Aguiar, Ken Edwards and Eric Mottram (Paladin, London, 1988), 265.
6. Randall Stevenson, *The Last of England?: The Oxford Literary History*, vol. 12: *1960–2000* (Oxford University Press, 2004), 171.
7. *The Faber Book of Modern Verse*, ed. Michael Roberts, revised Donald Hall (Faber, London, 1965), 31.
8. Hartley, *Philip Larkin, the Marvell Press and Me*, 78.
9. Jean Hartley writing to Jane Thomas, 13 October 2009 (unpublished private correspondence).
10. Amis, *The Letters of Kingsley Amis*, 105–6.
11. Motion, *Life*, 319. Such puerile but essentially de-inhibitive gestures were not confined to Movementeers like Larkin and Amis. In May 1962 – the very year that Larkin and Jones began their defacement of Murdoch's novel – the postmodern playwright Joe Orton and his companion (later murderer) Kenneth Halliwell were given six-month jail sentences for vandalizing public library books. Their joint venture began as anonymous protest against the suffocating banality of the holdings at their local Islington library. Sometimes it was the covers that received most attention, as when a John Betjeman volume had a photograph of an elderly tattooed man in swimming trunks collaged onto the dust jacket. Sometimes titles were doctored, as when *The Collected Plays* of Emlyn Williams listed *Knickers Must Fall* and *Fucked by Monty* among the contents. On other occasions back-cover blurbs were tastefully altered: Dorothy L. Sayers's *Gaudy Nights* represented the writer 'at her most imposing. At her most queer, and needless to say, at her most crude!'; while another of her Lord Peter Wimsey novels, *Clouds of Witness*, advised punters to 'have a good shit while you are reading!' In a perfect exemplification of the adage that after death one becomes famous for that which in life made one notorious, 40 of the volumes defaced by Orton and Halliwell were exhibited at Islington Local History Museum, October–February 2012. The Larkin–Jones collaboration, *The Shite from the Non-Enchanter*, awaits a similar accolade.
12. The Tourette Syndrome Classification Study Group, 'Definitions and Classification of the Disorders' (http://web.archive.org/web20060426232033). Accessed 30 March 2011.
13. Hardy, *Complete Poems*, 72.
14. Rambling Syd Rumpo was particularly associated with the BBC Radio comedy *Round the Horne*. His folk songs made suggestive use of little-known words like 'moulies' (as in 'The Ballad of the Woggler's Moulie', sung to the tune of 'Oh My Darling, Clementine') and neologisms like 'nadgers' ('Green Grow My Nadgers O!'). Other classic numbers include 'The Taddle Gropers' Dance', 'What Shall We

Do With the Drunken Nurker' and 'D'Ye Ken Jim Pubes'. Jim Orwin notes that 'Williams was a Larkin fan' who, according to Wikipedia, 'abandoned Christian faith following discussions with the poet'. In a letter of 10 April 2012, Orwin also draws my attention to the following passage from Williams's posthumously published diaries: 'Philip Larkin is dead. Surely the whole world must end now that this fine man has left it? I scribbled a quick poem in my notebook when I heard, although if anyone should ever read it I would squeal and die. Alright then, here it is. "Philip Larkin / I've thought about parking / My penis in your gob / Oh Mr. Larkin / The dog's are barking / Won't you suck my nob?" I call it O'd To Larkin. Of course, I would never have asked him when he was alive – he might have said yes, and the man was a rapist and a wife-beater.'

15. Hardy, *Complete Poems*, 349 and footnote 961.
16. Ibid., 228, 307, 154, 648, 16, 55, 216–17, 343, 51, 341.
17. Ibid., 603, 111, 532, 658.
18. John Ayto, *Twentieth Century Words* (Oxford University Press, 1999), 209.
19. Michael Millgate, ed., *The Life and Work of Thomas Hardy by Thomas Hardy* (Macmillan, London, 1984), 259; Millgate, *Thomas Hardy: A Biography Revisited* (Oxford University Press, 2004), 354. Hardy's tone-deafness extended to involuntary *doubles entendres* in the writings of others. His novel *A Pair of Blue Eyes* (1873) takes as a chapter epigraph Shelley's line 'He heard her musical Pants', the deadpan citation making no allowance for readers who picture the hero listening, not to his beloved's respiration, but to her melodious underwear. Thomas Hardy, *A Pair of Blue Eyes*, ed. Pamela Dalziel (revised edition, Penguin Books, London, 2005), 162. The allusion is to Shelley's *The Revolt of Islam*, Canto VI, verse xx, line 7. P.B. Shelley, *Poetical Works*, ed. Thomas Hutchinson (Oxford University Press, 1970), 99. It is only fair to add that in some unfathomable way Hardy's poetic greatness is intimately connected to this verbal fallibility. As Dylan Thomas remarked: 'I like the bus that Hardy misses more than the bus other poets catch.' See Seamus Perry's beautiful review article on the subject, 'So Striking a Miss-Hit', *Times Literary Supplement*, 1 April 2011, 8–9.
20. Hence the title of Beckett's remarkable 1972 play *Not I*. There is no connection with Robert Louis Stevenson's poem of the same name mentioned later in the chapter.
21. Sigmund Freud, *An Autobiographical Study* (1925), trans. James Strachey (Hogarth Press, London, 1935), 85.
22. See Mark Morton, *Dirty Words: The Story of Sex Talk* (2003; Atlantic Books, London, 2005), 202. Ford Madox Ford, *Some Do Not ...* (Sphere Books, London, 1969), 76.
23. W.E. Williams, ed., *Thomas Hardy: A Selection of Poems* (Penguin, Harmondsworth, 1960), 15.
24. S.W. Dawson, 'On Re-Reading *The Less Deceived*', in *Philip Larkin: A Tribute*, ed. George Hartley (Marvell, London, 1988), 180.
25. This last connection may be endorsed by the fact that when Larkin finished 'The Trees', carefully dating it '2 June 1967', he added the words 'Birthday of T Hardy 1840'.
26. Almack's was a London club founded in the Regency period and famous for its dinner-dances.
27. Two honourable exceptions: Clive James, 'On His Wit', in *Larkin at Sixty*, ed. Anthony Thwaite (Faber, London, 1982), 98–108; and John White, 'Philip Larkin: Funny Man', Part 1, *About Larkin*, 29 (April 2010), 20–4; Part 2, *About Larkin*, 30 (October 2010), 9–14.

28. Eric Homberger, *The Art of the Real: Poetry in England and America since 1939* (Dent, London, 1977), 74; Stan Smith, *Inviolable Voice: History and Twentieth Century Poetry* (Gill & Macmillan, Dublin, 1982), 176; Eagleton quoted in Christopher Hitchens, *Unacknowledged Legislation: Writers in the Public Sphere* (Verso, London, 2002), 250; ibid. Corcoran is similarly oblivious to Larkin's humour and the way it mediates his content: 'Philip Larkin is undoubtedly the most Movement of Movement poets in the sense that in him the true spirit of post-war English dispiritedness quickly reached, and subsequently maintained, its most quintessential form.' *English Poetry since 1940*, 87.

29. T.S. Eliot, *Selected Essays* (Faber, London, 1951), 296. A similar note is struck in Robert Frost's 1935 introduction to *King Jasper* by E.A. Robinson: 'If it is with outer seriousness, it must be with inner humour. If it is with outer humour, it must be with inner seriousness. Neither one alone without the other under it will do.' Robert Frost, 'Introduction' to *King Jasper*, by E.A. Robinson (Macmillan, New York, 1935), xi.

30. The Freud quotation and list of pre-Oedipal comedians are taken from *Comedy/Cinema/Theory*, ed. Andrew Horton (University of California Press, Berkeley, Los Angeles and Oxford, 1991), 10–12. I am indebted to James Zborowski for drawing this work to my attention.

31. Stevenson, not Stephenson, as Richard Palmer has it in his perspicacious but careless monograph *Such Deliberate Disguises*, 117. Palmer compounds the howler by insisting that the *Scottish* author is the grandson of George Stephenson, the *English* inventor of the steam engine. Elsewhere he attributes a 1954 article on 'The Movement' to Blake Morrison, who was four years old at the time; misspells the names of such thinkers as Castiglione, Nietzsche and Cassirer, and of the poets Shelley, Christina Rossetti, Michael Hamburger and LeRoi Jones; replaces Thom Gunn's arcane title *Moly* with the altogether more commonplace *Molly*; and makes errors in the titles of Larkin's 'Wedding-Wind', 'Next, Please', 'An Arundel Tomb', 'Self's the Man', 'The Card-Players', 'This Be The Verse' and 'Friday Night in the Royal Station Hotel'.

32. Robert Louis Stevenson, *Selected Poems*, ed. Angus Calder (Penguin, Harmondsworth, 1998), 122.

33. Compare with the final stanza of Housman's 'The Culprit', recounting the last words of a man about to be hanged:

> For so the game is ended
> That should not have begun.
> My father and my mother
> They had a likely son,
> And I have none.

A.E. Housman, *Collected Poems* (Penguin, Harmondsworth, 1956), 120.

34. Steve Clark, '"Get Out As Early As You Can": Larkin's Sexual Politics', in *Philip Larkin: A Tribute*, ed. George Hartley (Marvell, London, 1988), 242. In 1994, shortly before he went missing, *Select* magazine published a photograph of Richey Edwards, rhythm guitarist with the Manic Street Preachers, wearing a T-shirt inscribed with the first two lines of 'This Be The Verse'. The T-shirt was designed by one Jeremy Deller for the London boutique Sign of the Times. Deller went on to win the Turner Prize in 2004 and as I write is enjoying a major retrospective show at the Hayward Gallery, London (February–May 2012), which includes that iconic T.

35. Email from Jim Orwin, 22 March 2012. A reputable publisher really should approach Orwin with a view to preserving between hard covers his encyclopaedic knowledge of musical settings of Larkin poems.
36. Poem XL from *A Shropshire Lad*, which Larkin included in his Oxford anthology. Housman, *Collected Poems*, 70. Larkin was well aware that his demotion of childhood was not (or not only) a matter of personal animosity so much as a post-Romantic shift in society: 'children themselves have been devalued: we know them for the little beasts they are (a knowledge greatly amplified since 1945 by the forcible reintroduction of a servantless middle class to its offspring), and nobody would pretend there was anything angelic about them, so that one of the major illusions of the Romantic movement had thereby quietly disappeared, like knives and forks from a university refectory'. *RW*, 191.
37. Carol Ann Duffy, ed., *Answering Back* (Picador, London, 2007), xi.
38. Carol Rumens, 'This Be The Verse', in ibid., 9.
39. Rutherford, *Love is a Four-Letter World*, 57; *Flip Side to Philip Larkin*, 4. Something similar might be claimed for Daljit Nagra's 'This Be The Pukka Verse' whose 'kids' are 'fucked up' by being the mixed-race products of exploitative relations between the white administrators of the Raj and local Sikh women:

> sport that ends
> in the hushed-up bezti births
> of half-breed bastards growing up
> cursed as mad dogs and vagabonds
> in a jolly good lingam-land overflowing
> with Hobson-Jobsons of Holi,
> and opium and silk and spice
> and all the gems of the shafted earth!

Daljit Nagra, *Tippoo Sultan's Incredible White-Man-Eating Tiger Toy-Machine!!!* (Faber, London, 2011), 16–17. There may also be an echo of 'This Be The Verse' in the following excerpt from Kia Abdullah's first novel, *Assimilation*: 'any good psychiatrist will tell you: all our problems, insecurities, fears and fuck-ups stem from our parents'. The novel charts the rebellion of a young Muslim woman growing up in a British-Bangladeshi family in London. *Assimilation* (Toronto, Adlibbed, 2006),11.

40. This is another swipe at Stevenson, *A Child's Garden of Verses* (1885) being a volume of his poems about childhood.
41. Carey, 'The Two Philip Larkins', 51.
42. Osborne, *Larkin, Ideology and Critical Violence*, 220.
43. It is worth remarking that Larkin's formula 'They fuck you up, your mum and dad [...] // But they were fucked up in their turn' has been taken seriously by clinical psychologists. See Oliver James, *The Larkin Syndrome* (*The Observer*, London, n.d.). James reads the poem literally rather than as a strategic joke at the expense of hegemonic values.
44. 'All Things Bright and Beautiful' was published in *Hymns for Little Children* (1848) by Cecil Frances Humphreys Alexander and epitomizes the Victorian values scorned in 'This Be The Verse'. If Alexander's 'All Things Bright', 'We Are Little Christian Children' and 'We Are But Little Children Weak' encapsulate the 'soppy' side of Larkin's oxymoronic description, other of her hymns epitomize the 'stern' – 'Do No Sinful Action', for instance, or 'Souls in Death and Darkness Lying'.

The dual rejection of reproduction and religion which we are unpacking in 'This Be The Verse', and which makes it the polar opposite of 'All Things Bright', was made gloriously explicit in one of Larkin's reviews: 'It was that verse about becoming again as a little child that caused the first sharp waning of my Christian sympathies. If the Kingdom of Heaven could be entered only by those fulfilling such a condition I knew I should be unhappy there.' *RW*, 111.

45. Carey, 'The Two Philip Larkins', 51.
46. Robert Burns, *The Canongate Burns*, ed. Andrew Noble and Patrick Scott Hogg (Canongate, Edinburgh, 2001), 109. The poem has ten more stanzas, all as maudlin!
47. Wordsworth, *Poetical Works*, 378.
48. Hardy, *Complete Poems*, 513.
49. As Larkin wrote to Monica Jones, 'Why can't one stop being a son without becoming a father?' *LM*, 328. For an interesting elaboration of the argument see 'Philip Larkin or the Law of the Father' by Andy McKeown, *About Larkin*, 17 (April 2004), 16–20.
50. Lawrence S. Cunningham and John J. Reich, eds, *Culture and Values*, vol. II: *A Survey of the Humanities with Readings* (Cengate, Stamford, 2009), 492.
51. *Private Eye* magazine recognized as much in the following spoof (No. 1310, 23 March–5 April 2012, 27):

> *This be the verse*
> He fucks you up, the bard of Hull
> He may not try to, but he does
> Combines his rapt, seductive lull
> With bouts of misanthropic scuzz
>
> But he was fucked up in his turn
> By old-style poets he thought great
> Bleak symbols of the funeral urn
> Like crappy Auden and crappier Yeats
>
> Man hands on influence to man
> It deepens like a swelling ocean
> So get out quickly while you can
> And don't turn into Andrew Motion.

52. Alan Travis, *Bound and Gagged: A Secret History of Obscenity in Britain* (Profile, London, 2001), 218.
53. The element of shock attaching to the word 'cunt' in 'Love Again', which Larkin began in 1975 and completed in September 1979, derives from five centuries of its suppression. Its unproblematic status in the medieval period may be gauged by the fact that in the thirteenth century both London and Oxford had streets called *Gropecuntlane*, probably in recognition of the brothels located there. By the late eighteenth century the word was sufficiently indecent for Francis Grose's *Dictionary of the Vulgar Tongue* to only list it as 'c – t'. The *Oxford English Dictionary* did not include 'cunt' until the 1972 supplement, though 'prick' and 'cock' had been included in the 12-volume edition published in 1933. See Morton, *Dirty Words*, 207, 209.
54. As Larkin said: 'there *are* some odd poems in the Hardy canon – autobiographical stuff one can't account for. I don't think I could ever write poems like that – one

must make everything clear, present a picture or a story, not mutter about things you don't want known' (*LM*, 362).

55. J. Douglas Porteous, 'Sing-Along with Philip', *About Larkin*, 27 (April 2009), 31.

6   Radical Plot Deflation: 'Vers de Société'

1. George Kendrick, 'An Interview with Peter Easy', *Bête Noire*, 4 (Winter 1987), 23.

2. Nicholas Jenkins, 'The "Truth of Skies": Auden, Larkin, and the English Question', in *The Movement Reconsidered: Essays on Larkin, Amis, Gunn, Davie, and Their Contemporaries*, ed. Zachary Leader (Oxford University Press, 2009), 58.

3. Jonathan Raban, 'Philip Larkin', in *Driving Home: An American Scrapbook* (Picador, London, 2010), 88–9, 98, 99.

4. Jenkins, 'The "Truth of Skies"', 58–9. Christopher Ricks, 'The Whitsun Weddings', *Phoenix*, 11/12 (1973–74), 10.

5. Christopher Ricks, 'Like Something Almost Being Said', in *Larkin at Sixty*, ed. Anthony Thwaite (Faber, London, 1982), 121.

6. Ibid., 121–2.

7. Stevenson, *The Last of England?*, 552, 171, 173.

8. Kendrick, 'An Interview with Peter Easy', 22.

9. Steven Connor, *Postmodernist Culture: An Introduction to Theories of the Contemporary* (Blackwell, Oxford, 1989), 108.

10. Ibid., 115.

11. The eponymous heroine of Hardy's novel *The Hand of Ethelberta* (1876) has anonymously published a volume entitled *Metres by Me* which consists of 'a collection of soft and marvellously musical rhymes, of a nature known as the *vers de société*. The lines presented a series of playful defences of the supposed strategy of womankind in fascination, courtship, and marriage – the whole teeming with ideas bright as mirrors and just as unsubstantial, yet forming a brilliant argument to justify the ways of girls to men.' Thomas Hardy, *The Hand of Ethelberta* (Penguin, Harmondsworth, 1997), 26.

12. *Princeton Encyclopedia of Poetry and Poetics*, ed. Alex Preminger (Macmillan, London, 1975), 446.

13. Robert Conquest, 'A Proper Sport', in *Larkin at Sixty*, ed. Anthony Thwaite (Faber, London, 1982), 32.

14. This lack of specificity is a reason for rejecting the interpretations of biographicalists like James Booth who, by conflating author and narrator, reduce the array of vocations to just one, *poet*. See 'Two Guitar Pieces II' on the Philip Larkin Society website where Booth writes: 'In his later work the poet will frequently *depict himself* gazing out from a room' or 'rejecting the demands of the social world in favour of solitary self-possession ("Best Society", "The Whitsun Weddings", "Vers de Société").' My emphasis. (Accessed 2 July 2004.)

15. This passage benefitted from a reading of chapter 12, 'Narratology', in Peter Barry, *Beginning Theory* (Manchester University Press, revised edition 2002), 222–47.

16. Ezra Pound, *The Cantos of Ezra Pound* (Faber, London, 1975), 796.

17. Eliot, *Complete Poems and Plays*, 14; Yeats, *Collected Poems*, 228; MacNeice and Thomas, cited by Burnett, *TCP*, 470; Lawrence, *Lady Chatterley's Lover*, 123.

18. In the last year of his life Larkin asked me if I had read *Flaubert's Parrot* and seemed pleased that I had not so that he could urge the book upon me. In retrospect, his 'we old timers can still teach you young whipper-snappers a thing or two' tone reminds me of the description of the wrestling competition in 'Show

Saturday': 'Two more start, one grey-haired: he wins, though' (*CP*, 199). Larkin stressed the novel's emotional power but also the structural originality with which the emotion was conveyed – 'ingenious', he said. Contrary to the stick-in-the-mud persona he assiduously cultivated (*What do you mainly read?* '[N]ovels I've read before' (*FR*, 70)), he praised the fact that every Barnes novel was unique. How he would have responded to *Nothing to be Frightened of* (2008), a meditation upon death fit to mention in the same breath as 'Aubade'.

19. David Lodge, *The Modes of Modern Writing: Metaphor, Metonymy and the Typology of Modern Literature* (Edward Arnold, London, 1977), 226.
20. Alain Robbe-Grillet, *Last Year at Marienbad: A Cine-Novel*, trans. Richard Howard (Calder, London, 1962), 15.
21. Geoffrey Hill, 'Funeral Music, 8', in *Collected Poems* (Penguin, Harmondsworth, 1985), 77.
22. John Barth, 'Title', in *Lost in the Funhouse* (Penguin, Harmondsworth, 1972), 117.
23. Motion, *Life*, 338.
24. One of the first important analyses of postmodernist literature was Christopher Butler's *After the Wake: An Essay on the Contemporary Avant-Garde* (Oxford University Press, 1980).
25. Richard Ellmann, *James Joyce* (Oxford University Press, 1976), 725.
26. *Letters of James Joyce*, ed. Stuart Gilbert (Faber, London, 1957), vol. I, 123; *Finnegans Wake* (Faber, London, 1975), 628, 3; Ellmann, *James Joyce*, 716; Joseph Frank, *The Widening Gyre: Crisis and Mastery in Modern Literature* (Rutgers University Press, New Brunswick, 1963), 54.
27. The novel stands with Arnold Bennett's *Riceyman Steps* (1923) and Larkin's 'Mr Bleaney' as a devastating critique of the life-denial entailed to English frugality.
28. See Hans Bertens, *The Idea of the Postmodern: A History* (Routledge, London, 1995), 11: 'If there is a common denominator to all these postmodernisms, it is that of a crisis in representation: a deeply felt loss of faith in our ability to represent the real, in the widest sense.'
29. See chapter seven of Barnes's *Flaubert's Parrot* where Braithwaite mocks postmodernism's play with multiple endings and readerly choice.

7   Radical Citation: 'Aubade'

1. Edna Longley, 'Larkin, Decadence and the Lyric Poem', in *New Larkins for Old*, ed. James Booth (Macmillan, Basingstoke, 2000), 48.
2. Motion, *Life*, 372, 411.
3. Booth, *Philip Larkin: Writer*, 78.
4. Booth, *Philip Larkin: The Poet's Plight*, 10.
5. Booth, *Philip Larkin: Writer*, 79.
6. Booth, 'Philip Larkin: Lyricism, Englishness and Postcoloniality', 9.
7. Ibid., 10.
8. Booth, *Philip Larkin: The Poet's Plight*, 142–3.
9. Booth, 'Philip Larkin: Lyricism, Englishness and Postcoloniality', 19.
10. The ensuing paragraphs are indebted to a number of studies, quite the most useful of which was James William Johnson's entry on the 'Lyric' in the *Princeton Encyclopedia of Poetry and Poetics*, 460–70.
11. Although 'Aubade' was neither written to be sung nor presents itself as a work better received by ear than eye, Rowe goes too far in claiming that 'it is the kind

of poem which could not be sung' (Mark Rowe, 'Larkin's "Aubade"', in *Philosophy and Literature* (Ashgate, Aldershot, 2000), 189). Leading British postmodernist composer Thomas Adès did a setting of 'Aubade' as early as 1990, 14 years before Rowe's essay, and more recent versions include those of Per Nørgaard (for the Stuttgart Ballet) and Stephen Brown (an American composer who has set over 20 Larkin poems). David Whittle's *Bruce Montgomery/Edmund Crispin: A Life in Music and Books* (Ashgate, London, 2007) mentions Montgomery's musical settings of Larkin's early poems but it remains unclear if any of the latter were written with that in mind. I am grateful to Jim Orwin, the world authority on musical settings of Larkin, for sharing this information with me.

12. Lerner, *Philip Larkin*, 34.
13. In *Larkin, Ideology and Critical Violence* I offer an extended reading of 'I Remember, I Remember' as a sabotaging of that segment of the lyric inheritance associated with the English pastoral (see especially pp. 135–58). Trevor Tolley has offered a further instance: '"Poetry of Departures" is a translation of the phrase "poésie des départs" used to characterize a particular style of French nineteenth-century poem, such as Beaudelaire's [sic] "L'Invitation au Voyage", in which the poet contemplates leaving the everyday world for a more romantic setting. There is a light thumbing of the nose at foreign culture and cultural pretence on Larkin's part, though the main target is false expectations.' *My Proper Ground*, 76.
14. István Rácz, 'Agnosticism, Masks and Monologues in Philip Larkin', *Hungarian Journal of English and American Studies*, 1, 2 (1995), 116–17. Lerner, *Philip Larkin*, 37.
15. Rowe, 'Larkin's "Aubade"', 192.
16. Ibid., 206–7. Compare with Blake Morrison's discussion of 'Aubade' on the Philip Larkin Society's *Poem of the Month* website: 'Here he faces death head-on, with naked dread and almost shaming self-pity.' Or, again, Stephen Metcalf writing in *The New York Times* (30 May 2004): 'By the time he published "Aubade", near the end of his own life, there was no doubt to whom the opening lines were referring [...] an unblinking meditation on his approaching extinction.'
17. Booth's most considered statement on 'Aubade' may be found in his essay 'Why Larkin's Poetry Gives Offence', *English*, 46, 184 (Spring 1997), 1–19. Especially close to Rowe are such comments as this: 'The poet's contemplation of extinction has nothing to do with the quality of the life he has led, nor with any religious hopes or speculations. He is concerned only with the fact that he must die' (p. 16).
18. It is a testimony to the poets' successful eroticizing of the term that *Aubade* is now the brand name of a French luxury range of erotic underwear.
19. Larkin was long familiar with the concept of Courtly Love having read C.S. Lewis's classic account of the subject, *The Allegory of Love*, in 1942.
20. Rowe, 'Larkin's "Aubade"', 217, n. 13.
21. Andrew Marvell, 'To his Coy Mistress', in *The Metaphysical Poets*, ed. Helen Gardner (Penguin, Harmondsworth, 1966), 251–2.
22. John Donne, *The Songs and Sonets*, ed. Theodore Redpath (Methuen, London, 1967), 11, 34; *The Oxford Book of English Verse, 1250–1918*, ed. Sir Arthur Quiller-Couch (Oxford University Press, 1961), 231.
23. T.S. Eliot, 'American Literature and the American Language', in *To Criticize the Critic* (Faber, London, 1965), 58.
24. Ezra Pound, *The Spirit of Romance* (New Directions, New York, 1968), 11.
25. Pound, *Selected Poems, 1908–1959*, 53.
26. Amy Lowell, *The Complete Poetical Works* (Cambridge University Press, 1955), 73, 214.

27. *Imagist Poetry*, ed. Peter Jones (Penguin, Harmondsworth, 1972), 71.

28. Rowe, 'Larkin's "Aubade"', 189.

29. In a lecture to the Philip Larkin Society, 13 June 2009, Professor Marion Shaw persuasively linked 'Aubade' with Section VII of Tennyson's 'In Memoriam A.H.H.', a kind of funereal *alba* hidden in the larger elegy.

30. Tolley, *My Proper Ground*, 177.

31. George Orwell, *Down and Out in Paris and London*, in *The Complete Works of George Orwell*, vol. 1, ed. Peter Davison (Secker & Warburg, London, 1986), 89–90. Orwell's words had already been echoed in a Larkin letter to Monica Jones dated 10 March 1963: 'Home & got drunk, or half drunk, alone in flat' (*LM*, 317).

32. Conquest, 'A Proper Sport', 35.

33. Leggett, *Larkin's Blues*, 116.

34. Ibid., 47.

35. Ibid., 98.

36. Ibid., 99.

37. Whitehead, *Hardy to Larkin*, 238; Edward Thomas, *Collected Poems* (Faber, London, 1981), 84.

38. Siegfried Sassoon, *Collected Poems, 1908–1956* (Faber, London, 1984), 294–5.

39. Kingsley Amis, *The Green Man* (Triad/Panther, Frogmore, 1978), 77–8.

40. Terry Kelly, '"Aubade": The Making of a Poem, or the Dialectics of Despair', *About Larkin*, 26 (October 2008), 24.

41. I am indebted to Alain Sinner for this connection and quote from his translation of the Laforgue. See '"That chap Laforgue": Larkin and the Decadents', *English Studies*, vol. 11 (Centre Universitaire de Luxembourg, 2002), 23. An early version of this chapter was given at Dr Sinner's invitation as an address to the teachers of English in Luxembourg schools. An ensuing conversation with Vic Mousel furthered my thinking on the theme of mortality.

42. See Gilroy, *Philip Larkin: Selected Poems*, 91: 'The speaker in "Aubade" shares with Hamlet, in his famous soliloquy, the cast of mind which "slows each impulse down to indecision". "The anaesthetic from which none come round" has echoes of the "undiscover'd country, from whose bourn / No traveller returns", while the "Not to be" construction also suggests the connection.'

43. Robert Frost, *Selected Poems* (Penguin, Harmondsworth, 1963), 78.

44. Day Lewis, *The Complete Poems*, 372. Emeritus Professor of Physics George Cole recalls the evening of 14 February 1968 when Day Lewis gave a public lecture as Writer in Residence at the University of Hull after which there was to be a ceremonial signing of plates especially 'thrown' for the occasion: 'The Chairman for the lecture was Philip. His introduction of Day Lewis was as courteous, stylish and elegant as ever but it was very clear indeed that he really didn't approve of him at all. This was confirmed at the reception afterwards when he positively refused to sign a plate with C. Day Lewis. He was very happy to sign one by himself (in fact rather pleased) but in partnership – never. Day Lewis must have realised this because his willingness for a joint signing was totally rejected. There was no faint praise now. To try to pour oil over troubled waters I asked Day Lewis whether he thought it a good idea for his lecture to be published by the Hull University Press (we had a thriving Press in those days). He was horrified at the thought. He said the lecture had given good service over many years in the past and there was no good reason why it shouldn't give equally good service in the years to come: but this would be entirely ruined by publication. I had some sympathy with the spirit of Philip's introduction to the lecture.'

'C. Day Lewis and Philip each signed a plate and the potter left to fire them. A few days later he looked in to show me the finished plates. To my astonishment one plate had both signatures of Day Lewis and Philip clearly on it. There were three copied – one for me, one for the University (it was given to the Vice Chancellor, Dr Brynmor Jones) and the potter kept one for his own collection. He was extremely evasive when I asked him how he had persuaded the two poets to sign a single plate. Certainly, it seemed prudent not to tell Philip that he had, after all, shared a signing for antiquity with his fellow poet.' George Cole, 'Cigarette Cards', *About Larkin*, 21 (Summer 2006), 34.

45. Ford Madox Ford, *A Man Could Stand Up* (Sphere Books, London, 1969), 176; Randall Jarrell, *Selected Poems* (Faber, London, 1956), 214.
46. Dylan Thomas, *Collected Poems, 1934–1952* (Dent, London, 1967), 116.
47. Eliot, *Complete Poems and Plays*, 38. There may also be a more distant echoing of Empson's 'Courage Means Running'.
48. Richard Ellmann, *Oscar Wilde* (Penguin, Harmondsworth, 1988), 546. I am indebted to Toni Silver for drawing to my attention both this Oscar Wilde allusion and the Robert Frost echo mentioned above.
49. *Douglas Dunn and Philip Larkin: Faber Poetry Cassette* (ISBN: 0571131824). I am indebted to Jim Orwin for this information. Although it is not directly alluded to in 'Aubade', Hardy's poem 'Lying Awake' might be thought to corroborate Larkin's comments.
50. John Henry Newman, *The Dream of Gerontius and Other Poems* (Oxford University Press, 1914), 22; Eliot, *Complete Poems and Plays*, 38; Edward Fitzgerald, *The Rubaiyat of Omar Khayyam*, in *Selected Works*, ed. Joanna Richardson (Hart-Davis, London, 1962), 247; Virginia Woolf, *Between the Acts* (Hogarth Press, London, 1953), 173. Less direct but still well within the spectrum of echoes are lines 538–42 from Book XI of Milton's *Paradise Lost*:

> Thou must outlive
> Thy youth, thy strength, thy beauty, which will change
> To withered weak and gray; thy Senses then
> Obtuse, all taste of pleasure must forgoe,
> To what thou hast.

As early as 3 May 1956, 20 years before the poem, Larkin was using the same phrasing in a letter to Monica Jones: 'I have no house no wife no child no car no motor mower no holidays planned'; while six years later he alluded to the line from King Lear, 'Nothing will come of nothing' (*LM*, 160, 296).

51. Newman, *Apologia Pro Vita Sua*, quoted in B.C. Southam, *A Student's Guide to the 'Selected Poems' of T.S. Eliot* (Faber, London, 1994), 76; Hardy, *Complete Poems*, 797; Jerome Kern and Herbert Reynolds, 'They Didn't Believe Me', in *The Jerome Kern Song Book*, ed. Oscar Hammerstein II (Simon and Schuster, New York, 1955), 12; Llewelyn Powys, *Love and Death* (Bodley Head, London, 1939), 32; Powys, *Skin for Skin and The Verdict of Bridlegoose* (Bodley Head, London, 1948), 85; Woolf, *Orlando*, 24.
52. Keats, *Poetical Works*, 207–8. In his fascinating essay '"Fond of What He's Crapping On": Movement Poetry and Romanticism', Michael O'Neill detects a 'remote allusion' to the last stanza of 'Ode to a Nightingale' running through the second half of a different Larkin poem, 'Reasons for Attendance'. *The Movement Reconsidered: Essays on Larkin, Amis, Gunn, Davie, and Their Contemporaries*, ed. Zachary Leader (Oxford University Press, 2009), 289–90.

53. See Motion, *Life*, 202: 'Terry remembers Larkin enthusing about all these books [T.F. Powys, Anthony Powell, Cyril Connolly, Jules Laforgue, Henri de Montherlant], and wolfing down other favourites (William Cowper, Isherwood, Lawrence, Gladys Mitchell, John Dickson Carr) as well as new discoveries (Flann O'Brien, Conrad Aiken, John O'Hara). What impressed Terry wasn't just Larkin's eagerness, but the decisiveness of his opinions. "Philip had no very fixed ideas as to the nature of 'good literature'", he says; "everything he considered worth reading was a matter of personal choice, just as he made one feel that any book which had earned a place on his shelves [...] had helped to form what I was coming to recognize as his remarkable sensibility."' Larkin himself posited that 'a style is much more likely to be formed from partial slipshod sampling than from the coherent acquisition of a literary education' (*FR*, 14) – though the apparent amateurism is put in perspective by his first-class English degree from Oxford.
54. Booth, *Philip Larkin: The Poet's Plight*, 10. Booth repeats the point in his essay 'Philip Larkin: "The Card-Players"': 'After he found his poetic voice in 1946 Larkin saw into print only 112 mature poems, each of which aims to be "its own sole freshly created universe", with its own diction and imagery, and its own unique form.' See *Fourteen English Sonnets*, ed. Michael Hanke (Wissenschaftlicher Verlag Trier, 2007), 169.
55. Motion transcribes a manuscript poem dated 13 November 1972 and entitled 'Spare Time':

> In the old days
> I used to come home
> And settle to write
> In the famous evenings.
> Now I hit the jug
> And go out like a light,
> Waking, go to bed
> With a hangover. (*Life*, 424)

Whether 'Spare Time' is regarded as a separate poem that rehearses the later masterpiece or, more literally, a first draft of it, the fact that there are five years between the two once again challenges the view of Larkin as lyric poet spontaneously new-minting language in response to immediate sensation.
56. David Jones, *The Anathemata* (Faber, London, 1972), 24.
57. Duncan, *The Failure of Conservatism in Modern British Poetry*, 65; Appleyard, *The Pleasures of Peace*, 104; Roger Day, *Larkin* (Open University Press, Milton Keynes, 1987), 89.
58. Paulin, 'She Did Not Change', 234; Sean O'Brien, *The Deregulated Muse: Essays on Contemporary British and Irish Poetry* (Bloodaxe, Newcastle, 1998), 24.
59. William Cowper, *The Poems*, ed. John D. Baird and Charles Ryskamp (Oxford University Press, 1980), 136.
60. Epicurus, *The Extant Remains*, trans. Cyril Bailey (Oxford University Press, 1926), 85.
61. James Warren, *Facing Death: Epicurus and His Critics* (Oxford University Press, 2004), see especially pp. 154–9.
62. Powys, *Love and Death*, 147, 60.
63. To take an extreme analogy the better to dramatize the point: a prisoner on a train to Auschwitz who achieved a state of tranquillity by ignoring the terrible

fate to which he or she was being hurried might be admired for *sang froid* but not for responsiveness to their true positionality. Larkin believes we are all (so to speak) passengers on that train. As 'The Old Fools' asks of the elderly, those nearest the front of the train, soonest for disembarkation, 'How can they ignore it?' and 'Why aren't they screaming?' (*CP*, 196; *TCP*, 81). Or again, as he says in a letter to Monica Jones: 'You can look out of your life like a train & see what you're heading for, but you can't stop the train' (*LM*, 379).

64. Motion, *Life*, 468. Jim Orwin remarks that with passages such as this Motion set in place a simplification that has found favour with biographical critics like Booth, Warren Hope and Richard Bradford. In the interests of presenting Eva Larkin as his muse, Motion suggests that 'Aubade' was stalled until Larkin's mother died on 17 November 1977 and provided him with the impetus to finish the work. In the process, Motion elides the fourth of the poem's five stanzas: 'he added a final verse which is stoic where the previous three had been terrified'. The truth is more complicated, more text-centred. The first three verses of 'Aubade' were written in 1974 and the poem then set aside incomplete. Larkin resumed work on the piece on 18 May 1977 (six months before his mother's death) in response to a request from the American publisher Charles Seluzicki for a poem commemorating the fiftieth anniversary of Thomas Hardy's death. Larkin's introduction to the Faber cassette recording of 'Aubade', already quoted from in this chapter, underlines the likelihood that it was Hardy's death half a century earlier, rather than Eva's death half a year hence, that released his writer's block and allowed him to complete his last masterpiece. Appropriately, Charles Seluzicki, the catalyst in this process, published 'Aubade' in May 1980 in an edition of 250, every one of which Larkin initialled.

65. Palmer, *Such Deliberate Disguises*, 82. In a more general way, John Carey declared that 'Larkin is a modern stoic, today's Seneca.' Carey, 'Larkin: Poet of Deprivation', *The Sunday Times*, 13 November 1983, 39. I am grateful to the poet John Mowat for bringing this article to my attention.

66. Leggett, *Larkin's Blues*, 113.

67. John Macquarrie, *Existentialism* (Penguin, Harmondsworth, 1973), 155.

68. Martin Heidegger, *History of the Concept of Time: Prolegomena*, trans. T. Kisiel (Indiana University Press, Bloomington, 1985), 440.

69. Macquarrie, *Existentialism*, 153.

70. Ibid., 171.

71. Compare with this passage from a letter to Monica Jones: 'a sustained and unprejudiced contemplation of the passage of time, the inevitability of DEATH, the onset of incapacity & impotence. I think that [...] how one regards these facts settles one's whole life: if they seem distant & almost irrelevant then you are O.K.: if they seem closer to you than the name stitched on your underwear then you have had it, nothing else can possibly win yr concentration' (*LM*, 224).

Bibliography

Abdullah, Kia, *Assimilation* (Toronto, Adlibbed, 2006).

Ackroyd, Peter, 'Poet Hands on Misery to Man', *Times*, 1 April 1993, 35.

Alderman, Nigel, '"The Life with a Hole in it": Philip Larkin and the Condition of England', *Textual Practice*, 8, 2 (1994), 279–301.

Allcroft, Amber, 'Coincidences: Some Successful Detective Work South of the River', *About Larkin*, 21 (Summer 2006), 36.

Alldritt, Keith, *David Jones: Writer and Artist* (Constable, London, 2003).

Allott, Kenneth, ed., *The Penguin Book of Contemporary Verse* (Penguin, Harmondsworth, 1962).

Alvarez, A., ed., *The New Poetry* (Penguin, Harmondsworth, 1963).

Amis, Kingsley, *Lucky Jim* (1954; Penguin, Harmondsworth, 1962).

—— *The Green Man* (Triad/Panther, Frogmore, 1978).

—— *The Letters of Kingsley Amis*, ed. Zachary Leader (HarperCollins, London, 2000).

Amis, Martin, 'The Ending: Don Juan in Hell', in *The War Against Cliché* (Cape, London, 2001), 153–72.

Appleyard, Bryan, *The Pleasures of Peace: Art and Imagination in Post-war Britain* (Faber, London, 1989).

—— 'The Dreary Laureate of our Provincialism', *Independent*, 18 March 1993, 27.

Armstrong, Louis, *Louis Armstrong in His Own Words: Selected Writings*, ed. Thomas Brothers (Oxford University Press, 1999).

Ashbery, John, *Self-Portrait in a Convex Mirror* (Penguin, Harmondsworth, 1976).

Auden, W.H., *Collected Shorter Poems, 1927–1957* (Faber, London, 1966).

—— *Later Auden*, ed. Edward Mendelson (Faber, London, 1999).

Ayto, John, *Twentieth Century Words* (Oxford University Press, 1999).

Bainbridge, Beryl, *Sweet William* (Duckworth, London, 1975).

Barnes, Julian, *Flaubert's Parrot* (Picador, London, 1990).

—— *A History of the World in 10½ Chapters* (Picador, London, 1990).

Baron, Michael, ed., *Larkin with Poetry: English Association Conference Papers* (English Association, Leicester, 1997).

Barry, Peter, *Beginning Theory* (Manchester University Press, 2002).

Barth, John, *Lost in the Funhouse* (Penguin, Harmondsworth, 1972).

Barthes, Roland, *Camera Lucida: Reflections on Photography*, trans. Richard Howard (Fontana, London, 1984).

—— *Image – Music – Text*, ed. and trans. Stephen Heath (Fontana, London, 1984).

Baudelaire, Charles, *Fleurs du Mal/Flowers of Evil*, ed. Marthiel and Jackson Matthews (New Directions, Norfolk, 1955).

Bayley, John, *The Uses of Division* (Chatto & Windus, London, 1976).

—— 'Larkin's Short Story Poems', in *Philip Larkin: A Tribute*, ed. George Hartley (Marvell, London, 1988), 272–83.

Beauvoir, Simone de, *The Second Sex*, trans. H.M. Parshley (New English Library, London, 1970).

Benjamin, Walter, *Illuminations*, ed. Hannah Arendt (Collins, London and Glasgow, 1973).

Bennett, Alan, *Writing Home* (Faber, London, 1994).

—— *Untold Stories* (Faber, London, 2005).

Bertens, Hans, *The Idea of the Postmodern: A History* (Routledge, London, 1995).
Betjeman, John, *Collected Poems*, ed. Earl of Birkenhead (John Murray, London, 1958).
Booth, James, *Philip Larkin: Writer* (Harvester, Hemel Hempstead, 1992).
—— 'Philip Larkin: Lyricism, Englishness and Postcoloniality', in *Larkin with Poetry*, ed. Michael Baron (English Association, Leicester, 1997), 9–30.
—— 'Why Larkin's Poetry Gives Offence', *English*, 46, 184 (Spring 1997), 1–19.
—— 'From Here to Bogland: Larkin, Heaney and the Poetry of Place', in *New Larkins for Old*, ed. Booth (Macmillan, Basingstoke, 2000), 190–212.
—— *Philip Larkin: The Poet's Plight* (Macmillan, Basingstoke, 2005).
—— 'Philip Larkin: "The Card-Players"', in *Fourteen English Sonnets*, ed. Michael Hanke (Wissenschaftlicher Verlag Trier, 2007), 169–77.
Booth, James and Janet Brennan, 'Editorial', *About Larkin*, 29 (April 2010), 2.
Boucicault, Dion, *Plays*, ed. Peter Thomson (Cambridge University Press, 1984).
Bradford, Richard, *First Boredom, Then Fear* (Peter Owen, London, 2005).
Bray, Christopher, 'A Writer's Life: Clive James', *Telegraph* arts supplement, 5 November 2005, 12.
Brecht, Bertolt, *Brecht on Theatre: The Development of an Aesthetic*, trans. John Willett (Eyre-Methuen, London, 1964).
Brennan, Maeve, *The Philip Larkin I Knew* (Manchester University Press, 2002).
Bristow, Joseph, 'The Obscenity of Philip Larkin', *Critical Inquiry* (Autumn 1994), 156–81.
Browning, Robert, *Poems of Robert Browning*, ed. Sir Humphrey Milford (Oxford University Press, 1959).
Brownjohn, Alan, ed., *Departure* (Departure, Oxford, 1955).
—— *Philip Larkin* (British Council/Longman, Harlow, 1975).
—— 'Novels into Poems', in *Larkin at Sixty*, ed. Anthony Thwaite (Faber, London, 1982), 109–19.
—— 'Poet who Reluctantly Came to the Point', *The Listener*, 13 February 1986, 16.
Burke, Séan, *The Death and Return of the Author: Criticism and Subjectivity in Barthes, Foucault and Derrida* (Edinburgh University Press, 1998).
Burnett, Archie, ed., *The Complete Poems of Philip Larkin* (Faber, London, 2012).
Burns, Robert, *The Canongate Burns*, ed. Andrew Noble and Patrick Scott Hogg (Canongate, Edinburgh, 2001).
Butler, Christopher, *After the Wake: An Essay on the Contemporary Avant-Garde* (Oxford University Press, 1980).
Byron, Lord George Gordon, *The Works of Lord Byron*, ed. Rowland Prothero, 5 vols (John Murray, London, 1898–1904).
—— *Poetical Works*, ed. Frederick Page and John Jump (Oxford University Press, 1987).
Carey, John, 'Larkin: Poet of Deprivation', *The Sunday Times*, 13 November 1983, 39.
—— 'The Two Philip Larkins', in *New Larkins for Old: Critical Essays*, ed. James Booth (Macmillan, Basingstoke, 2000), 51–65.
Carpenter, Humphrey, *The Angry Young Men: A Literary Comedy of the 1950s* (Penguin, Harmondsworth, 2002).
Chambers, Harry, 'Some Light Views of a Serious Poem: A Footnote to the Misreading of Philip Larkin's "Naturally the Foundation Will Bear Your Expenses"', *Phoenix*, 11/12 (1973–74), 110–14.
Clark, Steve, '"Get Out As Early As You Can": Larkin's Sexual Politics', in *Philip Larkin: A Tribute*, ed. George Hartley (Marvell, London, 1988), 237–71.
—— '"The lost displays": Larkin and Empire', in *New Larkins for Old*, ed. James Booth (Macmillan, Basingstoke, 2000), 166–81.

Cole, George, 'Cigarette Cards', *About Larkin*, 21 (Summer 2006), 33–4.

Coleridge, Samuel Taylor, *Biographia Literaria* (Scolar, Menston, 1971).

—— *A Choice of Coleridge's Verse*, ed. Ted Hughes (Faber, London, 1996).

Connor, Steven, *Postmodernist Culture: An Introduction to Theories of the Contemporary* (Blackwell, Oxford, 1989).

Conquest, Robert, 'A Proper Sport', in *Larkin at Sixty*, ed. Anthony Thwaite (Faber, London, 1982), 31–7.

Cooper, Stephen, *Philip Larkin: Subversive Writer* (Sussex Academic Press, Brighton, 2004).

Corcoran, Neil, *English Poetry since 1940* (Longman, London, 1993).

—— ed., *Cambridge Companion to Twentieth Century English Poetry* (Cambridge University Press, 2007).

Cowley, Malcolm, 'Portrait of Mister Papa', *Life*, 10 January 1949, 101.

Cowper, William, *The Poems*, ed. John D. Baird and Charles Ryskamp (Oxford University Press, 1980).

Craik, Roger, 'Some Unheard Melodies in Philip Larkin's Poetry', *About Larkin*, 12 (2001), 11–13.

Crispin, Edmund, 'An Oxford Group', *Spectator*, 17 April 1964, 525.

Culler, Jonathan, *Barthes* (Fontana, Glasgow, 1983).

Cunningham, Lawrence S. and John J. Reich, eds, *Culture and Values*, vol. II: *A Survey of the Humanities with Readings* (Cengage, Stamford, 2009).

Davenport-Hines, Richard, *Auden* (Heinemann, London, 1995).

Davie, Donald, 'Larkin's Choice', *The Listener*, 29 March 1973, 420.

—— *Thomas Hardy and British Poetry* (Routledge & Kegan Paul, London, 1973).

—— *The Poet in the Imaginary Museum*, ed. Barry Alpert (Carcanet, Manchester, 1977).

Dawson, S.W., 'On Re-Reading *The Less Deceived*', in *Philip Larkin: A Tribute*, ed. George Hartley (Marvell, London, 1988), 178–83.

Day, Roger, *Larkin* (Open University Press, Milton Keynes, 1987).

Day Lewis, C., *The Complete Poems* (Sinclair-Stevenson, London, 1992).

Deleuze, Gilles, *Cinema 1: The Movement-Image*, trans. H. Tomlinson and B. Habberjan (Minnesota University Press, Minneapolis, 1986).

Derrida, Jacques, *Dissemination*, trans. Barbara Johnson (Athlone, London, 1981).

—— *Of Grammatology*, trans. Gayatri Chakravorty Spivak (Johns Hopkins University Press, Baltimore, 1997).

—— *Without Alibi*, trans. and ed. Peggy Kamuf (Stanford University Press, 2002).

Didsbury, Peter, *Scenes from a Long Sleep: New and Collected Poems* (Bloodaxe, Tarset, 2003).

Donne, John, *The Songs and Sonets*, ed. Theodore Redpath (Methuen, London, 1967).

—— *Devotions upon Emergent Occasions*, ed. A. Raspa (McGill-Queens University Press, Montreal, 1975).

Draper, Ronald, 'The Positive Larkin', in *Critical Essays on Philip Larkin: The Poems*, ed. Linda Cookson and Bryan Loughrey (Longman, London, 1989), 94–105.

Duffy, Carol Ann, *Standing Female Nude* (Anvil, London, 1985).

—— ed., *Answering Back* (Picador, London, 2007).

Duncan, Andrew, *The Failure of Conservatism in Modern British Poetry* (Salt, Cambridge, 2003).

Dunn, Douglas, *Under the Influence: Douglas Dunn on Philip Larkin* (Edinburgh University Press, 1987).

Eagleton, Terry, 'Larkin: A Left View', *About Larkin*, 9 (2000), 4–8.

Easthope, Antony, 'How Good is Seamus Heaney?', *English*, 46, 184 (1997), 21–36.

Eddy, Steve, *Philip Larkin: High Windows* (York Press, London, 2007).

Edwards, Ken, 'Some Younger Poets', in *The New British Poetry, 1968–88*, ed. Gillian Allnutt, Fred d'Aguiar, Ken Edwards and Eric Mottram (Paladin, London, 1988), 265–70.

Eliot, T.S., *The Sacred Wood* (Methuen, London, 1928).

—— *Selected Essays* (Faber, London, 1951).

—— *To Criticize the Critic* (Faber, London, 1965).

—— *The Complete Poems and Plays* (Faber, London, 1969).

—— *Selected Prose*, ed. Frank Kermode (Faber, London, 1975).

Ellmann, Richard, *James Joyce* (Oxford University Press, 1976).

—— *Oscar Wilde* (Penguin, Harmondsworth, 1988).

Enright, D.J., ed., *Poets of the 1950s: An Anthology of New English Verse* (Kenkyusho, Tokyo, 1955).

Epicurus, *The Extant Remains*, trans. Cyril Bailey (Oxford University Press, 1926).

Everett, Barbara, *Poets in Their Time: Essays on English Poetry from Donne to Larkin* (Faber, London, 1986).

—— 'Larkin and Dockery: The Limits of the Social', in *Philip Larkin: A Tribute*, ed. George Hartley (Marvell, London, 1988), 140–52.

—— 'Art and Larkin', in *Philip Larkin: The Man and his Work*, ed. Dale Salwak (Macmillan, London, 1989), 130–43.

—— 'Larkin's Money', in *New Larkins for Old*, ed. James Booth (Macmillan, Basingstoke, 2000), 11–28.

Ewart, Gavin, *The Collected Ewart, 1933–1980* (Hutchinson, London, 1980).

Fairclough, Norman, *Discourse and Social Change* (Polity, London, 1992).

Fenton, James, *The Strength of Poetry* (Oxford University Press, 2000).

Ferguson, Peter, 'Philip Larkin's XX Poems', in *Philip Larkin: A Tribute*, ed. George Hartley (Marvell, London, 1988), 153–64.

Fitzgerald, Edward, *Selected Works*, ed. Joanna Richardson (Hart-Davis, London, 1962).

Fitzgerald, F. Scott, *The Crack-Up and Other Pieces and Stories* (Penguin, Harmondsworth, 1965).

—— *The Great Gatsby* (Penguin, Harmondsworth, 1979).

Fletcher, Christopher, *Sunday Times, Culture* supplement, 11 May 2008, 14–15.

Ford, Ford Madox, *A Man Could Stand Up* (Sphere Books, London, 1969).

—— *Some Do Not ...* (Sphere Books, London, 1969).

Foster, Paul, Trevor Brighton and Patrick Garland, *An Arundel Tomb* (Otter Memorial Papers, Chichester, 1987).

Fraser, G.S., ed., *Poetry Now* (Faber, London, 1956).

Fraser, G.S. and I. Fletcher, eds, *Springtime: An Anthology of Young Poets and Writers* (Owen, London, 1953).

Freud, Sigmund, *An Autobiographical Study* (1925), trans. James Strachey (Hogarth Press, London, 1935).

Frost, Robert, *Selected Poems* (Penguin, Harmondsworth, 1963).

Gardiner, Alan, 'Larkin's England', in *Critical Essays on Philip Larkin: The Poems*, ed. Linda Cookson and Bryan Loughrey (Longman, London, 1989), 62–71.

Gardner, Helen, ed., *The Metaphysical Poets* (Penguin, Harmondsworth, 1966).

—— *The Art of T.S. Eliot* (Faber, London, 1968).

Gardner, Philip, 'The Wintry Drum', *Phoenix*, 11/12 (1973–74), 27–40.

Garland, Patrick, 'An Enormous Yes: A Memoir of the Poet', in *An Arundel Tomb*, by Paul Foster, Trevor Brighton and Patrick Garland (Otter Memorial Papers, Chichester, 1987), 23–6.

Giddins, Gary, *Satchmo* (Da Capo, New York, 1998).

Gilroy, John, *Philip Larkin: Selected Poems* (HEB, Penrith, 2009).

Goldsmith, Oliver, *The Poems*, ed. Austin Dobson (Dent, London, 1883).

Goodby, John, '"The Importance of Being Elsewhere", or "No Man is an Ireland": Self, Selves and Social Consensus in the Poetry of Philip Larkin', *Critical Survey*, 1, 2 (1989), 131–8.

Goring, Rosemary, ed., *Larousse Dictionary of Literary Characters* (Larousse, Edinburgh, 1994).

Greer, Germaine, 'A Very British Misery', *Guardian*, 14 October 1988, 27.

Gregson, Ian, *Contemporary Poetry and Postmodernism: Dialogue and Estrangement* (Macmillan, Basingstoke, 1996).

—— *Postmodern Literature* (Arnold, London, 2004).

Grubb, Frederick, 'Dragons', *Phoenix*, 11/12 (1973–74), 119–36.

Handley, Graham, *Brodie's Notes on Philip Larkin's Selected Poems* (Pan, London, 1991).

Hardy, Thomas, *Tess of the d'Urbervilles* (Macmillan Papermac, London, 1966).

—— *The Complete Poems*, ed. James Gibson (Macmillan, London, 1981).

—— *The Hand of Ethelberta* (Penguin, Harmondsworth, 1997).

—— *A Pair of Blue Eyes*, ed. Pamela Dalziel (Penguin, Harmondsworth, 2005).

Hartley, George, 'Nothing To Be Said', in *Philip Larkin: A Tribute*, ed. George Hartley (Marvell, London, 1988), 298–308.

—— ed., *Philip Larkin: A Tribute* (Marvell, London, 1988).

Hartley, Jean, *Philip Larkin, the Marvell Press and Me* (Carcanet, Manchester, 1989).

Hastings, Max, 'The Wages of Loyalty', *The Sunday Times*, *Culture* supplement, 19 August 2011, 32.

Hattersley, Roy, 'A Life in Parts', *The Guardian Saturday Review*, 6 May 2000, 6.

Hawthorn, Jeremy, *A Concise Glossary of Contemporary Literary Theory* (Arnold, London, 1998).

Heaney, Seamus, 'Englands of the Mind', in *Preoccupations* (Faber, London, 1980).

—— 'The Main of Light', in *Larkin at Sixty*, ed. Anthony Thwaite (Faber, London, 1982), 131–8.

—— *Finders Keepers: Selected Prose, 1971–2001* (Faber, London, 2002).

Hefferrnan, James W., *Museum of Words: The Poetics of Ekphrasis from Homer to Ashbery* (University of Chicago Press, 1993).

Heidegger, Martin, *History of the Concept of Time: Prolegomena*, trans. T. Kisiel (Indiana University Press, Bloomington, 1985).

Hemingway, Ernest, *The Sun Also Rises* (Pan, London, 1951).

—— *In Our Time* (Scribners, New York, 1996).

Hill, Geoffrey, *Collected Poems* (Penguin, Harmondsworth, 1985).

Hitchens, Christopher, *Unacknowledged Legislation: Writers in the Public Sphere* (Verso, London, 2002).

Holderness, Graham, 'Philip Larkin: The Limits of Experience', in *Critical Essays on Philip Larkin: The Poems*, ed. Linda Cookson and Bryan Loughrey (Longman, London, 1989), 106–18.

Hollander, John, *The Gazer's Spirit: Poems Speaking to Silent Works of Art* (University of Chicago Press, 1995).

Hollindale, Peter, 'The Long Perspectives', in *Critical Essays on Philip Larkin: The Poems*, ed. Linda Cookson and Bryan Loughrey (Longman, London, 1989), 50–61.

Homberger, Eric, *The Art of the Real: Poetry in England and America since 1939* (Dent, London, 1977).

Hope, Warren, *A Student Guide to Philip Larkin* (Greenwich Exchange, Holywood, 1997).

Horder, J., 'Poet on the 8.15', *Guardian*, 20 May 1965, 9.

Horton, Andrew, ed., *Comedy/Cinema/Theory* (University of California Press, Berkeley, Los Angeles and Oxford, 1991).

Housman, A.E., *Collected Poems* (Penguin, Harmondsworth, 1956).

Humm, Maggie, *Snapshots of Bloomsbury: The Private Lives of Virginia Woolf and Vanessa Bell* (Tate Publishing, London, 2006).

Ingelbien, Raphael, *Misreading England: Poetry and Nationhood since the Second World War* (Rodopi, Amsterdam, 2002).

James, Clive, 'On His Wit', in *Larkin at Sixty*, ed. Anthony Thwaite (Faber, London, 1982), 98–108.

—— 'Pretending To Be Him', *Times Literary Supplement*, 28 February 2003, 18–19.

Jardine, Lisa, 'Saxon Violence', *Guardian*, Section 2, 8 December 1992, 4.

Jarrell, Randall, *Selected Poems* (Faber, London, 1956).

Jenkins, Nicholas, 'The "Truth of Skies": Auden, Larkin, and the English Question', in *The Movement Reconsidered: Essays on Larkin, Amis, Gunn, Davie, and Their Contemporaries*, ed. Zachary Leader (Oxford University Press, 2009), 34–61.

Jennings, Elizabeth, *Collected Poems, 1953–1985* (Carcanet, Manchester, 1986).

Johnson, James Weldon, *The Book of American Negro Spirituals* (Da Capo, New York, 1977).

—— *The Second Book of American Negro Spirituals* (Da Capo, New York, 1977).

Jones, Alison, *A Student's Guide to High Windows and the Poetry of Philip Larkin* (Twin Serpents, Oxford, 2009).

Jones, David, *The Anathemata* (Faber, London, 1972).

Jones, Peter, ed., *Imagist Poetry* (Penguin, Harmondsworth, 1972).

Joyce, James, *Letters of James Joyce*, ed. Stuart Gilbert (Faber, London, 1957).

—— *A Portrait of the Artist as a Young Man* (Penguin, Harmondsworth, 1970).

—— *Ulysses* (Penguin, Harmondsworth, 1971).

—— *Finnegans Wake* (Faber, London, 1975).

Kaufmann, Walter, ed., *Existentialism: From Dostoevsky to Sartre* (Meridian, New York, 1975).

Kay, Jackie, 'Admirable Hornblower', *Observer Review*, 29 November 1998, 14.

Keats, John, *Poetical Works*, ed. H.W. Garrod (Oxford University Press, 1970).

Kelly, Terry, Review of Philip Larkin, *Collected Poems* (2003), *About Larkin*, 15 (April 2003), 28–30.

—— [untitled book review], *About Larkin*, 19 (Spring 2005), 32.

—— '"Aubade": The Making of a Poem, or the Dialectics of Despair', *About Larkin*, 26 (October 2008), 24–7.

—— 'Living with Larkin', *About Larkin*, 33 (April 2012), 15.

Kendrick, George, 'An Interview with Peter Easy', *Bête Noire*, 4 (Winter 1987), 9–27.

Kennedy, David, *The Ekphrastic Encounter in Contemporary British Poetry and Elsewhere* (Ashgate, Farnham, 2012).

Kern, Jerome, *The Jerome Kern Song Book*, ed. Oscar Hammerstein II (Simon and Schuster, New York, 1955).

King, Martin Luther, 'I have a dream', in *The Penguin Book of Historic Speeches*, ed. Brian MacArthur (Viking, London, 1995), 487–91.

Kuby, Lolette, *An Uncommon Poet for the Common Man: A Study of Philip Larkin's Poetry* (Mouton, The Hague and Paris, 1974).

Kynaston, David, *Family Britain, 1951–57* (Bloomsbury, London, 2009).

Larkin, Philip, *All What Jazz: A Record Diary, 1961–68* (Faber, London, 1970).

—— ed., *The Oxford Book of Twentieth Century English Verse* (Oxford University Press, 1973).

—— *A Girl in Winter* (Faber, London, 1975).
—— *Jill* (Faber, London, 1975).
—— *Required Writing: Miscellaneous Pieces, 1955–1982* (Faber, London, 1983).
—— *Collected Poems*, ed. Anthony Thwaite (Marvell and Faber, London, 1988).
—— *Selected Letters*, ed. Anthony Thwaite (Faber, London, 1992).
—— *Larkin's Jazz: Essays and Reviews, 1940–85*, ed. Richard Palmer and John White (Continuum, London, 2001).
—— *Further Requirements: Interviews, Broadcasts, Statements and Book Reviews, 1952–1985*, ed. Anthony Thwaite (Faber, London, 2001; revised and expanded, 2002).
—— *Trouble at Willow Gables and Other Fictions*, ed. James Booth (Faber, London, 2002).
—— *Early Poems and Juvenilia*, ed. A.T. Tolley (Faber, London, 2005).
—— *Letters to Monica*, ed. Anthony Thwaite (Faber, London, 2010).
—— 'Letter to *The Listener*', 15 October 1953, reprinted *About Larkin*, 31 (April 2011), 4.
—— *Poems*, selected and introduced by Martin Amis (Faber, London, 2011).
—— *The Complete Poems*, ed. Archie Burnett (Faber, London, 2012).
Latif, Tariq, *The Punjabi Weddings* (Arc, Todmorden, 2007).
Lawrence, D.H., *Lady Chatterley's Lover* (Penguin, Harmondsworth, 1960).
—— *Kangaroo* (Penguin, London, 1963).
—— *Sons and Lovers* (Penguin, Harmondsworth, 1964).
—— *Studies in Classic American Literature* (Mercury, London, 1965).
—— *Letters*, ed. James T. Boulton and Margaret H. Boulton, with Gerald Lacy, vol. VI (Cambridge University Press, 1991).
Leader, Zachary, ed., *The Movement Reconsidered: Essays on Larkin, Amis, Gunn, Davie, and Their Contemporaries* (Oxford University Press, 2009).
Leavis, F.R., *D.H. Lawrence/Novelist* (1955; Penguin, Harmondsworth, 1964).
Leggett, B.J., *Larkin's Blues: Jazz, Popular Music and Poetry* (Louisiana State University Press, Baton Rouge, 1999).
Lerner, Laurence, *Philip Larkin* (Northcote, Plymouth, 1997).
Levi, Peter, 'The English Wisdom of a Master Poet', in *An Enormous Yes: In Memoriam Philip Larkin (1922–1985)*, ed. Harry Chambers (Peterloo Poets, Calstock, 1986), 33–5.
Lodge, David, ed., *20th Century Literary Criticism: A Reader* (Longman, London, 1972).
—— *The Modes of Modern Writing: Metaphor, Metonymy, and the Typology of Modern Literature* (Edward Arnold, London, 1977).
Lomax, Marion, 'Larkin with Women', in *Larkin with Poetry*, ed. Michael Baron (English Association, Leicester, 1997).
Longfellow, Henry Wadsworth, *The Works of Henry Wadsworth Longfellow* (Wordsworth, Ware, 1994).
Longley, Edna, 'Larkin, Edward Thomas and the Tradition', *Phoenix*, 11/12 (1973–74), 63–98.
—— 'Poete Maudit Manque', *Philip Larkin: A Tribute*, ed. George Hartley (Marvell, London, 1988), 220–31.
—— 'Larkin, Decadence and the Lyric Poem', in *New Larkins for Old*, ed. James Booth (Macmillan, Basingstoke, 2000), 29–50.
Lowell, Amy, *The Complete Poetical Works* (Cambridge University Press, 1955).
Lyle, R.C., *Brown Jack* (Putnam, London, 1934).
Lyotard, Jean-François, *The Postmodern Condition: A Report on Knowledge* (Manchester University Press, 1987).
Macquarrie, John, *Existentialism* (Penguin, Harmondsworth, 1973).
Marsh, Nicholas, *Philip Larkin: The Poems* (Macmillan, Basingstoke, 2007).
McEwan, Ian, *Solar* (Jonathan Cape, London, 2010).

McGovern, Una, ed., *Chambers Dictionary of Literary Characters* (Chambers Harrap, Edinburgh, 2004).

McKeown, Andy, 'Philip Larkin or the Law of the Father', *About Larkin*, 17 (April 2004), 16–20.

Mellers, Wilfrid and Rupert Hildyard, 'The Edwardian Age and the Inter-War Years', in *The Cambridge Cultural History*, vol. 8: *Early Twentieth-Century Britain*, ed. Boris Ford (Cambridge University Press, 1989), 1–44.

Millgate, Michael, ed., *The Life and Work of Thomas Hardy by Thomas Hardy* (Macmillan, London, 1984).

——— *Thomas Hardy: A Biography Revisited* (Oxford University Press, 2004).

Morrison, Blake, *The Movement: English Poetry and Fiction of the 1950s* (Methuen, London, 1980).

Morton, Mark, *Dirty Words: The Story of Sex Talk* (2003; Atlantic Books, London, 2005).

Motion, Andrew, 'On the Plain of Holderness', in *Larkin at Sixty*, ed. Anthony Thwaite (Faber, London, 1982), 65–8.

——— *Philip Larkin* (Methuen, London, 1982).

——— 'This is Your Subject Speaking', in *Natural Causes* (Chatto & Windus, London, 1987), 49–57.

——— *Philip Larkin: A Writer's Life* (Faber, London, 1993).

Muldoon, Paul, 'This Be The Verse', *New York Times Sunday Book Review*, 22 April 2012, 1–2.

Mullan, John, *Anonymity: A Secret History of English Literature* (Faber, London, 2007).

Mulvey, Laura, *Visual and Other Pleasures* (Macmillan, Basingstoke, 1989).

Murdoch, Iris, *Sartre* (Collins, London, 1968).

Nagra, Daljit, *Tippoo Sultan's Incredible White-Man-Eating Tiger Toy-Machine!!!* (Faber, London, 2011).

Newman, John Henry, *The Dream of Gerontius and Other Poems* (Oxford University Press, 1914).

Nichols, Grace, *Picasso, I Want My Face Back* (Bloodaxe, Tarsent, 2009).

O'Brien, Flann, *At Swim-Two-Birds* (Penguin, Harmondsworth, 1975).

O'Brien, Sean, *The Deregulated Muse: Essays on Contemporary British and Irish Poetry* (Bloodaxe, Newcastle, 1998).

——— 'A Desolation Foretold', *Times Literary Supplement*, 8 June 2012, 9.

O'Driscoll, Dennis, *Troubled Thoughts, Majestic Dreams: Selected Prose Writings* (Gallery, Loughcrew, 2001).

O'Neill, Michael, '"Fond of What He's Crapping On": Movement Poetry and Romanticism', in *The Movement Reconsidered: Essays on Larkin, Amis, Gunn, Davie, and Their Contemporaries*, ed. Zachary Leader (Oxford University Press, 2009), 270–91.

Orr, Mary, *Intertextuality: Debates and Contexts* (Polity, London, 2003).

Orwell, George, *Down and Out in Paris and London*, in *The Complete Works of George Orwell*, vol. 1, ed. Peter Davison (Secker & Warburg, London, 1986).

Osborne, John, *Larkin, Ideology and Critical Violence: A Case of Wrongful Conviction* (Macmillan, Basingstoke, 2008).

Palmer, Richard, *Such Deliberate Disguises: The Art of Philip Larkin* (Continuum, London, 2008).

Parkinson, R.N., 'To Keep Our Metaphysics Warm: A Study of "Church Going"', *Critical Survey*, 5 (1971), 224–33.

Partridge, Eric, *The Penguin Dictionary of Historical Slang* (Penguin, Harmondsworth, 1978).

Paulin, Tom, Letter, *Times Literary Supplement*, 6 November 1992, 15.

—— 'She Did Not Change: Philip Larkin', in *Minotaur: Poetry and the Nation State* (Harvard University Press, Cambridge, MA, 1992), 233–51.

Payne, Michael and John Schad, eds, *Life.After.Theory* (Continuum, London, 2003).

Perry, Seamus, 'So Striking a Miss-Hit', *Times Literary Supplement*, 1 April 2011, 8–9.

Petch, Simon, *The Art of Philip Larkin* (Sydney University Press, 1981).

Phelps, Gilbert, 'Literature and Drama', in *The Cambridge Guide to the Arts in Britain*, vol. 9: *Since the Second World War*, ed. Boris Ford (Cambridge University Press, 1988), 196–236.

Picot, Edward, *Outcasts from Eden: Ideas of Landscape in British Poetry since 1945* (Liverpool University Press, 1997).

Plath, Sylvia, *Collected Poems*, ed. Ted Hughes (Faber, London, 1981).

Pollock, Alan, *Philip and Sydney*, play broadcast BBC Radio 4, 11 June 2010.

Porteous, J. Douglas, 'Nowhereman', *About Larkin*, 8 (1999), 12–16.

—— 'Sing-Along with Philip', *About Larkin*, 27 (April 2009), 31.

Pound, Ezra, *ABC of Reading* (Faber, London, 1951).

—— 'A Few Don'ts By An Imagist', in *Modern Poets on Modern Poetry*, ed. James Scully (Fontana, London and Glasgow, 1966), 31–5.

—— *The Spirit of Romance* (New Directions, New York, 1968).

—— *The Cantos of Ezra Pound* (revised and collected edition, Faber, London, 1975).

—— *Selected Poems, 1908–1959* (Faber, London, 1975).

Powys, Llewelyn, *Love and Death* (Bodley Head, London, 1939).

—— *Skin for Skin and The Verdict of Bridlegoose* (Bodley Head, London, 1948).

Preminger, Alex, ed., *Princeton Encyclopedia of Poetry and Poetics* (Macmillan, London, 1975).

Pugh, Sheenagh, *Sing for the Taxman* (Seren, Bridgend, 1993).

Punter, David, *Philip Larkin: The Whitsun Weddings and Selected Poems* (York Press, London, 2003).

Quiller-Couch, Sir Arthur, ed., *The Oxford Book of English Verse, 1250–1918* (Oxford University Press, 1961).

Raban, Jonathan, *Driving Home: An American Scrapbook* (Picador, London, 2010).

Rácz, István, 'Agnosticism, Masks and Monologues in Philip Larkin', *Hungarian Journal of English and American Studies*, 1, 2 (1995), 93–120.

—— 'Space in Larkin and Cézanne', *Hungarian Journal of English and American Studies*, 9, 2 (2003), 118–25.

Reading, Peter, *Stet* (Secker & Warburg, London, 1986).

Regan, Stephen, *Philip Larkin: The Critics Debate* (Macmillan, Basingstoke, 1992).

—— 'Larkin's Reputation', in *Larkin with Poetry*, ed. Michael Baron (English Association, Leicester, 1997), 47–69.

—— ed., *Philip Larkin: Contemporary Critical Essays* (Macmillan, Basingstoke, 1997).

—— 'The Movement', in *A Companion to Twentieth-Century Poetry*, ed. Neil Roberts (Blackwell, Oxford, 2001), 209–19.

—— 'Philip Larkin: A Late Modern Poet', in *The Cambridge Companion to Twentieth Century English Poetry*, ed. Neil Corcoran (Cambridge University Press, 2007), 147–58.

Rice, D. Talbot, *Teach Yourself to Study Art* (English Universities Press, London, 1955).

Richards, I.A., *Practical Criticism* (1929; Routledge & Kegan Paul, London, 1964).

Ricks, Christopher, 'The Whitsun Weddings', *Phoenix*, 11/12 (1973–74), 6–10.

—— 'Like Something Almost Being Said', in *Larkin at Sixty*, ed. Anthony Thwaite (Faber, London, 1982), 120–30.

—— *Allusion to the Poets* (Oxford University Press, 2002).

Ritchie, Harry, *Success Stories: Literature and the Media in England, 1950–1959* (Faber, London, 1982).

Robbe-Grillet, Alain, *Last Year at Marienbad: A Cine-Novel*, trans. Richard Howard (Calder, London, 1962).

Roberts, Michael and Donald Hall, eds, *The Faber Book of Modern Verse* (Faber, London, 1965).

Robinson, Jane, *Bluestockings: The Remarkable Story of the First Women to Fight for an Education* (Viking, London, 2009).

Rooney, Kathleen, *Live Nude Girl: My Life as an Object* (Arkansas University Press, Fayetteville, 2009).

Rossen, Janice, *Philip Larkin: His Life's Work* (Harvester, Hemel Hempstead, 1989).

Rowe, Mark, 'Larkin's "Aubade"', in *Philosophy and Literature* (Ashgate, Aldershot, 2004), 182–219.

Rumens, Carol, 'Distance and Difference in *A Girl in Winter*', *About Larkin*, 29 (April 2010), 7–12.

Rutherford, Maurice, *Slipping the Tugs* (Lincolnshire & Humberside Arts, Lincoln, 1982).

—— *Love is a Four-Letter World* (Peterloo, Calstock, 1994).

—— *This Day Dawning* (Peterloo, Calstock, 1994).

—— *Flip Side to Philip Larkin* (Shoestring Press, Nottingham, 2012).

Ruthven, K.K., *Feminist Literary Studies: An Introduction* (Cambridge University Press, 1984).

Salwak, Dale, ed., *Philip Larkin: The Man and his Work* (Macmillan, London, 1989).

Sassoon, Siegfried, *Collected Poems, 1908–1956* (Faber, London, 1984).

Schmidt, Michael, *Lives of the Poets* (Weidenfeld & Nicolson, London, 1998).

Scupham, Peter, 'A Caucus-race', *Phoenix*, 11/12 (1973–74), 173–82.

Shakespeare, John, 'A Few Suggestions', *Times Literary Supplement*, 3 April 2009, 12–15.

Shelley, P.B., *Poetical Works*, ed. Thomas Hutchinson (Oxford University Press, 1970).

—— *Shelley*, selected by Kathleen Raine (Poet to Poet, Penguin, Harmondsworth, 1978).

Simmons, James, 'The Trouble with Larkin', in *Philip Larkin: A Tribute*, ed. George Hartley (Marvell, London, 1988), 232–6.

Sinner, Alain, '"That chap Laforgue": Larkin and the Decadents', *English Studies*, 11 (Centre Universitaire de Luxembourg, 2002), 17–31.

Smith, Stan, *Inviolable Voice: History and Twentieth Century Poetry* (Gill & Macmillan, Dublin, 1982).

Snowman, Daniel, *The Hitler Emigres: The Cultural Impact on Britain of Refugees from Nazism* (Pimlico, London, 2003).

Sontag, Susan, *Styles of Radical Will* (Secker & Warburg, London, 1969).

—— *On Photography* (Penguin, Harmondsworth, 1979).

Southam, B.C., *A Student's Guide to the 'Selected Poems' of T.S. Eliot* (Faber, London, 1994).

Stapleton, Michael, *Cambridge Guide to English Literature* (Cambridge University Press, 1983).

Steinberg, Gillian, *Philip Larkin and His Audiences* (Macmillan, Basingstoke, 2010).

Steiner, George, *Heidegger* (Fontana, Glasgow, 1978).

Stevenson, Randall, *The Last of England?: The Oxford Literary History*, vol. 12: *1960–2000* (Oxford University Press, 2004).

Stevenson, Robert Louis, *Selected Poems*, ed. Angus Calder (Penguin, Harmondsworth, 1998).

Swarbrick, Andrew, 'The Less Deceived' and 'The Whitsun Weddings' by Philip Larkin (Macmillan, Basingstoke, 1986).
—— Out of Reach: The Poetry of Philip Larkin (Macmillan, Basingstoke, 1995).
Tennyson, Alfred, Lord, The Poems, ed. Christopher Ricks (Longman, London, 1969).
Terence, The Self-Tormentor (Heauton Timoroumenos), ed. and trans. A.J. Brothers (Aris and Phillips, Warminster, 1988).
Thomas, Dylan, Collected Poems, 1934–1952 (Dent, London, 1967).
Thomas, Edward, Collected Poems (Faber, London, 1981).
Thomas, Jane E., ed., 'Philip Larkin: Seven Verbal Snapshots', Bête Noire, 5 (1988), 87–92.
Thurley, Geoffrey, The Ironic Harvest: English Poetry in the Twentieth Century (Edward Arnold, London, 1974).
Thwaite, Anthony, 'The Poetry of Philip Larkin', in The Survival of Poetry, ed. Martin Dodsworth (Faber, London, 1970), 37–55.
—— 'The Poetry of Philip Larkin', Phoenix, 11/12 (1973–74), 41–58.
—— ed., Larkin at Sixty (Faber, London, 1982).
—— Poetry Today: A Critical Guide to British Poetry, 1960–1984 (Longman, London, 1985).
Timms, David, Philip Larkin (Oliver & Boyd, Edinburgh, 1973).
Tolley, A.T., My Proper Ground: A Study of the Work of Philip Larkin and Its Development (Edinburgh University Press, 1991).
—— Larkin at Work: A Study of Larkin's Mode of Composition as Seen in his Workbooks (Hull University Press, 1997).
—— 'Letter to the Editors', About Larkin, 34 (October 2012), 23.
Tomlinson, Charles, 'Poetry Today', in Pelican Guide to English Literature, vol. 7: The Modern Age, ed. Boris Ford (Penguin, Harmondsworth, 1961), 458–74.
Travis, Alan, Bound and Gagged: A Secret History of Obscenity in Britain (Profile, London, 2001).
Updike, John, 'Introduction', in Loving, Living, Party Going by Henry Green (Picador, London, 1978), 7–15.
Vaizey, Marina, The Artist as Photographer (Sidgwick & Jackson, London, 1982).
Wain, John, 'Engagement or Withdrawal? Some Notes on the Work of Philip Larkin', Critical Quarterly, 17, 4 (1975), 347–60.
Walpole, Horace, Anecdotes of Painting in England, ed. R.N. Wornum, vol. 2 (Bickers, London, 1888).
Warren, James, Facing Death: Epicurus and His Critics (Oxford University Press, 2004).
Watson, J.R., 'The Other Larkin', Critical Quarterly, 17, 4 (1975), 347–60.
—— 'Probably Neither Works: Negative Signifiers in Larkin's Poetry', About Larkin, 6 (1998–99), 14–17.
Watt, R.J.C., A Concordance to the Poetry of Philip Larkin (Olms-Weidmann, Hildesheim, 1995).
—— 'The Larkin Concordance', About Larkin, 3 (1997), 28.
Whalen, T., Philip Larkin and English Poetry (Macmillan, Basingstoke, 1986).
White, John, 'Philip Larkin: Funny Man', Part 1, About Larkin, 29 (April 2010), 20–4; Part 2, About Larkin, 30 (October 2010), 9–14.
Whitehead, John, Hardy to Larkin: Seven English Poets (Hearthstone, Munslow, 1995).
Whitman, Walt, The Viking Portable Walt Whitman, ed. Mark Van Doren (Viking, New York, 1966).
Wiemann, Birte, 'Larkin's Englishness: A German Perspective', About Larkin, 29 (April 2010), 25–7.

Williams, W.E., ed., *Thomas Hardy: A Selection of Poems* (Penguin, Harmondsworth, 1960).

Wood, James, 'Want Not, Write Not', *Guardian*, 30 March 1993, 20.

Woods, Tim, *Beginning Postmodernism* (Manchester University Press, 1999).

Woolf, Virginia, *Between the Acts* (Hogarth Press, London, 1953).

—— *Orlando* (Triad/Panther, London, 1977).

—— *The Waves* (Triad/Panther, Frogmore, 1977).

—— *A Room of One's Own* (Triad/Panther, Frogmore, 1978).

Wordsworth, William, *Poetical Works*, ed. Thomas Hutchinson and Ernest de Selincourt (Oxford University Press, 1988).

Yeats, W.B., *The Collected Poems* (Macmillan, London, 1965).

Yeazell, Ruth Bernard, *Art of the Everyday: Dutch Painting and the Realist Novel* (Princeton University Press, 2008).

Index

Principal entries are cited in bold type.

Printed and bound in Great Britain by
CPI Group (UK) Ltd, Croydon, CR0 4YY